LANCE LATTIG
SEPTEMBER 1987
NEW YORK

Architecture and Design: 1890-1939

Architecture and Design: 1890-1939

An International Anthology of Original Articles

Edited by Tim and Charlotte Benton
at The Open University
with Dennis Sharp

The Whitney Library of Design
An Imprint of Watson-Guptill Publications / New York

First published in the United States in 1975
by the Whitney Library of Design, an imprint of
Watson-Guptill Publications, a division
Billboard Publications Inc, One Astor Plaza,
New York, New York 10036

First published in Great Britain by Crosby Lockwood
Staples, in conjuction with The Open University Press
under the title of 'FORM AND FUNCTION: A Source Book
for the History of Architecture and Design 1890-1939'

Manufactured in Great Britain

Library of Congress Cataloguing in Publication Data
Benton, Timothy, comp.
Architecture and design, 1890-1939.
1. Architecture, Modern—20th century—Addresses, essays, lectures. 2. Architectural design—Addresses, essays lectures. I. Benton, Charlotte, joint comp. II. Sharp, Dennis. III. Title.
NA680.B.48 1975 724.9 74-30215
ISBN 0-8230-7045-X

Acknowledgements

We are grateful to the following for permission to include copyright material:

The Editor of *The Architectural Association Journal* for 'In Germany Now' by F. R. Yerbury from the A.A.J. Sept. 1933 and 'The Conditions for an Architecture of Today' by Wells Coates from the A.A.J. April 1938.

McGraw Hill Book Company for 'Streamlining' by Harold van Doren, from *Industrial Design: A Practical Guide* by Harold van Doren.

The Architectural Press Ltd., London for 'Suprematist Architecture' by Kasimir Malevich and 'Glass Architecture, August 1918' by Adolf Behne, both from *Fantastic Architecture* by U. Conrads and H. G. Sperlich.

The Architectural Review, London for 'Programme for the establishment of a Company for the Provision of Housing on Aesthetically Consistent Principles, 1910, by Walter Gropius from *The Architectural Review* Vol. 130.

Macmillan, London and Basingstoke for 'Modernismus' by Reginald Blomfield.

Horizon Press, New York for 'The Cardboard House' by Frank Lloyd Wright from *The Future of Architecture* 1953.

Ernest Benn Ltd., London for 'Reflections on a New Architecture, 1914-17' by Erich Mendelsohn from *Erich Mendelsohn: Structures and Sketches.*

Harvard University Press, Cambridge, U.S.A. for 'Declaration of the First Congress, La Sarraz, June 28, 1928' by CIAM, from *Can Our Cities Survive?* by J. L. Sert.

Athenaeum-Polak and Van Gennep, Amsterdam for 'Machinery' by Gino Severini, 'The Staatliche Bauhaus in Weimar' by Vilmos Huszar, 'Manifesto' by Frederick Kiesler and 'Architecture and Standardization in Mass Construction 1918' by J. J. P. Oud, from *De Stijl,* Vols. I–V.

Barrie and Rockliff, London for 'Glass in Modern Architecture, 1929' by Arthur Korn, from *Arthur Korn: Glass in Modern Architecture* edited by D. Sharp.

Mrs Hattula M-N. Hug for 'Constructivism and the Proletariat' by Lazlo Moholy-Nagy.

Studio International for 'Five Points' by Bruno Taut, 'Wood or Metal' by John Gloag, 'Wood or Metal – A Reply' by Charlotte Perriand, 'A Survey of Modern Tendencies in Decorative Art' by Maurice Dufrene, from *The Studio,* 1929 and 1931.

Prentice-Hall Inc., Englewood Cliffs, New Jersey for 'Purism' by Le Corbusier and Amedée Ozenfant.

The MIT Press, Cambridge, USA for 'Ten Years of Bauhaus' by Ernst Kallai, 'Address to the Student Representatives at the Bauhaus, 1928' by Hannes Meyer, 'Fine Art and Industrial Form 1926' by Georg Muche, 'The Value of the Teaching of Theory in Painting 1926' by Wassily Kandinsky, 'Bauhaus Dessau – Principles of Bauhaus Production 1926' by Walter Gropius, 'The State Garbage Supplies, 1924' by K. Nonn. 'The Staatliche Bauhaus in Weimar' by Oskar Schlemmer, 'Address to the Bauhaus Students, July 1919' by Walter Gropius, and 'Programme of the Staatliche Bauhaus in Weimar, April 1919' by Walter Gropius, from *The Bauhaus 1919-33* by Hans Wingler.

Naum Gabo for 'Realistic Manifesto 1920' by Naum Gabo and Antoine Pevsner and 'The Programme of the Productivist Group' by A. Rodchenko and V. Stepanova.

R. Piper and Co., Verlag, Munich for 'The Role of the Engineer in Modern Architecture', 'The New Ornament' and 'Design and Construction of Modern Furniture' by Henry van de Velde from *Zum Neuen Stil.*

Eugen Diederichs Verlag, Cologne for 'The Development of Modern Industrial Architecture 1913' by Walter Gropius, 'The Problem of Form in Engineering' by Hermann Muthesius, 'A Debate, 1911', and 'Ornament 1911' by Karl Grosz, 'Where Do We Stand?' by Hermann Muthesius, from *Deutscher Werkbund Jahrbuch,* 1912-13.

Verlagsgruppe Bertelsmann GmbH, Bertelsmann Fachverlag, Düsseldorf for 'The Future of German Form' by Hermann Muthesius, 'The Meaning of the Arts and Crafts' by Hermann Muthesius and 'The English House' by Hermann Muthesius, from *Anfange des Funktionalismus* by Julius Posener.

Museum of Modern Art, New York, for 'The Theory and Organization of the Staatliche Bauhaus' by Walter Gropius.

Lena Meyer-Bergner for 'The New World' by Hannes Meyer from *Hannes Meyer, Buildings, Projects and Writings* by Claude Schnaidt.

Thames and Hudson Ltd., London for 'The Will to Style' by Theo van Doesburg, from *De Stijl* by Hans L. C. Jaffe.

Musée Horta, Brussels for 'Reminiscences on the Maison du Peuple' by Victor Horta.

Miss Grace A. Crosby for 'Housing and Furnishing' and 'Modern German Architecture and What We May Learn From It', from *Form in Civilization* by W. R. Lethaby.

George Wittenborn Inc., New York for 'The Tall Office Building Artistically Considered' and 'Ornament in Architecture' by Lewis Sullivan from *Kindergarten Chats.*

Deutscher Werkbund Archives for 'Five Points of a New Architecture' by Le Corbusier from *Bau und Wolnung* 1927.

Foreword

This book has been prepared in conjunction with an Open University course entitled *History of Architecture and Design 1890-1939*. The book has been designed specifically to complement that course, and shares some of its peculiarities, such as the precise period covered and the general emphasis on certain architects and designers. However, we hope that it will prove of interest to a wider audience. The half century covered was selected for its homogeneity, with a cut-off at the Second World War for reasons of historical objectivity and to allow a sufficiently concentrated study of the rise of the Modern Movement in architecture and design. One of the features of the course, reflected in this book, is a concern to present some account of traditional architecture and theory to balance the rather one-sided chronicle of the rise and rise of the International Style often put forward as an account of the period. The two main alternatives to the International Style, stripped classicism and the vernacular tradition, are therefore given an airing, with a look at the political associations which they continue to have throughout the period.

Few of the 124 extracts printed in this book are cited intact, and this requires a word of explanation. We decided early on to try to go for breadth in obtaining representative statements from what we considered to be the most influential viewpoints, rather than quoting fewer articles or chapters in full. It is a fact that most of the more interesting statements of the period were long and thorough, of some 10,000 words on occasion. When the literature is more widely available in English, it will perhaps be time to reprint more of them in full. We have aimed at a thematic approach, but in sufficiently large sections to facilitate finding the extracts by date. At the head of each section, there is a short commentary on the selection, but otherwise we have left the extracts to speak for themselves. We have decided not to mark all the cuts in the original material, for reasons of typographical continuity. Where cuts are necessarily obtrusive, and where important material has had to be left out, we have marked them. Where speeches given in one year were reprinted in a subsequent year, we have given the first date in the title of the extract, and the date of publication in the list of sources.

As much as possible, we have looked to original source material for these extracts, but we have found a few collections of English language or translated extracts of great assistance. We have tried to overlap as little as possible with those which are already available, such as Ulrich Conrads' *Programmes and Manifestoes on 20th century Architecture*, Lund Humphries, 1970, which should be read as a complementary volume to this one. The following books contain valuable material, with which we assume the specialist reader will be familiar: U. Conrads and H. G. Sperlich, *Fantastic Architecture*, The Architectural Press, 1963; H. C. L. Jaffé, *De Stijl*,

Thames and Hudson, 1970; Le Corbusier and P. Jeanneret, *The Complete Architectural Works* (with English, French and German text), Thames and Hudson, 1966; Lewis Mumford, *Roots of Contemporary American Architecture*, Reinhold, New York, 1952; L. Munz and G. Künstler, *Adolf Loos*, Thames and Hudson, 1966; Dennis Sharp, *Glass Architecture by Paul Scheerbart and Alpine Architecture by Bruno Taut* (a translation of these two works), November Books, 1972; Hans Wingler, *The Bauhaus*, M. I. T. Press, 1969, and the various collections of Frank Lloyd Wright's writings of which the most accessible is Frederick Gutheim, *Frank Lloyd Wright on Architecture*, Duell, Sloan and Pearce, 1941.

The following German collections of source material provide a valuable extension to the material we have covered:

Akademie der Künste, Berlin, *Die Gläserne Kette* (Catalogue with letters and drawings of the expressionist 'Glass Chain' group), Berlin, 1963.

Adolf Loos, *Sämtliche Schriften*, Vol. I, Herold, Vienna, 1962.

Julius Posener, *Anfänge des Funktionalismus, Von Arts and Crafts zum Deutschen Werkbund* (Bauwelt Fundamente series, 11), Ullstein, Berlin, 1964.

F. Schwartz and F. Gloor, *'Die Form': Stimme des Deutschen Werkbundes* (Bauwelt Fundamente series, 24), Bertelsmann Fachverlag, Gütersloh, 1969.

Anna Teut, *Architektur im Dritten Reich 1933-45* (Bauwelt Fundamente series, 19), Ullstein, Berlin, 1967.

Henry Van de Velde, *Zum Neuen Stil* (edited Hans Curjel), Munich, 1955.

We have not listed source books which are mainly concerned with painting and sculpture rather than architecture unless, like Jaffé's *De Stijl*, they contain crucially important material for an understanding of architecture and design.

The editors would like to thank all those members of the course team who have contributed ideas and suggestions, and Susan Khin Zaw of the Open University, and Professor Reyner Banham and Stefan Muthesius. We would also like to thank all those who worked on the translations, both those whose names are listed under the translators' credits, and those who worked on material not eventually included. A special word of thanks to Lindsay Gordon is called for, whose organisation of the collating and photocopying of the mountain of paper involved before the final selection has been invaluable. Responsibility for all errors lies with us.

Tim and Charlotte Benton

Translations by Christopher Baggs
Charlotte Benton
Tim Benton
Colin Chant
J. Gawronska
Vivienne Menkes
Jennifer Monk
Translance
Susan Vaudin
Stephen Wilkins

Contents

List of Plates

Introduction

Albert Einstein opened a famous lecture with the advice: 'If you wish to learn from the theoretical physicist anything about the methods he uses . . . don't listen to his words, examine his achievements.' The same might broadly be said about architecture – after all, architecture confined to paper is a fantasy. Architectural history abounds with paper schemes, unfulfilled projects of the imagination that have not been realised because of their impracticability, lack of opportunity or restrictions of the purse. They are often supported by theories and polemical positions. Architecture is best experienced at first hand in its physical 'completeness'; written sources – observations, descriptions, explanations, criticisms – can only be used to expand our knowledge of a building, or place it in its context of time and circumstance. However, writings by architects, artists and designers are valuable in indicating their methods and modes of thinking.

An anthology of writings on architecture and design should not be seen as a substitute for experiencing an artefact. On the whole it is a fairly new activity to anthologise writings on these subjects; indeed, in terms of twentieth century ideas at least, it is a recent phenomenon born of the last twenty-five years or so. Collecting, sifting, selecting and compiling such material has usually been the prerogative of the critic intent on demonstrating his or her historical knowledge or on establishing a particular point of view about architecture or design, whose principal purpose has been to establish the pedigree of the so-called 'modern movement'. This has become a peculiarly fashionable pursuit, but the attitude is now tempered by a concern to investigate the framework of architectural and design ideas that were, up to a few years ago, entirely acceptable as working bases. They are clearly no longer so, and we must view the contents of this Reader as history having only marginal reference to the problems we face today.

The literature of architecture is exceedingly wide and covers a field that may, in its scope, be compared to that of the physical sciences. Not all of it contributes to knowledge; much of it is apologetic with only a residual significance. It ranges from the well-known architectural history books – Statham, Banister Fletcher and their like – to technical literature and to tediously written reports on architectural projects. This anthology falls somewhere in the middle ground, providing a cullender for comments (aesthetic, historical, technical, etc.) on architectural positions, theories, practices and procedures. It is arranged in such a way as to make possible a study of twentieth century viewpoints on architecture and design. It is international in scope but national in emphasis. It will not, we realise, meet all tastes. What has probably slipped through the holes are the perceptive comments about design that fall from the lips of the designer in the spontaneous interview or in reminiscences about particular projects. But in selecting material we have concentrated on appropriating the sources that best illustrate the standpoint of an attitude which has for more than 80 years been termed 'modern', for in dealing with the period from 1890 to 1939 one has inevitably to ask why the architecture and design of this period differs so radically from that which preceded it: why, in fact, the 'modern movement' was a product of a particular time; why it had lasting significance; why it changed the appearance of buildings and objects; and, above all, how it came to have historical validity in the modern world.

The Reader, while not necessarily arranged in strict chronological order, provides a basis for an examination of concepts and ideas. This skeleton outline of events and personalities will, I trust, put most of the writings in context and help towards an understanding of the main lines of development of the 'modern' view.

The changes which occurred in architectural attitudes immediately before the turn of the century were not uniquely or narrowly accidental. Architecture shared with the arts and the sciences an upheaval arising from within but conditioned by events and circumstances outside the art. Isolated pockets of resistance to the current concern with stylistic revivals and pastiches began to be formed in various parts in Europe and in Chicago in the 1890s, fed, in essence, by the social, artistic and craftsmanly notions of the English Arts and Crafts movement, which, although socially oriented, allowed the innovative as well as the individualistic element to predominate in design. Architecture was on the sideline of this movement but it represented in many ways the amalgam of attitudes to design. It promoted design changes on a much larger and more comprehensive scale, tuned to the requirements of human habitation (particularly those of the wealthier sections of society). Enhanced by modern notions of logical simplicity and refinement, architects provided a synthetic approach to design. The legacy of this Arts and Crafts approach can best be seen in the early New Towns of England (Letchworth, Welwyn Garden City, etc.).

As early as 1892 Louis Sullivan, the Chicago pioneer, was, as our first extract indicates, testifying to the aesthetic beauty to be found in a new architecture as 'well formed and comely in the nude'; ornamentation was to be conceived as an enhancement of its basic beauty. Simple geometric forms were to be ornamented just as the human figure carries well-thought-out clothing. It is an interesting analogy which some years later the Viennese irritant Adolf Loos was to pick up again with his notion of utilitarian simplicity. He admired the English and Americans and the kinds of society that could produce an architecture as handsome as that of the Georgian period – an art as simple as that of English cooking; to him the blue 'boiler suit' overall worn by the American plumber was the most obvious form of modern dress and the mechanical efficiency of the plumber himself epitomised for Loos the kind of rôle that he wished to commandeer for the arts, that of 'the quartermaster of Culture'.

Art and the machine, and the notions of applied decoration and utilitarian simplicity, were the concepts that polarised early 'modernist' attitudes (the title 'modern' gained its currency from Wagner's book *Moderne Architektur*, published in 1896). These notions engendered a desire for the honest expression of structure through material, line and form based on the imitation of nature: that is, wood should look like wood, metal like metal, glass like glass. Nature, as was realised by Eugène Vallin, an influential architect of the Nancy School, could be impounded to produce inspiration for formal design purposes; there was a quality to be found in natural forms that was *'non plus une forme tout faite, mais un principe formel, non plus un prétexte d'ornament, mais un élément structural pour les constructions* ... ('rather than a final form, a formal principle; rather than an excuse for embellishment, a basic element of construction').

Naturalistic ornament offered seemingly endless variations of shape and form that could be drawn on to prevent, as Emile Gallé wrote, 'the ornamentalist ...

from servile, insipid copying from objects devoid of meaning, reality and charm'. The Art Nouveau designers accentuated the delicate but vigorous twists found in plant forms and turned them into formally exaggerated design effects.

By 1900, the year of the Paris Exhibition (the year of triumph for the new style, Gallé himself was employing as many as 300 men in his workshops. With his emphasis on the simple idea that an article of 'art production' should bring joy to the man who made it, Gallé was re-expressing the ideas of the English Arts and Crafts movement. The way he developed his approach to decorative work is equally simple. He explains in a short article, 'Modern Furniture Decorated According to Nature', published in the *Revue des Arts Décoratifs* in 1900 [14], how he coupled the simple forms his father had introduced into glass and crystal making to his own love of flowers. He successfully adapted botanical motifs to a design end in his own glass and furniture productions. In common with many of his contemporaries in Nancy, and in common with the aim of artists in various other centres in Europe at that time, he demanded that art should be 'of its time'.

S. T. Madsen, in his book *Sources of Art Nouveau*, has suggested that Art Nouveau did not seriously affect architecture. But it did, he maintains, contribute to the development of new architectural ideas by enriching 'the architectural form language'. The decorative aspects of the interior design movement were developing side by side with the use of new constructional methods, as one can observe in Victor Horta's now destroyed *Maison du Peuple* in Brussels (1896-1899) [31]. Here, the ornamentation of the iron columns and balconies formed a sharp contrast to the carefully articulated and daring structural framing (see Plate 6).

The form language that was to become part of the inheritance of the later German and Dutch Expressionist architects was clearly suggested in the work of Horta in Brussels, in the work of van de Velde and in some of the buildings of Antoni Gaudi in Barcelona. Art Nouveau and Expressionism span the years from the 1880s to 1924. The term *L'Art Nouveau* itself, so Henry van de Velde claims, originated in Belgium towards the end of the 1880s, and was later first used to describe the work of the four designers, Sessurier-Bovy, Hankar, Horta and van de Velde himself. Van de Velde says in his memoirs:

> Although there was at the bottom little similarity in our aims, the work of the four of us was lumped together, judged and described by the one quality obviously common to the whole of it: its newness.

The name *L'Art Nouveau* was also used by the art dealer Bing for his gallery in the Rue de Provence, Paris, which was opened on 26 December, 1895. Van de Velde was responsible for the design of rooms for the gallery. Soon after his Parisian début van de Velde was invited to Germany, first to Hagen and later to Weimar to take over the Directorship of the School of Applied Arts. Thus, the *Veldische Stil* and the legacy of the Belgian movement, which had come to terms at least with a new attitude to architecture if not with a new style, reached Germany – via Paris. Van de Velde was to become, together with the Munich Jugendstil architect August Endell, one of the main influential forces on the later romantic trends in architecture; an influence that was shown particularly in the work and writings of Eric Mendelsohn [34].

The very diversity of epithets given to the 'new style' both before and after that date seems to imply that nobody was really prepared to own it; on the other hand, this same diversity does imply its wide European origins. The youthful aspects of the style were implied in the German epithet *Jugendstil,* which came from the name of the magazine, *Jugend,* founded in Munich in 1896. The title given to the style in Italy was *Stile Liberty* after the famous London shop of Liberty's, (a term that was revived in the 1950s by Italian architects with their so-called 'Neo-Liberty' style). In France and Belgium, besides the use of the term *L'Art Nouveau* itself, the connections with the English Arts and Crafts movement are indicated in such titles as *Style Anglais.*

The Austrian name *Secessionstil* comes from the breakaway group of artists who founded the *Wiener Secession* in 1897.

It was out of these national movements at the turn of the century that many of the precursors of the 'modern movement' emerged – men such as van de Velde, Hoffman, Behrens, Olbrich and Endell. Side by side with this logical sequence there were a number of developments which, although clearly related, were idiosyncratic in the extreme. Such a man as Hector Guimard is extremely difficult to place in any discussion of twentieth century architectural ideas. An ardent student of the work of Viollet-le-Duc, he was to become the best-known exponent of the Art Nouveau style in France. In 1894 he started to build the apartment block Castel Béranger in the fashionable Rue de la Fontaine in Paris. In this building the ornamental detail was quite extraordinary, although externally it was much the same kind of mixture as many of the other late nineteenth century Parisian apartments built in the same area. The elegant wrought-iron work of the entrance gates was surpassed in design ingenuity by those designed by Antoni Gaudi for the Guell Park in Barcelona of roughly the same date.

The designs for the *Métropolitain* in Paris show how clearly Guimard derived his structural ornament from nature. In an article in the *Architectural Record* of June 1902, he elicits three basic principles that determined his approach to architectural design:

1. Logic, which consists in taking into account all the conditions of the case, and they are infinite in variety and number, which the architect has to deal with.
2. Harmony, which means putting the construction into full accord, not only with the requirements to be met and the funds available, but also with the surroundings.
3. Sentiment, which, partaking at the same time of logic and harmony, is a complement of both, and leads to emotion, to the highest expression of the art.

In Glasgow at the turn of the century a small group of artists and architects came together under the leadership of Charles Rennie Mackintosh. This group – the Glasgow Four – consisted of Mackintosh, his wife Margaret McDonald, Herbert McNair and his wife Frances MacDonald. The Four had an important impact on Continental trends, principally through the publicity given to their work in the magazine *The Studio*. This magazine, founded in 1893, more than any other source was responsible for the widespread European interest in the work of British artists. Buildings and interior designs were featured by the Glasgow Four as well as by Baillie Scott, Voysey and Walton. *The Studio* was introduced just at the time when the first manifestations of the Art Nouveau style had appeared on the Continent. The real roots of the new Continental approach to architecture and interior decoration indeed go further back than the Glasgow school, to the ideas of John Ruskin and William Morris and to the Arts and Crafts movement (the Arts and Crafts Exhibition Society held its foundation meeting in 1888). Hermann Muthesius, in his trilogy on the English domestic architectural scene, *Das englische Haus,* went as far as to say that '... the whole of our movement is based on the results England achieved from 1860 up to the middle of the 1890s'.

The group at Glasgow worked virtually in isolation, with only the buildings of Charles Harrison Townsend in London showing any similar affinity to the embryonic Art Nouveau trends. The Glasgow group were interested, as Madsen and Howarth both indicate in their books, in all the prevailing trends current in the city during the 1890s; in the folk arts, in the Pre-Raphaelites, in the refined Oriental trends and in the nationalistic Celtic revival. Such inspirational sources as these helped to give the work of the group its own peculiar character, which involved a preoccupation with almost weightless naturalistic twisted forms and sinuously curved shapes enclosed in rectangular frames. The Four in fact did very little work on the Continent – a few exhibition rooms at Vienna and Turin, and a competition entry, a *Haus eines Kunstfreundes,* published by Alexander Koch in 1902. Their architecture cannot be judged as a distinct part of the Continental Art Nouveau. Their importance to later developments in architecture, particularly of the Individualistic and Expressionist kind, is, like that of the work of Antoni Gaudi in Barcelona, a prophetic one. The project by Mackintosh for a Concert Hall for the International Exhibition at Glasgow in 1901 is a remarkable example of a distinctly 'modern' building which depended for its effect on a domed roof and powerful buttresses between which were housed smaller vestibules. It was a building designed at the same time as the *Ernst-Ludwig-Haus* by Josef Maria Olbrich and Behrens's first building, his own house, both at Darmstadt.

It was probably Mackintosh who first used the phrase 'modern movement'. In a letter of 1903 to Fritz Warndörfer he wrote: 'The modern movement is not a silly hobby horse of a few who wish to achieve fame comfortably, it is something living, something good, the only possible art ...'. Such sentiments as these were echoed throughout Europe, but it was in Vienna that they were made reality. The Secession provided a place where the practical problems of craft production and aesthetic experiment could proceed side by side. By the end of 1903 the Werkstätte had been founded, financed by Fritz Wärndörfer (for whom Mackintosh had designed a music room in 1901) with Josef Hoffmann and Kolomon Moser as his main designers. Through these arts and crafts workshops, and similar ones in Germany, the problems of design and mass production were brought to a head and a foundation was laid for the formation of the Deutscher Werkbund in 1907. Kolomon Moser had predicted a period of intense art enterprise and the advent of a new style that would appear fitting for the times:

> We are now living in the times of
> automobiles: electric cars, bicycles
> and railways; what was good style in
> stage coach days is not so now, what
> may have been practical then is not
> so now, and as the times are, so must
> art be.

This adequately echoes the notion of the *Zeitgeist* implicit in the inscription by Hevesi on Olbrich's Secession House:

> To time its art,
> To art its freedom.

Otto Wagner (1841-1918) was at this time the best-known architect and engineer in Vienna. He had reduced his concept of architecture to the simple Vitruvian formula, 'purpose, construction and poetry'. It is claimed that Wagner was the first architect to introduce that most common of all stylistic motifs of modern architecture, the flat roof. His description of the characteristics of the future style was prophetic, and would, he wrote, be found in

> ... horizontal lines such as were prevalent in antiquity, table-like roofs, great simplicity and an energetic exhibition of construction and materials.

Such ideas as these, which were reflected in a building like his Post Office Savings Bank (1905), seem much closer to the ideas of the other famous Viennese architect, Adolf Loos (who had little sympathy with the Secession), than to the ideas of his Secession admirers.

Another factor that cannot be ignored in an assessment of the influences that formed a new attitude to architecture and design towards the end of the nineteenth century is the contribution made by structural engineers. They had a practical approach to design unalloyed by the necessity to master past architectural styles. Their structures were built with panache; they were uninhibited by aesthetic constraints.

The development of the engineer's structure was a logical one, with buildings superseding each other in creative skill, size and monumentality. Many examples could be cited of the inventiveness of the engineer from the early metal bridges, the columnated warehouses of the early part of the nineteenth century to glass and iron horticultural buildings. But clearly, in relation to the general argument later adopted by architects and critics in support of the 'functional' and spatial view of modern architecture, a line of pedigree can be seen linking the Crystal Palace design of Joseph Paxton (1851) with the work of Mies van der Rohe, Konrad Wachsmann and others a century later. It provides an argument fully exploited in the history books on modern architecture by Sigfried Giedion and Henry-Russell Hitchcock; it will be found partially substantiated in some of the extracts included in this anthology (see particularly Part Two).

World exhibitions from 1851 onwards probably best represent the changing attitudes to architecture fed by innovations in engineering. The year 1889 is significant with respect to this development as the World Fair in Paris of that year (earlier ones had been held in 1855, 1867 and 1878) brought to a head the desire of the engineers to exhibit their technical skill with a giant arched machine hall by Contamin, Pierron and Charton and the enormous vertical 'A'-frame tower by Gustave Eiffel. The height and breadth of these structures was amazing: the machine hall was as high (45 metres) as Amiens Cathedral and wider (115 metres) than anything built by man in a single span (its predecessor was the St Pancras, London, train shed, designed in 1865 and built in 1868 by Barlow and Ordish, which spanned 73 metres); while M. Eiffel's tower, reaching a height of nearly 1,000 feet, was the tallest structure in the world until the Empire State Building was erected in New York in 1931. The machine hall (and, one could add, the tower as well) represented, as Hans Sedlemayr has said, '... the focal point of a new conception of aesthetics, and crystallises all the deepest tendencies of the age'. The tower in particular broke down the aesthetic notion of enclosed space and demonstrated to later designers the idea of the interpenetration of space; the lattice ironwork of the structure in which 'outside space' and 'inner space', defined by the boundaries of structure, became one was to fascinate architects as well as designers and painters associated with the Cubist movement and, later, theorists associated with the Dutch 'De Stijl' group and the Russian Constructivists.

In summary, the characteristics of the first machine period which support later architectural views seem to be the following:

— There was a new concern with the lightness of structures which gives them the appearance of floating on minimal supports.
— A structure was no longer viewed as an enclosed object permanently confined by masonry walls with rectangular or arched openings.
— Internal and external spaces were in many examples fused (e.g. Eiffel's tower, numerous railway stations and glazed exhibition buildings).
— The dimensions of the structures were such that they produced an almost overwhelming effect in which man appeared diminutive and a distinct change of scale occurred (an effect that has not escaped the observers of central-area ideas of the post-1945 period and which helped to produce the current disenchantment with more recent 'big-scale' architecture). In the engineering examples, buildings related to the scale of machines (the 'iron horse' railway trains and manufacturing or exhibition machinery).
— Interest in prefabrication was from 1851 onwards implicit in the construction of repetitive column and beam or arched structures offered as a model for mass production (later to be introduced as a means of dealing with housing problems and referred to in extracts by Gropius, May and Schuster in Part Four [94, 99, 106, 111]).

It must be said that if these were the conditioning factors that helped to produce a new way of approaching architectural problems then it only needed the revolutionary zeal of a number of key innovators to make a new architecture a reality. This is what, in good measure, happened – even though we do sometimes get confused by the -isms and counter-isms that plagued modern architecture in the early part of this century. The design of objects went hand in hand with this development. At least, when we view it as a whole, we can now say that the 'modern movement' in architecture and design had continuity and a completely acceptable vocabulary. This new vocabulary, formulated in the mid-1920s, was at the end of the decade to be dubbed by Hitchcock and Johnson the 'international style'.

Prior to this, in 1927, Europe had witnessed the consolidation of international modern architecture at Stuttgart. It was the year in which the German Werkbund's pleas for a united front among the 'new architects' became reality, and in effect the year of acceptance of the canons of the new style for popular housing. The decision to plan a new settlement at Stuttgart was taken in 1926 by the Wurttemberg Chapter of the Deutscher Werkbund in conjunction with the town council of the city. The new settlement – the *Weissenhofsiedlung* – was presented to the public in the form of an exhibition called *Die Wohnung*, which not only included the house units themselves but also furniture and finishes designed to be appropriate to the interiors. With the acumen of a great impresario and the skill of a dedicated planner the co-ordinating director of the exhibition, Mies van der Rohe, invited the leading representatives of the 'modern movement' in architecture to make a contribution. He brought together the older generation Individualists, Peter Behrens and Hans Poelzig, the advocates of a hard-line modernism, Le Corbusier and Pierre Jeanneret, Ludwig Hilberseimer, J. J. P. Oud, Walter Gropius and Mart Stam, as well as the freer designers Hans Scharoun and Adolf Rading. Only the pressure of other work prevented Eric Mendelsohn, Adolf Loos, Hugo Häring and Heinrich Tessenow from contributing designs.

Mies van der Rohe felt at the time that planning could only be solved by the fusion of creative minds and it was with some alacrity that he brought together such a disparate group of individuals. Out of this team – which included among its German members keen experimentalists from the Bauhaus, the ex-Utopians from the eccentric Glass Chain Group, the *Sachlichkeit* fraternity of the Berlin Circle, as well as the famous international names, came a harmonious estate of cheap, minimally-sized dwellings for a new architecture of social universality; an architecture that was expressed in white cubic shapes and clean uncluttered surfaces. Architecturally, Le Corbusier's simple villa, which was a development of his ideas for the Citrohan unit of 1922, and his semi-detached house alongside embodied the principles of the new architecture. Following on from his earlier writings, Le Corbusier spelt out in no uncertain terms a warning to his critics at the exhibition that at Stuttgart he was not dealing with fashionable whims but with 'an absolutely new method of building' in which his five principles for a new architecture applied: (1) the Pilotis; (2) the roof-garden; (3) the free plan; (4) the long window; and (5) the free façade. His colleagues, in statements on their buildings, were not so forthright and it is worth noting that no other building in the exhibition followed the five points advocated by Le Corbusier. Each was a product of a creative mind that conformed only to a personal view about international 'functional' architecture. The total result of the exhibition was not, as some commentators have suggested, a moribund uniformity, or for that matter an *Ararbersdorf* as later depicted by the supporters of National Socialism (Plate 23). Rather, in its variety and inventiveness, it was a high point in modern architecture which was to inspire much of the architecture and design of the subsequent decade.

Functionalism was not a new doctrine or a distinctly twentieth century concept. Although the architecture of the 1920s and 1930s is now almost exclusively termed 'functionalist', it was not a new aesthetic idea; 'machine aesthetic' is probably a much better term. The Germans and Dutch called the 'pristine', clean, white, pure, logical and rational style of the late 1920s and early 1930s *sachlich* – objective.

The words 'functional' and 'functionalist' and the aphorism 'form follows function' had currency in America by the middle of the last century. The expression owes something, too, to the postulates of John Ruskin and to the philosophy of logical simplicity propounded by the English Arts and Crafts movement. But to Horatio Greenhough, an American sculptor who lived from 1802-1852, is laid the claim of the formation of a school of functionalist thought that goes through Richardson and Sullivan to Frank Lloyd Wright. However, this was largely in isolation and cannot be equated with the later Continental usage that sprang from the

German *Werkbund* and, in particular, Hermann Muthesius.

Greenhough's remarks on architecture and art, published in 1852 under the title *Form and Function*, were, he claimed, a 'search after great principles of construction'. He prophetically refers to the principle of functionalism: '... the character of a building has reference to its site – to its adaptation in size and form to that site. It has reference also to the external expression of the inward functions of the building: 'Instead of forcing the functions of every sort of building into one general form,' he goes on, 'without reference to the inner distribution, let us begin from the heart as the nucleus and work outwards' ... 'God's world has a distinct formula for every function, and we shall seek in vain to borrow shapes; we must make the shapes, and can only effect this by mastering the principles.' These thoughts proved to be a stimulus to architects; indeed, they express – as most certainly his own sculpture did not – the basic tenets of American organic functionalism.

As I have suggested, the industrial (engineer-designed) buildings of the nineteenth century also provided a further basis for the development of rational ideas. These buildings, economic and straightforward in their expression as warehouses, stations, bridges, etc., were to be linked with the massive grain silos and the products of the machines of the twentieth century: the car, the liner and even the English briar pipe which impressed adherents of functionalism like Le Corbusier to the extent that they used them to illustrate arguments on the kinds of simplicity that were sought after for a 'new architecture'. Le Corbusier expounded his functionalist theory in terms of the primary Platonist geometrical forms: 'cubes, cones, spheres, cylinders or pyramids'. With these forms, says Le Corbusier, 'the image ... is distinct and tangible within us and without ambiguity. It is for that reason that these are the beautiful forms, the most beautiful forms'. They became the forms symbolic of modern architecture.

During the early 1920s, through his writings and projects, Le Corbusier became the main figurehead in the movement for a new, rationally-based architecture. His influences had been Peter Behrens, Wright, Perret and of course the Viennese theorist Adolf Loos. The first few works of Le Corbusier show a great deal of simplification – largely through the influence of Loos – but very little suggestion of a new aesthetic. Only when he had absorbed the cubist aesthetic and had developed an expression of third dimensional organisation and interpenetration – during his Purist phase – did he finally free himself from his earlier eclectic manner. In the 'Citrohan' and 'Monol' housing schemes of 1920 he began experiments in constructional technique and massing. Within five years he published his revolutionary concepts in his articles in the magazine *L'Esprit Nouveau* under the title 'Vers une Architecture', later published in book form.

Reinforced concrete – ferro-concrete as it was called at the time – was the common material of most of the functionalist architects. As a material, it displayed in use the geometric precision required of the new architecture and adapted itself to the requirements of unbroken surfaces, column and cantilevered construction and (seemingly endless) shapes.

After the Stuttgart exhibition the formation of the CIAM Congress a year later at La Sarraz provided a firm basis from which to propagandise a functional and 'international' modern architecture. The other powerful architectural force at work on the Continent at that time was the Dutch De Stijl group. J. J. P. Oud (who became City architect to Rotterdam as early as 1918, and who claims never to have been a true member of the De Stijl group and later to have refused to join CIAM) was, with van Doesburg, van Eesteren and Gerrit Rietveld, involved in creating a powerful and influential movement in Holland.

Together with Gropius's Bauhaus building (1925-1926) and the Bauhaus system of education, these events were instrumental in changing design methods and attitudes to architecture throughout the world and encouraged the dispersal of ideas through national avant-garde groups.

Once the vocabulary of modernism was established,

its worldwide dissemination followed. In the USSR and later in Germany it was seen as a threat to the supposed nationalist styles of those countries by the ignorant politicians who assumed dictatorial control. For architects, artists and designers it proved a superlative answer to the problems of creative innovation. The 'international style' and its deviations (e.g. Mallet Stevens's half-hearted modernism) had in effect provided a shift from the aesthetic notion of *Kunstwollen* – the will to form – to an all-embracing idea of a *will to function.* If a building or an object was to appear 'right' as well as be 'beautiful' then this was to be measured by its functional efficiency (see the dialogue between Breuer and Perriand [116 and 120]). It is a point that is reiterated from the English point of view in the extract we include from Wells Coates's 'The Conditions for an Architecture of Today' [113] and from the American product designer's point of view in the extract on streamlining from Harold van Doren's book *Industrial Design* [124].

It was, I suppose, predictable that van Doren writing at this time should have looked back to the statement of Louis Sullivan that 'form follows function', for clearly Sullivan had himself seen – as van Doren notes – the danger of pure functionalism becoming an end in itself. Unfortunately, so often in the three decades after the period covered by the Reader this is precisely what happened: town centres became subservient to the demands of 'functional' traffic schemes and economically viable office projects and houses were designed (and in many cases still are) by means of functional plans laid down by government committees – almost everything in architecture has become formless, due principally to a change in scale which was only thought of during the formative years of the 'modern movement' in the more fantastical schemes of Sant'Elia, Chiattone, Le Corbusier, Taut and Scheerbart.

Dennis Sharp
January, 1975

One

Arts and crafts values

The dominant feature of all these extracts is the belief in reason or logic, whether in the Arts and Crafts conception of practicality, honest integrity and simplicity, combined with good craftsmanship (2, 3, 6, 7, 8, 9, 17, 18, 19, 22, 23), or in a tougher insistence on functionality (5, 16, 24, 25, 26) in which we approach the idea that fitness for purpose and perfect functioning might be a sure sign of beauty or even a worthwhile replacement for it. But all the extracts in Part 1 stop short of an explicitly functionalist aesthetic, despite very adventurous references to engineers as artists (16) and the possibilities of machine production (2, 8, 22). Rationality was often compared to the sensible, long-lasting values implicit in vernacular architecture and design, stressing the ability of the craftsman or architect, working within an instinctive tradition, to solve all the problems put to him (3, 4, 17, 20, 21, 24). There was a strong undercurrent of feeling that social factors should play a more important rôle in determining what kind of work should be produced. There was also a strong vein of regional or national pride which at times bordered on insularity (1, 4, 27 or 28). Because of all this, there are few precise recommendations offered as to what forms should be produced, relying on honest craftsmanship and instinctive good taste to solve that problem. Much of the polemic, in fact, is negative, intended to drive home the lessons to be learnt from the excesses of the facile eclecticism of the nineteenth century (11), about which all the authors are agreed. When searching for specific guidelines for form, most architects and designers either looked to vernacular prototypes, particularly Adolf Loos (21), or to the natural world, which played such an important part for Art Nouveau designers (1, 7, 9, 12, 14). We do find some examples of designers looking for abstract rules of composition and arrangement which will allow them to avoid turning to any outside source for formal inspiration, notably Endell (10) and, in very different ways, de Maillou (2) and Van de Velde (15). It is notable, finally, that men who would later develop something akin to a machine aesthetic, such as Gropius and Muthesius, were before the war committed to the idea of applying art to industry, the crafts and architecture, however much they might stress rationalism and logic (24, 26). It is also worth noting in general how the Art Nouveau designers and architects like Horta, Guimard and Van de Velde were determined to show that they had a reasoned argument to back up their creations, and that they were not concerned with mere formalism (8, 10, 12, 31), though the next generation would attack them on this point. Finally, we have included Hans Poelzig's excellent speech of 1931 (29) and Frank Lloyd Wright's defence of his own position against the International Style architects (30), because they help to show the mature and long-lasting strength of Arts and Crafts ideas, despite their modification by later concepts.

---

1 Louis Sullivan, *Ornament in Architecture,* 1892

I take it as self-evident that a building, quite devoid of ornament, may convey a noble and dignified sentiment by virtue of mass and proportion. It is not evident to me that ornament can intrinsically heighten these elemental qualities. Why, then, should we use ornament? Is not a noble and simple dignity sufficient? Why should we ask more?

If I answer the question in entire candour, I should say that it would be greatly for our aesthetic good if we should refrain entirely from the use of ornament for a period of years, in order that our thought might concentrate acutely upon the production of buildings well formed and comely in the nude. We should thus perforce eschew many undesirable things, and learn by contrast how effective it is to think in a natural, vigorous and wholesome way. This step taken, we might safely inquire to what extent a decorative application of ornament would enhance the beauty of our structures – what new charm it would give them.

If we have then become well grounded in pure and simple forms we will reverse them; we will refrain instinctively from vandalism; we will be loath to do aught that may make these forms less pure, less noble. We shall have learned, however, that ornament is mentally a luxury, not a necessity, for we shall have discerned the limitations as well as the great value of unadorned masses. We have in us romanticism, and feel a craving to express it. We feel intuitively that our strong, athletic and simple forms will carry with natural ease the raiment of which we dream, and that our buildings thus clad in a garment of poetic imagery, half hid as it were in choice products of loom and mine, will appeal with redoubled power, like a sonorous melody overlaid with harmonious voices.

I conceive that a true artist will reason substantially in this way; and that, at the culmination of his powers, he may realise his ideal. I believe that architectural ornament brought forth in this spirit is desirable, because beautiful and inspiring; that ornament brought forth in any other spirit is lacking in the higher possibilities.

That is to say, a building which is truly a work of art (and I consider none other) is in its nature, essence and physical being an emotional expression. This being so, and I feel deeply that it is so, it must have, almost literally, a life. It follows from this living principle that an ornamented structure should be characterised by this quality, namely, that the same emotional impulse shall flow throughout harmoniously into its varied forms of expression – of which, while the mass-composition is the more profound, the decorative ornamentation is the more intense. Yet must both spring from the same source of feeling.

I am aware that a decorated building, designed upon this principle, will require in its creator a high and sustained emotional tension, an organic singleness of idea and purpose maintained to the last. The completed work will tell of this; and if it be designed with sufficient depth of feeling and simplicity of mind, the more intense the heat in which it was conceived, the more serene and noble will it remain forever as a monument of man's eloquence. It is this quality that characterises the great monuments of the past. It is this certainly that opens a vista towards the future.

To my thinking, however, the mass-composition and the decorative system of a structure such as I have hinted at should be separable from each other only in theory and for purposes of analytical study. I believe, as I have said, that an excellent and beautiful building may be designed that shall bear no ornament whatever; but I believe just as firmly that a decorated structure, harmoniously conceived, well considered, cannot be stripped of its system of ornament without destroying its individuality.

It has been hitherto somewhat the fashion to speak of ornament, without perhaps too much levity of thought, as a thing to be put on or omitted, as the case might be. I hold to the contrary – that the presence or absence of ornament should, certainly in serious work, be determined at the very beginnings of the design. This is perhaps strenuous insistence, yet I justify and urge it on the ground that creative architecture is an art so fine that its power is manifest in rhythms of great subtlety, as much so indeed as those of musical art, its nearest relative.

If now we bring ourselves to close and reflective observation, how evident it becomes that if we wish to insure an actual, a poetic unity, the ornament should appear, not as something receiving the spirit of the structure, but as a thing expressing that spirit by virtue of differential growth.

It follows then, by the logic of growth, that a certain kind of ornament should appear on a certain kind of structure, just as a certain kind of leaf must appear on a certain kind of tree. An elm leaf would not 'look well' on a pine-tree – a pine-needle seems more 'in keeping'. So, an ornament or scheme of organic decoration befitting a structure composed on broad and massive lines would not be in sympathy with a delicate and dainty one. Nor should the ornamental systems of buildings of any various sorts be interchangeable as between these buildings. For buildings should possess an individuality as marked as that which exists among men, making them distinctly separable from each other, however strong the racial or family resemblance may be.

America is the only land in the whole earth wherein a dream like this may be realised; for here alone tradition is without shackles, and the soul of man free to grow, to mature, to seek its own.

But for this we must turn again to Nature, and hearkening to her melodious voice, learn, as children learn, the accent of its rhythmic cadences. We must view the sunrise with ambition, the twilight wistfully; then, when our eyes have learned to see we shall know how great is the simplicity of nature, that brings forth in serenity such endless variation. We shall learn from this to consider man and his ways, to the end that we behold the unfolding of the soul in all its beauty, and know that the fragrance of a living art shall float again in the garden of our world.

---

2 Rioux de Maillou, *The Decorative Arts and the Machine,* 1895

The English and the Americans would not be artists if they were not outstanding industrialists – if they were not eminently practical people. This is the faculty that enables them to discover the right form which bears a coherent relation to its function. When they make something, they make it well and they make it comfortable.

While the director of the *Revue des Arts décoratifs* was in America for the Chicago Exhibition, he happened to be visiting the showrooms of one of the largest furniture stores in the New World when the arrival of a customer allowed him to witness a typical scene. I feel sure he will not mind my relating it here as he described it.

The buyer was a hotelier engaged in fitting out one of those immense beehives for travellers, which seem to be the monopoly of the large American cities. He had come to choose furniture and wished to look at a type of armchair which rocks backwards and forwards rather like a seesaw – called a rocking-chair. This is still comparatively rare in France, but is used by all self-respecting Americans whenever they can snatch a few hours of leisure. The customer seemed little concerned about matters of good or bad taste and the tenor of the remarks he addressed to the manufacturer as he examined the different models, trying to make up his mind, bore exclusively on considerations of *comfort.*

One chair had arms which failed to allow a properly relaxed posture. The back of another was steep and would not mould the loins. The next had a very high back which would spoil *flirtation* with a person who might be rocking it from behind ...

At length, when the hotel proprietor stopped at the chair which most fully answered his requirements, the one most suited to its purpose, it turned out to be the very chair which had a structure most nearly approaching aesthetic perfection. The principle of the relation between function and form as the foundation of beauty was thoroughly borne out by the facts.

The essential characteristic of any production of the decorative arts is its ability to express itself, to state its *raison d'être* through lines which are meaningful, not arbitrary. A piece of furniture must reveal its purpose, allow it to be guessed. And there is another rule which is no less important for industrial designing. It is not enough merely to disclose the aim; an article must explain what it is, say plainly and in appropriate language of what it is made and by whom.

Wooden furniture must look like wood and if some parts have been machine-turned they must show signs of that type of manufacture. The mode of execution in a sense is what determines the peculiar quality, *sui generis.* Nothing can be hybrid in art. And the best partner of art is always honesty ...

Proudhon, whose penetrating abstract vision has shed light on this problem from within and without, in depth and to the full extent of its surface, and who cannot be quoted too often, wrote: 'The more a man can understand about things and their parts, letting others labour with execution and put finishing touches to detail, the more powerful will be his reasoning, the more his genius will develop and grow in strength.'

In industry this is an undisputed truth. Man raises himself by rendering his task less manual and more intellectual, progressing from being a factory-hand to a skilled worker, a foreman and a manager. In some respects the machines or mechanisms at our disposal thus aid the mind in its striving for something better, help it to rise towards its ideal. And as beauty is necessarily a category of the ideal, a machine can favour aesthetic progress. Indirectly it has an uplifting effect, relieving man of mechanical and physical strain by providing a material means of harnessing matter which liberates the mind, giving pride of place to ideas.

The individual work of art, however, is intended to preserve the artist's creative impulse. It lives on, so to speak, by protracting his life, the beating of his heart and the warmth of his breath, bearing the seal of his genius. The work of art is by nature aristocratic.

And the division of labour, that ineluctable law of economics which makes production accessible to all and therefore democratic, is its death-sentence.

Now a large majority of the population can only purchase articles which are cheap, that is, placed within reach of the budgets at the disposal of the cogs in the machine, in other words, they can only buy democratic products.

This brings the problem down to this: Which is better, a true *mechanistic* art or an art of imitation individuality?

For my part, I do not hesitate for one moment. *Imitation* is the worst enemy of art. It corrupts taste and scatters aspects of knowledge like weeds, whose harvest is quite predictable. The *petite bourgeoisie* of the Louis-Philippe era gave us a foretaste of what we can expect, as we are just now realising from what has survived from that time and what is still spreading. Anything rather than imitation!

Since a solution has to be found and since the democratic exigencies of modern times make not only cheap but the cheapest possible production a necessity, we have no alternative but to use machines. It remains for us to make the best use of them we can.

The way to begin is to be honest about our new methods. If a machine does the work, it should be allowed to leave its mark, to imprint its mode of expression on the things it produces.

There is a new decorative aesthetic to be developed from the arrival of industrialisation in the field of art. It is wrong to be mesmerised by the past when so much is fertile in the present. If the seeds are fostered wisely and allowed to flower, the unknown blooms which will emerge from this uncultivated ground will bring their own reward. Our efforts will have been worthwhile and we shall have won the key modern artistic victory.

No one can tell what industrial progress and discovery may have in store, or what great artistic revival may lie ahead.

The use of iron in building, for instance, has proved the greatest architectural event of the age. The way now looks superbly promising for harmonic associations of iron, ceramics and brick, and our central markets, for a start, were a stroke of genius. The lists are open and the valiant knights have but to join battle. Architects and engineers, men of arts and science alike, can safely be proud of wielding iron with a flourish. At the 1889 Exhibition in the *Gallérie des Machines* in Paris, science showed how much it could assist art by simply encouraging it to give linear expression to scientific laws. And the oriental dome boldly crowning the Palace of Fine Arts has been M. Formijé's triumphant demonstration of what art can offer science and what architecture, aided by science, is now in a position to achieve.

There is thus no reason why we should not expect equally inspired finds from other branches of the arts and aesthetic developments similar to those which have taken place in the art of building. New processes produce new art (*art nouveau*).

The great Swiss educator, Pestalozzi, wrote:

> Drawing consists in outlining forms which have been accurately and neatly defined in contour and content by means of perfect measurement. Before practising drawing, a child ought to have been taught how to measure and be capable of measuring more or less anything. If this has not been possible, it should at least be given training in the two together ... Then we must discover how this talent, which is the foundation of all the arts, can be developed, that is how children can be encouraged to grasp the exact measures of the things they see.

The brilliant recognition that *measuring is the foundation of all the arts* came from a man whose deep psychological insight made him the greatest of pedagogues. Measurement, as far as form is concerned, means, harmonically expressive proportions and harmonic proportions in colour as well. Both are placed at the service of thought: the field of art is marked out by this analysis which is one of measurement.

Machines also have a rôle to play in this respect. It is true that the new road eliminates the special preparation, the extra flavour added by the artist's *act*, but the way still looks sufficiently inviting for the critical and fastidious to find some consolation.

In conclusion, though the use of machines means losing the *living quality* which hand-execution can transmit through the tool, it can, in return, bestow a kind of abstract beauty by replacing physical effort with the sensitive manipulation, the masterly, *knowledgeable* and understanding urge of the man in charge. He uses material means to subject his materials to the superbly calm creative idea precisely because it consists of idea and will alone.

Idealism and mechanisation constitute the thesis and antithesis of an antimony, which we must strive to bring to a synthesis, to use academic language. And if mechanisation applied to art wishes to prevail in the future, it must adopt the *higher conciliation* of these two contradictory terms as its mission.

Since architecture is the most abstract of the arts, mechanical decorative productions should tend towards attaining equally abstract architectural qualities.

The charm and grace of ornamental detail has a pictorial appeal which is all very well, but the beauty which expresses the whole, that is, its construction, the logic of the composition, is better still, because it dominates and orders the whole. No decoration, however brilliant, can save a building which has failed architecturally. It will look no more than the accessory it is, just awkward outer trimming, whereas good proportions and a lucid design can often succeed in masking errors of detail. In a word, architectural simplicity is self-contained but there is no such thing as artistic decoration without an architectural basis. Before a thing can be decorative, it must exist in its own right, as an ornament, a piece of furniture, a building and so on. Art is justified in expecting a lot from machines, in asking a lot of them, and consequently in using them insofar as this is legitimately possible.

But there is one danger which ought not to be overlooked. Machines have their limitations and it is a mistake to believe that because they can do so much they can do everything. They must always obey the dictates of the raw material. For example, molten metal can be beaten or poured into a mould, but wood cannot. If wood is stamped, compressed and tortured, it will no longer be wood and, try as one may, will never produce more than a pasteboard effect. The peculiar quality and the beauty of wood lies in its grain and in the successful way the tool works the fibrous texture. If the fibres are crushed, the raw material is virtually lost. Beaten, compressed wood has not been worked, it has been destroyed. The result is similar when iron is not beaten, but rolled into a shape which no longer bears any relation to the action of the hammer striking the anvil. The effect is as painful as that achieved by certain misguided goldsmiths who apply the frail patterns of Renaissance metal-work to silver.

Different raw materials need different ways of fashioning. Each has its own language and it is the artist's task to find appropriate forms which will highlight rather than obscure this language.

Machines, then, can do a great deal for the decorative arts and for the education of taste in general, provided their true character, their appropriate fields of operation and their social implications are always remembered. Essentially they are economic forms, capable of benefiting art in two ways, first by elevating the worker and secondly by enlarging the public receptive to aesthetic feeling.

We must never forget that we are a democracy, that we live in a century oriented ever more towards democracy, and that there can be no art if there is no society to enjoy it, to want it, and by wanting it, to allow it to be produced.

In short, *art is social*: let us accept it as such, conceive of it as such, pursue it according to the measure of our democratic society ... and, forwards!

3 M. H. Baillie Scott, *An Ideal Suburban House,* 1895

Everyone who has experienced the discomforts of the average suburban house will admit that there is ample room for improvement in its arrangement; and it is with a view to show how a few of its most glaring defects at least may be corrected that the present writer has designed the house which is here illustrated. It is not supposed to be a model house, which may be built in any position or on any site – for the local conditions of almost any particular site will, or should, materially affect the plan of a house to be built on it; but it may be advanced as an example of certain points to be aimed at in planning a house to meet the requirements of the average householder. The key-notes of the design may be said to be simplicity and homely comfort, and the doll's-house-like prettiness of the so-called Queen Anne bijou residence has been held to be as undesirable on the one hand, as the stolid ugliness of the commoner box of bricks style of suburban house on the other. The study of the economical side of the question is also important in a house of this kind, where no money is to be wasted in useless ornament; and so we find simplicity desirable, not only from an artistic but from an economical point of view.

Turning to a consideration of the ground-plan, illustrated. On entering by the front door we find ourselves in a wide and low porch from which, through an archway to the right, we catch a glimpse of the staircase which rises from a wide corridor leading to the kitchen. On the left is a small cloak-room where hats, coats, and boots can be disposed instead of being hung up on the usual barbarous construction called a hat-stand, which generally bars the way to the entrance in the average house.

From the porch there are two doors, one into the drawing-room, the other into the hall, and the object of this arrangement will appear later on. It is difficult for me to picture to you the appearance of this porch with the vista-like effect of the broad corridor; but to get some idea of its general effect I must transport you

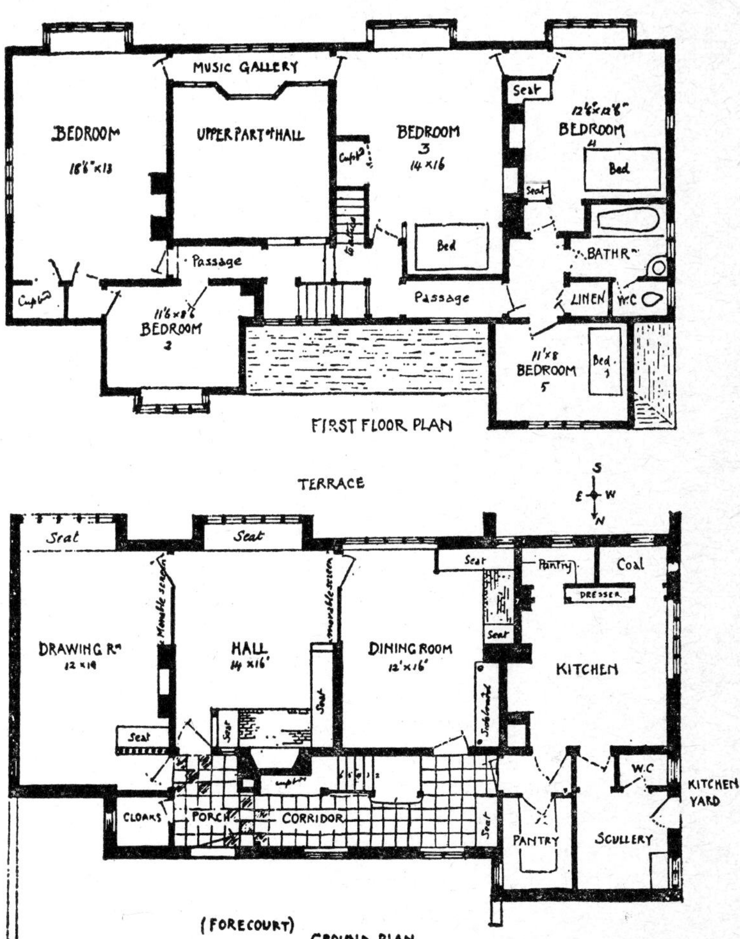

M. H. Baillie Scott, 'An Ideal Suburban House', 1894-5
First floor plan
Ground floor plan
The Studio, vol. IV, 1894-5

to some old Cheshire farmhouse, somewhere in the country where people have not yet grown to be ashamed of plain bricks and whitewash, and where the marbled wall-papers and oil-cloths which greet us on the threshold of so many modern villas are unknown.

The next portion of the house which claims our attention is what may be called the family sitting-rooms. These consist of the dining-room, hall, and drawing-room, all lighted from the sunny side of the house. These rooms are divided by panelled screens which are removable and when taken from their position may be used as folding screens in the various rooms. By this means the inconvenience which arises from the inevitable smallness of rooms in a house where economy is to be studied is obviated, and in a small house on festive occasions a large amount of space can be obtained.

The principal feature in the hall is the ingle.

I should like to picture to you a musical evening in this hall. In the ingle, seated on the broad seats, a company of friends are gathered around the blazing wood fire on the wide brick hearth, which lights up the burnished copper of the fire-dogs and the heaps of logs piled on each side of the hearth. There is no glaring gas, but here and there lamps and candles throw a soft suffused light. Above in the gallery are the musicians, and the strains of a violin are heard to their best advantage, while the position of the player gives an air of mystery to the music which greatly adds to its effect. Or if we imagine a more festive scene, we may picture the three sitting-rooms combined for a dance, and here again the central and elevated position of the musicians will be found appropriate to the occasion. This lofty hall may appear to be rather an expensive luxury for such a small house, but as it is not carried up quite through the two storeys it allows of a picturesque room partly in the roof over it, while it is a desirable relief to the comparative lowness of the ceilings of the other sitting-rooms. Of late years there has been a great revival of the hall as a central feature in a house, but as a rule it is practically a sitting-room where no one sits, a kind of show place forming a passage for the servants to the front door and for visitors to the drawing-room. This is all very well if we can afford to sacrifice a sitting-room in this way, but in our small house space is far too valuable. The hall is to be a place where the family may assemble round the fire in the evening, without being disturbed by servants passing through it, or without being obliged to hastily decamp on the arrival of an unwelcome visitor. So there is a separate door through which visitors may be shown to the drawing-room, and the servants never need pass through any of these three family sitting-rooms, as will be seen by a glance at the plan, so that our hall can form, as it should, a family gathering place.

The furniture is simple and dainty in design, and everything in the room is disposed with quiet dignity of effect, while conspicuously absent are the host of so-called decorative articles which make locomotion perilous in so many drawing-rooms, and which tempt one to exclaim with the carpenter through the looking-glass, 'If these were only cleared away, oh, wouldn't it be grand!' The pictures are few and choice, not dotted over the walls, but carefully grouped. Everything, in short, appears to have been specially designed to fit its particular position in the room, and we feel that the aim has been not to try and get as many pretty things as possible crowded together, but rather to eliminate as far as possible everything which is unnecessary. Here again simplicity is hand in hand with economy, and the price of the thousand and one nicknacks which destroy the repose of the average drawing-room is saved.

And here one may insist that the great advantage of a well-designed house is that it requires none of that palliative furniture which becomes a necessity in the average house to hide defects of proportion and construction. There are no large expanses of plate-glass windows to shroud in curtains, and no handsome marble mantelpiece to drape. Our object is, in fact, rather to display the beauties than hide the defects of the house, and so a far less amount of furniture is required than is usually considered necessary.

The kitchen of the average suburban house does not present so much room for improvements as the family rooms. Here at least, where things are for use and not for show, some approximation is made to a successful interior effect, and here we find perhaps a fine old copper scuttle and some brass candlesticks which have not been considered genteel enough for the front parlour. Our kitchen then presents a simple and homely character.

It is difficult for the architect to draw a fixed line between the architecture of house and the furniture. The conception of an interior must necessarily include the furniture which is to be used in it, and this naturally leads to the conclusion that the architect should design the chairs and tables as well as the house itself. Every architect who loves his work must have had his enthusiasm dampened by a prophetic vision of the hideous furniture with which his client may fill his rooms, and which looks all the more incongruous if the rooms themselves are architecturally beautiful.

It is a common belief that to build an artistic house a large sum of money is required. Art and ornament are often understood as synonymous terms, and the house which possesses the largest amount of ornament is often held to be the most artistic. It will therefore be necessary to state that the reverse of this is very often the case, and that a house is artistic in proportion to the amount of skill and thought displayed in its design, and not in proportion to the amount of decoration it possesses.

Again, the intrinsic value of the materials of which a house is built is often taken as the measure of its artistic merit without regard to beauty of workmanship or design. Such a method of judging is almost as unreasonable as if one estimated the value of a picture by the price per pound of paint or per yard of canvas.

What is really required is that we should spend more thought on our houses rather than more money, and that we should demand not only convenience of arrangement, but beauty of proportion and design. The English people pride themselves not a little on their love of home, a word which, indeed, hardly has an equivalent in other languages; but how can we dignify with such a title the cheerless dwellings in which so many of us live? Greater attention, it may be, is now being given to practical sanitation than formerly, but from an aesthetic point of view the healthy house is still an object of rarity. Let us hope that the time is not far distant when people who love this English home-life will refuse to associate it with the houses they now inhabit, and that the increased demand for a better class of buildings thus created will result in the erection of houses which we may be proud to call our Homes.

---

4 Alfred Lichtwark, *Palace Window and Folding Door,* 1896

The form of artistic development in Germany is still directed towards Athens and Rome or towards London and Paris. It is there that we feel at home and are fully acquainted with the situation and it is there that we find the measure by which to evaluate our own achievements, and the opinions by which we misconstrue them.

An interest in German things becomes less popular, the nearer to home and therefore of more actual importance it is. The German eye having become long-sighted, loves to linger on distant horizons and allow the fantasy free rein.

Millions of German readers are enthralled by a newspaper article concerning archaeological discoveries in Chaldaea. But nobody feels any excitement about the fact that, now more than ever before, a precious style of domestic architecture is falling into decay all over Germany, which has more significance for our artistic development in the future, than anything that lies buried under the ruins of Niniveh.

If the German character is only weakly represented in our artistic development, the local character is completely missing. A healthy artistic development should spring from Munich's soil in Munich, Nuremburg's soil in Nuremburg and Hamburg's soil in Hamburg . . .

If we wish to give the coming generation an artistic

education, which will be effective in practice then we must, as far as architecture is concerned, begin with the elements of middle-class and peasant building. First we must have the things which are essentials in our lives. The architectural education of the German must be inspired by fishermen's and seamen's houses, and from the peasants' or citizens' houses in the locality. It is of greater importance for him and for German art that he should understand the beauty of these basic forms of our architecture, rather than know all there is to know of the Greek temple or the Florentine Palace ...

Our civic architecture has made very great advances over the last twenty-five years. These advances have, however, been rather one-sided. For while the equipment of cellar, kitchen, bathroom and bedroom are vast improvements on those of our grandfather's generation, the design of the living-rooms and dining-rooms has seen little essential change. They have become neither more practical nor more beautiful. It is even quite possible that the artistic level has sunk to a lower level ...

If we wish to return to healthier conditions, we must try to identify the things which need improving. It is this and not the furnishing of a house which must be given priority treatment.

The form and lighting of room interiors are the great decisive factors.

They depend, however, on the treatment of the windows and doors, and if our architecture remains inadequate and makes no headway, despite using every stylistic device available, this is rooted in the basic mistake in the positioning of light apertures.

We must not expect a change for the better from the architect alone. More than any other artist he is dependent on the requirements, the taste and the goodwill of his clients.

It is therefore important to make more German people recognise that ninety out of a hundred of the rooms in our new buildings, with the best will in the world and great expense, cannot be furnished comfortably let alone artistically, because the windows and doors do not allow it.

The windows belong both to the exterior and the interior of a building. They are the hinge upon which the builder's plan turns, or should turn.

They form the rhythmical articulation of light and dark in the façade, which determines the character far more directly than the sum total of all the columns, ornaments and cornices. When seen from a distance, all decorative forms sink back into the mass of reflecting wall and yet the dark flecks of the windows, which reflect no light, still have something to say. And on the inside, neither paint, wall, ceiling nor door can match the window. It stands amongst them like something alive among dead things and has within it the power to make the room large or small, comfortable or unpleasant, artistic or banal.

Our modern architecture, however, allows this most expressive element of building to be ignored.

It basically only recognises one form, that of the Italian palace window, and has given up the many and varied developments of the last centuries, which have arisen from the needs of our climate, our customs and our artistic sensitivity.

The window is employed at present exclusively as a part of the façade, as if it consisted of a kind of embellishment similar to columns or woodwork. It no longer has the shape or size which the room requires to illuminate it, but rather must attune itself to the rhythm of the façade. It is no longer positioned where it is needed in the room, but rather where it is needed in the façade ...

If there was the possibility, that the windows of all the proud palaces of our cities could be re-built to suit the requirements of the interiors, our whole architecture would, at a stroke, be given a new face, for the tyranny of the façade, which is treated as a thing in itself and not as an expression of the ground plan, would be broken. There would be no more houses with columns ...

We must always return to these remnants of a foundering domestic culture. The English have built their town houses on the basis of the cottage, the simple country house, in which they have developed all the seeds of artistry, with great care and circumspection and with the most delicate taste. Our country house, which we pompously call a villa, is academic up to its neck, and instead of speaking Low German, Franconian, Swabian or Thuringian, it splutters forth a confused mixture of Greek, Italian and French.

---

5 Louis Sullivan, *The Tall Office Building Artistically Considered,* 1896

The architects of this land and generation are now brought face to face with something new under the sun – namely, that evolution and integration of social conditions, that special grouping of them, that results in a demand for the erection of tall office buildings.

It is not my purpose to discuss the social conditions; I accept them as the fact, and say at once that the design of the tall office building must be recognised and confronted at the outset as a problem to be solved – a vital problem, pressing for a true solution.

Let us state the conditions in the plainest manner. Briefly, they are these: offices are necessary for the transaction of business; the invention and perfection of the high-speed elevators make vertical travel, that was once tedious and painful, now easy and comfortable; development of steel manufacture has shown the way to safe, rigid, economical constructions rising to a great height; continued growth of population in the great cities, consequent congestion of centres and rise in value of ground, stimulate an increase in number of storeys; these successfully piled one upon another, react on ground values – and so on, by action and reaction, interaction and inter-reaction. Thus has come about that form of lofty construction called the 'modern office building'. It has come in answer to a call, for in it a new grouping of social conditions has found a habitation and a name.

Up to this point all in evidence is materialistic, an exhibition of force, of resolution, of brains in the keen sense of the word. It is the joint product of the speculator, the engineer, the builder.

Problem: How shall we impart to this sterile pile, this crude, harsh, brutal agglomeration, this stark, staring exclamation of eternal strife, the graciousness of those higher forms of sensibility and culture that rest on the lower and fiercer passions? How shall we proclaim from the dizzy height of this strange, weird, modern housetop the peaceful evangel of sentiment, of beauty, the cult of a higher life?

This is the problem; and we must seek the solution of it in a process analogous to its own evolution – indeed, a continuation of it – namely, by proceeding step by step from general to special aspects, from coarser to finer considerations.

It is my belief that it is of the very essence of every problem that it contains and suggests its own solution. This I believe to be natural law. Let us examine, then, carefully the elements, let us search out this contained suggestion, this essence of the problem.

The practical conditions are, broadly speaking, these:

Wanted – 1st, a storey below-ground, containing boilers, engines of various sorts, etc. – in short, the plant for power, heating, lighting, etc. 2nd, a ground floor, so called, devoted to stores, banks, or other establishments requiring large area, ample spacing, ample light, and great freedom of access. 3rd, a second storey readily accessible by stairways – this space usually in large subdivisions, with corresponding liberality in structural spacing and expanse of glass and breadth of external openings. 4th, above this an indefinite number of storeys of offices piled tier upon tier, one tier just like another tier, one office just like all the other offices – an office being similar to a cell in a honey-comb, merely a compartment, nothing more. 5th, and last, at the top of this pile is placed a space or storey that, as related to the life and usefulness of the structure, is purely physiological in its nature – namely, the attic. In this the circulatory system completes itself and makes its grand turn, ascending and descending. The space is filled with tanks, pipes, valves, sheaves, and mechanical etcetera that supplement and complement the force-originating plant hidden below-ground in the cellar. Finally, or at the beginning rather, there must be on the ground floor a main aperture or entrance common to all the occupants or patrons of the building.

Hence it follows inevitably, and in the simplest possible way, that if we follow our natural instincts without thought of books, rules, precedents, or any such educational impedimenta to a spontaneous and 'sensible' result, we will in the following manner design the exterior of our tall office building – to wit:

Beginning with the first storey, we give this a main entrance that attracts the eye to its location, and the remainder of the storey we treat in a more or less liberal, expansive, sumptuous way – a way based exactly on the practical necessities, but expressed with a sentiment of largeness and freedom. The second storey we treat in a similar way, but usually with milder pretension. Above this, throughout the definite number of typical office tiers, we take our cue from the individual cell, which requires a window with its separating pier, its sill and lintel, and we, without more ado, make them look all alike because they are all alike. This brings us to the attic, which, having no division into office-cells and no special requirement for lighting, gives us the power to show by means of its broad expanse of wall, and its dominating weight and character, that which is the fact – namely, that the series of office tiers has come definitely to an end.

I assume now that in the study of our problems we have passed through the various stages of inquiry, as follows: 1st, the social basis of the demand for tall office buildings; 2nd, its literal material satisfaction; 3rd, the elevation of the question from considerations of literal planning, construction, and equipment, to the plane of elementary architecture as a direct outgrowth of sound, sensible building; 4th, the question again elevated from an elementary architecture to the beginning of true architectural expression, through the addition of a certain quality and quantity of sentiment.

But our building may have all these in a considerable degree and yet be far from that adequate solution of the problem I am attempting to define. We must now heed the imperative voice of emotion.

It demands of us, what is the chief characteristic of the tall office building? And at once we answer, it is lofty. This loftiness is to the artist-nature its thrilling aspect. It is the very open organ-tone in its appeal. It must be in turn the dominant chord in his expression of it, the true excitant of his imagination. It must be tall, every inch of it tall. The force and power of altitude must be in it, the glory and pride of exaltation must be in it. It must be every inch a proud and soaring thing, rising in sheer exultation that from bottom to top it is a unit without a single dissenting line – that it is the new, the unexpected, the eloquent peroration of most bald, most sinister, most forbidding conditions.

The man who designs in this spirit and with the sense of responsibility to the generation he lives in must be no coward, no denier, no bookworm, no dilettante. He must live of his life and for his life in the fullest, most consummate sense. He must realise at once and with the grasp of inspiration that the problem of the tall office building is one of the most stupendous, one of the most magnificent opportunities that the Lord of Nature in His beneficence has ever offered to the proud spirit of man.

That this has not been perceived – indeed, has been flatly denied – is an exhibition of human perversity that must give us pause.

One more consideration. Let us now lift this question into the region of calm, philosophic observation. Let us seek a comprehensive, a final solution: let the problem indeed dissolve. [Sullivan summarises some of the theoretical attitudes to tall buildings of other architects and writers.]

. . . As to the former and serious views held by discerning and thoughtful critics, I shall, with however much of regret, dissent from them for the purpose of this demonstration, for I regard them as secondary only, non-essential, and as touching not at all upon the vital spot, upon the quick of the entire matter, upon the true, the immovable philosophy of the architectural art.

This view let me now state, for it brings to the solution of the problem a final, comprehensive formula.

All things in nature have a shape, that is to say, a form, an outward semblance, that tells us what they are, that distinguishes them from ourselves and from each other.

Unfailingly in nature these shapes express the inner life, the native quality, of the animal, tree, bird, fish, that they present to us; they are so characteristic, so recognisable, that we say, simply it is 'natural' it should be so. Yet the moment we peer beneath this surface of things, the moment we look through the tranquil reflection of ourselves and the clouds above us, down into the clear, fluent, unfathomable depth of nature, how startling is the silence of it, how amazing the flow of life, how absorbing the mystery. Unceasingly the essence of things is taking shape in the matter of things, and this unspeakable process we call birth and growth. Awhile the spirit and the matter fade away together, and it is this that we call decadence, death. These two happenings seem jointed and interdependent, blended into one like a bubble and its iridescence, and they seem borne along upon a slowly moving air. This air is wonderful past all understanding.

Yet to the steadfast eye of one standing upon the shore of things, looking chiefly and most lovingly upon that side on which the sun shines and that we feel joyously to be life, the heart is ever gladdened by the beauty, the exquisite spontaneity, with which life seeks and takes on its forms in an accord perfectly responsive to its needs. It seems ever as though the life and the form were absolutely one and inseparable, so adequate is the sense of fulfilment.

Whether it be the sweeping eagle in his flight or the open apple-blossom, the toiling work-horse, the blithe swan, the branching oak, the winding stream at its base, the drifting clouds, over all the coursing sun, form ever follows function, and this is the law. Where function does not change form does not change. The granite rocks, the ever-brooding hills, remain for ages; the lightning lives, comes into shape, and dies in a twinkling.

It is the pervading law of all things organic, and inorganic, of all things physical and metaphysical, of all things human and all things super-human, of all true manifestations of the head, of the heart, of the soul, that the life is recognisable in its expression, that form ever follows function. This is the law.

Shall we, then, daily violate this law in our art? Are we so decadent, so imbecile, so utterly weak of eyesight, that we cannot perceive this truth so simple, so very simple? Is it indeed a truth so transparent that we see through it but do not see it? Is it really then, a very marvellous thing, or is it rather so commonplace, so everyday, so near a thing to us, that we cannot perceive that the shape, form, outward expression, design or whatever we may choose, of the tall office building should in the very nature of things follow the functions of the building, and that where the function does not change, the form is not to change?

Does this not readily, clearly, and conclusively show that the lower one or two storeys will take on a special character suited to the special needs, that the tiers of typical offices, having the same unchanging function, shall continue in the same unchanging form, and that as to the attic, specific and conclusive as it is in its very nature, its function shall equally be so in force, in significance, in continuity, in conclusiveness of outward expression? From this results, naturally, spontaneously, unwittingly, a three-part division, not from any theory, symbol, or fancied logic.

And thus the design of the tall office building takes its place with all other architectural types made when architecture, as happened once in many years, was a living art. Witness the Greek temple, the Gothic cathedral, the medieval fortress.

And thus, when native instinct and sensibility

shall govern the exercise of our beloved art; when the known law, the respected law, shall be that form ever follows function; when our architects shall cease struggling and prattling handcuffed and vainglorious in the asylum of a foreign school; when it is truly felt, cheerfully accepted, that this law opens up the airy sunshine of green fields, and gives to us a freedom that the very beauty and sumptuousness of the outworking of the law itself as exhibited in nature will deter any sane, any sensitive man from changing into licence, when it becomes evident that we are merely speaking a foreign language with a noticeable American accent, whereas each and every architect in the land might, under the benign influence of this law, express in the simplest, most modest, most natural way that which it is in him to say; that he might really and would surely develop his own characteristic individuality, and that the architectural art with him would certainly become a living form of speech, a natural form of utterance, giving surcease to him and adding treasures small and great to the growing art of his land; when we know and feel that Nature is our friend, not our implacable enemy – that an afternoon in the country, an hour by the sea, a full open view of one single day, through dawn, high noon, and twilight, will suggest to us so much that is rhythmical, deep, and eternal in the vast art of architecture, something so deep, so true, that all the narrow formalities, hard-and-fast rules, and strangling bonds of the schools cannot stifle it in us – then it may be proclaimed that we are on the high-road to a natural and satisfying art, an architecture that will soon become a fine art in the true, best sense of the word, an art that will live because it will be of the people, for the people, and by the people.

---

6 Alfred Lichtwark, *Practical Application,* 1897

The needs of the housewife are coming to be recognised across the length and breadth of the kingdom. Whoever wants to test the new productions for their serviceability should examine them through the eyes of the housewife.

The young German woman has grown up under the influence of the studio style. It is therefore quite natural, that her taste should be easily inclined towards the opposite. Overcrowding, overloading, inflated style or empty pomp and cheap trimmings do not appeal to her. She does not wish to possess anything which will not serve a practical purpose, she hates pure decoration and finds pleasure in quiet and elegant simplicity. Wall plaques, bowls with high rims, superfluous curtains and drapes and cheap carvings are all repugnant to her.

She has a practical spirit. Even in the most magnificent surroundings she feels that the number of servants should be no more than absolutely necessary, for the reins are held in her own hands. She will examine all the products of decorative art from the point of view of practical serviceability and for their efficiency in the home, things which do not require an excessive amount of energy.

These already present tendencies will gain ground in the near future and at the same time take firm root. Decorative art must take this into account under all circumstances.

Part of the decorative work created by modern artists is not intended to serve any practical purpose and falls under a rubric of its own. We will only concern ourselves here with objects which claim to serve a purpose. If the exhibitions of furniture and devices designed by the artist are seen from the German housewife's point of view, certain new facts come to light.

There we have a wonderful chest, carved with beautiful figures or mounted with wrought iron, new in colour and form and a great work of art, the decorative content of which would keep an entire school busy. The housewife would say: that should be in a museum. I could not put it anywhere. My corridors are too narrow and I do not need storage furniture inside the rooms. And anyway the chest is an animal which became extinct long ago, like the dinosaur or the icthyosaur. It was practical in the Middle Ages, when it was necessary to pack one's belongings quickly on to a wagon, when there was a danger of floods, fire or war. The most we can do nowadays is to place it on the floor and store supplies inside it. But a trunk would serve the same purpose quite adequately. Even the successor of the chest, the chest-of-drawers, has already become a historical concept. We no longer store anything in the living-room, and in the bedroom our wardrobe with its many shelves is a far more convenient arrangement. Under no circumstances do we need a chest.

She is standing by a new dining-room suite, exceptionally beautiful from the artistic point of view. The colours are as wonderful as any picture or expensive dress, the form is new. The suite is very much to her liking. So she samples the expensive table, a delight to any artist, and suddenly she shakes her head. The thought of seeing her guests seated upsets her, for in accordance with the Gothic style the legs are slanting and are connected all the way around by angular cross bars. If someone moves thoughtlessly, they will injure their shin-bone and if they then jump up in pain, their knee will also be injured, for the edge is far too deep. At one glance she can also see the dangers of using the dining-room chairs. The back rest is high enough for the person sitting in the chair to rest the back of his neck against it. Such chairs make serving difficult. One clumsy movement and the sauce is spilt, and if the chairs have to be moved closer together for once, the meat-dish can no longer be passed in between them. Also, at the point where the occupant's back should be supported, there is a concave movement in the back-rest in place of a convex one. When the guest therefore attempts to lean backwards he will find his chest constricted. No, no, not these chairs. Dining-room chairs must have a low back rest and always support the small of the back.

In another ensemble, she finds herself standing in front of a delightful fireplace, with a high wooden mantelpiece. The shape could have been the design of a great sculptor. She cannot see enough of it. But how can one keep the smooth surfaces, which require daily cleaning, free from dust? What about the angles and niches? A feather duster would not suffice. A high step ladder would be needed. And so a long list of complications appears before her: Where should the ladder be stored, so that it would be readily available for use first thing in the morning? Which of the servants should carry it there and bring it back? What would it bump against on its way? What could be used to protect the carpet on which the ladder would stand? How much time would all this cost? And the fireplace is found wanting.

In another fascinating room, wide pieces of brass have been set into the floor. The effect is novel and artistic. But the brass has to be polished, and more and more as time goes on. But the housewife knows, that brass and wood cannot be cleaned at the same time. There is no way round it, the wood would become smudged. Perhaps she would have purchased the room otherwise, but now she goes on her way with a sigh ...

Does this have to be so?

---

7 Thiébault-Sisson, *An Innovator, – Victor Horta,* 1897

The architect has been the last to respond to the movement which is currently driving all artists to search for new forms, dictated by a new ideal. Schooled in the past, fed on respect for tradition and crammed from early youth with formulas to meet every kind of usage the architect abandoned the habit of research, and thereby personal expression, under the July Monarchy and the Empire ...

All around people are now emerging who are not without originality and ability, but there have not appeared anywhere such bold new inventions, and such a logical yet deeply personal art, as in the works of a young architect, Victor Horta – of whom Belgium can be justly proud.

This is his first attempt, built for a bachelor. It is the Tassel house in the Rue de Turin. [There follows a detailed description of the house, outside and in] . . .

You will realise that the house is composed of two quite distinct parts; the main part is at the back, being separated from the front by a glazed court.

Victor Horta, Tassel House: first floor landing, 1893
Art et Décoration, vol. 1, 1897

The architect has made this glazed court, which is sunny all day long, the centre and the bright focal point of the residence. As far as possible, he has avoided having solid walls around it. Masonry pillars, which would

Victor Horta, Tassel House: salon, 1893
Art et Décoration, vol. 1, 1897

have made it seem like a well, have been replaced by an exposed metal framework which is reinforced here and there by colonettes. Their light green colour and their shape, so carefully considered and so charmingly achieved, closely match the general decoration. Light stems, leafy on top, and rising as if from a stalk at the base, pleasantly prolong the sensation of greenery and coolness with which the winter garden has charmed your eye. And it's a wonder to see a whole flower bed of stylised foliage running over the walls in capricious arabesques of colour, prolonging the illusion further and uniting with the supple ironwork scrolls in harmonious arrangements ...

You arrive at the mezzanine floor; there are still more surprises in store for you. The architect has made a smoking-room of the central part, lit by a coloured glass window overlooking the street, and flanked by a bathroom on one side and a laboratory on the other.

Before returning to the landing, halt in this sort of vestibule which serves as lobby to the smoking-room and lean out over the large bay which links it to the central glass-walled court. Your gaze travels easily beyond the space of the living-room which commands the ground floor, to the end of the dining-room. On social evenings, if you wish to smoke a cigar, you will still be in constant communication through this bay with the melomaniacs sitting in the living-room. The smoke of your havanas will not bother them and the noise of your conversation will not disturb them, yet you will hear the sound of their instruments or the muffled tone of their voices, and you will appreciate this arrangement, which was of no small importance to Horta ...

It is not the only one of Horta's buildings where the interior organisation reveals such carefully thought out harmony, a house so perfectly adapted to the character and life style of its owner, and such true originality in the decorative detail. In fact, the artist is careful not to follow the bad example of so many of his contemporaries by endlessly reproducing the same work.

For him, the *maison type* does not exist. None of those houses built by him resemble each other, except in the following respects: in the scrupulous care with which he designed them and in the successful utilisation of all the corners and awkward irregularities of the site; in the elegant simplicity of the façades and the underlying unity of the decoration in which the use of harmonious curves plays a large part; in his preoccupation with lighting all the rooms directly by distributing them around a central point, the focal point of the home, where daylight floods in, making everywhere bright and cheerful ...

However, certain points are worth making. The point of departure of these innovations is the observation of nature. But although the artist observes nature and is inspired by her for this or that motif, and seizes from plants the secret of the delicate undulations or graceful curves of their stems, nevertheless, his ambition has never been to do anything which might directly resemble nature.

When he is designing some fanciful decoration, he follows the secret law obeyed by vegetation, which grows in immutable and ever harmonious forms, but he compels himself with the same strictness never to draw a motif, nor to describe a single curve which could be seen as a pastiche of a natural form ...

---

8 Henry Van de Velde, *A Chapter on the Design and Construction of Modern Furniture,* 1897

The nature of my entire industrial and ornamental production springs from the single source of reason, rationality in essence and appearance, and this is no doubt what accounts for my oddness and the peculiar position I occupy. Certainly I could scarcely have found a better means of being different, though evidently my aims go farther than that. We must endeavour to work out the foundations on which to build a new style and in my opinion the origin clearly lies in never creating anything which has no valid reason for existing, even with the almighty sanction of industry and the manifold consequences of its powerful machines.

But I could be prouder of the certainly far more individual principle of systematically avoiding designing anything that cannot be *mass-produced.* My ideal would be to have my projects executed a thousand times, though obviously not without strict supervision, because I know from experience how soon a model can deteriorate through dishonest or misguided handling until its effect is as worthless as the one it was destined to counteract. I can thus only hope to make my influence felt when more widespread industrial activity will allow me to live up to the maxim which has guided my social beliefs, namely that a man's worth can be measured by the number of people who have derived use and benefit from his life's work.

We can succeed in modernising the appearances of things by carrying out the simple intention to be strictly rational, by following the principle of rejecting without exception all forms and ornamentation which a modern factory could not easily manufacture and reproduce, by plainly stating the essential structure of every piece of furniture and object and by constantly bearing in mind that they must be easy to use. Is there anything which has been the object of keener striving for new forms than a hall-stand, a folding-table, or an armchair? And yet these articles simply show that new results can be obtained by using means and materials which are as old as the hills. And I must confess that my own means are the same as those which were used in the very early stages of popular arts and crafts. It is only because I understand and marvel at how simply, coherently and beautifully a ship, weapon, car or wheel-

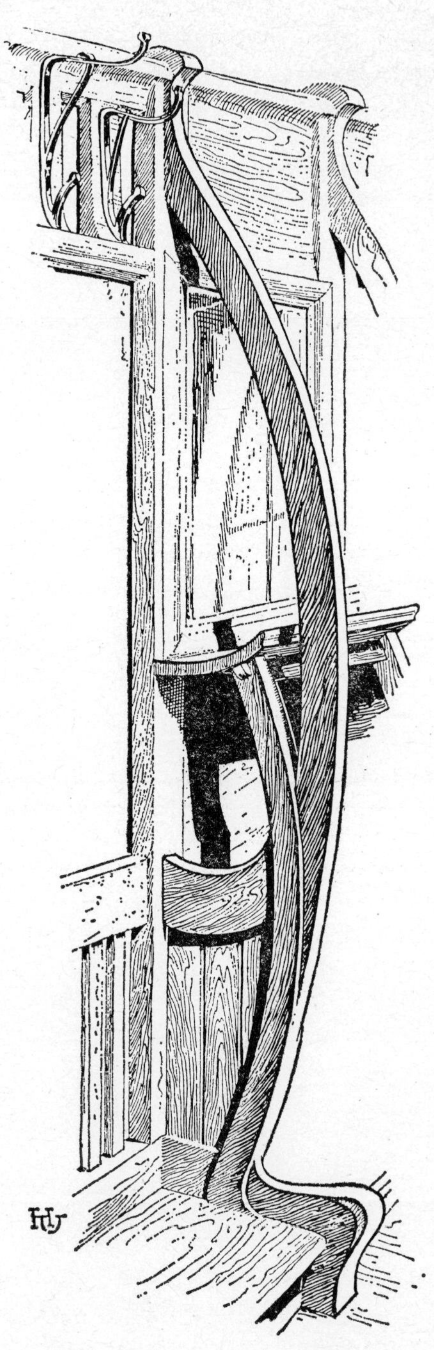

Henry Van de Velde, Hallstand, 1897-8
Drawing by Hugo Ulbricht in *Pan*, vol. III, Part 2, 1897-8

barrow is built that my work is able to please the few remaining rationalists who realise that what has seemed odd to others has in fact been produced by following unassailable traditional principles, in other words unconditionally and resolutely following the functional logic of an article and being unreservedly honest about the materials employed, which naturally vary with the means of each.

---

9 S. Bing, *Where are we Going?* 1897-8

Before new sources of life could be opened up in the field of commercial art, blessed with such a distinguished past, and in order to prevent its final decline, one thing was essential. Our eyes had first to learn to see again. And, secondly, we had to grasp the great danger, arising from the comfortable indolence in which we slumbered in the shade of the past quietly watching one generation follow another, leaving no trace of its own individuality.

Today we have already reached this stage. A new wind blows over the art of interior design. A spring breeze blows even in the sleepiest corners and shakes the dear old traditions so much, that they are beginning to totter precariously. But even if new seeds are sown everywhere, nobody yet knows what they will bring with them. Will it be a Renaissance, which will encourage with its new juices the old roots to flower anew, or will something completely new sprout from the earth which will contradict everything from the past and perhaps shoot widely over the mark in its mad haste?

This is where the danger lies. The moment is decisive: There has seldom been a more critical moment in the history of art. The position requires quiet contemplation. The movement, the birth of which we are now witnessing, will be either fruitful or disastrous for that which it wishes to serve, depending upon whether it is left to the mood of coincidence, the caprice of more or less good ideas – or the consistent seriousness of logical, healthy law.

Where are these laws to be found? Where are the elements of this logic? ... The sole means of probing the future is to clarify the past. We must look for the harmful elements (in nineteenth-century eclecticism, when tradition was broken) and see if they can be made harmless. We will approach the right path only when we realise which paths are false. [Bing cites the slavish return to nature as one such blind alley and Ruskin's attachment to the Middle Ages as another.]

In great times of crisis, when one becomes aware of the depths to which one has unconsciously sunk, and the root of the evil which paralyses creativity becomes obvious, remedies in the form of new theories spring up, which forthwith become immovable principles. Nothing is more dangerous than an excessive application of these universal remedies.

From the principle, that all art is of equal value and is interconnected, it was inferred, that all art had to strive for one and the same aim and possessed a common ideal. And finally this point of view maintained that even the most different works of art were sufficiently close for them to require only one more step for one type of art to merge with another.

We have all welcomed the liberation of painters and sculptors from their hierarchical prejudices and are thankful to them that they offer their influence to elevate trade and to prevent it from sinking. A flock of artists and indeed some of the most noteworthy, have given up the exclusive attitude to art, not only to create prototypes and models but even to complete objects with their own hands, which are intended to serve a purpose. By now, a number of years have elapsed since the beginning of this movement, and we have sufficiently tangible results available for this trend to be recognisable.

We must admit, that the results have remained far behind our original expectations. Indeed, the movement, which filled all hearts with the hope of a rising sun, has given something to the pleasure to be derived from the Arts and Crafts. Great value is attributed to its work, if it is judged by the aesthetic of abstract art, but only very few have adhered to the original practical programme. Let us seek the causes of this disillusionment. There is a principle, which is so simple that one hesitates to put it into writing: the rule that the structure of every object must be primarily subjected to the strict requirements of its precise function. Perhaps it is the very simplicity of this precedent which deludes the complex artistic imagination which is always directed towards the ideal. The necessity, in the creation of a commodity, to create the fundamental nature of the thing in such a way as to respect the means of manufacture, the practical purpose to which it will be put, the question of whether the object once produced can be reproduced economically; all those problems have to be solved before one can think of external embellishments, the artistic originality value, or the symbolic or literary significance. But they are obviously considerations too trivial for minds accustomed to living in the clouds to occupy themselves with thoroughly, without impairing their true temperament.

The contrast between the two types of quality is immediately striking. How can one expect this privileged group, whom nature has gifted with an imaginative power of elevated sensibility, used to attributing deep significance to material things, to giving us ideal forms – how can one expect these dreamers to give us a weighty understanding of the exact requirements of practical life?

In everything that they undertake, their dreamlike style, the indestructible stamp of their accustomed tradition, will appear, even against their own will and knowledge. All such artists, who work at the rejuvenation of craft, with valuable inspiration but without a strict obedience to the discipline of the metier, will find their patronage in the tight circle of devotees who find pleasure in owning the sole examples of highly sophisticated works and who do not concern themselves as to whether these works at the same time represent examples of value in use ...

The moral is, that one should not be afraid to keep the old division of art with its two separate fields and should only consider that a new factor has thereby come to light, which changes the nature of the classification.

In the one camp we place everything which is created under the principle *Art for Art's Sake*: that art which only aims to please the eye or the spirit. In this category we have firstly, in accordance with the old division, the great sculptures and easel paintings and to this, we must add each and every object which has arisen from a fantasy – or poetic imaginary power, under whatever name it might appear. On the other hand we have *Practical Art* (it is not important whether we call it this or whether we say 'decorative' or 'applied' art), art which must adhere to satisfying exclusively ornamental or purely practical purposes and which rationally should also include architecture.

With this tidy allocation of each thing to the group in which it belongs, we will see things more clearly, and if each artist were to know, before starting his work, into which of these two groups he intends it to fall, then the immense number of mistakes which darken the future and endanger the campaign for beauty, of which the end of our century is so proud, will disappear.

---

10 August Endell, *The Beauty of Form and Decorative Art*, 1897-8

In the ever more vehement yearning for a new style in architecture and applied art, and in the new, original and independent style of decoration, the dissonant warning voices of the cautious can be heard. From the dizzy heights of their experience, they smile down sympathetically upon the foolish exploits of their juniors and still remain ready to show to the general public the only path of truth. They teach us that there can be no new form, that all possibilities have been exhausted in the styles of the past, and that all art lies in an individually modified use of old forms. It even extends to selling the pitiful eclecticism of the last decades as the new style.

To those with understanding, this despondency is simply laughable. For they can clearly see, that we are not only at the beginning of a new stylistic phase, but at the same time on the threshold of the development of a completely new Art. An Art with forms which signify nothing, represent nothing and remind us of nothing, which arouse our souls as deeply and as strongly as music has always been able to do.

The barbarian finds our music distasteful; culture and education are necessary for its full appreciation. Appreciation of visual form is also something that must be acquired. We must learn to see it and really immerse ourselves in form. We must discover how to use our eyes. It may well be that man has for a long time delighted in form subconsciously. In the history of the fine arts this development can be clearly studied but it has not yet reached the point where it has finally taken root never to be forgotten. Painters have taught us a great deal, but their primary aim has always been colour, and where they were concerned with form, they mainly searched for the conceptual quality by the exact reproduction of the object, and not the aesthetic quality, which nature only rarely and by chance offers in the dimensions which the painter requires.

If we wish to understand and appreciate formal beauty we must learn to see in a detailed way. We must concentrate on the details, on the form of the root of a tree, on the way in which a leaf is connected to its stalk, on the structure of the bark, on the lines made by the turbid spray on the shores of a lake. Also we must not just glance carelessly at the form. Our eye must trace, minutely, every curve, every twist, every thickening, every contraction, in short we must experience every nuance in the form. For there is only one point in our field of vision which we can see exactly, and it is only that which is clearly seen, which can hold some meaning for us. If we see in this way, an immensely rich new world is revealed to us, full of totally new experience. A thousand sensations are awakened within us. New feelings and shades of feeling, continual unexpected transformations. Nature seems to live and we begin to understand that there really are sorrowing trees and wicked treacherous branches, virginal grasses and terrible, gruesome flowers. Of course, not everything is going to affect us in this way, there are also things which are boring, meaningless and ineffectual, but the alert eye will everywhere observe forms of superb, soul-shattering magnificence.

This is the power of form upon the mind, a direct, immediate influence without any intermediary stage, by no means an anthropomorphic effect, but one of direct empathy. If we speak of a sorrowing tree, we do not at all think of the tree as a living being which sorrows, but mean only that it awakens the feeling of sorrow within us. Or when we say that the pine tree aspires upwards we do not animate the pine tree. It is just that the expression, of the act of aspiring, produces more easily in the mind of the listener a clearer image of verticality. We are employing nothing more than a verbal aid to make up for an inadequate vocabulary and to produce a living concept more quickly.

'How can the feelings aroused by form be explained?' is a question voiced most loudly by those who have never experienced them. I could answer, that there is no place for this here, that one can enjoy music without having to know why the chords can possibly move us so greatly. But in order to pacify those who doubt and to pave their way into the world of form, I should like to attempt to describe the emotive effect of the elements of form and their constituent parts, and also to at least outline the psychological explanation, so far as is possible without lengthy discussion . . .

The straight line is not only mathematically but also aesthetically superior to all other lines. If we follow a straight line, for instance the vertical, with our eyes, this always retains the same direction in our field of vision. In contrast to this, a curved line, perhaps that of a round-headed archway for instance, alters its shape continually: first vertical, then slanting upwards, then horizontal, then slanting down and finally descending vertically. Whereas during the observation of curved lines there is always something new to grasp, the straight line always looks the same. As we look, our perception is quickened, and this is accelerated, the further the straight line extends, since every extra second of looking appears to add nothing to our perception. But since more familiar things are grasped more readily still, urging the eye on, the speed with which we perceive a straight line rises continuously.

Every quick motion gives us a certain feeling which we will call for the moment 'the feeling of speed'. The straight line awakes this feeling in us; it looks quick and the more so the longer it is. The width of the straight line, however – we are here speaking of real and not mathematical lines – has the effect of slowing it down. For a wide straight line requires more time for it to be appreciated than a narrow one, since it requires more perception. The straight line therefore appears faster or slower depending on whether it is narrow or broad.

The effect of direction is of a completely different nature. The vertically descending straight line (i.e. the straight line which we follow from the top downwards) has a light and effortless effect. The horizontal has a quiet strength, and the vertically ascending line gives the effect of strong exertion. The slanting positions, slanting downwards or upwards, offer intermediary nuances, so that we have a continual table of characteristics stretching from a feeling of minimum effort to the strongest feeling of all. This emotional appeal is probably based on the fact that directing the eye upwards requires more effort than looking downwards. The reason for this is not quite clear. The mid-point of the eye is in front of the pivoting point, and probably of the centre of gravity. This in fact would mean that raising the eyeball requires effort but that lowering it does not. Besides this, certain assumptions about the processes in the retina enable us to give a second reason for the emotional effect which we are discussing. This however can only be developed in a more comprehensive description.

Be that as it may, the straight line gives the feeling of speed. The effect is lessened the wider and shorter the line is and strengthened the narrower and longer it is. At the same time, the feeling of effort is at its weakest when the line drops vertically and at its strongest when it rises vertically. Indeed effort (tension) and speed (tempo) are the two constituent parts of all feeling.

Straightforwardness, sincerity, warmth, solemnity, profundity and sublimity all have a slow tempo in common, whereas frivolity, provocation, arrogance, harshness, violence and savagery are transmitted to us by speed and suddenness. In both cases, however, there is a step by step gradation of tension, effort, force, intensity or whatever one wishes to call it. An element of lightness and effortlessness is present in all simplicity and frivolity, whereas that which is savage or inspired call forth within us extremes of effort. And just as with these extremes, there is a certain tempo for every emotion and a corresponding degree of exertion. We have attempted in the accompanying Table to organise the main nuances of emotion. In the horizontal rows, the effort rises from left to right whereas it is the tempo which rises in the vertical lines from bottom to top. The inner rectangle contains feelings of gaiety, those outside it are feelings of apathy. Apathy results in us from everything which is too weak or too strong, too slow or too fast for our endurance . . .

And because all sensations are only tempo and tension, form is able to awaken all shades of emotion within us. For we saw that the straight line always awoke within us not only these two kinds of sensation, but indeed every other possible variety. And it will be seen later that all forms are basically only modifications and combinations of the straight line.

However, the impression made by a single line is too short-lived to occupy us intensively. It is not until we come across richer images that our attention is arrested for a lengthier period and only in these do the individual elements have a fuller and more intensive effect, due

TEMPO	Light ← EFFORT → Heavy							
Quick	Malicious	Scornful	Haughty	Pathetic	Frigid	Pitiless	Cruel	Terrible
	Facetious	Frivolous	Provocative	Arrogant	Harsh	Violent	Savage	Hideous
	Coquettish	Chic	Ebulliant	Daring	Reckless	Majestic	Awesome	Dreadful
	Affected	Gracious	Elegant	Energetic	Vigorous	Firm	Brutal	Bestial
	Sweet	Dainty	Flexible	Fiery	Strong	Rugged	Powerful	Frightful
	Insipid	Delicate	Devoted	Generous	Distinguished	Mighty	Monstrous	Awful
	Vacuous	Straightforward	Sincere	Warm	Solemn	Profound	Sublime	Gruesome
Slow	Dim	Weak	Tired	Troubled	Sad	Melancholic	Sombre	Desperate

* It is impossible, of course, to translate the German words precisely: this Table is intended to give the essence of Endell's idea.

to their contrast with the remainder. I therefore dispense with giving a table of the various grades and will immediately deal with complicated straight-lined images, to demonstrate the emotional effect which we have discussed.

Straight-line Compositions

... We shall start with a row of window divisions.* Windows are mainly at eye level and are therefore in the first instance seen from bottom to top. Let us do this here. (a) is a simple rectangle i.e. a wide straight line which stresses the ascending direction but is limited by the extent of its width, thus, in a middling tempo allied with effort – an impression of energy. This basic form is adhered to everywhere. (b) is horizontally divided, which cuts the upward direction; the tension is reduced but the speed, too, is slower than (a). (c) is divided vertically, faster as the parts are less wide: more energetic and stronger than (a). The cross shape (d) is more peaceful than the shape (c), approaches (a) but is more delicate than this because the tension and tempo of the parts are evenly reduced, more energetic than (a). In (e) we move from the quiet quality of the lower part to the stronger quality of the upper, the first example of a contrast. The transition in (f) is even stronger, if not *too* strong. In contrast to this the upper part at (g) is even more forceful because it is a longer shape and yet the contrast does not have such a strong effect because the lower section gains more tempo from the vertical division. The remaining windows show the contrast the other way round. Energy and peace have faded away, (h) is a poor solution, the upper part being too weak; (i) is better and (k) more so; in contrast (l) is again worse because the division into thirds is too forceful at the base, which is the reason for lowering the cross bar as in (m).

If we now observe the same structure from top to bottom, then the impression changes greatly; the tempo remains but the effort is lowered and the sequence of the parts also changes. As a result, completely meaningless contrasts occur here and there, such as at (g), where the tempo of the upper parts is too strong in order to blend harmoniously with the calm lower parts. One must not think that any window is objectionable for this reason. On the contrary, the stronger the character of an image is, the more it makes you look at it in a certain way. The practised eye instinctively examines an object in the way which gives it maximum

* See illustration, p. 24.

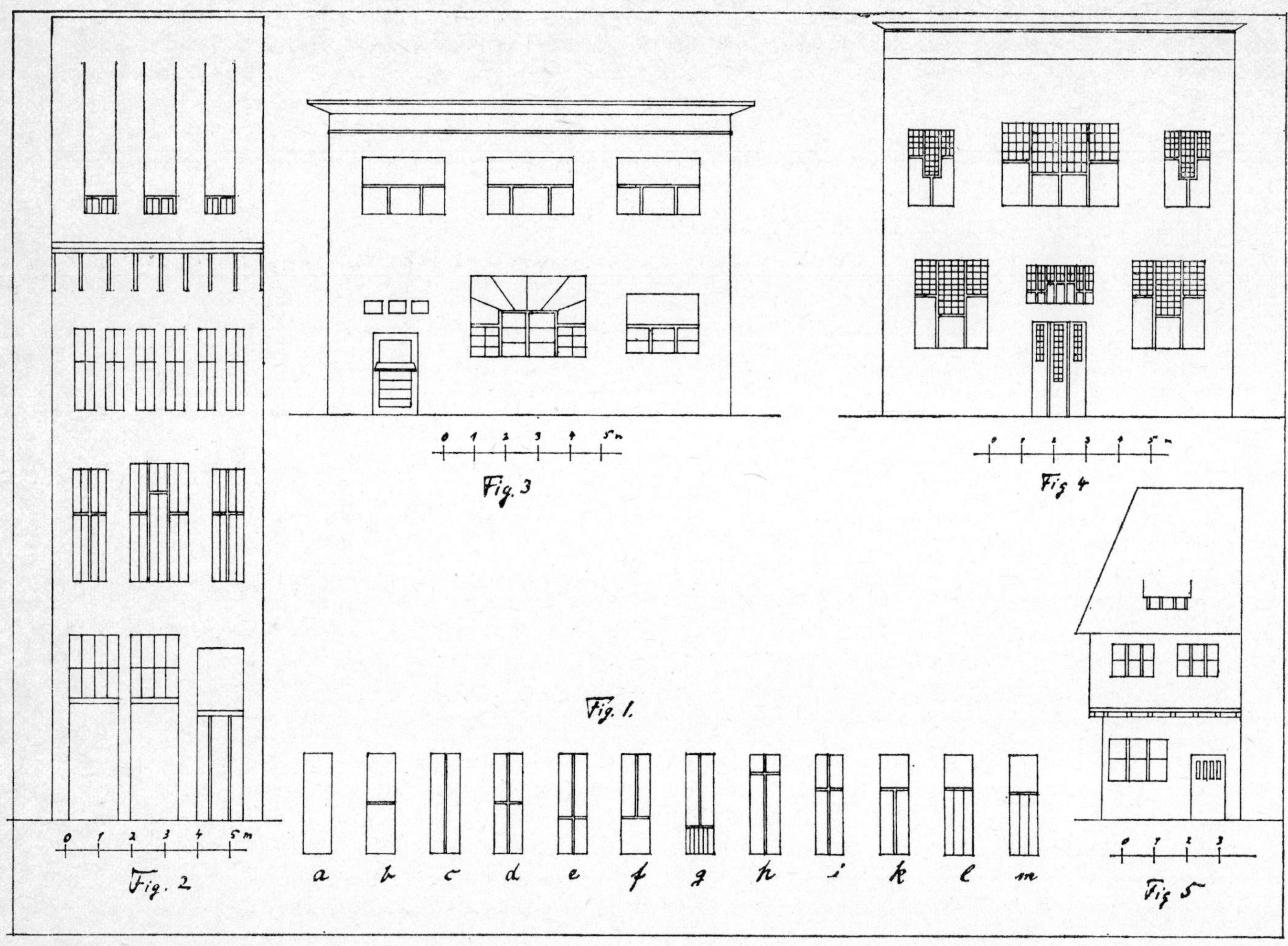

August Endell, Diagram of window proportions
Dekorative Kunst, vol. II, 1898

impact, and when it is forced to look in a different way in order to examine a certain detail, it momentarily ignores its observation. In any case we see by fits and starts, if only because our eyelids close every other second. It is a matter of aesthetic education to see things always at once from the most effective angle. What makes it easier for us to learn this, is that we get more pleasure from things in this way. At this point we can understand why one so frequently speaks of the movement of a line. As I progressively take in the form of a line, I am doing something which is not identical but is similar to following a moving body with the eye. Two parts of the line which in fact coexist, appear one after the other to the observer and this is enough to create the impression of movement. This is an extremely convenient but only a figurative expression, which can never explain the basis of aesthetic form.

We shall now discuss the illustrated façades. They are, in the first place, drawn for maximum impact. However, real proportions are used as a basis which can be seen from the measurements. Fig. 2, has its height strongly developed i.e. high tension and fast tempo. These are slightly limited by the width, especially by the horizontal lines of the cornice and the upper row of windows, which create a wide effect. But, reinforced by the narrow, high windows and window divisions, the vertical timber struts under the cornice and the roofing of the dormer windows, we get an overwhelmingly vertical thrust with minimal horizontality. And indeed the impression develops in a certain way from bottom to top. Below, there is a certain calm in the wide display windows and the skylight above the door. Much more energetic are the narrow divisions on the first floor, the middle window being calmer than the side ones; more energetic still the top row of windows, but the horizontal lines here lie at the same height everywhere. They dampen the tempo and in this way lead us to the horizontal of the cornice. Once again the dormer windows and the strips of roof which cover them take up the strong vertical movement, which then fades away upwards into the width of the roof. Therefore, a crescendo which is followed by a double diminuendo. The façade is not attractive, it is too harsh for that, but it undeniably has character.

Its exact opposite is Fig. 3. This has limited tension and a slow tempo, a comfortable width in the proportion of the whole and in the parts. All the windows are divided up into horizontally orientated shapes, the lower window in the centre being the only one with slightly more force, the height being more emphasised but dampened here by the ray-shaped division of the top piece, the slanting glazing bars leading into the general horizontal movement. And so the whole appears somewhat too comfortable.

Façade Fig. 4 is stronger without lapsing into the excited intensity of Fig. 2. Everywhere the vertical direction is emphasised but the tempo is limited by the development of the width. The sharp energy of the small window divisions is dampened by cutting the upper halves into small squares. In order not to produce a dull impression by the damping down effect, the horizontal glazing bar is not taken in a straight line. The middle section is always set deeper, to enhance the calm of the lower opening and simultaneously giving an enriching effect. In the side windows of the first floor the upper divisions into thirds are intentionally changed to a halving below. A division into three throughout would have resulted in too strong a tempo. The door has proved a little too lively, even the wide skylight does not achieve a slow enough tempo. At least the lower floor gives an effect of strength and calm due to its large windows. This trait is more obvious in the large central window of the first floor, whereas the small windows to right and left are a little more lively. The cornice is too simple and too weak, a gayer frieze or a richer line for the roof should have been in its place, but it was worth while sticking to simple straight lines. Damped energy and peaceful security – not without liveliness – this is probably the character of this façade.

The last façade, Fig. 5, also shows an emphasis on height but the cantilevering of the first storey and the projecting roof allow no energetic impression to persist. The two floors have an effect of calm and strength due to their two prominent wall surfaces, without completely dispensing with tempo, this being strengthened in particular by the window mullions. Even the roof adapts to this character of quiet strength and simple solidity. It gives us our first example of a narrowing surface, the tempo rises as it runs its course and at the same time the slanting line limits the tension, so that the surface becomes lighter and more free. The low dormer window works to counteract this impression, just as the small square heads of the beams give a humorous contrast to the wall surfaces.

Of course these comments only examine the effects of

the façades as drawn here. With an executed façade some of the impact is altered and new factors emerge which we can only come to understand in three-dimensional forms.

---

11 Adolf Loos, *Potemkin's Town,* 1898

Everyone has heard of the canvas and pasteboard villages which Potemkin built for Catherine the Great in the Ukraine. It was the favourite's way of transforming the wildnerness into a flowering landscape that would gratify the gaze of the Empress, but whether the shrewd minister was expected to produce an entire city or not is another matter.

But then, such things can only happen in Russia!

The Potemkin city I should like to speak about here is none other than our own dear Vienna. That is a hard accusation and one which it will be hard for me to prove, because I should need hearers with a finer sense of justice than is commonly found among us.

A swindler is a person who claims to be important when he is not, and the community at large will despise him for his duplicity even if no one has been harmed. But supposing someone were to use spurious stones and other artificialities in order to obtain the same effect, what would happen? In some countries he would have a similar fate, but Vienna does not seem to have reached that stage yet. In fact only a very limited circle would be aware that there was anything fraudulent or immoral going on. And yet there are persons who are constantly trying to be what they are not, not only with false watch-chains, not only with their title or decoration, which are imitation in any case, but also with their apartment and their apartment building itself.

Whenever I stroll along the Ring, I always feel as if a modern Potemkin had wanted to make somebody believe he had been transported into a city of aristocrats.

All that the Italian Renaissance could produce in noble mansions has been plundered in order to conjure up for her Highness the common people, a New Vienna which only people in a position to own an entire palace from the cellars to the chimney-pots could inhabit. There are stables on the ground floor, servants' quarters in the low-ceilinged mezzanines, fine reception-rooms in the architecturally fully elaborated first floor, and the living-rooms and apartments at the top. Viennese landlords were delighted with the idea of owning a mansion and the tenants were equally pleased to be able to live in one. A kind of feudal splendour and lordliness overcame even the ordinary man who had rented a studio-flat in the upper storey whenever he contemplated his residence from outside. But then, doesn't the owner of a false diamond gaze fondly on its scintillating glass? And how much more could we not say about the deceiver deceived!

People will argue that I am wrong in ascribing these intentions to the people of Vienna. The architects are the ones to blame; they ought never to have built in such a style. But it is my duty to protect architects. Every city has the builders it deserves because building is governed by the law of supply and demand. The man who most completely satisfies the reigning taste will build the most and the most gifted architect may leave this world without ever having been offered a commission. But unfortunately this sets a fashion and architects build in the same way because this is what people are used to and this is the way to build. The estate agent would really prefer to have the façade stripped bare from top to bottom because it would be cheapest and that would be the honest, correct and most artistic way of proceeding. But then no one would pay any attention to the building. Bearing future tenants in mind, the architect has no alternative but to nail on these and only these façades.

And I mean literally nail on, because not a single

one of these Renaissance and Baroque mansions is actually made of the materials it suggests. Some look as if they are in stone, like the Roman and Tuscan houses, and some in stucco like the buildings of Viennese Baroque, but they are of neither. Their ornamental elements, their consoles, festoons, cartouches and indentations are made of cast cement and have been simply nailed on. This technique was first used in this century and is perfectly legitimate but that is surely not a reason for applying it to forms which are specifically related to another material simply because no practical difficulties stand in the way. The artist's duty must always be to find new plastic language for new materials. Anything else is imitation.

But to the Viennese of the last generation this did not matter in the slightest. On the contrary they were overjoyed at being able to copy nobler materials so cheaply, believing, like the upstarts they were, that no one would notice the fraud. The parvenu has always been convinced that the detachable shirt-fronts, imitation furs and all the substitutes with which he surrounds himself amply fulfil their task. Only those who are immediately above him, who have already risen a stage further and are thus in the know, smile over his futile exertions. And in time even the parvenu opens his eyes, noticing that his friends possess this or that which is not so genuine as he had originally thought, until he too resigns himself and stops pretending.

Poverty is not a disgrace. Not everyone can have been born lord of a great feudal demesne. To try to act as if one has is both absurd and immoral. We must not be ashamed of the fact that we rent a flat in a building with many other people on the same social level as ourselves. We should not be ashamed of the fact that there are some building materials which are too expensive for us, nor be ashamed of the fact that we live in the nineteenth century and do not want to have a house built in the style of another period. This would be the way to see just how quickly we would be given a style of architecture suited to the times. You will argue that this is what we have got. But I mean a style which can be handed on to posterity with a clear conscience and be singled out with pride even in the distant future. Such a style has not been found in Vienna this century. Whether you try to build wooden huts with canvas, pasteboard and paint, where peasants live happily, or use tiles and cement to raise stone mansions for feudal aristocrats, basically it amounts to the same. It is the spirit of Potemkin that has haunted nineteenth-century architecture in Vienna.

---

12 Victor Champier, *The Castel Béranger by Hector Guimard*, 1899

The present period has reached a stage of aristocratic *cacophony* which corresponds fairly well to the atmosphere of moral and intellectual anarchy created by our individualistic society in its attempts to find its way. The panic-stricken quest for novel artistic ideas is just one of the consequences and should not be regarded with too much alarm. We must at least be thankful that there are those who show common sense in their frantic searchings and a respect for method by trying to devise a general plan and a programme.

In the Castel Béranger, Guimard has not limited his aims simply to applying the principles of his teachers with verve and competence, as he so often did at the beginning. Believing that he was taking a step forward, he has carried their conclusions to the point of absurdity. To me, the wrought-iron gate at the entrance with its zig-zag bars breaking the equilibrium and its upward-lacing stems seems the most glaring kind of error.

Furthermore, as a decorator, Guimard has inaugurated a system which he conceived three or four years ago when he took advantage of a travel scholarship to spend some time in Belgium. Naturally, such an ultramodernist would not have thought it worthwhile to study architecture in Italy. In Brussels, like so many, he came under the spell of the poetic imagination of Victor Horta, the celebrated Belgian architect, and was able to admire the Maison Tassel, one of this refined and sensitive artist's most ingenious achievements. Then one day, in conversation with Horta, he heard him come out with the following sally, 'It is the stem that I like to use for decoration, you know, not the flower!'

St Paul on the road to Damascus could not have been more suddenly touched by grace than Guimard at this revelation. His mind immediately began to seethe with ideas about the expressive values of lines and colours for buildings and furniture as well as in interior decoration. In order to understand how he reached the Olympian certainty that he can now solve the problems of discovering a new style, you would have to listen to him explaining his theory with his own inimitable boundless enthusiasm.

It is useless to argue that an art form which limited itself to borrowing its decorative elements from the stems of plants and the roots and branches of trees and give them realistic interpretation would be exceedingly impoverished. And equally useless to repeat some of the epigrams that the effects of certain sculptures adorning the Castel Béranger have inspired, such as, 'skeletons dancing a jig' or 'a game of knuckle-bones'.

'Oh yes, I know,' Guimard will reply, spreading his huge arms in an expansive gesture. 'I know what people say and could not care less. I shall go on working because I am convinced I am right. I believe you must always turn to nature for advice, you see. When I design a house, or a piece of furniture, or carve something, I think of the outside world. Beauty there is perpetually changing. Nothing is parallel or symmetrical. Forms grow out of other forms, in ever-varying movements. Consider the forest with its profusion of species, its myriad shades of greenery and its carpets of flowers and you have a feeling of unity born of infinite variety. Surely no setting could be finer, more entrancing? Then contemplate just one of the plants which make up the forest and you will see that each tree, each bush differs from its neighbour. Not one branch resembles another and no flowers are alike. Surely this is a lesson for the architect, for the artist who knows how to look at such a remarkable display of forms and colours? The branches of trees and these stems which are straight and wavy by turns surely provide us with the right models for building? ... So why don't we follow these general laws? Perhaps the great architect of the universe is the true master of us all, so why don't we respect his example?'

When Guimard pours forth his reforming theories with such grandiloquence we can say no more. No doubt there is folly in much of what he calls his 'doctrine', but then, what do words matter? It is the artist's work that counts. And the work of this particular architect is indeed often disconcerting. But there is a basic soundness in what he is doing. If he can let off steam and forget his more idle fancies, he will convince us yet.

---

13 Charles Plumet, *The Modern Home,* 1899

The working man also needs a comfortable happy home, but on no account must it resemble the one he lives in at present. His house is often so squalid that it would be hard to say whether the atmosphere where he toils all day long is the more harmful, or the place where he falls asleep at night. We must be capable of designing healthy, airy houses, so that when our workers return home they will find cleanliness and joy.

By choosing deliberately *simple* plastic forms, we mean to express our artistic and social idea in language which will be intelligible to all. We hope to attract the public's attention by a demonstration based on pure reason, showing how modern building materials can be used to attain humanitarian and democratic ends.

We proudly and sincerely believe that the artist, who by nature is a lover of his fellow-men, has a wholly altruistic mission to accomplish. *It is his duty to place the greatest sum of rationality before men's eyes, down to the humblest articles, and never to design anything for everyday use which is not based on the notion of utility allied with beauty.*

The day is not far off when every man possessed of sound and lucid judgement will come naturally to admire a fine civic action and the beautiful shapes of utensils by the same process of deduction and analysis.

Our faith in our aims has been singularly fortified by our immense respect for integrity, our hatred of all those who wish to implant the colonnades, archways and attics of an alien art as the basis of the modern style, and our disgust at the degenerate art daily displayed in our streets.

Our aims are too high from the sociological standpoint and our moral interest in completing the proposed task too great, for us not to recognise and feel glad that we must serve them with a saint's devotion and that, if we are to succeed, we must summon up all the creative passion we possess, every scrap of determination and unquestioning self-denial.

We shall be rewarded beyond all measure by the profound and rapid evolution that the reform of modern housing will bring in its train.

Then man will take possession of the new surroundings created for him and the good land of France will see the return of the principles of sound logic, rationalism and clarity. A rehabilitated better man will recognise the old frank qualities of his race, which will never perish, whatever some may say.

---

14 Emile Gallé, *Modern Furniture Decorated according to Nature,* 1900

Fortunately, a love of flowers was conspicuous in my family: it was an inherited passion. It was my salvation. I had some smattering of the natural sciences and had followed the botanising excursions of Godron, the author of *Flora of Lorraine and France.* My father had used motifs from nature, representations of grasses and flowers on his crystal glass and his china. I carried on my father's tradition in the way I moulded and decorated glass and clay. All this was done by trial and error, with lack of experience and infinite blunders, which I might have been spared if I had been specially taught. In the end, I was led to repeat exactly the same experiment in furniture, and to try out the same applications of principles, the same adaptations of decoration taken from life, using other materials. This was all.

And, when I produce some examples of modern furniture decorations based on my studies from nature, the first lesson I draw from them is that in decorative art, as well as in other arts, it is fitting to understand the word Beauty in the sense of Truth, and never in the false and mediocre meaning of prettiness without character, or opulence devoid of feeling. The most useful advice which can be given to the decorator who is looking for representational elements for furniture, is to look for them in the living world and to treat them truthfully.

What then is modern furniture?

It must be *modern,* that is, invented by the living generation, made *to be used* and decorated to *please.* Conceived by our contemporaries and not by men from other ages with other customs, it must be made according to our ideas, for our pleasure, to our size, and to fit in with present day life. And, above all it must be constructed topically and practically, according to the constraints of the material used, namely wood. Hence it will be the predominance of reason over illogicality, of sound construction over what would be a futile task: the destruction of the organic wholeness of furniture.

It will also be the advent of naturalistic observation in furniture, after the reign of false and conventional decorative elements. From the most restrained patterns, from the simple curve to rich details, the decoration of modern furniture must reflect life. It will prefer natural truth to any artificial combinations.

It will have character, that is, it will have the 'lines of life' – specific outlines, drawn from the physiological forms of the different species of flora and fauna. These outlines will then be adapted to each material, to the means of construction and to suitability by means of the broad and necessary syntheses which they require.

The decoration of modern furniture will not be deliberately melancholy. It will be sincere. It will therefore be spontaneously happy, since it will be a popular art, that is, an art in which the worker, the maker, instead of being reduced to the state of a machine and knowing only the 'hard labour' of sweating over parts (never the whole) of someone else's design will be given the dignity of a thinking being. He will also be called upon to participate both in the remuneration due to intelligent work and in these free joys of the spirit; understanding, conception, invention, the interpretation of a plan, of a work, and the adaptation of living models to the work of his hands. Hence this art can be happy because it will be carried out by the worker, with pleasure and with awareness, and the ornamentalist will hence be spared from servile, insipid copying from objects devoid of meaning, reality and charm.

In brief, modern furniture must be logical, convenient, artistic with an art full of natural health, living, human, and true, otherwise it will not exist at all, any more than, in our opinion, many a product catalogued among classified styles, represents art.

Such proposals, I know, would not appeal to the various partisans of artificiality in decoration, neither to the defenders of traditional styles, and even less perhaps to those who count on snobbery establishing among the French, as among the Belgians and the Germans, a blind allegiance to modern cosmopolitanism, a bumptious pretension to art, a whiplash art – if indeed the name of art can be given to these virtuoso deformations of nature, typical of every debauched dauber, every wayward draughtsman. [Gallé goes on to give three Arts and Crafts principles for all designs: (a) the design should meet the precise functions required of it, (b) the design should take into account the materials and means of construction, and (c) the construction should not be masked by unnecessary ornament. He goes on as follows.]

Now let us go on to superficial decoration and the form of the details. I like to think that the modern designer is careful to establish in advance, which the artist of former times did not always do, a general theme inspired by the purpose of furniture, or simply by a leading motif of decoration, for example the type of plant with which it is associated.

At this juncture I know very well that there is an objection which will certainly be made to our predilection for truth in furniture decoration: those wits who always like to anticipate the way in which a principle good in itself can be abused, will predictably reproach our incursions among real plants as botanical pedantry, finicky observation of nature. Hence we must forewarn the designers who, after so long an absence are returning gratefully to nature, against the dangers of importing into decoration what properly belongs to science. In painting nudes, the artist must not let his knowledge of anatomy show through to the detriment of the reality and beauty of the flesh. Similarly, it is not fitting that the idea of natural shapes and organic functions, from which so many charming applications for furniture can arise, should become a parade of pedantic science. It is in his studies from nature that the decorative artist must concentrate on rigorous accuracy. However, as a general rule in furniture, it is advisable for this information to remain latent or rather synthesised. As you can imagine, there is no question of transforming an armchair into a piece of botany!

These are the basic ideas from which I have shown that the panels of a linen cupboard can be decorated with the scented plants dear to our ancestors: lavender, rosemary, iris, and mignonette. Let us imagine that we have to decorate the back of a drawing-room sofa. What prevents us from using as our decorative theme the cereals and their florula, realised in some choice silk? We will base the modelling of the armrests, the feet and the framework, on the stems of grasses which can be in turn straight and slender or twisted. If we prefer to upholster a back made from pierced wood, the way it is cut can be inspired by the interlacing of stalks of corn, adapted to the working of the wood, just as they are blown symmetrically by the breeze or bent by the burden of ripe grains. A few ears of corn, the pale blue of the corn flower and fennel-flower, and the dark blue of larkspur will provide variety among the severity of the mouldings. The latter can even be enriched here and there with overlapping blades of corn, the ears, the husks and the glumellae ...

We will thus obtain a living whole, in which the form will no more be sacrificed to the decoration than the decoration will be sacrificed to the form. Each will be subordinated to the other in the cause of unity ... [He goes on to describe various ways of making complex mouldings.]

There can be no doubt that the architects and the stone carvers in the thirteenth century drew their exquisite inspirations from this very subject. Let us not imitate them, let us follow their example. Take the stalk of the leaf or the flower of certain umbelliferous plants, or certain orchids from our woods. Study the grooves with which they are furrowed. They are alternately wide and narrow. Examine them at a large magnification: they have the appearance of actual carpenter's or architect's mouldings, with light opposed to dark; round surfaces contrasted with plane surfaces. You will also find other shapes than the torus and cyma borrowed unchanged from the Greeks. Moreover, this structure is built up sometimes from top to bottom, sometimes from left to right, in opposing directions. It is interrupted here and there, regularly, magisterially by the putting forth of leaves and branches. To surprise the secrets of these combinations, make a whole series of sketches, but compare them with the living model. You will be astonished to find that these anatomies are far more full of charm and secrets, that their beauty is always superior to the adaptations which we make from them. You will be filled with astonishment that man has so little drawn upon this immense repertoire for rejuvenation of the art of designing furniture ... [Gallé discusses ways of decorating joints in furniture.]

To summarise, modern decorations, carved and sculptured from nature, display the construction. Their design will break up and disguise the jointing and assembly points as little as possible.

On the other hand, the aim of decoration will be to enhance the material, and to draw the attention to the joins in a lively and economical manner.

The ornamentation of these parts in relief will be inspired preferably by the shapes of living organisms, which can be adapted in a lifelike and graceful manner to the same angles of our wooden structures. Indeed, Nature, who does not need brackets and attachment pieces to lighten the burden of her flower heads, does not moreover give us examples of these abaci, these rectangular coping stones, these rectangular blocks which, in stone structures, stop the flow of sap of the acanthus and form a join and a block between the capital of the column and the architrave of the entablature ...

So it now seems that we are in a position, even before we have been able to study flat decoration, to define what our ornamental style for furniture consists of, purely according to the sculptural quality of the works which have been accomplished.

It is the step by step rendering of nature herself by decorative contrivances. It is the application, preserving discretion in forms and delicacy in colouring, of the miraculous clothing of nature to the logical and sane construction of the objects of our homes. Our style is the beautification of the working parts of our silent servants, furniture, vases, hangings, in the same way that we see the bony framework of the animal clothed in flesh – and with what art, with what a decorative effect!

Would that we could have worked several times in the past, and may we work in the future, in such a way that our contribution could be recognised by this double character: a true and simple ornamentation, spreading as of its own accord over the surface of the structure, under the influence of a naive examination of nature.

This would be our ideal realised: furniture treated like a naked body, decorated in harmony with its structure, with its limbs spreading out like those of the animal or the plant, with their nerves, their flesh, their hide, plumage, tissues, membranes, bark, in their burgeoning, their flowering, their fruiting; this is the work of the sculptor, the work of intellect, of truth, of freedom: a work of tact, which is difficult, durable and beautiful, which we advocate, which we propose for our own and last efforts.

---

15 Henry Van de Velde, *The New Ornament,* 1901

The ornamental style is subject to no laws other than those it sees itself, which are imposed by its striving for harmony and balance. It does not aspire to represent anything in particular. It needs the freedom to represent nothing, and without this freedom it cannot survive. There are times when it sets itself the task of arousing a particular feeling to correspond to the function of a room. At these times it confirms to linear principles, and gives expression to a scheme whose framework is established, but which still retains flexibility and can be swayed by external influences which it neither can nor wishes to evade.

On uniform surfaces, all its influences are intrinsic, and the ornament will necessarily be created from the two or three lines which we, driven by a subconscious force, as by a scream, commit to paper without further thought. Once the decisive lines are set, however, one needs only to follow on from there to be able to clarify which lines are called for by the design, which are forbidden, and which are necessary for its completion. This is a perception which has never forsaken me. I know that lines have complementary values, just like colours. A line imposes a certain direction on another, just as violet demands orange, red demands green, etc.

At the moment I am guided by three principles. They are still empirical, but this empiricism is as sure as the empiricism which resulted in the wonderful discoveries of the laws governing colour and which, starting from the painter Delacroix's experiments, finally led to the principles formulated by Chevreul, Helmholtz and O. N. Rood.

These are the three rules:

(i) Complementary contrasts
(ii) Repulsion and attraction
(iii) The desire to give the negative forms (ground) the same degree of significance as the positive forms (figure).

---

16 Henry Van de Velde, *The Role of the Engineer in Modern Architecture,* 1901

There exists a class of persons whom we can no longer refuse to call artists. Their work rests on the one hand on the use of materials which were previously unknown and on the other on an extraordinary boldness which even surpasses the daring of the builders of cathedrals. The artists I am referring to, who have created a new architecture, are the engineers.

The essence of what these people are doing is reason and their means is calculation. It is their employment of reason and calculation that can lead to the purest and most certain beauty! It becomes all the more amazing and ludicrous to think that such men should be denied the name of artist when those who previously carried out the tasks they are now accomplishing laid open claim to it. The only difference between the two is that whereas the earlier builders used stone and wood, modern engineers adopt metal, glass and ceramics. They build houses and mansions for us for the same purposes as those designed by architects and moreover use all kinds of materials to produce totally new objects such as locomotives, bicycles, automobiles, adventurous steamboats and the machines that make up the overwhelming might of our industry.

The laws I have mentioned are never discussed because the effects of their sound logic are so certain and undisputed that they seem the only ones truly capable and certain of producing ever new and beautiful things, with the result that the engineers are to be regarded as the only ones who have offered the world new and beautiful things. The exceptional beauty which engineering has inspired derives from the fact that it remained as unconscious of its potentialities as the beauty of Gothic cathedrals became self-aware. A few farsighted learned contemporaries were the first to discover it, especially J. K. Huysmans and Zola. Both, in their own way, one lyrically and the other more thoroughly and with shrewdness, have praised the aesthetic achievements of modern engineering but they have failed to lay sufficient emphasis on the unavoidable necessity of its forms and the peculiar nature of its hitherto unknown beauty.

The basic principle of the beauty of these necessary forms could be formulated in a very everyday manner by saying that objects or things become beautiful when they are what they should be, as they would have been if someone who for the first time wondered what use and service might be expected of them had designed them spontaneously.

In point of fact any consideration other than utility and function can be dangerous and soon lead to a failure, because afterthoughts breed on each other continuously, in an irrational way.

This stern theory is the only one which can guarantee permanently sound craftsmanship and allow us to enjoy modern beauty where it genuinely lies, in the procession of articles which have come into being in the age of engineering, electricity and metallurgy.

I have already made frequent mention of locomotives, steamers, machines and bridges, but the first English perambulators, the different bath-room fittings, electric hanging-lamps and surgical instruments should also be remembered among the modern inventions which attract by their beauty.

All these articles are beautiful because they are exactly what they should be and their forms become even more beautiful when they are made out of beautiful raw materials which have been properly treated. They remain beautiful until greedy mischief-making manufacturers choose to embellish them in their own way and then, utterly disregarding their original necessity, rob them of their forms. These highly dangerous afterthoughts, which are evil, always know on which sources to draw in order to appeal to the masses who have no experience of the real character of modern beauty and are always mesmerized and immediately taken in by the myriad guises of outward ornamental fantasy.

The time will come when we shall be able to hinder actively such profanation. As soon as people know where the true source of formal beauty lies, and who the people who provide it are, they will begin to understand and honour the engineers as they now honour the poets, painters and sculptors and as they honoured the architects in the past. But their respect for architects will suffer because they will realise that the aesthetic renaissance of practical articles of everyday use has nothing to do with architects.

17 Hermann Muthesius, *The English House,* 1904-5

[From Vol. II, *The Development of the English House*]

Conclusion

English domestic architecture today is an amalgamation of the revived tradition of old rural architecture and of the modern Arts and Crafts movement. But let me repeat once more that the modern English artistic movement has no trace of those fanciful, superfluous, and often affected ideas with which a part of the new continental movement is still engaged. Far from this, it tends more towards the primitive and the rustic; and here it fits particularly well with the type of traditional rural house. Moreover this outcome is perfectly to the taste of the Englishman for whom there is nothing better than plain simplicity, who finds the unspoilt original poetically attractive because it appeals to his rural tendencies and who finds random fanciful extravagances at their most obnoxious when he has to live daily surrounded by them. The Englishman in his house wants peace. A tidy cosiness, fully developed comfort, that is what is important to him. A minimum of 'forms' and a maximum of peaceful, comfortable and yet lively atmosphere, that is what he aims for. His unalterable preference is for the rural and the rustic. Such accord seems to him to be a link with beloved mother Nature, to whom, despite all higher cultures, the English nation has remained more faithful than any other people. And today's house is proof of this. The way in which it is situated far back from the road, surrounded by flower gardens, the way it opens itself behind broad, luxuriant lawns which exude the fresh vigour and calm of nature, the way in which its broadly spreading mass is more expressive of protection and shelter than of striving for pomp and architectonic deployment, the way in which it lies far away hidden from all civilisation and demands from the inhabitants the daily sacrifice of covering great distances (which they willingly undertake out of love), the way in which it fits so admirably into surrounding Nature in the happiness of its colouring and the solidity of its form: in all these ways it stands there today as cultural proof of the healthy tendencies of a nation which amid all its wealth and advances in civilisation has retained to a remarkable degree its appreciation of what is natural. Urban civilisation, with its destructive influences, with its senseless haste and press, with its hothouse stimulation of those impulses towards vanity which are latent in man, with its elevation of the refined, the nervous, the abnormal, to unnatural proportions, all this has had practically no harmful effect on the English nation.

The leading sector of the people in intellectual, spiritual matters is in particular given to the country life—precisely that sector which with us runs the greatest risk of falling prey to urban life. Great emphasis was placed upon untreated wooden surfaces. Primitive peasant forms were revived, construction details were always apparent, often in a most obtrusive fashion, and little heed was paid to comfort or refined modes of life. The thinking behind this was that one must go back and start at the beginning in order to get over the degenerate state of culture which the nineteenth century had brought about. The only room in the house to which the so-called artistic strivings of the time had not penetrated was the kitchen. So they went back to kitchen furniture: kitchen chairs gave them ideas for new forms of chair, kitchen cupboards for new forms of cupboard. This new furniture differed from the genuine kitchen pieces in that it was ten times more expensive because it was produced under the economic conditions of works of art. In the London Arts and Crafts Exhibition they are displayed with the claim that they are works of art, not only because their retail price corresponds to that of works of art, but also because in the catalogue, apart from the name of the 'designer' there is given the name of every single craftsman who was associated with the product. Is it any wonder that the public laughs at such exhibits?

To call it modern would be an anachronism: it is

reactionary. They have got so caught up in this ideal of handicraftsmanship that they have no ears for anything else. As there are no strong personalities who could surpass these goals of craftsmanship with that little bit extra which constitutes a work of art, the craftsmanship ideal in its most meagre form fulfills all the demands of London's craft-artists. The curse which weighs on their products is one of economic impossibility. So it is the furniture which is the part of the London Arts and Crafts achievement which is bound to be disappointing. One searches for modern art, that is for pieces which will suit perfectly our modern conditions, and one finds offered rough-jointed kitchen cupboards for which one is supposed to pay as many pounds as they would be worth in Thalers.*

Both the furniture of the London Arts and Crafts Group and the other art furniture will only be found in houses whose owners wanted to have artistically chosen furnishings. And even in England these houses are few. So, what should be the chief aim of a new movement in the industrial arts, namely the introduction of artistically satisfactory objects into the normal house, has not occurred in England either.

But the general standard of English house furnishings differs greatly from its continental counterpart. England is the only country in which it is possible today to find in furniture shops a selection of furniture which, even if it does not always come up to high artistic standards, at least fully satisfies general good taste. And that is something ...

In Germany one is brought to the edge of despair by the effort which the man well educated in matters of taste has to expend in order to get his house furnished, when faced by our businessmen's total lack of any understanding for what is simple and good. The Englishman is spared this labour. In shops such as Liberty's, Story's, Heal and Sons, and many others, he can easily find what he needs. These are the results of the new movement in the arts and crafts which should not be underestimated. Indeed, in this raising of the general level, which shows itself eventually in the improvement in the contents of the commercial furnishing business, one can clearly see the most valuable results of what our arts and crafts movement has been striving for.

The Bathroom

Water pipes and waste pipes, pipes of the most varied sort for hot water, for heating, for electric light, for communication, are beginning to weave their way through the house and give it the character of a refined organism, with as many arteries, veins and nerves as the human body has. The aesthetic beauty of earlier ideals has had to take a back seat for the moment; but perhaps in time a completely new sort of beauty will take its place, the beauty of the refined practical purpose. There are signs of this in those parts of the house concerned with matters of health ...

The observance of this principle creates a noble and in the best sense of the word artistic style for the bathroom, and by refraining from all ornamental additions (which always upset the overall picture), an impression of genuine modernity can be achieved. It is genuine and it will last because it has been developed in a strictly logical fashion and takes no account of sentimental or deliberate attempts at atmosphere. Such a modern bathroom is like a piece of scientific apparatus in which ingenious technology celebrates its triumph and any imported 'art' can only have a disturbing effect. Form developed purely from purpose is by itself so ingenious and expressive that it evokes a feeling of aesthetic well-being that differs in no way from a feeling of artistic pleasure. Here we have a really new art which needs no creation or atmosphere to succeed, an art based on actual modern conditions and modern achievements, and which perhaps one day, when all contemporary fashions purporting to be modern artistic movements have passed away, will be seen as the most eloquent expression of our age.

* Obsolete German coin worth 15p, [*Translator's Note*]

18 Josef Hoffmann and Koloman Moser, *The Work-Programme of the Wiener Werkstätte,* 1905

Josef Hoffmann, Monogram of the Wiener Werkstätte
Österreichisches Museum für Angewandte Kunst

The boundless evil, caused by shoddy mass-produced goods and by the uncritical imitation of earlier styles, is like a tidal wave sweeping across the world. We have been cut adrift from the culture of our forefathers and are cast hither and thither by a thousand desires and considerations. The machine has largely replaced the hand and the business-man has supplanted the craftsman. To attempt to stem this torrent would seem like madness.

Yet for all that we have founded our workshop. Our aim is to create an island of tranquillity in our own country, which, amid the joyful hum of arts and crafts, would be welcome to anyone who professes faith in Ruskin and Morris. We are calling for all those who regard culture in this sense as valuable and we hope that the errors we are bound to commit will not dissuade our friends from lending their support.

We wish to create an inner relationship linking public, designer and worker and we want to produce good and simple articles of everyday use. Our guiding principle is function, utility our first condition, and our strength must lie in good proportions and the proper treatment of material. We shall seek to decorate when it seems required but we do not feel obliged to adorn at any price. We shall use many semi-precious stones, especially in our jewellery, because in our eyes their manifold colours and ever-varying facets replace the sparkle of diamonds. We love silver and gold for their sheen and regard the lustre of copper as just as valid artistically. We feel that a silver brooch can have as much intrinsic worth as a jewel made of gold and precious stones. The merit of craftsmanship and artistic conception must be recognised once more and be valued accordingly. Handicrafts must be measured by the same standards as the work of a painter or sculptor.

We cannot and will not compete with cheap work, which has succeeded largely at the expense of the worker. We have made it our foremost duty to help the worker recover pleasure in his task and obtain humane conditions in which to carry it out, but this can only be achieved step by step.

In our leather-work and book-binding, just as in our other productions, we shall aim at providing good materials and technical finish. Decoration will obviously only be added when it does not conflict with the nature of the material and we shall make frequent and varied use of the different techniques of leather-inlay, embossing, hand gilding, plaiting and steeping.

The art of good binding has completely died out.

Wiener Werkstätte trademark
Österreichisches Museum für Angewandte Kunst

Hollow backs, wire sewing, carelessly-cut, loosely-bound leaves and poor quality have become ineradicable. The manufactured so-called first edition, with its brightly printed jacket, is all that we have. The machines work away busily and swamp our bookshelves with faulty printed works and hold the record for cheapness. And yet any cultivated person ought to be ashamed of this material plenty, because he knows that on the one hand easy production means fewer responsibilities and on the other excess can only lead to superficiality. And how many of these books can we really call our own? Ought we not to possess them in their finest apparel, printed on the best paper and bound in the most beautiful leather? Have we so soon forgotten that the love with which a book is printed, put together and bound totally alters our relationship with it, that lasting acquaintance with beauty can only improve us? A book should be a work of art through and through and its merit be judged in those terms.

Our carpenters' workshops have always insisted upon the exactest and most reliable craftsmanship. But nowadays people have unfortunately grown so used to catchpenny trash that a piece of furniture executed even with a minimum of care seems quite out of reach. But it must be pointed out once and for all that we should have to assemble a pretty big house, not to mention everything inside it, if we were to equal the cost of building a railway sleeping-compartment, for example. This shows just how impossible it is to work out a sound basis for comparison. Only a hundred years ago, people were already paying hundreds of thousands for a period cabinet in a mansion, whereas today, when the most unexpected effects might be achieved if only the necessary commissions were forthcoming, they are inclined to reproach modern work with lacklustre inelegance. Reproductions of earlier styles can satisfy only the parvenu. The ordinary citizen of today, like the worker, must be proud and fully aware of his own worth and not seek to compete with other social stations which have accomplished their cultural task and are justified in looking back on an artistically splendid heritage. Our citizens have still far from carried out their artistic duties. Now it is their turn to do full justice to the new developments. Just striving to own pictures, however magnificent, cannot possibly suffice. As long as our towns, houses, rooms, cupboards, utensils, clothes, jewellery, language and feelings fail to express the spirit of the times in a clear, simple and artistic manner, we shall remain indefinitely far behind our ancestors and no pretence will conceal our lack. We should also like to draw attention to the fact that we too are aware that, under certain circumstances, an acceptable article can be made by mechanical means, provided that it bears the stamp of manufacture, but it is not our purpose to pursue that aspect yet. We want to do what the Japanese have always done, and no one could imagine machine-made arts and crafts in Japan. We shall try to accomplish what lies within our power, but our progress will depend on the encouragement of all our friends. We are not free to follow fancy. We stand with both feet in reality and await the commissions.

19 Hermann Muthesius, *The Meaning of the Arts and Crafts,* 1907 *

Nowadays the meaning of arts and crafts is artistic, cultural and economic at one and the same time. I should like to discuss the artistic aspect first, because it is the most obvious to a very great extent and also because it has been the source of inspiration for our entire movement, until quite recently. The various cultural forces at work are only just beginning to make themselves felt and their relevance is not yet very visible. Any economic significance must still lie almost exclusively in the future, though the hopes we can perhaps entertain in this respect are founded on parallels in history . . .

If the artist is to do justice to the new needs, he must first of all do justice to the individual requirements of each piece he creates. The essence of modern arts and crafts was thus seen to lie initially in a firm grasp of each item's particular purpose and then, as a logical consequence, in devising the appropriate form. But as soon as the artist's attention had been diverted from the outward imitation of earlier styles, in other words as soon as he had faced reality, he became aware that there were other needs as well. Different materials must evidently be handled in different ways. Stone could not have the same dimensions and forms as wood, and wood could not be treated as if it were metal. Similarly, within the metals cast iron must be worked in a different manner from silver. Forms had to be evolved according to their function and according to the character of the material employed. The new respect for the nature of materials naturally involved a corresponding concern for the best way of assembling the different parts. Function, material and structure thus became the basic principles guiding the work of the modern craftsman.

In practice, new forms are never determined solely in respect of these three laws. The question of feeling invariably intervenes in the passage from mind to hand and is especially important when a piece must be designed to please. An engineer may perhaps be capable of banishing the element of feeling, but it is doubtful. In any case it would be completely absurd to ask an artist to control his sensibility to produce logical mathematical forms at the expense of his imagination. Feeling is an important factor in modern arts and crafts and possibly enters into the process to a greater degree than it did formerly. A very different order of sensibility is needed in order to create in total independence of historical influences than to reproduce the outward appearance of older styles. It is in guarding against any irrelevant backsliding into sentimentalism and inappropriateness that the iron rules of function, material and structure prove a bastion. Attempts to resuscitate the past can scarcely fail to injure the efficiency of these laws. The quality of the arts and crafts produced in the second half of the nineteenth century, the chief period of historical imitation, has made this quite plain. This period, with its swiftly changing fashions, was the heyday of the worst ornamental aberrations and indiscriminate adoption of substitute materials. Stamped pasteboard was used for wood; stucco, or even sheet-zinc, to suggest stone; and tin castings simulated bronze. Even the most elementary sense of propriety was lost. Now why should this have happened? The main reason seems to have been that the entire generation had become bemused with appearances and, in keeping with the reigning mood of historical nostalgia, preferred them to everything else. Modern craftsmen have certainly managed to break away from the conceptions of those decades but the rest of the community has not. Both the public at large and the manufacturers are still thoroughly ensnared in it . . .

The arts and crafts are called upon to restore an awareness of honesty, integrity and simplicity in contemporary society. If this can be achieved, the whole of our cultural life will be profoundly affected, and the way will have been paved for the most far-reaching consequences. The success of our movement will not

---

* These extracts are from the opening speech Muthesius gave to his course of lectures on contemporary arts and crafts at the Berlin commercial academy in the Spring of 1907. This lecture aroused protests from the craft corporations and led ultimately to the founding of the Deutscher Werkbund in October of the same year.

only alter the appearance of houses and flats but will have direct repercussions on the character of an entire generation. A true understanding of the art of decoration is bound to provide a form of social training because it will ultimately eradicate the pretentious parvenu ambitions that have had such a harmful effect on our surroundings ...

Our movement is in the process of creating what might be called a new style of living. This is the true purpose of modern arts and crafts. Creating a new interior is only a step away from altering the design of the flat or house which contains that interior. It is perfectly easy to observe, in point of fact, that domestic architecture, especially the design of small country houses, has already taken inspiration from the ideas being developed in the arts and crafts. The most recent trend can be defined largely by the fact that a simple house which fits into its local context and is built to the principles of sound logic has begun to replace the ornate villa heavily laden with the merchandise of the past ...

Though the new movement is spreading so rapidly to the other arts that it can be regarded as a general trend no longer exclusively concerned with arts and crafts, the fact nevertheless remains that its influence has been almost entirely intellectual up to now and as yet has not had any significant repercussions on the economy of the country. The movement began in intellectual circles and that is where it has thrived, as new ideas were exchanged and passed on. But in a field which is commercial as well as artistic, any lasting success is bound to depend on whether or not the movement finds the proper economic outlet.

Moreover it is already becoming possible to point out that helping the modern movement is by no means a commercially unsound proposition. The large number of industrialists who followed the new path as a logical decision have obtained significant financial success. It is enough to mention the Dresdner Werkstätten für Handwerkskunst, which in the space of eight years developed from very humble beginnings into a concern with a colossal turnover, capable of employing hundreds of carpenters. But an essential condition, of course, is the sincerity of the manufacturer. If he joins the new movement because he believes in it and not on purely material grounds, his business cannot fail to benefit. It is legitimate to say that the industrialists who do not waste time signing protests will be the men of the future, because they will have kept pace with the movement of the times whereas the others are engaged in sterile attempts to stem it.

Solving the economic future of arts and crafts nevertheless remains the most urgent question at the present moment. Simply persuading manufacturers to adopt the so-called new manner instead of continuing to make reproductions is by no means going to settle it. Many have in fact attempted to do this already by exchanging the Art Nouveau and Secession styles for Empire and Biedermeier. The ideas inherent in our movement are too serious for us to indulge in frivolous dalliance with changing fashions and with novelty for its own sake. Our movement has nothing to do with the so-called 'modern style' at all as a matter of fact and we regard it as premature and irresponsible to proclaim one as such. Styles do not grow up overnight and cannot be invented to order. They can only be the fruit of periods of serious striving, when inner forces are made explicit. If the new trends are genuine, then an original, lasting style will emerge, and if they are superficial and vain they will ultimately lead to something resembling the fickle imitations of the last fifty years. It is impossible to foresee the kind of style that will spring from the determined efforts of contemporary arts and crafts. It can only be sensed. It is not our duty to try our utmost to force a style out of our period; we must simply work away with as much dedication and honesty as we possess and as our conscience demands. Nor can style be anticipated; it can only grow up as the all-embracing expression of the spirit of the age. It is up to the next generation to sort out what exactly our style was, that is to say to detect the common ground in the most meaningful achievements of our best artists and craftsmen.

So far the industrial art manufacturer has been resolutely opposed to applying ethics and morals to his business, which he claimed to run by satisfying the presumed demands of the public. As a result he produced articles which looked as if they were expensive but which cost next to nothing, and consumers at every level eagerly swallowed the bait. Similar professional practices, and the buyer's connivance, had a mutually demoralising effect on industry and on the public. After all, manufacturers can scarcely enjoy devoting their lives to producing trash and in the long run customers will cease to be pleased with things which are worthless. A thorough revision of attitudes must be brought about and it has to begin with the manufacturer. All he needs to do is to transfer the honest principles he observes in his private life to his business and, just as he would not be slipshod at home, refuse to produce shoddy goods, that is, not manufacture imitations and substitutes or articles which look as if they are valuable when they are not. Anyone who is at all familiar with English life and attitudes knows to what extent such principles can become the common good of the community. The English manufacturer operates according to his higher instincts almost without exception and thus produces honest goods.

However terrible and unpatriotic it may sound, anyone with proper knowledge of our neighbours must realise that today Germany simply does not count in either painting or sculpture. The painters we regard as heroes at home are not even known by name abroad, whereas the French impressionists are on everybody's lips. And even a foreign connoisseur would be at pains to think of a German sculptor when asked, though Meunier and Rodin spring to mind all over the world. In architecture we rank as the most backward country in Europe, because German taste in general is regarded as being at the very bottom of the ladder. In fact our artistic reputation has sunk so low that 'German' and 'bad taste' have become practically synonymous. There is nothing to be gained by refusing to admit this. We need to look the bare facts in the face, especially as the arts and crafts movement may be sacrificed on account of this reputation. It cannot be disputed that the exponents of our movement have produced something which will cause other countries to revise their judgement hastily. The exhibition of German arts and crafts in St Louis acted as a revelation for everybody and it is fair to say that people are already beginning to speak of a new flowering in German arts and crafts. Any increase in our exports is bound to depend on whether or not the new esteem can be consolidated.

---

20 Adolf Loos, *Cultural Degeneracy,* 1908

Hermann Muthesius, whom we have to thank for a series of instructive books on English life and housing has set forth the aims of the Deutscher Werkbund and attempted to give reasons for its existence. The aims are good, but the Deutscher Werkbund in particular will never achieve them.

The Deutscher Werkbund would be the last body to achieve them. The members of this confederation are men who are trying to replace our present-day culture with another. Why they are doing this I do not know. But I know that they will not succeed. No one yet has thrust his podgy hand into the spinning wheel of time without having it torn off by the spokes.

We have our culture, our ways of life and the commodities which enable us to live this life. No man – nor any association – had to create our wardrobes, our cigarette boxes, our jewellery. Time created them for us. They change from year to year, from day to day, from hour to hour. For we ourselves change from hour to hour, and with us our attitudes and habits. This is how our culture has changed. But the people of the Werkbund are confusing cause and effect. We do not sit in a particular way because a carpenter has made a chair in such and such a manner. A carpenter makes a chair in a particular manner because that is how we wish to sit. And for this reason the activities of the

Werkbund are useless – to the joy of all who love our culture.

The aims of the Deutscher Werkbund, as set forth by Muthesius, can be summed up in two phrases: excellence of workmanship, and the creation of a contemporary style. These aims are a single aim, for whoever works in the style of our time works well. And whoever does not work in the style of our time works carelessly and badly. And that is how it should be. For a bad form – by which I mean any form which does not conform to the style of our time – can be excused if one has the feeling that it will soon be done away with. But when rubbish is produced for posterity, its effect is doubly unaesthetic. It is the aim of the Werkbund to produce things for posterity which are not in the style of our time. That is bad. But Muthesius also says that through the cooperative work of the Deutscher Werkbund, the style of our time will be discovered. This is a waste of effort. We already have the style of our time. We have it everywhere where the designer, and therfore a member of this very movement, has not yet interfered. Ten years ago these artists set out in search of new fields to conquer, and having laid low the carpenter's art, attempted to gain control of tailoring. Those who are now members of the Werkbund belonged then to the Secession. They wore frock coats made of Scottish materials with velvet facings and they stuck a piece of cardboard in their stand-up-turn-down collars covered with black silk (Ver-Sacrum style) to give the illusion of a cravat wound three times round the neck. With a few forceful articles on this subject I drove the gentlemen in question out of the tailor's and cobbler's shops and saved other as yet uncontaminated crafts from the unsolicited attentions of the 'artists'. The master tailor who had shown himself so amenable to these cultural and artistic endeavours was abandoned and gentlemen took out a credit account with a well-known Viennese tailor.

Can anyone try to deny that our leather goods are in the style of our time? And our cutlery and glasses? And our bathtubs and American washstands? And our tools and machines? And everything, I repeat everything, which has not fallen into the hands of the artists!

---

21 Adolf Loos, *Architecture,* 1910

May I lead you to the shores of a mountain lake? The sky is blue, the water green and everything is profoundly peaceful. Mountains and clouds are reflected in the lake, and so are houses, farm-yards, court-yards and chapels. These do not seem man made, but more like the product of God's workshop, like the mountains and trees, the clouds and the blue sky. And everything breathes beauty and tranquillity.

Ah, what is that? A false note in this harmony. Like an unwelcome scream. In the centre, beneath the peasants' homes which were created not by them but by God, stands a villa. Is it the product of a good or a bad architect? I do not know. I only know that peace, tranquillity and beauty are no more.

For there are no good or bad architects in the eyes of God. Near to his throne, all architects are equal. In the towns, in the realms of Belial, there you will find fine distinctions, as you would expect among the depraved. And therefore I ask: how is it that every architect, however good or bad, violates the lake?

The peasant does not do this. Nor the engineer who builds a railway to the shores of the lake or draws deep furrows through the clear mirror-like surface, with his ship. They create in a different way. The peasant cuts out the spot on the green grass where the house is to be built and digs out the earth for the foundation walls. Then the mason appears. If there is loamy soil in the vicinity, then there will also be a brickworks to provide the bricks. If not, then the stone from the river banks can be used for the same purpose. And while the mason places brick upon brick and stone upon stone, the carpenter has established himself nearby. The strokes of the axe ring out merrily. He makes the roof. What kind of a roof? One that is beautiful or ugly? He does not know. The roof.

And then the joiner takes the measurements for doors and windows, and all the others appear and take measurements and go to their workshops and work away. And then the peasant mixes up a large vat with lime-white and whitewashes the house. He keeps the brush, however, for it will be needed again next year at Easter.

His aim was to build a house for himself, his family and his livestock and in this he has succeeded. Just as his neighbours or his ancestors succeeded. As every animal, which allows itself to be led by its instincts, succeeds. Is the house beautiful? Well, it is just as beautiful as the rose or the thorn, the horse or the cow.

And I ask yet again: Why does the architect both good or bad violate the lake? Like almost every town dweller, the architect possesses no culture. He does not have the security of the peasant to whom this culture is innate. The town dweller is an upstart.

I call culture, that balance of inner and outer man, which alone can guarantee reasonable thought and action. Next, I am going to give an answer to the question: 'Why do the Papuans have a culture and why do not the Germans?'

Until now, the history of mankind has never had to record a period devoid of culture. This period was reserved for the town dwellers of the second half of the nineteenth century to create. Until then, the development of our culture continued as an even flow. One did not look forwards or backwards, the present was all important.

But then false prophets arose. They said, 'How ugly and joyless our lives are!' And they gathered together everything from the old cultures, established them in museums and said, 'Look, that is true beauty. You have been living among wretched ugliness.'

Then there was velvet and silk and columns and mouldings inside the house. Above all there was ornamentation. And as the craftsman, because he was a modern, cultured man, was not capable of drawing ornaments, schools were founded, where healthy young people were warped until they could produce a satisfactory result. Just as in China children are placed in a vase and fed for many years until they escape their cages as horrible freaks. These dreadful, spiritual freaks were then duly admired, just like their Chinese brethren, and were easily able to earn their daily bread, thanks to their defects.

There was no one, at the time, who could call out to mankind and say, 'Remember, the path of culture is the path away from ornamentation towards the elimination of ornament'. The evolution of culture is synonymous with the separation of the ornamental from the functional. The Papuan covers everything within his reach with decoration, from his face and body down to his bow and rowing boat. But today tattooing is a sign of degeneration and is only used by criminals or degenerate aristocrats. And the cultured man finds, in contrast to the Papuan negro, that an untattooed face is more attractive than a tattooed one even if the tattooing were the work of Michelangelo or Kolo Moser himself. And man in the nineteenth century wants to feel that not only his face, but also his suitcase, his dress, his household effects and his house are safe from the artistically trained latter day Papuans. The Gothic? We have reached further than Gothic man. The Renaissance? We have reached further. We have become more refined and noble. We no longer have the strong nerves needed to be able to drink from an ivory goblet, carved with an Amazon slaughter. We have lost the old skills? Thank goodness! In exchange we have the heavenly notes of Beethoven. Our temples are no longer painted blue, red, green and white, like the Parthenon. No, we have learnt to discover the beauty of bare stone.

But as I have already said, there was no one around at the time, and the enemies of our culture and those who praised old cultures had an easy task. What is more, they were mistaken. They misunderstood the past epochs. It was only those objects of excessive ornamentation, preserved in good condition due to their lack of use, which were handed down to us and it was thus assumed that in the past there had only been ornamental things. Moreover, the age and origin of the objects could easily be determined from the ornamentation and this type of categorisation was one of the best loved pastimes of this God-forsaken time.

But the craftsman could not keep up. He was supposed to make and discover anew everything that had been made by people throughout the ages. These things were in each case an expression of their own particular culture and had been created by the masters then in the same way as the peasant now builds his house. The master of today can work as well as any master of any age. But the contemporary of Goethe could no longer make ornaments. So those who had the new warped ideas were sought out and placed before the masters as guardians.

The master mason and the builder were each given a guardian. The builder could only build houses in the style of his day. But the man who could build in a style of the past, who had lost all contact with his own time, uprooted and bent, he, the architect, became the new leader.

The craftsmen did not have a great deal of interest in books. The architect took everything from books. An immense literature provided him with his source of knowledge. One had no idea what a poisonous effect this immense number of publications would have on our town culture, for it hindered every form of self-assessment. Whether the architect had imprinted the forms in his mind so strongly that he could draw them from memory, or whether it was necessary for him to have the copy before him during his moments of 'artistic creation', was all one and the same thing. The effect was always identical: an abomination. And this abomination went on and on. Everyone wanted to see their work immortalised in new publications, and a large number of architectural periodicals met the conceited needs of the architect. And so things have remained, right up to the present day.

But the architect also ousted the builder-craftsman for another reason. He learnt to draw, and as he had learnt nothing else, in this at least he was competent. The craftsman cannot do this. His hand has become heavy. The designs of the old masters are unwieldy, any student of the architectural profession can do it better. And especially the so-called 'high-flyers', sought after by every architect's office, and inevitably offered a very high salary.

The architect has caused architecture to sink to a graphic art. It is not the man who can build best who gets most orders but rather the man who cuts the finest figure on paper. And yet these two are complete opposites.

If we line up all the different art forms, and begin with graphic art, this shades off into painting. This then leads through coloured sculpture to plastic art, and from plastic art we arrive at architecture. Graphic art and architecture are at opposite ends of the line.

The best draftsman can be a poor architect and the best architect a poor draftsman. But a talent for graphic art is already needed when the career choice, to become an architect, is made. Our whole new architecture is worked out on the drawing board and the resulting drawings produced in this way are simply translated into three dimensions like a painting turned into a waxwork tableau ...

Today, however, the 'high flyer' is supreme. It is no longer the craftsman's tools which create the forms, but rather the pencil. From the detailing of a building it can be seen whether the architect has used pencil number 1 or pencil number 5. And what disastrous taste results from a pair of compasses! The marks of the drawing pen have produced an epidemic of squares. No window frame or marble slab remains unmarked in the scale of 1 : 100, and bricklayers and stone-masons must hack out this graphic nonsense in the sweat of their brows. If water colour accidentally accompanies the artist's drawing pen, then the gilder is also inconvenienced ...

The second half of the nineteenth century was filled with the cry of the uncultured, 'We have no style of building!' How wrong, how incorrect! More than ever before, this period had an accentuated style, most easily differentiated from any period of the past; it was a change without precedent in our cultural history. As, however, the false prophets could only recognise a product by its ornamental nature, the ornament became a fetish, and they falsely attributed this changeling with the name of style. We already had true style but we had no ornamentation. If I could knock down all the ornaments of our old and new houses, so that only the bare walls remained, it would be difficult indeed, to differentiate between the house of the fifteenth and the house of the seventeenth century. But the houses of the nineteenth century can be picked out at a glance by any layman. We had no ornamentation and there were complaints that there was none. And they copied ornaments of so long past, that even they began to find them ludicrous, and when this was no longer possible, they discovered new ornamentation for themselves, that is to say, they had sunk to such cultural depths that they were capable of making these discoveries. And they were then delighted that they had found the style of the twentieth century.

But that is not the style of the twentieth century. There are many things which show the style of the twentieth century by pure form alone. They are made by craftsmen, with whom the warped architects were not acquainted. For instance, the tailors. And the cobblers, the purse-makers, saddlers, waggon builders, instrument makers and all those, who only escaped the general uprooting because their craft did not seem refined enough to the uncultured, and who therefore did not allow them to become a part of their reform. What real luck! From these remains, which the architects left to me, I was able to reconstruct modern joinery, twelve years ago. The joinery which we would possess if the architects had never stuck their noses into the joiner's workshop. For I did not approach the work as an artist, creating freely and leaving free play to the fantasy. Or so artistic circles seem to express themselves. No. Instead, I approached the workshop gingerly, like an apprentice, and I reverently gazed up at the man in the blue apron. And asked, 'Let me into your secret!' For modestly hidden away from the eye of the architects, many pieces of workshop-tradition still remained. And when they sensed my intentions, and saw that I was not one who would disfigure their beloved wood with my drawing board fantasies, and realised that I did not wish to violate the pure colour of their awesomely respected material with green or violet stains, their proud work-shop consciousness came to the surface and their carefully hidden tradition came to the forefront and their hate for their oppressors was given free vent. And I found the modern wall facings in the panels, which hid away the water tanks of the old waterclosets. I found the modern corners on the canteens, in which the silver cutlery was stored. I found locks and metal fittings at the trunk- and piano-makers. And most important of all, I found, 'That this style of the year 1900 is only as different from the style of the year 1800, as the tailcoat of the year 1900 differs from its century old predecessor'.

That is, not a great deal. The one was of blue cloth and had gold buttons, the other of black cloth with black buttons. The black tailcoat is in the style of our time. No one can deny that. The new movement, in its arrogance, omitted to reform our clothing. They were, you see, all serious men who found it beneath their dignity to concern themselves with such things. And so our clothes have stayed in the style of our time. These worthy serious men found that the only thing befitting to them was to discover ornaments.

When it finally became my lot to build a house, I told myself, 'The external appearance of a house can only have changed as much as the tailcoat, that is, not a great deal'. And I looked at the old buildings, and saw how they emancipated themselves from ornamentation from century to century and year to year. I therefore had to resume, from the point where the chain of development had been broken. One thing I knew: I had to become significantly less complicated in order to remain within the line of development. I had to replace the gold buttons with black ones. The house must look inconspicuous. Was it not I who had said, 'He who is modernly dressed is always least conspicuous'? ...

A house should appeal to everybody, as distinct from works of art which do not have to appeal to anyone. The work of art is the artist's private affair. A house is not. The work of art is put into the world without there being a function for it. A house supplies a need. The work of art is answerable to no one. The work of art aims at shattering man's comfortable complacency. A house must serve one's comfort. The work of art is revolutionary, the house conservative. The work of art points man in the direction of new paths and thinks to the future. The house thinks of the present. Man loves everything that serves his comfort. He hates everything that wants to tear him away from his secure and safe position, and is burdensome. And so he loves the house and hates art.

Does the house therefore have nothing to do with art, and should architecture not be classified under the arts? This is so.

Only a very small part of architecture belongs to art: the tomb and the monument. Everything else, everything which serves a purpose should be excluded from the realms of art.

Only when the great misunderstanding, that art is something which serves a purpose, can be overcome, only when the deceptive slogan 'applied art' has disappeared from popular parlance, only then will we have the architecture of our times. The artist has only himself to serve; the architect must serve the general public. But the fusion of art with craft has caused both them and all mankind untold damage.

Mankind no longer knows what art is. 'Art in the service of business' was the name given to an exhibition in Munich recently, and there was no one who would correct the brazen word. And nobody laughed at the splendid phrase 'applied art'.

But whoever realises that the purpose of art is to guide man ever onwards and upwards, making him ever more God-like, senses that the fusion of art with functional ends is a profanation of the highest degree. Man does not allow the artist free play because he is not in sufficient awe of him and the crafts cannot unfold freely while loaded down by the heavy burden of idealised demands. The artist cannot have a majority behind him amongst the living. His realm is that of the future.

Architecture arouses feelings in people. The task of the architect is therefore, to define what the feelings should be. The room must look comfortable, the house cosy. The court-house must make a threatening impression on the furtive criminal. The bank building must say, 'Here your money is securely safeguarded by honest people'.

The architect can only achieve this if he makes use of the same type of buildings, which have always produced these feelings in people, in the past. The Chinese colour of mourning is white, while for us it is black. It would therefore be an impossible task for our architects to arouse a joyous mood by the use of black paint. If we find a mound in the forest, six foot long and three foot wide, formed into a pyramid shape by a shovel, we become serious and something within us says, 'Someone lies buried here'. This is architecture.

---

22 C. R. Ashbee, *A Chapter of Axioms,* 1911

Axiom I.—Modern civilisation rests on machinery, and no system for the endowment, or the encouragement, or the teaching of art can be sound that does not recognise this.

Axiom II.—The craft cannot be learned in the school, the craft can only be learned in the life of the workman in the workshop.

Axiom III.—The purpose of the 'arts and crafts' is to set a standard of excellence in all commodities in which the element of beauty enters. The tendency of machine industry is to 'standardise', that is to say, to create as many pieces of any commodity to a given type as is economically possible.

Axiom IV.—Standard of excellence in the industrial arts acts in competitive industry as Gresham's law acts in coinage. The bad coin tends to drive out the good. So the bad product tends to drive out the good product, the unskilled workman and the machine tend to drive out the skilled craftsman.

Axiom V.—Machinery is neither all good nor all bad. An intelligent community will distinguish which is which, and the aesthetic education of the community in our day should be directed towards this distinction between the bad and the good.

Axiom VI.—The experience of the last twenty-five years has shown that in many trades and crafts the distinction between what should and what should not be produced by machinery has already been made.

[Ashlee goes on to discuss each Axiom in turn.]

Axiom III.—The purpose of the 'arts and crafts' is to set a standard of excellence in all commodities in which the element of beauty enters. The tendency of machine industry is to 'standardise', that is to say, to create as many pieces of any commodity to a given type as is economically possible.*

It is often supposed that the two principles [the 'standard of excellence' and 'standardisation'] here involved are irreconcilable; that there cannot be beautiful machine products, or that the beauty of a mechanical object lies in its conformity to the standard of a hand-made piece. But experience does not bear out this supposition. In modern mechanical industry 'standard' is necessary, and 'standardisation' is necessary. The principle in each is sound, and the community needs both. But if we try in practice to mix them up, the result is failure. For instance, if we make, by the process of 'standardisation', commodities whose intrinsic excellence depends upon human fancy and individuality, or if we make by hand commodities whose serviceableness depends upon rapidity, uniformity, and mechanical precision, we get into hopeless difficulty and economic confusion.

The discovery of this truth has been the work of the English Arts and Crafts movement. It has been left to the artists to test the truth of the axiom. And this they have done, not by the writing of economic text books, nor by the delivery of University Extension Lectures, but in all the little workshops of the hundred-and-one craftsmen who have tackled one craft after another in the modern revival of the Arts, and sought to drag it out of the quagmire in which the industrial revolution of the eighteenth and nineteenth century left it.

23 Karl Grosz, *Ornament*, 1911

The richness and variety of ornamental art treasures, which have come down to us over the centuries, is extremely great. But have we ourselves entered into the spirit of this cultural heritage? Have we really taken full mental possession of this wealth? Some people say 'of course we have', others would dispute this, and yet others want nothing to do with this inheritance as they consider themselves men enough to be able to produce a contemporary ornamental art on their own.

In any case one thing is certain and that is that we find ourselves today in a very difficult situation vis-á-vis ornamentation. Strictly speaking this has been the situation not just from today but for some time past.

Certain things however have no need of ornamentation and never will have in the future. One need only think of the developments in the shape of our means of transport, especially the car, and also in our weaponry. Here the pure and fine forms and shapes sensitively fulfil definite requirements. It is just the same with many items of daily use, where the complete

* Arthur Penty, in his excellent little book on the *Restoration of the Guild System*, has rightly shown how the distinction between these two is that one is qualitative, the other quantitative.

artistic penetration of the form and the high quality of the materials and workmanship would satisfy even spoiled claims for luxury. It is true that in the past, weapons, means of transport, implements, buildings and even tools were decorated, but only to raise them sufficiently from the mass of the common or garden. But at the time of the industrial style these articles as well were submerged in cheap decoration, so that any further development could only be sought for by returning to simplicity. We have just been through this reaction.

Now, once again, we long for more decoration, for ornamentation. But experience has taught us that decoration must introduce questions of quality, that it constitutes a mark of special value, which may only be turned into common currency with great care. Immediately the question arises; must decoration necessarily always be ornamentation?

Indeed not! The first embellishing feature of any building is the correct division of proportions. A good composition and elevations, good use of cornices and pilasters are themselves means of decoration and often suffice without any additional ornaments. Similarly with furniture. The man who has studied antiques does not immediately think of ornaments when talking about decoration, for he has seen how often the panelling alone, right through from simple flat designs to complex rich relief patterns, itself produces a sufficiently decorative effect. In the same way, there are many decorative possibilities in metal and ceramic work which simply result from a sensitive appreciation of the techniques involved. If, in developing shapes and forms for our ornamental art, we are to avoid an unnatural leap, then we too must first of all cultivate this 'decoration without ornamentation', a feature which has always been understood by the sensitive expert ...

Within the last few decades we have tried out and studied the ornamental motifs of every single style. We have attempted to derive ornaments either directly from motifs found in nature or via abstract shapes and lines. But we still have not made any real progress forward.

The reason for this must surely lie in the one-sided attempts at tackling the problem of ornamentation. Three things are needed for the final, successful solution. We need to study nature on two scores; firstly for motifs which should be collected with an eye to making us as independent as possible of those motifs used in former periods and, secondly, to help us acquire a sensitive feel for form and colour. Further we must make a study of the effects of every decorative feature on every artistic work of whatever period and from whatever race. This study is necessary in order to become fully aware of the wealth of extant works of art; but this process should not be mistakenly used for imitative copying of ornamental motifs. Whether we have the strength to add still further to this wealth, by creating really original ornamental effects capable of further development, remains to be seen. In any case experiments of this kind are only tolerable if a mature artistic perception is behind them. And finally it is necessary that the new ornamental art fits organically into the given problems and discussions about form in general. Like the actual working of the ornaments themselves this assumes a creative ability. Only as time goes by will new ways of employing them gradually crystallise ...

In matters of contemporary ornamental art artistic conditions are accompanied by economic considerations as well.

The use of ornamental decoration for objects of mass consumption is strictly speaking a devaluation. Yet the masses instinctively reach for decorated things and these should not be withheld from them. Industry can only achieve its real goals if the following principle is remembered: everything of a decorative nature must possess artistic and technical quality. Then the grading of articles from modest to fastidious, according to effect, will just be a matter of money; even the simplest thing can be beautiful. However, industry will not be able to attain healthy economic goals if it wants to pretend to offer things with sophisticated decorative value for little money, as it will deceive the undiscerning masses and in the end will undermine itself and its reputation ...

Unfortunately for the time being this is just wishful theorising, which marches forward swiftly on paper but, contained as it is within the bounds of economic possibilities, is forced to move along at a snail's pace.

Let us not give up hope! The Werkbund was founded for this very purpose, namely to keep all those people together, who despite everything will not give in.

The Werkbund will have to devote special attention to this problem of how to produce an ornamental art which corresponds in its forms to the way we feel.

---

24 Hermann Muthesius, *Where do we Stand?* 1911

. . . The Deutscher Werkbund was founded at a time when closer cooperation among all those participating in the new movement proved necessary to withstand the attacks of our opponents. The militant years in this sense are over because our ideas have ceased to be disputed and now meet with general approval, though this does not mean that the Werkbund is in danger of becoming superfluous, as has been suggested. This might seem the case if we were only to consider the narrower field of the industrial arts, but it would be taking a very limited view to imagine that it was enough to have made our sofa cushions and chairs look presentable. We must also think ahead; because it is now, with the end of hostilities, that the real tasks of the Deutscher Werkbund are making themselves felt. The Werkbund's first consideration has always been quality and it is true that a sense of quality is definitely on the increase, at least as far as technical and material matters are concerned, but even this does not mean that our mission is over. Far more important than the material world is the spiritual; in other words, form stands higher than function, material and technology. No matter how impeccably these three latter principles were carried out, we should still be living in a coarse crude world if there were no form. It thus becomes more and more obvious that our real goal is the greater, more far-reaching task of reawakening an understanding for form and bringing about the revival of architectural sensibility.

Architecture is and remains the true yardstick of the cultural level of a country. If a people is capable of producing perfectly good furniture and lighting systems but daily comes out with the worst architectural constructions to put them in it is because there is a lack of harmony and clarity in general; this very eclecticism proves the absence of rigour and organisation. What we are pleased to call culture is unthinkable without an uncompromising respect for form; and formlessness is just another name for philistinism. Form is a higher intellectual need in the same way that cleanliness is a higher physical need, because the sight of crude forms will cause a really cultivated person something resembling bodily pain and the same uncomfortable sensation that is produced by dirt and foul smells. As long as educated people fail to experience as urgent a need for form as for clean clothes, we shall remain a very long way away from conditions which can be even remotely compared with the great periods of artistic flowering.

In order to discover the real position in this respect, you only need to glance at the houses belonging to educated Germans, which generally afford the same cheerless prospect we get from a residential suburb. People who have houses built nowadays do not feel the need to engage qualified assistance when a building contractor will do just as well. A man who goes to the best tailors, loves good music and keeps an exquisite winecellar will invariably allot so little importance to his housing that he will regard the first mason's foreman to hand as adequate for his needs. This is an almost general practice in Germany nowadays, unlike England and France where cultivated people naturally choose good architects just as they go to the best doctors when they are ill and not to a first-aid centre. But our leading citizens continue to shun the qualified architect although this does not prevent them from sitting on cultural development committees and becoming members of building advisory boards.

The thought of all that remains to be done merely to mitigate the worst of these evils is quite overwhelming. The problem is where to begin first. The two most obvious areas of action are to influence the producer on the one hand and the user on the other, in other words, train the younger generation of architects properly and help clients to acquire a truer grasp of architectural values.

The training of future architects seems to be the comparatively lighter task because a certain amount of progress has already been made in this direction. The improvements introduced have had a noticeable effect on younger architects with very positive results and the reforming hand laid upon secondary education as a whole and on training schools has at least succeeded in removing the dross of pretentiousness. The question of whether or not the further education given in technical universities may also be in need of reform can only be touched upon here, but there is no doubt that overemphasis on external considerations largely bound up with social distinctions can severely damage a student's inner development. These courses seem to aim at producing fourth-rate advisers rather than first-rate performers. It is also evident that no good can come from the present view that a student should be allowed to decide that he is going to 'study' architecture at the age of twenty rather as someone chooses law or medicine. Some evidence of artistic talent at least should be made the primary condition and there should be some means of putting these gifts to the test. Similarly the general tendency to insist on the mere assimilation of architectural externals that have little to do with the practice of art as such seems to leave a great deal to be desired.

But since most educated Germans still circumvent qualified assistance altogether, it seems more urgent to concentrate on the other line of attack for the time being, namely to try to exert an influence on the consumer. Any public interest in architecture has been allowed to lie completely fallow for a very long time in our country. The newspapers deal with every first-night at the theatre as if it were an international event and devote long columns to exhibitions of painting and sculpture but they still behave as if architecture simply did not exist. Reporters know nothing at all about it and younger art critics have only quite recently begun to bother about winning it even a tradesman's entrance into the market-hall of opinion. The average reader prefers to avoid any references to architecture, almost as if he were being asked to appreciate the merits of Sanskrit dialects.

Lately however it has proved possible to earn something of a hearing from the public at large by a rather roundabout route. The magic word that has roused everyone from their architectural apathy is conservation (*heimatschutz*). The ideals inspiring this movement have now fortunately almost become universally accepted and we are bound to acknowledge that the associations which spread these ideas have done a good job. The fact that the principles of conservation have been generally accepted is at least one important way of admitting that the constructions which have sprung up all over our countryside in the last five years have been officially recognised as unsuitable ...

It is all very well to say that conservation is just another substitute for genuine artistic feeling, but we happen to be in the needy position where even substitute for genuine artistic feeling, but we happen to be in the needy position where even substitute measures must be accepted gratefully. Nothing would be more dangerous than to attempt to draw a line through all these side-attempts to cure our ills because of some mistaken subservience to higher artistic claims. And I must insist once and for all that in view of our present sorry state the way the Kunstwart and the Dürerbund are popularising the understanding of art by distributing comprehensive literary propaganda, which is so often criticised by the artists themselves, must be admitted as an absolutely necessary educational medium that cannot be dispensed with and that the concern of those who tend to regard such activities as 'inferior' and even dangerous to art is decidedly premature. The principle of art for art's sake has little practical relevance in architecture in any case, since building is an essentially popular and social form of art.

But one thing which must be made quite clear in connection with recognising the services of propaganda, is the fact that the artist must go his own way unperturbed about fleeting popular notions which have nothing to teach him and nothing to forbid. It is, after all, the artist who must produce the art, and hope in the artistic future of the nation rests with him alone; he is the one who holds our artistic destiny in his hands, now just as before. All attempts to spread the knowledge of art are bound to be short-lived if we lack the creative power which sincerely gives of its best with its blood, unconcerned about passing trends.

This is what accounts for the inviolability of art and, as a consequence, the immense responsibility of the creative artist.

Perhaps it also falls within the Werkbund's province to attempt to bring out the artist's knowledge of his responsibility as sharply as possible ...

A number of practical jokers have come to the fore even among the ranks of those who contributed towards producing the present good, who have begun to perform grotesque turns to convince the public that this is the desired swing into the latest phase of interior design. They are people who claim that 1850 was the time when the most amusing articles were made and that the period is worth exploiting and imitating! Fifteen years ago they were the first to heap abuse on the owners of the very pieces they now declare as models of style. However this happened, the fact remains that fashionable society, as fickle as ever and incapable of recognising permanent values is beginning to tire of its beloved Biedermeier and has taken up 1850 as its latest ideal. But the artist must realise that we are in a serious position and place our aims above the ability to adapt to such passing fancies.

Great values are at stake in fact, because Germany is a country where present achievements can have a determining influence on the future development of style. After England laid the foundations for a thorough reorganisation of the industrial arts, Germany proved capable of employing its remarkable yield of strength and energy to gain a leading position in the field. For a moment it really seemed as if it might be possible to transform the wasteland wrought by a century which had turned away from art. There was hope that time might be cancelled out and that a new feeling for beauty could be resuscitated, founded on achievements stemming from a genuine feeling for the age, the only achievements worth having. Surely we cannot now allow ourselves to slip back into producing imitations of our worst artistic periods.

If people want imitations and if there is an inclination to provide them, then why not follow the example of France, which is busily copying its own best periods over and over again. Why do we have to show the world that Germany's reputation for bad taste was well founded, because we have proved capable of reverting to the very style which revealed us bankrupt in London in 1851. Even if the imitations of 1850 are accepted at home, there is no doubt that they will have a disastrous effect on our reputation abroad ...

It is evident that the ephemeral is incompatible with the true essence of architecture. The peculiar qualities of architecture are constancy, tranquillity and permanence and its thousand-year-old traditions of expression have almost come to represent what is eternal in human history. The present impressionistic attitude towards art in a sense is unfavourable to its development. Impressionism is conceivable in painting, literature, sculpture to some extent and perhaps even music, but in architecture it does not bear thinking about. The few individualistic attempts already tried out by some architects to illustrate what might be an impressionist manner are simply horrifying. Of all the arts, architecture is the one which tends most readily towards a type [*typisch*] and only thus can it really fulfil its aims. It is only by steadily striving for a single target that we shall be able to recover the quality and unerring surety of touch that we admire in the achievements of the past, where singleness of purpose was inherent in the age. This is also valid for painting and sculpture to a certain extent ...

The recovery of a feeling for architectural form is the first condition in all the arts nowadays and the indispensable foundation for what we hope will be a general process of artistic regeneration. The tremendous significance of the movement we have brought half-way along the road to completion lies in this direction because the outcome of our efforts may come to fulfil directly the destiny of the period. It is all a matter of restoring order and rigour in our modes of expression, and the outward sign can only be good form ...

Germany has the reputation for being more precise and rigorous in the organisation of its businesses, industries, and public services than other countries (this has been put down to its military upbringing). If that is true, it is perhaps a sign that Germany is called upon to provide a solution for the important problems posed in the field of architectural form. How well the modern economy as a whole begins to comprehend the new architectural needs will depend on whether or not its corporations and businesses will at last cease to believe that they can do without advice from the best architects. If it should prove possible to convince certain circles of the necessity of form, especially rich private persons, a further great step forward will have been taken.

When wealth becomes simply the amassing of material plenty it has no meaning for progress. Its imperative duty should be to succour want and provide inner enrichment. Such aims are inconceivable without art, and architecture is the handmaiden able to bestow meaningful forms on our poverty. Only when every member of the population instinctively clothes his basic needs with the best forms available, shall we as a nation have attained the level of good taste which the otherwise advanced activities of Germany deserve. The extent to which we develop our taste, that is our handling of form, will have decisive significance for Germany's reputation in the future. And the process has to begin at home. Only when our own standards have become clearly defined and harmonious can we hope to influence others. Only then will the world respect us as people who, among other things, can be relied upon to solve the problem of restoring the lost values of architectural culture.

---

25 From the debate following Muthesius's speech, 1911

K. E. Osthaus

[Picking up Muthesius's point about architecture tending towards a Type.] Adopting the stance of a refined aesthetic what position can be taken towards this question? I believe that I can answer it in this way: standard patterns will always develop whenever requirements are exactly the same. On the whole, standard designs show a concern only for satisfying needs and not for satisfying the dictates of art. Wherever similar human groups have similar needs it is clearly more than likely that the result will be the development of standard designs. I have just come back from France. There, to my great surprise, I found a number of towns whose development has almost completely followed some form of artistic planning. I would specially like to mention Rennes. This town was razed to the ground by fire in the middle of the eighteenth century and then rebuilt according to a coherent architectural plan. Strictly speaking there are only standard designs in the town. It is almost impossible to distinguish one house from the next. And yet the town makes a more impressive impact than almost any other town in the world. Despite the complete external uniformity, looking at the town gives you the impression that it had an extremely lively artistic life. The standard design which emerges here has been formed by a careful balancing and refining of personal requirements. Thus, following standard patterns is not necessarily an obstacle to artistic presentation. It is simply a question of whether the standard design is coped with artistically or not ...

C. J. Fuchs, (A member both of the Bund für Heimatschutz and the Werkbund)
We understand by the word *Heimatschutz* [conservation] in a broader sense, everything which, whilst new, allies itself harmoniously with existing old forms but without being identical with them. If new styles are developed by real artists then former aesthetic values will never be destroyed. Works of art are always compatible with each other, even if their styles are completely different. We must give thought to the problem as a whole and realise the practical tasks which still exist. The number of artists who can produce such works of art and know how to add something extremely new to something old and beautiful, is small. It is precisely the rôle of the Werkbund to take into account the average job of a large number of builders and foremen, and I believe we would be on much surer ground if we could bring these people to employ established forms and native building methods and arrangements. More would come from this than if they tried to imitate distinguished artists. We saw the unfortunate results of doing this in the Jugendstil period. I think we can clearly distinguish here between the two above mentioned aspects. Surely the Werkbund does not merely wish to promote the independent use of artists in the sphere of economic production and industrial work. It also wants to bring a large number of operatives in this field to the point where they can produce something good which the artist generally would not undertake and for which it would be too costly to call him in. The Werkbund must want to raise the spiritual level of the large mass of things produced. This undoubtedly happens best when the old and proven forms are adhered to, forms which have developed over centuries following certain traditions. And all this is what the Heimatschutz movement wants.

If you were to see the problem from this angle then you will appreciate that there is no opposition between the Werkbund and Heimatschutz movements.

Hermann Muthesius
If a new conception in today's architecture can be detected then it is this; we are in the process of returning from an individual to a standard way of thinking. We are endeavouring to construct whole housing estates in a uniform style. I consider this emphasis on standard designs in architecture to be extremely important for its whole future. We can learn something here by drawing a parallel with England. Developments there were in advance of ours by several decades. Similar attempts to reassert the values of vernacular building methods were being made in England in the 1860s. One can produce English lectures and essays from that period which show exactly the same lines of thought as those put forward by our own Heimatschutz movement today. Architecture as well conformed with this formula. Despite this, a new tradition grew up then, which bore a completely modern stamp. If you look at an English detached house today, you will encounter a complete uniformity of style, a national tradition which we must regard as an ideal state. Imitations of older styles are no longer to be seen, although at the time they were at least popularly thought to have provided the point of departure for the whole movement. A modern means of expression has developed from the tendencies of the native building methods. And that, gentlemen, strengthens my hope for a successful future for those efforts which inspire us in the Deutscher Werkbund and which are shared by the German Heimatschutz organisations.

26 Walter Gropius, *The Development of Modern Industrial Architecture,* 1913

There is no doubt that a desire for outward beauty of form is growing up in all branches of trade and industry alongside the hitherto exclusive demand for technical perfection and commercial value. Aesthetic considerations such as unity of form, choice of colour and a general feeling of elegance are automatically being taken into account in the designing of machinery, vehicles and factory-buildings, which serve purely utilitarian purposes, as well as in the manufacture of articles for everyday use ...

Earlier, the separate activities of technician, salesman and artist were concentrated in the single person of the craftsman. And as long as the artist's contribution was regarded as unnecessary for industry, machine-made products inevitably remained inferior substitutes for handicrafts. Very gradually, however, certain members of the business world began to see just how much could be gained by enlisting the intellectual labour of the artist.

The artist has the power to give the lifeless machine-made product a soul; it is his creative force which will live on, actively embodied in its outward form. His collaboration is not just a luxury, generously thrown in as an extra, it is an indispensable part of the industrial process and must be regarded as such ...

The really brilliant ideas are precisely the ones which most merit reproduction and should be brought within reach of the community at large, not reserved solely for private appreciation. In practice, it has already proved a shortsighted policy to attempt to economise on the artist. The experience of a number of leading firms has shown quite plainly that it pays in the long run to give thought to the artistic worth as well as the technical perfection and saleability of a product, because their goods have become a means of carrying tastefulness and quality among large numbers of people. Not only have they earned themselves a reputation for promoting culture but, which is equally as important in business, have considerably increased their pecuniary gain ...

For a long time factories were regarded as belonging to the unavoidable evils one had to bear and a bleak tumble-down establishment was thought to suffice. It was only with the general growth of prosperity that something more began to be expected. The first steps were taken with improved lighting, heating and ventilation, though now and again an architect was called in somewhat belatedly to adorn the bare utility structure with what were invariably unsuitable trimmings, a procedure which unfortunately is still a favourite one today. This misguided approach simply conceals the unsolved difficulties from the outside distorting the true character of the building by allowing it to masquerade in borrowed garments from an earlier period which have absolutely nothing in common with the sterner purposes of a factory. The good name of the firm can only suffer from a building got up in fancy-dress. It is not by administering such inexpensive remedies that the difficulties are likely to be solved. The problems facing modern architecture need to be grasped from within, not superficially. If a building is not just to remain an outer shell, it must have a coherent basic structure which has been conceived artistically and there must be no decorative afterthoughts. Unless the architect is consulted when the plant is actually being laid out, he will never be able to fill his employer's organisational needs and interpret the manufacturing process in a way which will bring out the true merit of the establishment and its methods of work. The value of his intellectual contribution lies in the neat ordering of the ground-plan and the proportioning of the masses, not (as many still believe) in superabundant ornamentation.

Rococo and Renaissance styles just will not do for the functional rigour of our modern world and its judicious use of materials, money, labour and time. They would simply reduce what may be an intrinsically dignified structure to a sentimental and meaningless paraphrase. The new times demand their own expression. The modern architect must develop his aesthetic repertoire from forms stamped with precision, with nothing left to chance: clear contrasts, the ordering of the members, symmetry and unity of form and colour – this is what the energy and economics of public life require.

But these are only guiding principles. They will not crystallise into a powerful artistic whole unless they are handled by a gifted builder. It is the total newness of industrial architecture which will capture the lively imagination of the artist, precisely because there is no traditional heritage to cramp his style. The more freely he is allowed to display his originality in the new language the more the building will provide the asset and advertisement the firm desires. A handsome outfit reflects on its wearer and the new design will encourage positive conclusions as to the character of the firm as a whole. The public's attention will certainly be more attracted by the artistic beauty and compelling original outlines of the actual factory-building than the vulgar propaganda of slogans and brochures which can only weary an already jaded eye. Once an artistic idea has been embodied in three-dimensional form it never loses its effect.

A factory which has come into being through the combined energies of employer and architect will possess advantages which the organisation as a whole is bound to share. If the rooms have been lucidly arranged inside – clearly reflected in the outward appearance as well – they will considerably simplify the process of manufacture. It should not be forgotten that from the purely social point of view it is of the utmost importance whether or not a factory-hand carries out his work in airy well-proportioned rooms or squalid forbidding quarters resembling a barracks. A worker will find that a room well thought-out by an artist, which responds to the innate sense of beauty we all possess, relieves the monotony of the daily task and he will be more willing to join in collective undertakings. If the worker is happy, he will take more pleasure in his duties and the productivity of the firm will increase.

One or two enterprising owners who have recently been calling in architects with training in the fine arts as well are plainly deriving incalculable reward from their farsightedness. And now that cultivated circles outside the business world have begun to hear of their activities, their reputation for following an ideal that goes beyond the mere material gratification of the masses is spreading more and more rapidly. The first and most important step taken in this direction was made when the General Electric Company in Berlin (A.E.G.) appointed Peter Behrens as artistic adviser on every aspect of the business. In five years the happy union of bold organisation and exceptional artistic gifts has produced achievements which, by their grasp of changing and sometimes totally new values up to now seem to rank as the most powerful and purest examples of a thorough rethinking in European architecture. Simply by basing its designs on the elementary principles of tectonics, A.E.G. has set up buildings which are monuments of sovereign strength, commanding their surroundings with truly classical grandeur and which no one can pass by without being involved emotionally. This was an event which set an example for industry as a whole and others lost no time in following suit. With the growing interest, it is becoming more and more common to find the right architect in conference with his employer. The new factory buildings, such as the Coffee Marketing Company in Bremen (built by H. Wagner), the Delmenhorster Anker linoleum factory (built by Stoffregen), the chemicals factory in Luban near Posen (by Hans Poelzig), to mention only a few, convey the impression of coherent architecture which has at last discovered the right dress for the life style of the times and firmly rejects the romantic residue of past styles as cowardly and unreal.

Compared with the rest of Europe, Germany seems to have taken a considerable stride ahead in the field of artistic factory-building, but America, the home of industry, possesses some original majestic constructions which far outstrip anything of a similar kind achieved in Germany. The compelling monumentality of the

Canadian and South African grain silos, the coal silos built for the large railway companies, and the totally modern workshops of the North American firms almost bears comparison with the buildings of Ancient Egypt. Their individuality is so unmistakable that the meaning of the structure becomes overwhelmingly clear to the passer-by. But the impact of these buildings does not depend on their superior material extent. That is certainly not where to look for an explanation of their monumental originality. It seems rather to lie in the fact that American builders have preserved a natural feeling for large compact forms fresh and intact. Our architects might take this as a valuable hint and refuse to pay any more heed to fits of historical nostalgia or other intellectual considerations under which European creativity continues to labour and which stand in the way of true artistic naïveté.

---

27 W. R. Lethaby, *Modern German Architecture and what we may learn from it,* 1915

My right to speak of German architecture and arts and crafts comes from my having visited the country about half a dozen times, and having seen many of the most important cities, including Berlin. It was many years ago that I came to the personal conclusion that Germany was racing; that she had consciously divided up human activities and knowledge into departments, and had definitely set herself to outrun all other competitors in all of them. The guardians and directors of the State had, it seemed to me, substituted for the old customary methods and detached competitions in arts and sciences a clear and definite purpose of beating down all rivals and surpassing all emulation. This is not far-fetched; it has simply been the result of bringing in the Prussian war spirit into every phase of life. German science, of which I can only speak concerning archaeology, German industry, German architecture, have all been recast under the dominating desire to attack and to conquer. Think what this means if it is true – and something like it must be true – that at some time, forty or fifty years ago, the real leaders of the Prussian Power should have gathered together in some room and have decided to enter on such a definite campaign. German museums, German books, German machine industry and factories, the German theatre, and all the rest to outclass the spontaneous productions of neighbour States. This being the end in view, all the necessary means were easy to see and to apply. The efforts of other people were studied, reported on, absorbed, and their mistakes in many cases rectified. For it has been an essential part of the position that Germany, coming into the field as an attacking party, was able to select and experiment in a way that was impossible for those who, in many cases, had been the pioneers. This conquering spirit certainly carries far; we do not know how far, but it must have its limitations – it will, I think, dry up the sources of originality. It seems to me, although there is a certain absurdity in uttering individual opinions on the psychology of a colossal Empire, that the Prussian spirit runs to extremes; even organisation may perhaps be over-organised, specialisation be too specialised, and thoroughness be too thorough. Germany perhaps tends to the unmeasured. Domesticity and feeding seem to an outsider to be done without measure – education and erudition are perhaps carried beyond due measure, and violence is certainly made violent beyond measure ...

The first thing in the arts which we should learn from Germany is how to appreciate English originality. Up to about twenty years ago there had been a very remarkable development of English art in all kinds.

It is equally true or even more true that the German advances in industrial design have been founded on the English arts and crafts. They saw the essence of our best essays in furniture, glass, textiles, printing, and all the rest, and, laying hold on them, coined them into money, while our Press, caught up into an eddy of devilish bright writing, set about to kill the whole thing. Just as we gave Germany many of the industrial ideas which she has so thoroughly exploited – the extracting of aniline dyes, for example; just as she took up the arts and crafts experiments, which we employed critics to destroy at home; so we first seem to have arrived at the thought of an architecture which should develop in its own sphere, and not be for ever casting back to disguise itself in the skins which it had so long ago sloughed off – or, like the dog of Scripture, eat its dinner twice over. (Even this image, however, is inadequate; the ideal seems to be that the architectural dog should for ever and ever re-swallow the same meal.) German architects have seized on this theory of a 'real architecture' – or they have reached it for themselves. Meanwhile we have been caught up in one of our recurring reactions. Architecture is not seen as one of the forms in which the national energy, intellect, and spirit shall expand, but it is diverted and maimed and caged into formulas which are not only dead, but never had life ...

---

28 Hermann Muthesius, *The Future of German Form,* 1915

As far as England is concerned, the war has furnished irrefutable evidence that she has passed the peak of her development. There is no need to discuss how far this peak is already behind her. Signs of old age have been observable for decades. In all areas Germany has taken England's place ...

Nevertheless one could almost say that the benefits of trade are by no means the most valuable things acquired by a nation leading in matters of taste. More important than money is reputation, higher than wealth stands esteem, and highest of all, love. And all these will be offered to the nation which leads the way in matters of art.

The particular qualities needed for this are in evidence at their clearest in modern Germany: adaptability, close and careful adjustment to the circumstances, subordination to important criteria, in a word, organisation.

But just as, on the battefield, in our war policies, in our finances and economy, we venture everything in order to gain victory with the help of an organisation worked out to the finest detail, so in our art we must introduce our carefully considered marshalling of forces in order to attain German Form, which is awaited by many people with hope and yearning.

More important than ruling the world, more important than supporting it financially, is to educate it, to flood it with goods and wares. It is a matter of giving the world an image. Only the nation which can achieve this task stands truly at the head of the world, and Germany must be this nation. [Author's italics.]

---

29 Hans Poelzig, *The Architect,* 1931

Technology has taught us to reflect anew on the concept of architecture.

Liebermann says: 'Painting is leaving things out', and in modern architecture we have come to essentially the same conclusion, whereas formerly architecture was generally understood to be a process of adding on.

Does this, then, sum up the concept of architecture? The road to present-day architecture began with the reform of industrial building methods. We older ones, who seized on industrial building a generation ago, were frankly hungry for a field which had not yet been ploughed, which was not ruled by preconceived, historicising, stylistic opinion. At that time people were accustomed to seeing Gothic churches, Oriental synagogues, and German Renaissance post-offices. Law courts even appeared in monastic Baroque. Every attempt to make a breach in these conventions failed, and industrial building was merely the area in which we found the least resistance, one which was willingly left to us since it seemed unimportant to the stylists of official architecture.

Undoubtedly the first buildings produced in this spirit made an impression; people now saw that industrial buildings could develop a beauty of their own, a beauty which was essentially related to that of old warehouses, bridges, and so on.

In the works which were characteristic of him – bridges, railway stations etc. – the engineer's calculations had led him to produce forms whose beauty had hitherto been overlooked. Considered mechanical, they could only be rendered worthy of artistic consideration by the addition of formal 'architectural' appendages. Now this kind of form is recognised as valid not only from a mechanical and constructional point of view, but also as giving industrial buildings an artistic status of their own.

And this is where we stand today. We have come a long way in a remarkably short time. The formalistic bonds of a traditional architecture have been broken. Where do we go from here? The modern style is now recognised, whereas only a few years ago a building which rejected historically established canons of taste would find almost insuperable obstacles placed in its path by the authorities in Berlin. This new objective reality is acknowledged; now it must simply be built, 'cost what it may' as the humorous saying goes.

Is this objective reality really so objective and realistic?

The play of ornament, surface and decoration in the earlier sense is now so to speak forbidden. But has it really, totally ceased? Instead of hand-wrought, or even machine-produced ornaments, we now see the use of valuable materials: lacquer, glass, metal, stone. The interplay of these different surfaces now replaces the interplay of ornament, and undoubtedly they are better suited to the naked, slender forms of modern building; the unity of form is retained, but heightened through surface polish and colour.

I can see no danger in this – but there is a danger that the architect, having been denied the use of ornament by the development of present-day architecture, will begin to play with construction methods instead. This is an expensive game to play and the seduction of ornament was scarcely less intoxicating than that of the constructional methods placed in the hands of the present-day architect, with their seemingly limitless possibilities.

In fact this new kind of 'objective' practicality or realism contains just as much false romanticism, and ultimately as much *un*practicality as any period which has fallen under the spell of a slogan. It is totally unpractical if I use expensive beams to span wide areas, leaving out intermediate supports which would make the construction cheaper and easier. The use of gigantic window areas without reason is no less intrinsically foolish than the previous attitude of architects who felt obliged to use heavy masses and large expanses of wall for the sake of architectural propriety.

The concept of play arises again and again, and this is inevitable. Building is one of the earliest forms of play in children. Architecture is play in the highest sense, just as the world is the play of God. *Dum ludere videmur* – while we appear to be playing – we produce our most sublime creations. No art was ever created with furrowed brow and intellectual ponderings. Of course the architect is ever and again torn from his daydreams, and he needs the highest degree of discipline to adjust his inner vision to the demands of the outside world ...

Most of us know that our buildings demand a distinctly economical and technical approach, and that our solution of the problem in hand must make the minimum demands on space, material and time. Apart from that we are free, and we should never allow ourselves to be overtaken by a form of mechanistic romanticism which would result in technology becoming as holy to us as perhaps the Renaissance tradition was to the architects of the nineteenth century. Should one forget that technology is there to be used when necessary and not to be glorified for its own sake, one would only too easily find oneself rejoicing in every gas-pipe and heating appliance, in every detail of concrete construction, revealing everything in as naked a fashion as possible, confident that one had thereby proved one's modernity. One so easily forgets that technical forms have only a relative significance, in contrast to the absolute significance of art, and that some new construction technique may demand quite different forms again. Indeed, the most effective technological achievement is that which is the least intrusive in a formal sense, and which conforms to the technical ideal with the minimum of materials and forms.

In 1898, old Schäfer, my unforgettable teacher, gave an address at the Berlin Industrial Exhibition on the subject of Architecture – and in it he said something which has always stuck in my mind. He gave the opinion – and in this he was naturally a child of his time – that steel construction could not be used for stylistic expression in architecture, that the ideal of that form of technology lay in reducing and refining the form more until it disappeared altogether, while architecture as an art form needed heavy masses. That was old Schäfer's opinion. Today we know that steel construction has afforded us a type of structure offering extreme refinement of the skeleton without the material itself needing to appear on the outer surface.

Schäfer was thus quite wrong about the development of present-day architecture, since he was still grounded in the traditions of hand craftsmanship; but was he completely wide of the mark in relation to technological form in itself?

In fact the more it progresses, the more technology tends to reduce its own formalistic status. The turbines of today are minute compared with the gigantic machines which we used to have. And all the technological forms which we architects strive so vainly to dispose in an orderly fashion today (heating units, piping conduits etc.,) will, I am firmly convinced, disappear or become so small that they will cease to have any formal significance. It is therefore quite pointless to try and stabilise their form as some kind of artistic norm, thereby falling once more into the mistake of the Jugendstil, which tried to extract a generally valid ornamental and architectural style from the rapidly changing forms of technology.

What, after all, is architecture all about? Surely it is about form, indeed about symbolic form. But are technological forms symbolic, and can they ever be? Are art forms transitory? Certainly they can be destroyed. But is their effect transitory?

A motor car or bicycle which has outlasted its usefulness is thrown on the scrap heap; no one sheds a tear for their form, for the form of the car of ten years ago. A pure art form, a temple, the interior of a Gothic cathedral, a picture by Rembrandt; these lose nothing of their impact on the human psyche. Technological forms rise and fall, change and are destroyed, becoming valueless and ineffectual. They stem from and serve the practicalities of life. Technology follows the laws of nature, it is an extension of nature. Indeed, devices such as the airship, or the aeroplane, seem like some fantastic crystallisation of prehistoric natural forms, as if demonic powers were trying to take concrete shape once more. Such demonic grandeur is an extension of nature, but it is never art.

The divine Word which inspires art is never a form of calculation – it is against all calculation but is mathematical in a higher sense. The logic of art goes against Nature, against her laws. A Greek temple has nothing to do with architectural structure in a mathematical sense; not one of its lines expresses a definite mathematical formula; the curves follow a higher order than the mathematical one. Nor is there anything practical about the structure of a Gothic cathedral in a technological sense at least. Particularly in its vaulting, it represents an assault on the principles of stone construction. The Gothic style is and always will be an extraordinary game, a theatrical manipulation of space.

The engineer goes imperturbably on his way, but his creations are Nature – they do not become symbolic, they do not become style. Their validity stems only from technological considerations. They can and must influence pesent-day style, just as natural forms have influenced style in the past, just as Nature produced a different architecture among the Nordic peoples from that of the Greeks.

And as technology and technological forms are today spread throughout the world, to the extent that no one can erect a present-day building without technical knowledge, it is logical that the new style of building should show an international face, that for the first time in the history of the earth the architectural forms of the different parts of the world should resemble one another. But present-day architecture is naturalistic; in musical terms it is atonal.

We must get through this atonality, we must not quickly settle down with a modern building style which relies cheaply for its harmonies on crude contrasts and pleasing rhythms. This modern melody quickly makes an impression, offending some, exciting others, but its effect is short-lived and its enthusiasts soon come to look on it with scorn.

And is there anything which has not been declared kitsch at some point or other? The Biedermeier style was once considered pretty bourgeois kitsch, while the products of the Jugendstil were high art. Then the tables were turned, Jugendstil became kitsch and Biedermeier was treasured as folk-art. Today the wheel has given another half turn, and folk-art in the widest sense is falling back into the realm of kitsch. Who can guarantee that a substantial proportion of the present-day Modern Movement will not suffer the same fate in some fifteen years' time?

Soon enough, many people will be longing to sink back once more and slumber in the bed of a historical style. A new Classical age is not yet upon us, but we are gravely threatened by a new classicism, which closes its eyes to the difficult problems which still confront us and must be resolved. If we do not want a naturalistic, atonal architecture, which has no symbolic or practical value, neither do we want forms steeped in the symbolism of another cultural tradition, a resurrected mummy which, however aesthetic in appearance, contains no living elements. This would mean shutting our eyes to technical progress, placing ourselves in opposition to the new and natural forms of technology ... And it shows a lack of awareness, a regression into naturalism, if technical forms intrude unmodified into architectonic (and therefore symbolic) space. In art, man puts himself outside nature; in technology he extends nature ... The essence of art lies in the manipulation of spacc and form. Its laws are on a different level from those of technology.

Take for example an ordinary, present-day villa. Does anyone dare to judge it purely on its technological merits? Are purely technical considerations allowed to govern the shape and size of the rooms, and the general layout of the house? And if they were taken to be the only governing factor, would the result be a house? Would it even amount to a 'machine for living in'? The people who invented this expression surely meant only that one should first think out the whole ensemble with all the rigorousness of an engineer designing a machine. In the final analysis, the natural materials, such as wood and stone, are only extended by technological ones, such as steel and concrete; the earlier, simpler methods of heating, lighting, and so on, are replaced by more complex and comprehensive technological methods; and the architect merely has to make use of all these possibilities in order to create the most humanly proportioned dwelling that he can ...

And why, after all, is the current style of building successful? For practical reasons? Are the large window areas practical? Is the flat roof preferred on purely practical grounds? This particular form predominates because it is the new symbol of a new way of life, which corresponds to the current hunger for light and air. The sensitive layman would sooner be palmed off with a house by some gifted artist which is completely unpractical but has the form which he likes, than move into some perfectly practical form of housing which nevertheless seems to him without form: he seeks an enrichment of his emotional life ...

The effect of true architecture can only be emotional, non-technical, independent of any yardstick, like the effect of music. And its responsibilities are as great as those of music also, for just as a popular song sticks in the mind and obsesses you, so man cannot escape from an inferior, tormenting architectural environment. The architect's responsibility is enormous, his work can enhance the whole appearance of a town or ruin it for centuries. We are now beginning to grasp this responsibility once more, but we are afraid of the consequences, of the difficulty of embodying this responsibility in rules and regulations. What then is architecture? In Paul Valéry's *Eupalinos, or, On Architecture,* a dialogue between Socrates and Phaidros in Hades, Phaidros says:

> Have you not observed in walking round this city that among the buildings of which it is composed, some are silent, while others speak, and others still – strangest of all – even sing? This extreme animation does not arise from the function of the buildings, or from their general form, any more than does that which makes some of them silent. It is something which comes from the talent of their builder, or even more from the favour of the muses. Now those of the buildings which neither speak nor sing deserve nothing but contempt. They are dead things, lower in rank than those heaps of rubble discharged by contractors' carts, which at least attract the inquisitive eye by the arbitrary patterns which they take on falling. As for the monuments which only speak, I have nothing but respect for them so long as their speech is clear. They say for example, 'This is where the traders meet. This is where the judges hold their deliberations. Here, prisoners sigh. Here, those who love debauchery can ... (at this point I told Eupalinos that I had seen some quite remarkable examples of this last kind. But he did not hear me.) These markets, these law-courts, these prisons speak a most explicit language when those who build them know what they are about. The first kind visibly attract a jostling, ever-renewed crowd, offering them vestibules and entrances; they invite them to enter through their doors, to mount their easy accessible flights of stairs into their roomy and well-lit halls, to form groups and abandon themselves to the ferment of commercial intercourse ... The residences of justice, on the other hand, should impress the severity and justness of our laws upon the eye.

Throughout this fine profound dialogue there is not a word about technology, even in the old sense of craftsmanship, and not a word about economics!

Therefore render unto Caesar the things which are Caesar's, and to God the things which are God's! It would be laughable, falsely romantic and quite counterproductive to bury our heads in the sand and try to brush aside the demands of technology and economics – they must be given their due, but they must not enslave us. Our works must transcend the demands of technology and economics and not offer an abrupt but short-lived impact, which does not shout loudly for attention, but speaks, or even sings, in a way that will still be understood by posterity. Posterity, after all, will have forgotten all the surprises which we have been given by new technological discoveries, and will only understand whatever portion of that eternal melody we have managed to capture in our creations.

---

30 Frank Lloyd Wright, *The Cardboard House,* 1931

Any house is a far too complicated, clumsy, fussy, mechanical counterfeit of the human body. Electric wiring for nervous system, plumbing for bowels, heating system and fireplaces for arteries and heart, and windows for eyes, nose and lungs generally. The structure of the house, too, is a kind of cellular tissue stuck full of bones, complex now, as the confusion of Bedlam and all beside. The whole interior is a kind of stomach that attempts to digest objects – objects, 'objets d'art' maybe, but objects always. There the affected affliction sits, ever hungry – for ever more objects – or plethoric with over plenty. The whole life of the average house, it seems, is a sort of indigestion. A body in ill repair, suffering indisposition – constant tinkering and doctoring to keep alive. It is a marvel, we its infestors do not go insane in it and with it. Perhaps it is a form of insanity we have put into it. Lucky we are able to get something else out of it, though we do seldom get out of it alive ourselves.

But the passing of the Cornice with its enormous 'baggage' from foreign parts in its train clears the way for American homes that may be modern biography and poems instead of slanderous Liars and poetry-crushers.

A house, we like to believe, is *in statu quo* a noble consort to man and the trees; therefore the house should have repose and such texture as will quiet the whole and make it graciously at one with External Nature.

Human houses should not be like boxes, blazing in the sun, nor should we outrage the Machine by trying to make dwelling-places too complementary to Machinery. Any building for humane purposes should be an elemental, sympathetic feature of the ground, complementary to its nature-environment, belonging by kinship to the terrain. A House is not going anywhere, if we can help it. We hope it is going to stay right where it is for a long, long time. It is not yet anyway even a moving-van. Certain houses for Los Angeles may yet become vans and roll off most anywhere or everywhere, which is something else again and far from a bad idea for certain classes of our population.

But most new 'modernistic' houses manage to look as though cut from cardboard with scissors, the sheets of cardboard folded or bent in rectangles with an ocassional curved cardboard surface added to get relief. The cardboard forms thus made are glued together in box-like forms – in a childish attempt to make buildings resemble steamships, flying machines or locomotives. By way of a new sense of the character and power of this Machine Age, this house strips and stoops to conquer by emulating, if not imitating, machinery. But so far, I see in most of the cardboard houses of the 'modernistic' movement small evidence that their designers have mastered either the machinery or the mechanical processes that build the house. I can find no evidence of integral method in their making. Of late, they are the superficial, badly built product of this superficial, New 'Surface-and-Mass' Aesthetic falsely claiming French Painting as a parent. And the houses themselves are not the new working of a fundamental Architectural principle in any sense. They are little less reactionary than was the Cornice – unfortunately for the Americans, looking forward, lest again they fall victim to the mode. There is, however, this much to be said for this house – by means of it imported Art and Decoration may, for a time, completely triumph over 'Architecture'. And such Architecture as it may triumph over – well, enough has already been said here, to show how infinitely the cardboard house is to be preferred to that form of bad surface-decoration. The Simplicity of Nature is not something which may easily be read – but is inexhaustible. Unfortunately the simplicity of these houses is too easily read – visibly an attitude, strained or forced. They are therefore decoration too. If we look into their construction we may see how construction itself has been complicated or confused, merely to arrive at exterior simplicity. Most of these houses at home and abroad are more or less badly built complements to the Machine Age, of whose principles or possibilities they show no understanding, or, if they do show such understanding to the degree of assimilating an aspect thereof, they utterly fail to make its virtues honourably or humanly effective in any final result. Forcing surface-effects upon mass-effects which try hard to resemble running or steaming or flying or fighting machines, is no radical effort in any direction. It is only more scene-painting and just another picture to prove Victor Hugo's thesis of Renaissance architecture as the setting sun – eventually passing with the Cornice.

The Machine – we are now agreed, are we not – should build the building, if the building is such that the Machine may build it naturally and therefore build it supremely well. But it is not necessary for that reason to build as though the building, too, were a Machine – because, except in a very low sense, indeed, it is not a Machine, nor at all like one. Nor in that sense of being a Machine, could it be Architecture at all! It would be difficult to make it even good decoration for any length of time. But I propose, for the purposes of popular negation of the Cornice-days that are passed and as their final kick into oblivion, we might now, for a time, make buildings resemble Modern bath-tubs and aluminium kitchen-utensils, or copy pieces of well designed machinery to live in, particularly the liner, the aeroplane, the street car, and the motor-bus. We could trim up the trees, too, shape them into boxes – cheese or cracker – cut them to cubes and triangles or tetrahedron them and so make all kinds alike suitable consorts for such houses. And we are afraid we are eventually going to have as citizens Machine-made men, corollary to Machines, if we don't 'look out'? They might be face-masqued, head shaved, hypodermically rendered even less emotional than they are, with patent-leather put over their hair and aluminium clothes cast on their bodies, and Madam herself altogether stripped and decoratively painted to suit. This delicate harmony, characteristic of machinery, ultimately achieved, however, could not be truly affirmative, except insofar as the negation, attempted to be performed therein, is itself affirmative. It seems to me that while engaging cardboard houses may be appropriate gestures in connection with 'Now What Architecture,' they are merely a negation, so not yet truly conservative in the great Cause which already runs well beyond them. *Organic simplicity* is the only simplicity that can answer for us here in America that pressing, perplexing question – Now What Architecture? This I firmly believe. It is vitally necessary to make the countenance of simplicity the affirmation of reality, lest any affectation of simplicity, should it become a mode or Fashion, may only leave this heady country refreshed for another foolish orgy in surface decoration of the sort lasting thirty years 'by authority and by order', and by means of which Democracy has already nearly ruined the look of itself for posterity, for a half-century to come, at least. Well then and again – 'What Architecture?' ...

When 'in the cause of Architecture', in 1893, I first began to build the houses, sometimes referred to by the thoughtless as 'The New School of the Middle West', (some advertisers' slogan comes along to label everything in this our busy woman's country), the only way to simplify the awful building in vogue at the time was to conceive a finer entity – a better building – and get it built. The buildings standing then were all tall and all tight. Chimneys were lean and taller still, sooty fingers threatening the sky. And beside them, sticking up by way of dormers through the cruelly sharp, saw-tooth roofs, were the attics for 'help' to swelter in. Dormers were elaborate devices, cunning little buildings complete in themselves, stuck to the main roof slopes to let 'help' poke heads out of the attic for air ...

The whole exterior was be-devilled – that is to say, mixed to puzzle-pieces, with corner-boards, panel-boards, window-frames, corner-blocks, plinth-blocks, rosettes, fantails, ingenious and jigger work in general. This was the only way they seemed to have, then, of 'putting on style'. The scroll-saw and turning-lathe were at the moment the honest means of this fashionable mongering by the wood-butcher and to this entirely 'moral' end. Unless the householder of the period were poor indeed, usually an ingenious corner-tower on his house eventuated into a candle-snuffer dome, a spire, an inverted rutabaga or radish or onion or – what is your favourite vegetable? Always elaborate bay-windows and fancy porches played 'ring around a rosy' on this 'imaginative' corner feature. And all this the building of the period could do equally well in brick or stone. It was an impartial society. All material looked pretty much alike in that day. Simplicity was as far from all this scrap-pile as the pandemonium of the barnyard is far from music. But it was easy for the Architect. All he had to do was to call: 'Boy, take down No. 37, and put a bay-window on it for the lady!' So – the first thing to do was to get rid of the attic and, therefore, of the dormer and of the useless 'heights' below it. And next, get rid of the unwholesome basement, entirely – yes, absolutely – in any house built on the prairie. Instead of lean, brick chimneys, bristling up from steep roofs to hint at 'judgement' everywhere. I could see necessity for one only, a broad generous one, or at most, for two, these kept low down on gently sloping roofs or perhaps flat roofs. The big fireplace below, inside, became now a place for a real fire justified the great size of this chimney outside. A real fireplace at that time was extraordinary. There were then 'mantels' instead. A mantel was a marble frame for a few coals, or a piece of wooden furniture with tiles stuck in it and a 'grate', the whole set slam up against the wall. The 'mantel' was an insult to comfort, but the *integral* fireplace became an important part of the building itself in the houses I was allowed to build out there on the prairie. It refreshed me to see the fire burning deep in the masonry of the house itself.

Taking a human being for my scale, I brought the whole house down in height to fit a normal man; believing in no other scale, I broadened the mass out, all I possibly could, as I brought it down into spaciousness. It has been said that were I three inches taller (I am 5 ft. 8½ in. tall), all my houses would have been quite different in proportion. Perhaps.

House-walls were now to be started at the ground on a cement or stone water-table that looked like a low platform under the building, which it usually was, but the house-walls were stopped at the second storey window-sill level, to let the rooms above come through in a continuous window-series, under the broad eaves of a gently sloping, overhanging roof. This made enclosing screens out of the lower walls as well as light screens out of the second-storey walls.

Here was true *enclosure of interior space*. A new sense of building, it seems. The climate, being what it was, a matter of violent extremes of heat and cold, damp and dry, dark and bright, I gave broad protecting roof-shelter to the whole, getting back to the original purpose of the 'Cornice'. The undersides of the roof projections were flat and light in colour to create a glow of reflected light that made the upper rooms not dark, but delightful. The over-hangs had double value, shelter and preservation for the walls of the house as well as diffusion of reflected light for the upper storey, through the 'light screens' that took the place of the walls and were the windows.

At this time, a house to me was obvious primarily as interior space under fine *shelter*. I liked the sense of shelter in the 'look of the building'. I achieved it, I believe ...

The house began to associate with the ground and become natural to its prairie site. And would the young man in architecture ever believe that this wall was all 'new' then? Not only new, but destructive heresy – or ridiculous eccentricity. So New that what little prospect I had of ever earning a livelihood by making houses was nearly wrecked. At first 'they' called the houses 'dress-reform' houses, because Society was just then excited about that particular 'reform'. This simplification looked just like some kind of 'reform' to them. Oh, they called them all sorts of names that cannot be repeated, but 'they' never found a better term for the work unless it was 'Horizontal Gothic', 'Temperance Architecture' (with a sneer), etc., etc. I don't know how I escaped the accusation of another 'Renaissance'.

What I have just described was all on the *outside* of the house and was there chiefly because of what had happened *inside*. Dwellings of that period were 'cut-up', advisedly and completely, with the grim determination that should go with any cutting process. The 'interiors' consisted of boxes beside or inside other boxes, called *rooms*. All boxes inside a complicated boxing. Each domestic 'function' was properly box to box. I could see little sense in this inhibition, this cellular sequestration that implied ancestors familiar with the cells of penal institutions, except for the privacy of bed-rooms on the upper floor. They were perhaps all right as 'sleeping boxes'. So I declared the whole lower floor as one room, cutting off the kitchen as a laboratory, putting servants' sleeping and living quarters next to it, semi-detached, on the ground floor, screening various portions in the big room, for certain domestic purposes – like dining or reading, or receiving a formal caller. There were no plans like these in existence at the time and my clients were pushed towards these ideas as helpful to a solution of the vexed servant-problem. Scores of doors disappeared and no end of partition. They liked it, both clients and servants. The house became more free as 'space' and more liveable, too. Interior spaciousness began to dawn ...

The main motives and indications were (and I enjoyed them all):

First— To reduce the number of necessary parts of the house and the separate rooms to a minimum, and make all come together as enclosed space – so divided that light, air and vista permeated the whole with a sense of unity.

Second— To associate the building as a whole with its site by extension and emphasis of the planes parallel to the ground, but keeping the floors off the best part of the site, thus leaving that better part for use in connection with the life of the house. Extended level planes were found useful in this connection.

Third— To eliminate the room as a box and the house as another by making all walls enclosing screens – the ceilings and floors and enclosing screens to flow into each other as one large enclosure of space, with minor subdivisions only.

Make all house proportions more liberally human, with less wasted space in structure, and structure more appropriate to material, and so the whole more liveable. *Liberal* is the best word. Extended straight lines or stream-lines were useful in this.

Fourth— To get the unwholesome basement up out of the ground, entirely above it, as a low pedestal for the living-position of the home, making the foundation itself visible as a low masonry platform on which the building should stand.

Fifth— To harmonise all necessary openings to 'outside' or to 'inside' with good human proportions and make them occur naturally – singly or as a series in the scheme of the whole building. Usually they appeared as 'light-screens' instead of walls, because all the 'Architecture' of the house was chiefly the way these openings came in such walls as were grouped about the rooms as enclosing screens. The *room* as such was now the essential architectural expression, and there were to be no holes cut in walls as holes are cut in a box, because this was not in keeping with the ideal of 'plastic'. Cutting holes was violent.

Sixth— To eliminate combinations of different materials in favour of mono-material so far as possible; to use no ornament that did not come out of the nature of materials to make the whole building clearer and more expressive as a place to live in, and give the conception of the building appropriate revealing emphasis. Geometrical or straight lines were natural to the machinery at work in the building trades then, so the interiors took on this character naturally.

Seventh—To incorporate all heating, lighting, plumbing so that these systems became constituent parts of the building itself. These service features became architectural and in this attempt the ideal of an organic architecture was at work.

Eighth— To incorporate as organic Architecture – so far as possible – furnishings, making them all one with the building and designing them in simple terms for machine work. Again straight lines and rectilinear forms.

Ninth— Eliminate the Decorator. He was all curves and all efflorescence, if not all 'period'.

Standing here, with the perspective of long persistent effort in the direction of an organic Architecture in view, I can again assure you out of this initial experience that Repose is the reward of true simplicity and that organic simplicity is sure of Repose. Repose is the highest quality in the Art of Architecture, next to integrity, and a reward for integrity. Simplicity may well be held to the fore as a spiritual ideal, but when actually achieved, as in the 'lilies of the field', it is something that comes of itself, something spontaneously born out of the nature of the doing whatever it is that is to be done. Simplicity, too, is a reward for fine feeling and straight thinking in working a principle, well in hand, to a constituent end. Solomon knew nothing about it, for he was only wise. And this, I think, is what Jesus meant by the text we have chosen for this discourse – 'Consider the lilies of the field', as contrasted, for beauty, with Solomon.

Now, a chair *is* a machine to sit in.

A home *is* a machine to live in.

The human body *is* a machine to be worked by will.

A tree *is* a machine to bear fruit.

A plant *is* a machine to bear flowers and seeds.

And, as I've admitted before somewhere, a heart *is* a suction-pump. Does that idea thrill you? ...

Therefore, now let the declaration that 'all is machinery' stand nobly forth for what it is worth. But why not more profoundly declare that 'Form follows Function' and let it go at that? Saying, 'Form follows Function', is not only deeper, it is clearer, and it goes further in a more comprehensive way to say the thing to be said, because the implication of this saying includes the heart of the whole matter. It may be that Function follows Form, as, or if, you prefer, but it is easier thinking with the first proposition just as it is easier to stand on your feet and nod your head than it would be to stand on your head and nod your feet. Let us not forget that the Simplicity of the Universe is very different from the Simplicity of a Machine ...

Truly ordered simplicity in the hands of the great artist may flower into a bewildering profusion, exquisitely exuberant, and render all more clear than ever. Good William Blake says exuberance is *beauty*, meaning that it is so in this very sense. This is for the Modern Artist with the Machine in his hands. False Simplicity – Simplicity as an affection, that is, Simplicity constructed as a Decorator's *outside* put upon a complicated, wasteful engineer's or carpenter's 'Structure', outside or inside – is not good enough Simplicity. It cannot be simple at all. But that is what passes for Simplicity, now that startling Simplicity-effects are becoming the *fashion*. That kind of Simplicity is *violent*. This is for 'Art and Decoration'.

Soon we shall want Simplicity inviolate. There is one way to get that Simplicity. My guess is, there is *only* one way really to get it. And that way is, on principle, by way of *Construction* developed as Architecture. That is for us, one and all.

---

31 Victor Horta, *Reminiscences of the Maison du Peuple,* (undated)

I was greatly moved when a deputation of three delegates arrived to ask me to take charge of the plans ... I was weighed down by quite enough responsibilities as it was, but rubbish! I was young, I could easily take on this as well ... Anyway, it was an interesting commission, as I saw straight away – building a palace that wasn't to be a palace but a 'house' whose luxury feature would be the light and air that had been missing for so long from the working-class slums ...

As the shape of the site was extremely irregular, when I produced a feeling of regularity in all this chaos with my design for the ceiling joists [of the Café], it seemed like pure fantasy. Similarly, people approve from the decorative point of view of elements that arise directly from constructional needs, such as the brackets on the stanchions transferring the load to a greater or lesser height. Elements that the design had put in the second rank in allocating the premises gave way to elements that were reckoned to be more important from the functional point of view. Thus the auditorium that was to be used for special occasions took a back seat in favour of offices in which people were to work every day. The original plan was to site it on the first floor, but now it was transferred to the upper floors ... It was essentially one *vast attic,* but it was not to look like one and the acoustics had to be satisfactory. The result was a complete success – a whisper can be heard from the back of the auditorium ...

There are two main reasons for this – the horizontal ceiling, and the sharply sloping floor raised at the far end to break the reverberation of the sound. This delighted the audience, who thought that this arrangement was designed solely to enable them to see the stage better. Breadthwise the cross-section corresponded to the man-

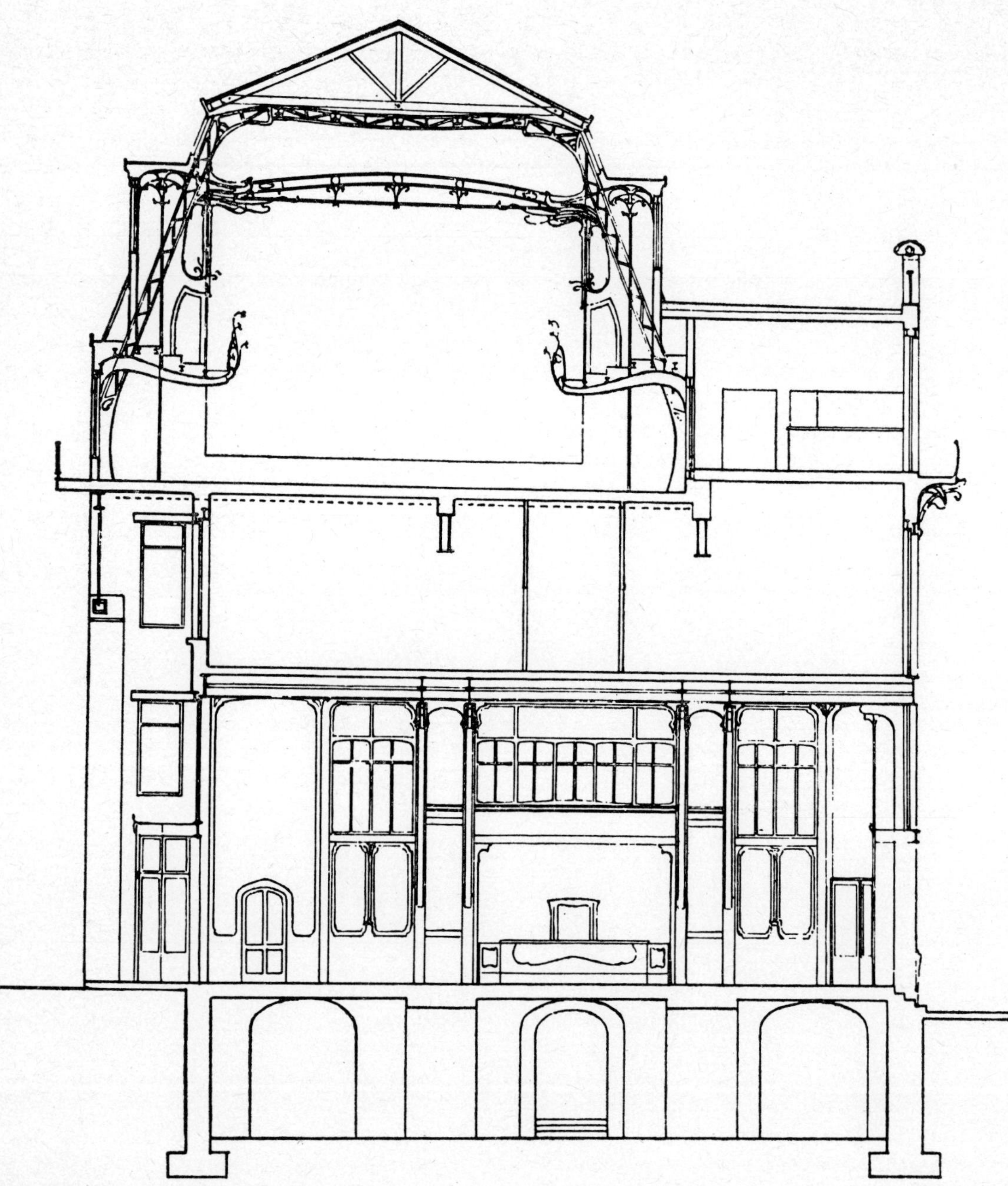

Victor Horta, Section of Maison du Peuple
Musée Horta, Brussels

sard-style shape lit by vertical windows, which enabled the architect to hang a double gallery from the roof trusses. As for the clarity of the acoustics, this was obtained by means of the upper gallery along which passed the pipes that radiated a blanket of heat on to the ceiling, which was corrugated to allow the sound to reverberate on to the seats. 'What a fanatasist this architect is – he must have his alternating lines and curves – but he really is a "master" at them.' People praise him to the skies: but I am fuming: ... 'You idiot, don't you see that everything is thought out in terms of architecture as construction, faithful to the brief to the point of sacrifice?' ...

If it had to be done all over again it would have to be made completely different, since it is no longer in keeping with the requirements of one dominant party. Yesterday's slogan is no longer the slogan of today. I should not really be surprised if they were to demolish it, because in that case it would suffer the same fate as several of my other buildings have already suffered ...

But there's the rub – if I had dreamed of building a lasting work of art, since I am not incapable of doing what is appropriate in the circumstances I should have geared my work to a durable quality that dwells more or less on the past ... The same went for the architectural forms, since I was not aiming to create a style but simply to express my tastes and my capabilities without sham, the tendency being to make the work seem temporary rather than permanent ...

Two

The artistic vision and architecture

These extracts are grouped rather loosely by context rather than by any shared set of assumptions. That is, all the extracts here are the products of artistic ideas developed just before or after the First World War and are all more or less influenced by it. They are connected in varying degrees with the following 'isms': Futurism (32), Expressionism (34, 35, 36, 37, 38, 39, 52), Constructivism, (and Productivism, de Stijl etc.) (40, 41, 43, 44, 45, 46, 47, 50, 51, 54, 55) and Purism (42, 49). This categorisation, if scrutinised, shows how much overlap these artistic movements had and how imprecise their basic tenets were. Two of the most influential, Paul Scheerbart (33) and Frederick Kiesler (53), do not fit usefully into any of these categories except by the association of those who were influenced by them. Many of the writings of the constructivists and realists sound as romantic as those of the expressionist circle (e.g. 41 and 54), while many of the expressionist texts are based on a solidly rational and practical framework (34, 36, 39,). All these extracts have in common some element of irrational romanticism, usually of a fairly extreme sort and mostly brought on by collapse after the War and the blame associated with the pre-War materialistic attitudes which had in many cases degenerated into a driving determination to outsell and out-produce all rivals. Adolf Behne's article (35) stresses the need for a renewed spirituality and imagination after the War and is a key to the period. The Russian Revolution had, of course, an even more overwhelming effect on artists and architects there, but ideological issues channelled the desire for change and fantasy into various forms of machine romanticism, each claiming greater realism and more extensive social awareness than the next. The constructivists were mainly involved in the search for an appropriate symbolism for a revolutionary society (40, 41, 43, 44, 50). The European version of Constructivism, drawing artistic material from Cubism and de Stijl was characterised by a sometimes excessive polarisation between the demand for greater factual reality and the creation of an abstract aesthetic based on primary colours and the conflict between horizontal and vertical (47). It is interesting that in almost all the extracts in this section, there are eager tributes to the almost magical powers ascribed to new materials and new techniques, and I have included two extracts specifically about the machine aesthetic which became quite fashionable in France. This is the idea that mechanical forms were *ipso facto* beautiful (48, 49), although this idea underlies many of the other extracts as well. One idea which is shared by all the authors of these extracts is that the main goal of the artist should be architectural, that is, should lead to a great work of construction which should either be taken literally to mean building, or more symbolically to refer to the work of spiritual and artistic reconstruction. Furthermore, Cubism, de Stijl and the various forms of Constructivism were all seen as 'architectural' art movements, in the sense that they all dealt with form as a construction of planes, solids and spaces. The influence of the artistic movements after the War was important not only because it focused artists' minds on architecture as the supreme challenge, but also because it raised the temperature of polemic to a white heat which would enable the mature aesthetic of the International Style to be welded together from the most disparate elements. It supplied the key ingredients which had been missing in the Arts and Crafts period, extreme enthusiasm, inventiveness, iconoclasm and a determination to make really dramatic changes once and for all. All the major figures of the Modern Movement were affected, for a time at least, by the kind of ideas presented here.

32 Antonio Sant'Elia, *The New City*, 1914

The problem of modern architecture is not one of linear rearrangement.

It is not a question of finding new mouldings, new door- and window-frames, of replacing columns, pilasters and corbels with caryatids and gargoyles; nor is it a question of leaving a façade in bare brick, or plastering it or facing it in stone; it is not, in a word, a question of establishing formal differences between the new building and the old, but of creating entirely afresh the newly constructed house, treasuring every resource of science and technique, elegantly satisfying every requirement of our habit and our spirit, trampling underfoot whatever is grotesque. oppressive and antithetical to us (tradition, style, aesthetics, proportion), establishing new forms, new lines, a new harmony of profiles and volumes, an architecture whose *raison d'être* must stem solely from the particular conditions of modern life and whose aesthetic values match our sensibilities.

This architecture naturally cannot be subject to any law of historical continuity. It must be new as our state of mind and the contingencies of our historical moment are new.

The art of building has been able to evolve through time and to pass from one style to another while maintaining the general characteristics of architecture intact, because changes in fashion and those determined by alterations of religious convictions and by the succession of political decrees are frequent in history; but those causes of profound changes in our conditions of life, which discard and renew, are very rare, like the discovery of natural laws, the perfection of technical methods, the rational and scientific use of materials.

In modern life the process of sequential stylistic development is halted. *Architecture breaks with tradition*; of necessity it begins again from the beginning.

The calculation of the resistance of materials, the use of reinforced concrete and of iron, rule out 'architecture' as understood in the classical or traditional sense. Modern constructional materials and our scientific ideas absolutely do not lend themselves to the discipline of the historical styles and are the principle cause of the grotesque appearance of modish constructions which attempt to obtain from the lightness and superb grace of girders and the fragility of reinforced concrete, the suggestion of a load-bearing arch and the bulky appearance of marble.

The formidable antithesis between the modern world and the old is determined by everything that was not there before. Elements whose existence the ancients could hardly have imagined have entered our lives. Material contingencies have been established and new attitudes of mind have come into being which have thousands of repercussions; most important of these is the formation of a new ideal of beauty which is still obscure and embryonic, but whose attraction is already felt even by the masses. We have, in effect, lost the sense of the monumental, the heavy and the static, and we have enriched our sensibility with a taste for the light and the practical. We no longer feel ourselves to be the men of the cathedrals and public forums, but men of the grand hotels, railway stations, huge roads, colossal ports, covered markets, illuminated arcades, straight roads, and beneficial slum-clearance.

We must invent and build *ex novo* the modern city, like an immense and tumultuous building site – flexible, mobile and dynamic in its every part – and the modern house like a gigantic machine. The lifts must no longer be hidden away like tapeworms in the stairwells; but the stairs – which have become useless – must be abolished, and the lifts must clamber up the façades like snakes of iron and glass. The house of concrete, glass and iron, without painted or sculptured decoration, rich only in the inherent beauty of its lines and modelling, extraordinarily 'ugly' in its mechanical simplicity, its height and width determined by need – and not as municipal regulations prescribe – must rise up on the brink of a tumultuous abyss: the street, which will no longer extend like a doormat at entrance level but will plunge storeys further into the earth. These storeys will gather up the metropolitan traffic and will be linked for necessary transfers by metal gangways and very fast moving pavements.

For these reasons I affirm that it is necessary to abolish the monumental and the decorative; that it is necessary to resolve the problem of modern architecture not by pilfering from photographs of China, Persia or Japan, or by imbecilic dependence on Vitruvian rules, but by strokes of genius and equipped only with scientific and technical expertise. I affirm that everything must be revolutionised; that we must exploit the rooftops, utilise the basements, reduce the importance of the façade; we must transfer problems of good taste from the field of the trivial moulding, fussy capital and fiddly doorway to the broader field of bold groupings of masses and the large-scale layout of sites. I affirm that it is time to have done with monumental, funereal, commemorative architecture; that architecture must be something better and more vital; and that to obtain this something we must begin by overturning monuments, pavements, colonnades and flights of steps, by submerging streets and squares, by raising the level of the city, by altering the earth's crust to reduce it at last to serve our every need, our every whim.

And I conclude in disfavour:

Of modish architecture of every country and every kind;

Of classical, solemn, hieratic, theatrical, decorative, monumental, frivolous, charming architecture;

Of the preservation, reconstruction and reproduction of monuments;

Of perpendicular and horizontal lines, cubical and pyramidal forms, which are static, solemn, oppressive and quite foreign to our newest sensibility;

Of the use of materials that are bulky, ponderous, durable, obsolete, expensive and incompatible with the complex of modern culture and modern technical experience.

And I affirm:

That the new architecture is the architecture of cold calculation, of reckless daring and of simplicity; the architecture of reinforced concrete, of iron, glass, cardboard, textile fibres and all those surrogates of wood, stone and brick which enable us to obtain the maximum of elasticity and lightness.

That true architecture is not, for all this, an arid combination of expediency and utility, but remains art – i.e. synthesis, expression.

That decoration as something superimposed on or attached to architecture is an absurdity, and that the decorative value of truly modern architecture depends solely on the use and original arrangement of raw or bare or violently coloured material.

And finally I assert that, just as the ancients drew inspiration for their art from the elements of nature, so we – who are materially and spiritually artificial – must find this inspiration in the elements of this totally new mechanical world we have created, of which architecture must be the most beautiful expression, the most complete synthesis, the most effective artistic integration.

---

33 Paul Scheerbart, *Glass Architecture,* 1914

Chapter 1 Environment and its influence on the development of culture

We live for the most part in enclosed rooms. These form the environment from which our culture grows. Our culture is to a certain extent the product of our architecture. If we want our culture to rise to a higher level, we are obliged, for better or for worse, to change our architecture. And this only becomes possible if we take away the closed character from the rooms in which we live. We can only do that by introducing glass architecture, which lets in the light of the sun, the moon and the stars, not merely through a few windows, but through every possible wall, which will be made entirely of glass – of coloured glass. The new environment, which we thus create, must bring us a new culture.

Chapter 4 Double glass walls, light, heating and cooling

As air is one of the worst conductors of heat, the double glass wall is an essential condition for all glass architecture. The walls can be a metre apart – or have an even greater space between. The light between these walls shines outward and inward, and both the outer and the inner walls may be ornamentally coloured. If, in so doing, too much light is absorbed by the colour, the external wall may be left entirely clear; it is then advisable simply to provide the light between the walls with a coloured glass shade, so that the wall light in the evening does not dazzle the outside.

To place heating and incandescent elements between the walls is in most cases not to be recommended, since by this means too much warmth or cold is lost to the outer atmosphere. Heating and cooling elements, however, can be suspended like lamps in the interior, where all hanging lights are to some extent superfluous, since light is distributed by the walls.

In the first instance, it is clearly advisable to build glass houses only in temperate zones, and not in the equatorial and polar regions as well; in the warmer climates one could not do without a white reinforced concrete roof, but in temperate zones this need does not arise. To provide floor heating and cover, electrically-heated carpets are recommended.

Chapter 33 Lighting between the double walls (which do not exclude suspended fittings in the room)

I have frequently said that the double walls are there, not merely to maintain the temperature of the room, but to accommodate the lighting elements. I must ask to be forgiven for repetition but I want to stress and underline it.

With this type of lighting the whole glass house becomes a big lantern which, on peaceful summer and winter nights, shines like fireflies and glow-worms. One could easily become poetic. But lighting can also be installed inside the room. This interior lighting also illuminates the walls – if not so strongly as the light between the double walls.

Chapter 13 The functional style

The reader might gain the impression that glass architecture is rather cold, but in warm weather, coolness is not unpleasant. Anyhow, let me make it clear that colours in glass can produce a most glowing effect, shedding perhaps a new warmth. What has been said up to now takes on a somewhat warmer atmosphere. I should like to resist most vehemently the undecorated 'functional style' ('Sachstil'), for it is inartistic. It has often been adopted before in other contexts, and this is happening once again.

For a transition period, the functional style seems to me acceptable; at all events it has done away with imitations of older styles which are simply products of brick architecture and wooden furniture. Ornamentation in the glass house will evolve entirely of its own accord – the oriental decoration, the carpets and the majolica will be so transformed that in glass architecture we shall never, I trust, have to speak of copying. At least, let us hope so!

Chapter 18 The beauty of the earth, when glass architecture is everywhere

The face of the earth would be much altered if brick architecture were ousted everywhere by glass architecture. It would be as if the earth were adorned with sparkling jewels and enamels. Such glory is unimaginable. All over the world it would be as splendid as in the gardens of the Arabian Nights. We should then have a paradise on earth, and not need to watch in longing expectation for the paradise in heaven.

Chapter 29 Hollow glass elements in every possible colour and form as a wall material (the so-called 'glass-brick')

So-called glass-bricks make a wall material which may become an interesting speciality of glass architecture. Large industrial undertakings have been formed already which could have a big future. Everything fireproof and transparent is aesthetically justifiable as a wall material. Glass bricks should make many iron skeletons superfluous.

Chapter 35 Ventilators, which are ousting the customary windows
It will seem very natural that ventilators should have a principle part to play in a glass house, and will supplant everything window-like. When I am in my glass room, I shall hear nothing of the outside world. If I long for the sky, the clouds, woods and meadows, I can go out or repair to an extra-veranda with transparent glass panes.

Chapter 106 More coloured light!
We must not strive to increase the intensity of light – today it is already too strong and no longer endurable. But a gentler light is worth striving for. Not more light! – 'more coloured light!' must be the watchword.

Chapter 111 Glass culture
After all the above, we can indeed speak of a glass culture. The new glass environment will completely transform mankind, and it remains only to wish that the new glass culture will not find too many opponents. It is to be hoped, in fact, that glass culture will have even fewer opponents; to cling to the old is in many matters a good thing; in this way at any rate the old is preserved. We, too, want to cling to the old – the pyramids of ancient Egypt should most certainly not be abolished.

But we also want to strive after the new, with all the resources at our disposal; more power to them!

---

34 Eric Mendelsohn, *Reflections on a New Architecture,* 1914-17

In general

Architecture is the only tangible expression of space of which the human spirit is capable. Architecture seizes upon space, encompasses space and is space itself. Out of the three-dimensional infinitude of universal space – which is beyond human conception – Architecture brings us, by means of its spatial delimitation, the concept of space and mass.

Its values are those of space and surface and it is founded wholly upon mathematical actuality. The geometry of space, the law of the seizure and the penetration of space, of corporeal determination and of constructed bulk, embrace all fabrics: the simplest equation from the cube to the sphere, and the highest, arising from some cosmic blossoming-forth.

The living quality of Architecture depends upon sensuous seizure by means of touch and sight: upon

Eric Mendelsohn, Sketch for the Einstein Tower
Structures and Sketches, London, 1924

the terrestrial cohesion of mass, upon the superterrestrial liberty of light.

It is light that first gives movement to mass and sublimates it to a supersensuous expression of dynamic and rhythmical agitation. It is light that first rounds out mathematical precision and space consciousness to

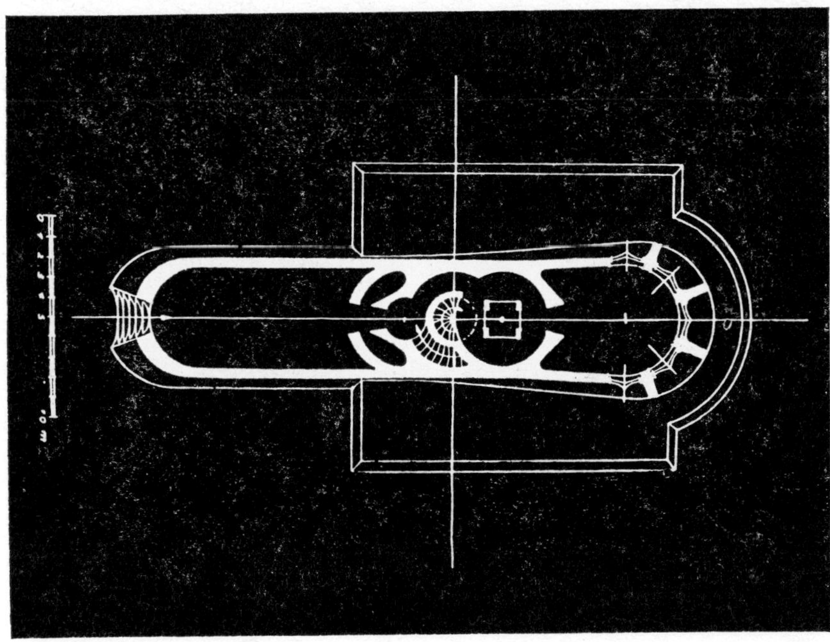

Eric Mendelsohn, Plan of the Einstein Tower

the freedom, independence and law of architectonic creation.

Out of its own laws Architecture lays down the conditions that govern its active masses: the dynamic condition – the movement of space – to visualise its linear elements by means of its contours; the rhythmic condition – to visualise the relation of the masses – by means of the projection of surfaces, and the static condition – the equalisation of movement to visualise this as elements of construction by means of ground plan and section.

Architecture determines its own standard from time to time, a standard that instinctively apperceives, compares and coordinates, a standard that scientifically tests, measures, divides and proves.

This standard by virtue of the objectivity inherent in its corporeal detachment, and its absolute attitude, serves to resolve mysterious secrets into predestined law and order.

Closely related to this law and order we find the extra-human and inconceivable, things that bow and erect themselves, that burrow beneath and overtop one another, in grotesque accentuation from the building blocks of the child to the tower spawned by chaos.

Miracles of measurement, of consummated coincidences and harmonies as well as layers and series of inspired proportions are discovered; mutual corrections and equalities of will, sacred things that the law of creation bestows upon its creature, and the artist upon his creation. Profound necessity decrees that all artistic creation should be subject to the same stern law of Life.

The inner and outer wall

The outer wall acts upon the visible universe: its physical compactness operates upon the illimitableness of space. It is part of the eternal law, the united voice of spatial and constructive demands, a section in space towards a certain direction. Its law of limitations is imposed by the building as a whole. Its decomposition is subject to the law of superficies in space. The outer wall collects light, in order to let it penetrate fully through its openings.

The inner wall determines the centre of gravity of the room by means of its limitations. This wall is an independent surface, and is related to its companion walls, with the floor and with the ceiling. Its decomposition brings about the sliding of surface into surface. When this wall happens to be a functional part of the construction, of a framework, of a vault or a span – a burden-bearer or a burden-conductor – then it becomes subject to a structural inhibition.

The unique nature of architectonic space conditions the unique quality of its effects. Its final consummate expression is independent of decoration and dress. Its being fettered to material media implies no lessening of its innate worth; Architecture demands freedom of space in order to stretch its limbs, it demands the freedom of the Will-to-Build in order to assert itself. It portends a transformation into the future, it becomes a great event governed by new laws.

Architecture is the expression of the will of an epoch and of the spirit of that epoch. It binds its single law to the fate of a nation. It bears witness to this nation's needs and hopes, its achievements, longings and its God. It bears witness to origin, to growth and decay. Architecture is proof of its inherited, its nourished and its spontaneous, self-engendered will. It is a document of its political history, its spiritual mission, its intrinsic culture.

The singleness of its general operation corresponds to the responsibility of all architectonic work; the reshaping of vision into actuality, the uniting of free creation with expedient objectivity. Only the well-rounded, self-contained personality will be able alike to dominate intuition and calculation.

---

35 Adolf Behne, *Review of Scheerbart's 'Glass Architecture'*, 1918-19

The concept that architecture is a so-called useful art has so thoroughly penetrated the consciousness of Europeans that everyone here is dismayed when this point of view is challenged and the opinion ventured that architecture is a free and sublime art, drawing upon its own deep sources and glorifying the world. Not the commission of a Consistory or the Ministry of Housing is the origin and incentive for an architectural work of art, but rather what Paul Scheerbart, the guardian angel of true architecture, has called the 'superior passion for building'.

Building ... a word that should resound in us like a jubilant cry, which calls us to our most proper and highest vocation, has become such a commonplace triviality for us that its sound falls wearily to the ground.

Building ... which ought to be the cooperative effort of many enthusiastic people who, out of their love for the world, add something new to it, something great and splendid, a work which towers far above the individual, has instead become merely an everyday matter. What should be ecstasy has become only a concern for the pay cheque. Today, building is a bit like the opening of a large umbrella. But an association which is not moved by a superior drive to build, is weak, disintegrated, and poor. For what is, in the last analysis, this lofty impetus to build? It is the most profound and ultimate vital power.

The world consists primarily of building – not of painting or carving. Building is the world-art. Building is the elemental art. The products of the other arts have to be sheltered, and this shelter is in turn created by building. That which is built, however, stands in the sun, in the wind, and in the rain. Its environment is not its enemy, but its playmate. And only the art of building can play with the great existing wonders around us. It attracts the sun to where there should be glitter and sparkling, it places its building stones high in the sky, angular or curvilinear, smooth or ornamented, blunt or sharp-edged, light or dark – and there the elements work the stones. Birds fly between them, the rain drenches them, the wind dries them, the frost splits them. Architecture is the only art which deals directly with the elements. The formation of the world is a kind of building, and through individuals filled with love of mankind, humanity builds a self-perfecting form of the world.

If the practitioners of today's building art ask what they should do, the answer is: Do at least build! What you have accomplished so far has been a dull pastiche. Nobody will stop you if you build full of imagination rather than full of melancholy. No one is going to withdraw commissions from you if, instead of building in terms of stereotypes, you build daringly; nobody will have a grudge against you if you construct a radiant, inspiring, magnificent architecture instead of a dull one. You will not sink in anyone's esteem – if this were conceivable – when you build far more beautifully than anybody had imagined you to be capable of. The possibilities for wonderful, handsome building already exist – even today. We have iron and concrete and glass. Yet experience proves that you do not utilise them, even when they are served you on a silver platter.

I realise that the European of today is not quite ready for glass architecture. How could it be otherwise after what we have just observed. To begin with, he cannot help but consider this idea comical. It is impossible for the modern European to think of glass architecture as anything but a grotesque practical joke. He may consent to consider the matter from an aesthetic point of view, or, at best, take it as profoundly symbolic. Yet this is all wrong. The idea of a glass architecture is perfectly simple and is to be understood just as Scheerbart presents it ... in the light of gayest optimism. It is not the crazy caprice of a poet that glass architecture will bring a new culture.

No material overcomes matter to such an extent as glass. Glass is a completely virgin material; to produce it, matter has been melted down and transformed. It has the most elementary effect of all the materials we possess. It reflects sky and sun, it is transparent like water, and it has a wealth of possibilities as regards colour, shape, and quality that are really inexhaustible and to which no one can remain indifferent. In comparison with glass all other materials seem to be derivative or trifling – merely man-made. Glass has an extra-human, super-human quality.

Therefore, the European is right when he fears that glass architecture might become uncomfortable. Certainly, it will be so. And that is not its least advantage. For first of all the European must be wrenched out of his cosiness [*Gemütlichkeit*]. Not without good reason the adjective '*gemütlich*' intensified becomes '*saugemütlich*' (swinishly comfortable). Away with comfort! Only where comfort ends, does humanity begin. Comfort is of no value. It is true that glass as a material is hardly suitable for an alcove in which to play cards or to sit down for the evening beer – unless one would abuse it by imitating the romanticism of bull's-eye panes. Yet such glass panels are not at all what we mean by glass architecture. Glass architecture rules out the dull vegetative state of jellyfish-like comfort in which all values become blunted and worn, and it substitutes a state of bright alertness, a daring activity, and the creation of ever fresher, ever more beautiful values.

Its profoundest effect, however, will be that it breaks down the inflexibility and harshness of the European. The European is easy-going where he has no responsibility; where he has it, however, he is harsh. Underneath a jelly-like exterior he is dull and brutal. Glass will transform him. Glass is sheer and angular, yet in its hidden potential it is gentle and delicate. The new

European will have these qualities too: clear determination and utmost gentleness.

Glass is not going to bring us a new morality, perhaps because we do not need it, since it stands to reason that people will help each other, not out of sentimentality (sentimentality will disappear from Europe), but out of an abundance, out of a *joie de vivre*, out of a desire for beauty, out of love. The craving for beauty will not tolerate any sorrow, any distress anywhere, for they would be blemishes on the clear pure radiance of life. Love will be not so much a love between individuals as a love for the infinite universe of which every being is a tiny part. Because all particles love the whole, they embrace each other in such a way that one defends the other. To love more than one individual will not only be lawful, but the command. This love, however, is not of a sexual sort, and never makes people cruel, but only gentler and more helpful. Glass architecture is going to eliminate all harshness from the Europeans and replace it with tenderness, beauty, and candour.

---

36 Walter Gropius, *Programme of the Staatliche Bauhaus in Weimar,* April, 1919

The ultimate aim of all visual arts is the complete building! To embellish buildings was once the noblest function of the fine arts; they were the indispensable components of great architecture. Today the arts exist in isolation, from which they can be rescued only through the conscious, cooperative effort of all craftsmen. Architects, painters, and sculptors must recognise anew and learn to grasp the composite character of a building both as an entity and in its separate parts. Only then will their work be imbued with the architectonic spirit which it has lost as 'salon art'.

The old schools of art were unable to produce this unity; how could they, since art cannot be taught. They must be merged once more with the workshop. The mere drawing and painting world of the pattern designer and the applied artist must become a world that builds again. When young people who take a joy in artistic creation once more begin their life's work by learning a trade, then the unproductive 'artist' will no longer be condemned to deficient artistry, for their skill will now be preserved for the crafts, in which they will be able to achieve excellence.

Architects, sculptors, painters, we all must return to the crafts! For art is not a 'profession'. There is no essential difference between the artist and the craftsman. The artist is an exalted craftsman. In rare moments of inspiration, transcending the consciousness of his will, the grace of heaven may cause his work to blossom into art. But proficiency in a craft is essential to every artist. Therein lies the prime source of creative imagination. Let us then create a new guild of craftsmen without the class distinctions that raise an arrogant barrier between craftsman and artist! Together let us desire, conceive, and create the new structure of the future, which will embrace architecture and sculpture and painting in one unity and which will one day rise towards heaven from the hands of a million workers like the crystal symbol of a new faith.

Programme of the Staatliche Bauhaus in Weimar

The Staatliche Bauhaus resulted from the merger of the former Grand-Ducal Saxon Academy of Art with the former Grand-Ducal Saxon School of Arts and Crafts in conjunction with a newly affiliated department of architecture.

Aims of the Bauhaus

The Bauhaus strives to bring together all creative effort into one whole, to reunify all the disciplines of practical art – sculpture, painting, handicrafts, and the crafts – as inseparable components of a new architecture. The ultimate, if distant, aim of the Bauhaus is the unified work of art – the great structure – in which there is no distinction between monumental and decorative art.

The Bauhaus wants to educate architects, painters, and sculptors of all levels, according to their capabilities, to become competent craftsmen or independent creative artists and to form a working community of leading and future artist-craftsmen. These men, of kindred spirit, will know how to design buildings harmoniously in their entirety – structure, finishing, ornamentation, and furnishing.

Principles of the Bauhaus

Art rises above all methods; in itself it cannot be taught, but the crafts certainly can be. Architects, painters, and sculptors are craftsmen in the true sense of the word; hence, a thorough training in the crafts, acquired in workshops and in experimental and practical sites, is required of all students as the indispensable basis for all artistic production. Our own workshops are to be gradually built up, and apprenticeship agreements with outside workshops will be concluded.

The school is the servant of the workshop, and will one day be absorbed in it. Therefore there will be no teachers or pupils in the Bauhaus but masters, journeymen, and apprentices.

The manner of teaching arises from the character of the workshop: Organic forms developed from manual skills.

Avoidance of all rigidity; priority of creativity; freedom of individuality, but strict study discipline.

Master and journeyman examinations, according to the Guild Statutes, held before the Council of Masters of the Bauhaus or before outside masters.

Collaboration by the students in the work of the masters.

Securing of commissions, also for students.

Mutual planning of extensive, Utopian structural designs – public buildings and buildings for worship – aimed at the future. Collaboration of all masters and students – architects, painters, sculptors – on these designs with the object of gradually achieving a harmony of all the component elements and parts that make up architecture.

Constant contact with the leaders of the crafts and industries of the country. Contact with public life, with the people, through exhibitions and other activities. New research into the nature of the exhibitions, to solve the problem of displaying visual work and sculpture within the framework of architecture.

Encouragement of friendly relations between masters and students outside of work; therefore plays, lectures, poetry, music, costume parties. Establishment of a cheerful ceremonial at these gatherings.

Range of Instruction

Instruction at the Bauhaus includes all practical and scientific areas of creative work.

A. Architecture,
B. Painting,
C. Sculpture

including all branches of the crafts.

Students are trained in a craft (1) as well as in drawing and painting (2) and science and theory (3).

37 Walter Gropius, *Address to the Bauhaus Students,* July, 1919

In his opening remarks Gropius declared that the exhibition revealed both 'talent and disruption'. One noticed that the convulsions caused by the war had not yet been mentally overcome. He had especially asked the students for design and idea sketches, but what had been submitted kept close to academic conventions. No one had 'brought forward a compositional idea'.

* * *

I suggest that, for the time being, we refrain from public exhibitions and work from a new point of departure, so that, in these turbulent times, we can collect our thoughts anew and become first of all self-sufficient, and that will hopefully be a great deal ... The main thing for all of us is undoubtedly experience, and what we as individuals make out of it. We find ourselves in a colossal catastrophe of world history, in a transformation of the whole of life and the whole of inner man. This is perhaps fortunate for the artistic man, provided he is strong enough to bear the consequences, for what we need is the courage to accept inner experience, then suddenly a new path will open for the artist ... Indifference, dozing, and indolence are the worst enemies of art.

Some day you will break free of your own limitations and will know where you have to go. We will encounter surprises, some will make decisions to start anew, even if they have already gained some renown. Since I feel all this so distinctly, I, for my part, do not want to do anything by force. It will all come from yourselves.

[During the period before the war] we designed artistic ashtrays and beermugs, and in that way hoped to work up to the great building. All that by smooth organisation. That was an incredible presumption on which we were shipwrecked, and now things will be reversed. No large spiritual organisations, but small, secret, self-contained societies, lodges. Conspiracies will form which we will want to watch over and artistically shape a secret, a nucleus of belief, until from the individual groups a universally great, enduring, spiritual-religious idea will rise again, which finally must find its crystalline expression in a great *Gesamtkunstwerk*. And this great total work of art, this cathedral of the future, will then shine with its abundance of light into the smallest objects of everyday life. We will not live to see the day, but we are, and this I firmly believe, the precursors and first instruments of such a new, universal idea. Up to now, the artist has stood by himself, for in these chaotic times there is no rallying idea discernible which would spiritually and materially reverse the order of things. On the strength of his visual gifts, the artist reads the spiritual parallels of his time and represents them in pure form. When such spiritual common property is lacking, there is nothing left for him but to build up his metaphysical element from his own inner resources. He stands aloof, and at best a few friends understand him, but not the general public. We artists therefore need the community of spirit of the entire people as much as we need bread. If the signs are correct, then the first indications of a new unity which will follow the chaos are already to be seen. I am dreaming now of the attempt to gather a small community from the scattered isolation of the individual; if this succeeds, we will have achieved a great deal.

The coming years will show that for us artists the crafts will be our salvation. We will no longer stand by the side of the crafts but be a part of them, since we have to earn money. For great art, this is a historically inevitable process, a necessity. All great works of art in past ages sprang from absolute mastery of the crafts. You will ask what my intentions are for the crafts so that an exodus from our midst by those unable to support themselves with free-lance art may be prevented. I work ceaselessly on the realisation of my plans. To begin with, a practical workshop outfitted for sculptors will be ready in the fall, and for painters, hopefully an apprentice course with a painter and decorator. Then it will also gradually become clear who will want to stay with us and who will rightfully be an apprentice, journeyman, or junior master, for at this moment these terms are just a game, since they still lack meaning in regard to the crafts. Much now depends on my being able to get our budget passed, despite the gloomy economic prospects. If successful, I will throw myself this fall into the task of reorganising the Bauhaus, and I hope to create a basic plan for you, with which you will be quite content.

38 Bruno Taut, *'Ex Oriente Lux': Call to Architects,* 1919

German architecture! – does such a thing exist?

First came all the styles, Renaissance, Gothic, Baroque, Biedermeier, Empire, Schinkelesque – but no calmness, it was all rush, rush. Then the Jugendstil and chaos. Heavy, sticky waves of sloppy style broke over us, and, to avoid drowning we clung to the solid rock of understanding. Despairing cries were heard, sharp dry words pierced the air. But they could not dispel the muddy waters and they covered them like a poisonous cloud. Those struggling for air choked. The words were: 'purpose ... material ... purpose ... construction ... purpose ... organism ... purpose ... homeland ... purpose ... purpose'. And, 'space, space' echoed through the air. Greatest wisdom: build space! not walls, ceilings, floors but 'negative' and 'positive' space. In fact: build with air!

'And the wolf laughed like a happy bunch of thieves and the whole wood – and meadow-land joined in the laughter. The dromedary turned the next corner in bewilderment – there came the loud cry "this wolf" ...'

Paul Scheerbart! Your laughter was not scorn. You alone knew the essence of building. You lived in the sparkling palaces and shining domes and between the giant buildings with their towers of angular glass.

Architects! here is your world. Step into the sparkling world of the poet and laugh, far away from all that is a torment to the mind and it has nothing to do with building. Let Paul Scheerbart take the blindfolds from your eyes and you will see. What you had no faith in before – how oppressively dark it was then! – you can see now in the magnificent world of the fantasy. Yes, can you see it? Man could build all this if he wanted to. But first you must want it, you, the creators!

And a new miracle reveals itself to your seeing eyes. Turning your gaze inwards upon yourself, the living magnificent world of fantasy lights up the surrounding gloom. The earth itself shines forth anew and hard 'reality' is unveiled – the impossible becomes possible – a miracle! How could we miss it, the paradise of the artist in the womb of all culture! Where Man – not human nature – was born!

India! Europe! push the dirty rubbish of establishment aside, the sticky, stinking shrouds which cover your people, be naked and kneel in humility before the radiant sun of art!

How could we have allowed our judgement to be so clouded that we could not see the light long ago! Classical forests of columns were erected in the way before us, a Greek–Roman–Italian wall of marble dolls and temple façades. But it is beginning to crack and will crumble.

Tuba mirum spargens sonum – per sepulcra regionum: the trump of doom! Resurrection of art! We rub our eyes, those of us blessed to see again. Yes, it is reality, we are not dreaming – that was once built by man. The Indian says, that the buildings were the creation of Gods. And truly they were Gods. If building is Indian, and also Classical, Roman, Gothic, Renaissance and Baroque, how does the whole European culture compare! Kill the European, kill him, kill him, kill him off! Sings St Paulus [Scheerbart].

Are we exaggerating? Take a look at any of the photographs of the great pagodas of Madura, Udepur, the Schiwa-pond of Tschillambaram, the grotto temples of Elefanta, the magnificent temple of Angkor-Vat in Cambodia, the beautiful great Choay-Dagone Pagodas in Rangoon – like sand dunes eroded into form – the large temple of Chamukte in Palitana, the great pagoda of Bangkok or the architectural mountain of Borobudur on Java! Each tiny part of the great culture from the fourth to the sixteenth century in Upper India, Ceylon, Cambodia, Annam, Siam and on Insulinde – what melting of form, what fruitful maturity, what restraint and strength and what unbelievable fusion with plastic art! Adornment overflowed, it overstepped all limits, tender from an inward devotion and strong and rich in the extreme. Tense, angular stratification; heavy, richly soft bulk; enormous soaring towers and most tender finesse – ecstasy!

Sunk into this magical world, engulfed in its honey – and where is Europe? In contrast to this Florence is thin, Syria raw, Egypt mathematical, Baroque unbalanced, St Gereon a box of stone bricks and even Gothic is only a constructed transcendency. How little remains? Yes, Strasbourg and its Gothic glass art and the Zwinger at Dresden – but can this beat India? Bow down in humility, you Europeans!

Humility will redeem you. It will give you love, love for the divinity of the earth and for the spirit of the world. You will no longer torment your earth with dynamite and grenades, you will have the will to adorn her, to cultivate and care for her – culture! Be one with her in subordination, and let her transport you to the stars. It will be a kingdom. Be good, and then the world will be beautiful and all a paradise! And you yourself become a paradise. Only glory within you!

We will grow wise – we will know how high man can build – can, if he wishes. We architects must lead mankind towards this aim. We must courageously bring that which is highest before man's senses and drive a nail through his flat world. It should collapse in ruins, turn to dust and allow a new Phoenix to arise from the ashes, a new light to shine afar, art which is happiness and life.

Formulas and recipes disappear. The architect with this fire within, feels the oneness within himself, unity with his people and with all mankind. His eyes are open, he puts each thing in its place, a hut remains a hut and nothing more and no longer does he overestimate department stores, office buildings and factories. He also does not underestimate them. The fire illuminates all things. In the subordination everything finds its place, truthfulness is once more, and a beam of eternal light falls on to even the most humble hut. Serenity and purity in all things!

Our protector Paul Scheerbart, shall lead us.

> Wherever you fly,
> You ne'er will reach the ultimate aim,
> Treasure this world and also the stars!
> Everything, that you here do spy,
> Is only of light a delicate game,
> A great lantern of a wonderworld.

---

39 Bruno Taut, *The City Crown*, 1919

We must have the same today as in ancient townscapes: The highest, the crown must be embodied in the religious structure. The house of God remains for all time the building to which we always aspire, which can bear our deepest emotion in the face of man and the world.

Why in the last few years, since the heyday of Jesuitism, has no large Cathedral been built or at least seriously planned? Schinkel's romantic line of thought led him to a great cathedral project on the Templowerberg near Berlin, driven by the feeling of finally creating something which would bring together the longings and hopes of man in community. But his impulse found no echo.

In the concept of the new town the church is missing. Churches are probably provided for in the plans, but they are arranged in such a way that they have no outstanding significance.

The idea of God also dissolves like the new town itself. It should not be asserted that religious life has waned in sincerity. But it is dissolving more and more into small canals; the common prayer, the liturgic deed has lost its unifying strength ...

But one belief definitely holds good. It is inconceivable that millions of people should lapse completely into materialism, vegetating, without knowing why they are here. Something must live within every human heart which will lift it beyond the temporal and which allows man to feel his associations with his contemporaries, his nation, all people and the entire world? Where does it reside? ...

There is one word which follows rich and poor alike, which echoes everywhere and which at the same time promises a new form of Christendom: the social thought. The feeling of having to help towards the good of mankind in some way, of somehow achieving salvation for oneself and therefore also for others and feeling at one and in solidarity with all people – it lives or at least slumbers in us all. Socialism, in the unpolitical, superpolitical sense, as far removed from any form of domination as the simple, straightforward relationship of men to one another, steps over the rift of feuding classes and nations and binds man to man. If there is anything today which can provide a crown for the town then it is the expression of this thought.

This is what the architect must create should he not wish to make himself superfluous and if he wants to know his purpose in life ...

All study of the old styles of building is of no help here; for this leaves architects with the individual forms only, for their eyes are blind to the light which shines through all the beautiful, unique things. The architect must recall his high priestlike, godly vocation and must seek to raise the treasure which lies buried in the depths of men's hearts. Discarding himself completely, he should merge into the soul of the people as a whole and find himself and his high vocation, whereby in aim at least, he gives expression to that which slumbers in every man. A star-crossed architectural ideal should once more arise and lead everyone to the consciousness that they are but the limbs of a great architecture, just as in the days of old.

Then colour blossoms forth once more, the colourful architecture today craved by only the few. The range of pure unbroken colours again falls over our houses and delivers them from their dead-on-grey. And a love of brightness awakens; the architect no longer avoids the bright and shiny. He knows how to value it from his new standpoint, far from the old prejudice, can divide everything and each thing into new effect ...

If we see the possibility of the city-crown in social thought then we must examine the type of action in which this thought is already known today. What does the public want today? What is it doing? Are there not organisations in which the longings of the crowd at least find expression in veiled form? If we go to the places to which they repair in order to spend their leisure time

Bruno Taut, The City Crown: view to the east
Die Stadtkrone, Jena, 1919

away from material desires, we come to the leisure spots, from the cinema upwards to the theatre, or to inns and assembly houses, to which they are drawn by a political urge or by the desire for communal experience. There are two motives then, pleasure and community spirit, which have already caused numerous buildings to be erected. These instincts are clearly recognised by the leaders and with some luck have been purified. The desire for pleasure which drives men to the theatre in such great throngs (in Brussels the number of theatregoers according to newspaper reports is 20,000 each night out of a population of about 600,000), should not be interpreted as an uncultured search for entertainment, for contained therein is the story of the soul for the lofty, to be raised above everyday life. But the German theatregoer is seen by theatre people as an appreciative attentive guest who goes to the theatre with the feeling that it is Sunday. The other side of people's urges, which leads to public houses, is also based upon a noble, inner trait. It is the will to shape oneself to the common interest and to feel at one in one's environment, as a man amongst men ...

It is clearly a single, completely homogeneous, large movement which exhibits these tendencies. And it is certainly this trend which encompasses many – perhaps all – sections of the public most broadly and strongly. Veiled within it lies the meaning of the longings of our time, trying to reach the light and calling for a visible transfiguration. That is the architectural will of our world.

We have the concept of the new town, but it is a town without a crown. We do however know how its head, its crown, must be.

The Town Crown

The design shown in the following is an attempt to show how perhaps the crowning, the highest element in the new town could be aimed for. It could appear, from the examples shown and mentioned here, bold and even presumptuous to attempt something lying in this direction. But the attempt has to be made once even at the risk of being called imprudent and Utopian. It should merely clarify the tendencies pressing towards the heights in a concrete vision, and should not be seen so much as an end in itself but as an encouragement towards the realisation and further establishment of goals, of that which has already been recognised ...

The centre, the town crown itself shows a grouping of all the buildings towards which the social trends already mentioned aim and which a town of this size requires for artistic and entertainment purposes.

Four large buildings forming a cross, austerely orientated towards the sun, comprising opera house, theatre, large public house or public hall and small assembly hall, crown the layout and have exits which point in the four different directions in order to allow a rapid dispersal of crowds. There are open places to the sides in consideration of possible panic. In its centre there is a square with extensions for storehouses for the theatre scenery, supply rooms, business rooms, etc. They are connected and surrounded by a colonnade which, at its four corners to right and left of the public hall, forms communal houses for smaller, more intimate gatherings (weddings and suchlike) with garden terraces, and on the other side forms an aquarium and plant house with like gardens. This gallery allows the most compact use of the whole to be made; one can spend the afternoon on the garden terraces and the evening at a concert or the theatre or at a meeting ...

The whole is graduated from top to bottom in a similar way to people being graded in their inclinations and their dispositions. Architecture becomes a crystallised image of the stratas of man. Everything is accessible to everyone, everyone goes in the direction to which he is drawn. There are no conflicts because the people who find themselves together are all in the same mood.

The uppermost crown is formed by the mass of the four large buildings, as a visible expression of fulfilment, symbolised in its cruciform. The socially directed hopes of the people find their fulfilment here in the heights. The drama, the musical, animates the souls of the people here united, in a way which they have longed for in everyday life, and the gatherings in the public halls show them what they as people can give one another and results in a refining of the herd instinct, the primitive force of alliance ...

The cross made by these four large buildings is the highest crown of the whole group of buildings; but this built mass does not yet form the crown. It is firstly a base for the highest building, which reigns over the whole as pure architecture, completely dissolved from its purpose. It is the crystal house, constructed from glass, the building material; matter, and yet signifying more than usual matter in its shimmering, transparent, reflecting being. A reinforced concrete construction lifts it above the mass of the four large buildings and forms its structure, in which the whole rich scale of glass architecture shines within glass prisms, coloured glass and enamelled plates. Within the house there is nothing but a beautiful room, accessible by steps and bridges to right and left of the theatre and the small public hall. How can one possibly hint at what one can achieve by building! All tender and all great sensations should waken here when the full sunlight pours over the high room and breaks up into numerous fine reflections, or when the evening sun fills the upper dome of the roof and deepens the rich colours of the glass pictures and sculptures, with its red glow. Here architecture will renew its wonderful link with sculpture and painting. Everything will be a work of art, in which the achievement of the architect in the conception of the whole, that of the painter in the glass pictures of an enraptured, world-pervading fantasy, and the work of the sculptor, will be inseparable from the whole, and so wholly connected with it that everything is just a part of great architecture which fulfils all artists equally and forces them to ultimate expression. Cosmic, divine thoughts are mirrored in the colours of the artist, 'world-parts', and a new sculptural form decorate all architectural structures, views, connections, shores, supports, etc., and show that sculpture can once more be more than the carving of stone figures and suchlike. It will awaken once more and unveil all its precious riches which have been neglectfully withheld for so long. The whole free world of form released from the spell of realism, that element found in waves, clouds, mountains, all elements and beings, which leads the soul of the artist far above the figures and naturalism of the present, arises once more and shines and shimmers in all colours and materials, metals, precious stones and glass in all the parts of the room where it is provoked by the play of light and shadow. This room is not smooth and walled but rather filled with the harmony of a rich, complete formation. From its galleries great music resounds acoustically unimpeded; a form of music which only serves the highest and is as far removed from domestic as it is from pictorial art.

Infused with the light of the sun, the crystal house reigns over all like a glittering diamond which shines in the sun as a sign of the heights of pleasure and the purest peace of mind. In this room a lonely wanderer will find the pure delight of architecture, and ascending by the steps in this room to the upper platform, he will see at his feet his town and behind it the sun, towards which this town and its heart is so strictly directed, rising and setting.

'The light that tries to infuse the universe is alive in the crystal.' Coming from infinity it catches in the highest point of the town, breaks up and shines in the coloured plates, edges, surfaces and arches of the crystal house. This shall be the bearer of a cosmic experience, a religiousness, which offers a reverential silence. It does not stand isolated but is supported by buildings which serve the nobler feelings of the people, and which furthermore are again separated from the profane wheels by outer courts: as in times of old there was a fair and kermis in front of the church, so here we find realism and the joy of living around the crystal. The shine, the reflection of the pure, transcendental, shimmers above the festiveness of the unbroken, radiating colours. And the area of the town spreads out around as a sea of colour and a sign of the delight in the new life ...

When the city is first set up the area will be left open; then with the growing expansion of the town in accordance with the fixed plan, the necessities will be built little by little until eventually the ultimate will be built. The building may stretch through generations, the means are found in the measures of progress and this agreement of tempo and need will also produce the harmony of the style. Many architects may work together as long as they fit into a large overall plan. Wonderful, to play one's part without knowing which ecstatic Brunnelleschi will once form the highest crown! ...

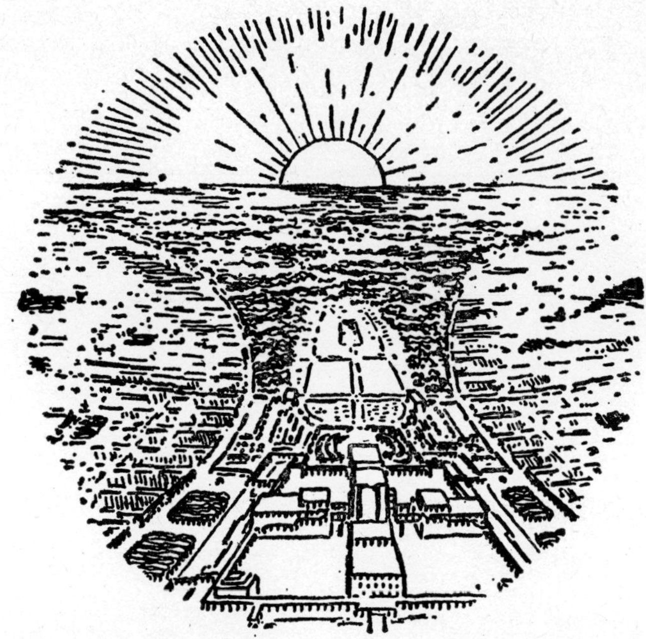

Bruno Taut, The City Crown: bird's eye view to the west
Die Stadtkrone, Jena, 1919

---

40 Nikolai Punin, *On Tatlin's Monument to the Third International,* 1919

Tatlin, the most forceful and clear-sighted master of our age, has entirely denied the artistic value of the monuments now being erected; he proposes an entirely new and, as I see it, mathematically true form of monument ...

Artist Tatlin proposes a project, already worked out in its essentials, for a monument to the great Russian Revolution. As regards its appearance, the form of the monument corresponds to all the artistic forms discovered in our age. These forms are the simplest possible: cubes, cylinders, spheres, cones, segments of circles, and spherical planes, sections from these etc. It is desirable that the monument should be made as large as possible, as is only natural in view of the size of buildings in our towns. A succession of the simplest forms (cubes) is to contain halls for lectures and gymnastics, premises for agitation, and other rooms which can be used for different purposes as required; these premises, however, are not to be museums or libraries of any kind, their character should preferably be shifting the whole time. The monument contains also an agitation centre, from which one can turn to the entire city with different types of appeals, proclamations and pamphlets. Special motorcycles and cars could constitute a highly mobile, continuously available tool of agitation for the government, and the monument therefore contains a garage ... On one of the monument's wings (if these are built, and this is surely necessary – if I have properly understood the modern principles for the construction of artistic form) one can also catch a giant screen, on which it would be possible in the evenings with the help of a film reel – visible from a great distance – to send the latest news from cultural and political life throughout the world. For the reception of instant information, a radio receiver of worldwide range is to be installed in the monument, together with its own telephone and telegraph station (not too large) and other possible information apparatus. In accordance with the latest invention, one part of the monument is to be equipped with a projector station that can write letters in light in the sky (there are particularly good opportunities for this towards the north); with such letters, it would be possible to compose different slogans in connection with current events . . .

This project shows in what direction the artist is to work, when he has grown tired of heroes and busts. Above all the artist must forget sculpture in the more restricted sense of this term; the forms of the human body cannot today serve as an artistic form: form must be discovered anew. I am not a sculptor. I don't know what form it will be, but it will surely lie very close to the simplest forms discovered by artists in recent years.

---

41 Naum Gabo and Antoine Pevsner, *The Realistic Manifesto,* 1920

Neither Futurism nor Cubism has brought us what our time has expected of them. Besides those two artistic schools our recent past has had nothing of importance or deserving attention.

But Life does not wait and the growth of generations does not stop and we who go to relieve those who have passed into history, having in our hands the results of their experiments, with their mistakes and their achievements, after years of experience equal to centuries . . . we say . . .

No new artistic system will withstand the pressure of a growing new culture until the very foundation of Art will be erected on the real laws of Life.

Until all artists will say with us . . .

All is a fiction . . . only life and its laws are authentic and in life only the active is beautiful and wise and strong and right, for life does not know beauty as an aesthetic measure . . . efficacious existence is the highest beauty.

Life knows neither good nor bad nor justice as a measure of morals . . . need is the highest and most just of all morals.

Life does not know rationally abstracted truths as a measure of cognisance, deed is the highest and surest of truths.

Those are the laws of life. Can art withstand these laws if it is built on abstraction, on mirage, and fiction?

We say . . .

Space and time are re-born to us today.

Space and time are the only forms on which life is built and hence art must be constructed.

States, political and economic systems perish, ideas crumble, under the strain of ages . . . but life is strong and grows and time goes on in its real continuity.

Who will show us forms more efficacious than this . . . who is the great one who will give us foundations stronger than this?

Who is the genius who will tell us a legend more ravishing than this prosaic tale which is called life?

The realisation of our perceptions of the world in the forms of space and time is the only aim of our pictorial and plastic art.

In them we do not measure our works with the yardstick of beauty, we do not weigh them with pounds of tenderness and sentiments.

The plumb-line in our hand, eyes as precise as a ruler, in a spirit as taut as a compass . . . we construct our work as the universe constructs its own, as the engineer constructs his bridges, as the mathematician his formula of the orbits.

We know that everything has its own essential image; chair, table, lamp, telephone, book, house, man ... they are all entire worlds with their own rhythms, their own orbits.

That is why we in creating things take away from them the labels of their owners ... all accidental and local, leaving only the reality of the constant rhythm of the forces in them.

1. *Thence in painting we renounce colour as a pictorial element, colour is the idealised optical surface of objects; an exterior and superficial impression of them; colour is accidental and it has nothing in common with the innermost essence of a thing.*

We affirm *that the tone of a substance,* i.e. *its light-absorbing material body is its only pictorial reality.*

2. We renounce *in a line, its descriptive value; in real life there are no descriptive lines, description is an accidental trace of a man on things, it is not bound up with the essential life and constant structure of the body. Descriptiveness is an element of graphic illustration and decoration.*

We affirm *the line only as a direction of the static forces and their rhythm in objects.*

3. We renounce *volume as a pictorial and plastic form of space; one cannot measure space in volumes as one cannot measure liquid in yards: look at our space ... what is it if it is not continuous depth?*

We affirm *depth as the only pictorial and plastic form of space.*

4. We renounce *in sculpture, the mass as a sculptural element.*

It is known to every engineer that the static forces of a solid body and its material strength do not depend on the quantity of the mass ... example a rail, a T-beam etc.

But you sculptors of all shades and directions, you still adhere to the age-old prejudice that you cannot free the volume of mass. Here (in this exhibition) we take four planes and we construct with them the same volume as of four tons of mass.

Thus we bring back to sculpture the line as a direction and in it we affirm depth as one form of space.

5. We renounce *the thousand-year-old delusion in art that held the static rhythms as the only elements of the plastic and pictorial arts.*

We affirm *in these arts a new element, the kinetic rhythms as the basic forms of our perception of real time.*

These are the five fundamental principles of our work and our constructive technique.

Today we proclaim our words to you people. In the squares and on the streets we are placing our work convinced that art must not remain a sanctuary for the idle, a consolation for the weary, and a justification for the lazy. Art should attend us everywhere that life flows and acts ... at the bench, at the table, at work, at rest, at play; on working days and holidays ... at home and on the road ... in order that the flame to live shall not be extinguished in mankind.

We do not look for justification, neither in the past nor in the future.

Nobody can tell us what the future is and with what utensils one eats it.

Not to lie about the future is impossible and one can lie about it at will.

We assert that the shouts about the future are for us the same as the tears about the past: a renovated day-dream of the romantics.

A monkish delirium of the heavenly kingdom of the old attired in contemporary clothes.

He who is busy today with the morrow is busy doing nothing.

And he who tomorrow will bring us nothing of what he has done today is of no use for the future.

Today is the deed.

We will acount for it tomorrow.

The past we leave behind as carrion.

The future we leave to the fortune-tellers.

We take the present day.

42 Le Corbusier and Amadée Ozenfant, *Purism,* 1920

Introduction

Logic, born of human constants and without which nothing is human, is an instrument of control and, for he who is inventive, a guide towards discovery; it controls and corrects the somewhat capricious march of intuition and permits one to go ahead with certainty. It is the guide that sometimes precedes and sometimes follows the explorer; but without intuition it is a sterile device; nourished by intuition, it allows one 'to dance in one's fetters'.

Nothing is worthwhile which is not general, nothing is worthwhile which is not transmittable. We have attempted to establish an aesthetic which is rational, and therefore human.

It is impossible to construct without fixed points. We already sought in an earlier article* to determine some of these.

The Work of Art

The work of art is an artificial object which permits the creator to place the spectator in the state he wishes; later we will study the means the creator has at his disposal to attain this result.

With regard to man, aesthetic sensations are not all of the same degree of intensity or quality; we might say that there is a hierarchy. The highest level of this hierarchy seems to us to be that special state of a mathematical sort to which we are raised, for example, by the clear perception of a great general law (the state of mathematical lyricism, one might say); it is superior to the brute pleasure of the senses; the senses are involved, however, because every being in this state is as if in a state of beatitude.

The goal of art is not simple pleasure, rather it partakes of *the nature of happiness.*

It is true that plastic art has to address itself more directly to the senses than pure mathematics, which only acts by symbols, these symbols sufficing to trigger in the mind consequences of a superior order; in plastic art, the senses should be strongly moved in order to predispose the mind to the release into play of subjective reactions without which there is no work of art. But there is no art worth having without its excitement of an intellectual order – of a mathematical order; architecture is the art which up until now has most strongly induced the states of this category. The reason is that everything in architecture is expressed by order and economy.

The means of executing a work of art is a transmittable and universal language.

One of the highest delights of the human mind is to perceive the order of nature and to measure its own participation in the scheme of things; the work of art seems to us to be a labour of putting into order, a masterpiece of human order.

Now the world only appears to man from the human vantage point, that is, the world seems to obey the laws man has been able to assign to it; when man creates a work of art, he has the feeling of acting as a 'god'. But a law is nothing other than the verification of an order.

In summary, a work of art should induce a sensation of mathematical order, and the means of inducing this mathematical order should be sought among universal means.

System

We established in our article 'On the Plastic' that there are two quite distinct orders of sensation:

(i) Primary sensations determined in all human beings by the simple play of forms and primary colours. For example, if I show to everyone on Earth – a Frenchman, a Negro, a Laplander – a sphere in the form of a billiard ball (one of the most perfect human materialisations of the sphere), I release in each of these

* 'Sur la plastique' in *Esprit Nouveau,* I, 15 October 1920.

individuals an identical sensation inherent in the spherical form: *this is the constant primary sensation.* (ii) There are secondary sensations, varying with the individual because they depend upon his cultural or hereditary capital. Thus, if I hold up a primary cubic form, I release in each individual the same primary sensation for the cube; but if I place some black geometric spots on the cube, I immediately release in a civilised man the idea of dice to play with, and the whole series of associations which would follow. A Papuan would only see an ornament. *There are, therefore, besides the primary sensations, infinitely numerous and variable secondary sensations.*

What we have said for the cube and the sphere is true for all the other primary forms, for all the primary colours, for all the primary lines; it is just as true for the cube, the sphere, the cylinder, the cone and the pyramid as for the constituent elements of these bodies, the triangle, the square, the circle, as for straight, broken, or curved lines, for obtuse, right or acute angles, etc. – all the primary elements which react unthinkingly, uniformly, in the same way, on all individuals.

The great works of the past are those based on primary elements, and this is the only reason why they endure.

Superior sensations of a mathematical order can be born only of a choice of primary elements with secondary resonance.

Composition

Composition is our stock-in-trade; it involves tasks of an exclusively physical order. Composition comprises choice of surface, division of the surface, co-modulation, relationships of density, colour scheme.

A painting is an association of purified, related, and architectured elements.

Space is needed for architectural composition; space means three dimensions. Therefore we think of the painting not as a surface but *as a space.*

Our mind reacts to colours as it reacts to basic forms. There are brutal colours and suave colours, each appropriate to its object. Moreover, given the play of memory, acquired in looking at nature, logical and organic habits are created in us which confer on each object qualifying, and hence constructive colour; thus blue cannot be used to create a volume that should 'come forward', because our eye, accustomed to seeing blue in the depths (sky, sea), in backgrounds and distant objects (horizons), does not permit with impunity the reversing of these conditions. Hence a plane that comes forward can never be blue; it could be green (grass), brown (earth); in summary, colours should be disciplined while taking account of these two incontestable standards:

(i) The primary sensory standard, immediate excitation of the senses (red and the bull, black and sadness).

(ii) The secondary standard of memory, recall of visual experience and of our harmonisation of the world (soil is not blue, the sky is not brown, and if sometimes they may seem so, it would only be an accident to be disregarded by an art of invariables).

Purism

The highest delectation of the human mind is the perception of order, and the greatest human satisfaction is the feeling of collaboration or participation in this order. The work of art is an artificial object which lets the spectator be placed in the state desired by the creator. The sensation of order is of a mathematical quality. The creation of a work of art should utilise means for specified results. Here is how we have tried to create a language possessing these means:

Primary forms and colours have standard properties (universal properties which permit the creation of a transmittable plastic language). But the utilisation of primary forms does not suffice to place the spectator in the sought-for state of mathematical order. For that one must bring to bear the associations of natural or artificial forms, and the criterion for their choice is the degree of selection at which certain elements have arrived (natural selection and mechanical selection). The Purist element issued from the purification of standard forms is not a copy, but a creation whose end is to materialise the object in all its generality and its invariability. Purist elements are thus comparable to words of carefully defined meaning; Purist syntax is the application of constructive and modular means; it is the application of the laws which control pictorial space. A painting is a whole (unity); a painting is an artificial formation which, by appropriate means, should lead to the objectivication of an entire 'world'. One could make an art of allusions, an art of fashion, based upon surprise and the conventions of the initiated. Purism strives for an art free of conventions which will utilise plastic constants and address itself above all to the universal properties of the senses and the mind.

---

43 Nikolai Punin, *Tatlin's Monument,* 1922

In 1919 the Department of Plastic Art under Narkompros commissioned V.E. Tatlin to design a project for a monument for the Third International. Artist Tatlin started work immediately, and completed this project.

The main idea of the monument is based on an organic synthesis of the principles of architecture, sculpture and painting. It was to comprise a new type of monumental construction, combining a purely creative form with a utilitarian form. In agreement with this principle, the monument consists of three great rooms in glass, erected with the help of a complicated system of vertical pillars and spirals. These rooms are placed on top of each other, and have different, harmonically corresponding forms. They are to be able to move at different speeds by means of a special mechanism. The lower storey, which is cubic in form, rotates around its own axis at a rate of one revolution per year. This is intended for legislative assemblies. The next storey, which is pyramidal, rotates around its axis at the rate of one revolution per month. Here the executive bodies are to meet (the International's executive committee, the secretariat, and other administrative executive bodies). Finally, the uppermost cylinder, which rotates one revolution per day, is reserved for centres of an informative character: an information office, a newspaper, the issuing of proclamations, pamphlets and manifestoes – in short, all means of informing the international proletariat; it will also have a telegraphic office and an apparatus that can project on to large screens. These can be fitted around the axes of the hemisphere. Radio masts will rise up over the monument. It should be emphasised that Tatlin's proposal provides for walls with a vacuum in between (Thermos), which will make it easy to keep the temperature in the various rooms constant.

---

44 A. Rodchenko and V. Stepanova, *The Programme of the Productivist Group,* 1920

[This programme was published several months after the 'Realistic Manifesto' as a reply to it, in a catalogue for an exhibition organised by Rodchenko and Stepanova and signed by them.]

The task of the Constructivist group is the communistic expression of materialistic constructive work.

It tackles the solution of this problem on the basis of scientific hypotheses. It emphasises the necessity of synthesising the ideological and formal part so as to direct the laboratory work on to the tracks of practical activity.

When the group was first started the ideological part of its programme was as follows:

1. The sole premise is scientific communism, based on the theory of historical materialism.

2. The cognition of the experimental trials of the Soviets has led the Group to transplant experimental activities from the abstract (transcendental) to the real.

3. The specific elements of the group's work, namely 'tektonika', construction, and 'faktura', ideologically, theoretically, and by experience justify the changing of the material elements of industrial culture into volume, plane, colour, space, and light.

These constitute the foundations of the communistic expression of materialistic construction.

These three points form an organic link between the ideological and formal parts.

'Tektonika' is derived from the structure of communism and the effective exploitation of industrial matter.

Construction is organisation. It accepts the contents of the matter itself, already formulated. Construction is formulating activity taken to the extreme, allowing, however for further 'tektonical' work.

The matter deliberately chosen and effectively used, without however hindering the progress of construction or limiting the 'tektonika', is called 'faktura' by the group.

Among material elements are:

Matter in general. Recognition of its origin, its industrial and productional changes. Its nature and its meaning.

Intellectual materials: light, plane, space, colour, volume.

The Constructivists treat intellectual and solid materials in the same way.

The future tasks for the group are as follows:

1. Ideologically:

(a) Proving by word and deed the incompatibility of artistic activity and intellectual production.

(b) The real participation of intellectual production as an equivalent element, in building up communist culture.

2. In practice:

(a) Agitation in the press.

(b) Conception of plans.

(c) Organisation of exhibitions.

(d) Making contact with all the productive centres and main bodies of unified Soviet mechanism, which realise the communistic forms of life in practice.

3. In the field of agitation:

(a) The group stands for ruthless war against art in general.

(b) The group prove that evolutionary transition of the past's art-culture into the communistic forms of constructive building is impossible.

The slogans of the Constructivists

1. Down with art.
   Long live technic.
2. Religion is a lie.
   Art is a lie.
3. Kill human thinking's last remains tying it to art.
4. Down with guarding the traditions of art.
   Long live the Constructivist technician.
5. Down with art, which only camouflages humanity's impotence.
6. The collective art of the present is constructive life.

---

45 Theo Van Doesburg, *The Will to Style,* 1922

... We are not the first to struggle for a solution of the problem of art: it has been the struggle of many generations. The proof of that can be found in all the significant works of art in our heritage. However different these expressions of artistic endeavour may seem to our optic sense, our inner senses recognise every human creation to be only the upper surface of a battle waged in our very being. Not waged in art, science, philosophy and religion alone, but in our daily life where it takes the form of the struggle for spiritual and material existence.

What is the nature of this struggle?

Every work of art, of the past or of the present, provides an answer.

This conflict, which has its foundations in the structure of life, is a conflict between two polar forces. You may call them Nature and Spirit, or the Feminine and Masculine principles, Negative and Positive, Static and Dynamic, Horizontal and Vertical – they are the invariable elements in which the contradictions of our existence are rooted and which can be seen in variability. To bring about an end to the conflict, a reconciliation of the extremes, and agreement between the polarities – that is the stuff of life, the basic object of art. This reconciliation, which appears in art as harmony or vital repose, contains in itself the criterion for the essential significance of every work of art; not indeed for a work of art as an individual expression, but for art as the collective expression of a race, for a style ... In the new plastic art the expressive impulses become more profound, abstract, and are applied to architecture. The struggle for an elemental style with elemental means which I have briefly described, takes a path parallel to that of the progressive development of technology. From the most primitive tools of the Stone Age (e.g. the primitive drill) there has developed the electrical machine, perfect in its form and in its function (e.g. the latest model of drill). In the same way the primitive drawings of the Stone Age have developed into the elemental works of art of our own age.

Where these two lines of development (the technical and the artistic) meet in our age the application of the machine to the new style is a matter of course. The machine is the purest example of balance between the static and the dynamic, between intellect and instinct. If culture in the broadest sense really means independence of nature, it is no wonder that the machine takes pride of place in the concept of cultural style. The machine is the supreme example of intellectual discipline. Materialism, as a philosophy of life and art, considered hand craftsmanship to be the purest expression of the soul.

The new spiritual philosophy of art not only saw at once its limitless potentialities for artistic expression. For a style which is no longer concerned with the production of individual pictures, ornaments or private houses, but makes a collective assault on whole districts of cities, skyscraper blocks and airports, with due consideration of the economic circumstances – for such a style there can be no question of employing hand craftsmanship. The machine is all-important here: hand craftsmanship is appropriate to an individualistic view of life which has been overtaken by progress. Hand craftsmanship, in the age of materialist philosophy, debased man to a machine; the machine, used properly in the service of cultural construction, is the only means of bringing about the converse: social liberation. This is by no means to say that mechanical production is the only requirement for creative perfection. A prerequisite for the correct use of machines is not quantity alone but, above all, quality. To serve artistic ends the use of machines must be governed by the artistic consciousness.

The needs of our age, both ideal and practical, demand constructive certainty. Only the machine can provide this constructive certainty. The new potentialities of the machine have given rise to an aesthetic theory appropriate to our age, which I have had occasion to call the 'mechanical aesthetic'. Those who believe that the spirit will only overcome nature in some sphere beyond the boundaries of reality will perhaps never admit that the general form of our life today provides the necessary condition for a style of life and art in which the religious truths which transcend the individual can be realised. The style which we are approaching will be, above all, a style of liberation and vital repose. This style, far removed from romantic vagueness, from decorative idiosyncrasy and animal spontaneity, will be a style of heroic monumentality (e.g. the American grain silo). I should like to call this style, in contrast to all the styles of the past, the style of the perfect man, that is, the style in which the great oppositie are reconciled ...

Let me give you some examples of the characteristics of the new style in opposition to those of the old.

Certainty instead of uncertainty.
Openness instead of enclosure.
Clarity instead of vagueness.
Religious energy instead of faith and religious authority.
Truth instead of beauty.
Simplicity instead of complexity.
Relationship instead of form.
Synthesis instead of analysis.
Logical construction instead of lyrical constellation.
Mechanisation instead of manual work.
Plastic form instead of imitation and decorative ornamentation.
Collectivism instead of individualism, etc.

The urge to establish the new style is seen in numerous phenomena. Not only in painting, sculpture and architecture, in literature, jazz and the cinema, but most significantly of all in purely utilitarian production.

All those various artefacts which serve a particular purpose do not start out with any artistic intentions. And yet they move us by their beauty ...

---

46 Vilmos Huszar, *The Staatliche Bauhaus in Weimar,* 1922

The aim which the Bauhaus has set itself, and which corresponds to the will of our age, is good. After four years of existence, how near has the Bauhaus got towards an actual realisation of this aim?

In the Weimar Museum I visited the exhibition of Thuringian artists, to which the Bauhaus masters have contributed.

What the masters can accomplish, they teach. What do they accomplish? Each one does what his mood suggests, far from any binding discipline. Where are at least some attempts at communal work by even two participators? Where is the combination of several disciplines? Where are the attempts to create a unified work of art, a homogeneous creation of space, form and colour?

Pictures; nothing but pictures and miniatures, graphics and individual sculptures.

The things Feininger is exhibiting were done better ten years ago in Frankfurt (1912 cubism). His latest watercolours are dilute Klee-infusions! Klee himself scribbles morbid dreams, which one can find as beautifully portrayed if not more so in Prinzhorn's paintings of the mentally ill. Kandinsky is still producing his intermingled decorations. Waste of material – with no positive reason. Arbitrary and capricious! Even more arbitrary and capricious, as also intellectual and without intuitive power, uneasily mottled together, are the works of G. Muche. The emptily gorgeous daubings of Itten are designed purely for external effect. Schlemmer's works are experiments which we already know from other sculptors. What he has in the way of personal emphasis shows so little strong conviction as regards creative intentions that it cannot be considered for the collective architectural concept. In the Weimar cemetery there stands an expressionist monument by Herr Director Gropius which, as a product of a cheap literary brainwave, cannot even compete with Schlemmer's sculpture.

These masters, with a few others, intend to train the young generation to create the unified work of art – *the great building*!

Is it not strikingly clear that if they do not relate to each other or to life each of these masters is wrapping himself up in his own solitary world? Since these masters lack a homogeneous background or a common intellectual attitude, there is no possibility of collective discipline in the training of the pupils. Educational discipline based on subjective individual conceptions can only lead to dead dogma.

To attain these goals set out by the Bauhaus in its prospectus other masters are needed, masters who know what is required for the creation of the unified work of art, and who can prove their competence thereto by their achievements.

To sum up one must ask oneself the following questions.

Faced with the predominance of a crass individualism, in which each works according to his mood, can the desired goals be reached?

Can one hope for the reunification of all the disciplines of practising artists while there is no common ideal to establish ties?

In a country which is torn politically and economically, can one justify the spending of large sums of money on an institute such as the Bauhaus is today?

My answer is: No – No – No!

The unproductivity of the Bauhaus as it is today makes it clear that to let the institute continue as a '*Meisterschule*' would be a *crime against the state and civilisation*. The atmosphere of the Bauhaus is corrupt. An improvement is only possible through the application of radical methods. These 'artistic masters' must be dismissed and a new start made on the only rational basis – workshop principles (joinery, etc.).

---

47 Laszlo Moholy-Nagy, *Constructivism and the Proletariat,* 1922

Reality is the measure of human thinking. It is the means by which we orient ourselves in the Universe. The actuality of time – the reality of this century – determines what we can grasp and what we cannot understand.

And this reality of our century is *technology* – the invention, construction and maintenance of the machine. To be a user of machines is to be of the spirit of this century. It has replaced the transcendental spiritualism of past eras.

Before the machine, everyone is equal – I can use it, so can you – it can crush me and the same can happen to you. There is no tradition in technology, no consciousness of class or standing. Everybody can be the machine's master or its slave.

This is the root of socialism, the final liquidation of feudalism. It is the machine that woke up the proletariat. In serving technology the worker discovered a changed world. We have to eliminate the machine if we want to eliminate socialism. But we all know there is no such thing. This is our century – technology, machine, socialism. Make your peace with it. Shoulder its task.

Because it is our task to carry the revolution towards reformation, to fight for a new spirit to fill the forms stamped out by the monstrous machine. Material well-being does not depend on manufactured goods. Look around. The proletariat is not happy today in spite of the machine.

Material well-being is caused by the spirit that is superior to the demand of routine work; it is a socialism of the mind, a dedication to the spirit of the group. Only a proletariat, educated to this grasp of essential community, can be satisfied.

Who will teach them? Words are heavy, obscure. Their meaning is evasive to the untrained mind. Past traditions hang on to their meaning. But there is art. Art expresses the spirit of the times; it is art that crystallises the emotional drive of an age. The art of our century, its mirror and its voice, is *Constructivism*.

Constructivism is neither proletarian nor capitalist. Constructivism is primordial, without class and without ancestor. It expresses the pure form of nature, the direct colour, the spatial element not distorted by utilitarian motifs.

The new world of the proletariat needs Constructivism; it needs fundamentals that are without deceit. Only the natural element, accessible to all eyes, is revolutionary. It has never before been the property of civilised man.

In Constructivism form and substance are one. Not substance and tendency, which are always identified. Substance is essential, but tendency is intentional. Constructivism is pure substance – not the property of one artist alone who drags along under the yoke of individualism. Constructivism is not confined to the picture frame and the pedestal. It expands into industrial design, into houses, objects, forms. It is the socialism of vision – the common property of all men.

Only the today is important for the Constructivist. He cannot indulge in the luxurious speculations of either the Utopian Communist who dreams of a future world domination, or of the bourgeois artist who lives in splendid isolation. It cannot be either proletarian art or art of the precious salons. In Constructivism the process and the goal are one – the spiritual conquest of a century of technology.

---

48 Gino Severini, *Machinery,* 1922

The precision of machines, their rhythm and their brutality have no doubt led us to adopt a new form of realism that we can express without painting train engines.

The inventor is also a creator, and the artist is first and foremost an inventor, but up to now I believe that the two forms of creation, although similar, cannot be considered to be identical.

Yet there is an analogy between a machine and a work of art. For instance, all the various material components that go to make up an engine are directed by a single will – that of its inventor, which adds another kind of life, action, or movement to the integral vitality of these various materials. *The method used for constructing a machine is similar to that for constructing a work of art.*

If we also consider a machine from the point of view of the effect it creates on the beholder we will again discover that there is an analogy here with the work of art. In fact, unless you are completely blinded by some form of prejudice, you cannot fail to experience a feeling of pleasure, of admiration, when you are confronted by a well-built machine.

Admiration is in itself an aesthetic pleasure, and as the aesthetic pleasure created in us by a machine can be thought of as Universal, we may conclude that the effect created by a machine on the beholder is analogous to that produced by a work of art.

---

49 Fernand Léger, *The Machine Aesthetic: The Manufactured Object, the Artisan and the Artist,* 1924

Modern man lives more and more in a preponderantly geometric order.

All man-made mechanical and industrial creation is dependent on geometric forces.

I want to discuss, above all, the prejudices which blind three-quarters of mankind and totally prevent it from arriving at a free judgement of the phenomena, whether beautiful or ugly, which surround them.

I consider that formal beauty in general is totally independent of sentimental, descriptive and imitative values. Each object, painting, building and ornamental arrangement has an intrinsic value, strictly absolute, which is independent of what it may represent.

A number of individuals would be responsive to beauty (visual object) without reference to anything else if they were not blindfolded by a preconceived idea of the art object. The cause of it is poor visual education and the modern mania for classification at all costs, for categorising individuals like tools. People are *afraid to judge freely*, which is, nevertheless, the only state of mind possible for the appreciation of beauty. Victims of a critical, sceptical, intellectual era, they are consumed by the wish to understand rather than give in to their feelings. They believe in '*makers of art*', because these are professionals. Titles and distinctions seduce them and cloud their view. My aim is to try and establish this: that there is no such thing as a catalogued or hierarchical beauty; that is the worst possible error. Beauty is everywhere: more perhaps in the arrangement of your saucepans on the white wall of your kitchen than in your eighteenth-century drawing-room or in the official museums.

What I have to discuss, then, is a new architectural order: the architecture of mechanisation. Architecture, both ancient and modern, also originates from geometric forces.

Greek art made horizontal lines dominant. It influenced the entire seventeenth century in France. Romanesque art made vertical lines dominant. The Gothic achieved an often perfect balance between the play of curved and straight lines. The Gothic even achieved that astonishing thing: architectural movement. There are Gothic façades which are articulated like a dynamic picture – it is the interplay of complementary lines which are put in opposition by contrast.

One can assert this: that a machine or a manufactured object can be beautiful when the relationship of the lines which inscribe the volumes is balanced in an order equivalent to that of earlier architecture. We are not, therefore, strictly speaking, confronted by the phenomena of a new order, but quite simply by an architectural manifestation like any other.

Where the question becomes more complex is when one considers mechanical creation in the context of its results, that is its *aim*. If the aim of earlier architecture was Beauty rather than function, it is undeniable that in the mechanical order the dominant aim is *function*, strictly function. Everything is rigorously directed towards function. *The thrust towards function thus does not prevent the establishment of a state of beauty.*

The case of the evolution of the form of the automobile is a significant illustration of my theory; it is, moreover, interesting by virtue of the fact that the closer the form of the car has approached its functional purpose the more beautiful it has become. That is to say, that at the beginning when vertical lines dominated the form (and which were opposed to its function) it was ugly. People were still looking for the horse; they called cars 'horseless carriages'. When, because of the necessity of speed, the car was lowered and elongated and when, as a result, horizontal lines balanced by curves came to dominate, it became a perfect whole, logically organised for its function; it was beautiful. This definition of the relationship between beauty and utility in the car does not prove that functional perfection must lead to perfect beauty; I deny it until there is a conclusive demonstration of the contrary. I can't remember them, but I have seen frequent examples of the loss of beauty through the accentuation of function.

Chance alone governs the incidence of beauty in the manufactured object.

You may perhaps regret the loss of fantasy; but the geometrical austerity which could put you off is compensated for by the play of light on bare metal. Every machine-object possesses two material qualities: one, which is often painted and light absorbant, is fixed (architectural value) and the other (most frequently bare metal) which reflects light and fulfils the rôle of limitless fantasy (painterly value). Thus light is the determinant of the degree of variety in the machine-object. This quality of colour leads me to consider this second formal aspect of the machine, that is to say the arrival of polychrome mechanical architecture.

There, undoubtedly, we find ourselves confronted by the birth of an ill-defined but the nonetheless real formal taste; a *renaissance of the artisan* or, if you prefer, the birth of a new artisan.

The absolutely indispensable manufactured object did not need, from the functional or commercial point of view, to be coloured; it sold in any case, in response to an absolute need. *Before this occurrence, what do we see?* The decoration of useful objects has always existed to some degree, from the peasant who decorates the handle of his knife to the modern industries of 'decorative art'. The aim was and still is to create a hierarchy among objects, artistic and commercial plus-values in the quality of the object.

It is this area which is exploited by these productions of objects (decorative arts) with the intention of creating *objets de luxe* (which is a mistake in my opinion) and expanding the market by creating a hierarchy of objects. This has brought us to such decadence in the 'decorative object' (professional artists) that the few people who have sure and healthy taste are discouraged and turn naturally to the mass-produced objects, in white wood or rough metal, which are beautiful in themselves, or which they can work on or have worked according to their taste. *The polychromed machine object is a new beginning, a kind of renaissance of the primitive object.* The machine, I know, also creates ornaments itself; but being by its function condemned to work within the geometric order, I have more faith in it than in the longhaired gentleman with a floppy cravat intoxicated with his own personality and his own imagination.

The charm of colour works, and it cannot be overlooked; commercially and from the point of view of sales, the manufacturer knows this very well. It is so important that the question should be considered from this point of view: 'The reaction of the public in front of the object in question.' How does the public judge the object thus presented? Does it consider beauty or utility first? What is the order of its judgement? This is what I personally think: that the initial reaction to the manufactured object, particularly amongst the masses, frequently concerns its beauty. It is indisputable that a child makes aesthetic judgements, so much so that he puts the thing he likes in his mouth and wants to eat it to prove his desire to possess it. The young man says: 'The lovely bicycle', and only afterwards examines it from the point of view of usefulness. People say: 'the beautiful car', of the car which passes by and disappears (thus giving voice quite spontaneously to an aesthetic judgement which transcends professional aesthetic prejudice).

The manufacturer is aware of this quality and uses it more and more for his commercial ends. He has gone on from there to put colour on strictly utilitarian objects. We are now confronted by an unprecedented invasion of multicoloured utilitarian objects. Even agricultural machinery is becoming agreeable in character, decked out like a butterfly or a bird. Colour is such a vital necessity that it is reasserting its rights everywhere.

All these coloured objects compensate for the loss of colour which can be observed in modern dress. The old, highly colourful fashions have disappeared; contemporary clothing is grey and black. The machine is dressed up and becomes a spectacle and compensation. This observation leads us to envisage the *inherently beautiful* manufactured object as having a decorative value in the street. For, after the manufacturer who employs colour as a means to attract and sell, there is the retailer, the shopkeeper, the display artist who, in turn, arranges his window.

So we come to *the art of window display* which has assumed great importance over recent years. The street has become a permanent display of ever increasing intensity.

The window-display has become a major anxiety in the retailer's activities. Frantic competition reigns: to be seen more than the neighbouring shop is the compulsive desire which animates our streets. Can you doubt the extreme care that goes into this work?

My friend Maurice Raynal and I have witnessed these ant-like exertions, not on the main boulevards under the brilliance of arc lamps, but at the end of a dimly lit arcade.

The objects were modest (in the well known hierarchical sense of the word): *they were waistcoats* in a haberdasher's small display window. This man, this artisan, had seventeen waistcoats to display in his window, with as many cuff-links and neckties to go with them. He spent about eleven minutes on each. After the sixth we left, exhausted; we had been there for *an hour* in front of that man who, when he had adjusted these articles by one millimetre, would come out to see the effect. Each time he came out he was so absorbed that he did not see us. With the dexterity of a master of composition and arrangement he set up his display, with his brow wrinkled, his gaze fixed, as if his whole future depended on it. When I think of the sloppiness and lack of discipline in the work of certain artists, well known painters, whose pictures are sold at high prices, we should deeply admire this splendid artisan who carefully and conscientiously fashions his own work. It is more valuable than the other, which will disappear, and he will have to renew it in a few days with the same care and keenness. Amongst such men, these artisans, there is an undeniable concept of art which is closely linked to commercial ends, but is a formal phenomenon of a new order and the equal of any other existing artistic manifestations.

We find ourselves confronted by a thoroughly admirable renaissance, a world of artisan-creators who gladden our eyes and transform the street into a permanent and endlessly variable display. I can imagine the theatres emptying and disappearing, and people spending their time out of doors if there were no prejudices about *hierarchies in art*. On the day when the work of this world of workers is understood and appreciated by people who are free of prejudices, who have eyes to see, we will truly witness an extraordinary revolution. The false masters will fall from their pedestals, and values will at last be put in their proper place. *I repeat: there is no hierarchy* in art. A work is worth what it is worth in itself and it is impossible to establish a criterion. It is a question of taste and individual emotional capacity.

In the face of these artisans' achievements, what is the position of the so-called professional artist?

Before considering the position in question, I will allow myself a backward glance at a monstrous formal mistake which still weighs heavily on people's artistic judgement.

The arrival of mechanical beauty, of all these beautiful objects which have no pretension to art, justifies a quick revision of the traditional representational values classified as definitive.

The Italian Renaissance (the *Mona Lisa*, the sixteenth century) is considered by the whole world as an apogee, a summit, an ideal to strive for. The *raison-d'être* of the *Ecole des Beaux-Arts* is based entirely on servile imitation of that period; *it is the most colossal error possible*. The sixteenth century is a time of almost total decadence in all the visual arts.

It is the error of *imitation*, of servile copying of the subject, in opposition to the preceding so-called Primitive period which is great and immortal precisely because it invented its forms and means. The Renaissance took the means for the ends believing, moreover, in the beautiful subject. It thus combined two fundamental errors: the spirit of imitation and the copying of the *beautiful subject*.

The men of the Renaissance believed themselves superior to their predecessors, the Primitives; in imitating natural forms instead of inventing their equivalents, they complacently described the most exaggerated and theatrical gestures and actions of their time in their vast pictures. *They were victims of the beautiful subject. If a subject is beautiful*, a form is beautiful, it is an absolute value in itself, austere, intangible.

One does not imitate or copy a beautiful thing; one admires it, and that is all. At the very most one can, through one's talent, create an equivalent work.

It was the Renaissance, in ecstatically pursuing the beautiful subject, which engendered the kind of malady that is the Ecole des Beaux-Arts. They wanted something which is actually materially impossible. A beautiful object is uncopiable, unreproducible, in the scientific sense of the word. The banal experience of the thirty pupils in front of a beautiful object under the same light at the same time but all thirty of them producing different 'copies' is conclusive enough. Scientific methods such as casting or photography are not any better. Every manifestation of beauty, of whatever kind, contains within it an unknown quantity which will always be mysterious to the creator who, caught between his conscious and unconscious, is incapable of defining the boundaries of these two feelings: the objective and subjective collide continually, and interact in such a way that the result, which is the creation, always remains a partial enigma to the artist. *The beautiful machine* is the modern *beautiful subject* par excellence; it too is uncopiable.

Two producers are thus face to face: are they going to destroy each other? I believe that the need for beauty is more widespread than it seems. From childhood to the adult state, the demand for Beauty is considerable; three quarters of our daily gestures and hopes are activated by this desire. Here too the law of supply and demand functions; but, at the present time, the demand is addressed primarily to the *professional artist,* thanks to the prejudice which I have mentioned already, from which he benefits. This means that people are scarcely aware yet of all the beautiful artisan-made objects – because they are not the work of an 'artist'.

I have just been to see the display at the Paris Fair in which invention bubbles over at every step, and the effort to show off the quality of the execution is prodigious.

I was astonished to see that all these men who, for example, have arranged these splendid panels of free-standing pieces, these amazing fountains of letters and lights, these powerful or furious machines did not understand, did not feel that they were the true artists, that they have overturned all the modern formal principles. They are unaware of the formal quality they create, they do not realise it.

In such a case, ignorance is perhaps healthy, but it is truly a sad matter this disturbing question of the unconscious in artistic creation, and one which will continue to disturb the mystery seekers.

Let us suppose, all the same – as I suggested earlier – that this whole immense world of engineers, workmen, shopkeepers and display artists, became aware of the beauty that they make and amongst which they live. Their need for beauty would be almost satisfied: the peasant would be happy with his beautiful polychrome mechanical harvester and the salesman with his melody of neckties. *Why is it that these people go into ecstasies on Sundays over questionable pictures in the Louvre or elsewhere? Out of a thousand pictures are two beautiful? Of a hundred machine-made objects thirty are beautiful* and, beautiful and useful at the same time, they resolve the problem of Art.

The artisan regains his place, which he should always have kept, because he is the true creator. It is he who daily, modestly, unknowingly, creates and invents these pretty knick-knacks and beautiful machines which enable us to live. His unselfconsciousness saves him. The great majority of professional artists are despicable for their pride in individualism and their self-consciousness; they make everything barren. It is always in periods of decadence that people have observed the hideous hypertrophy of the individual amongst false artists (the Renaissance).

Take a tour around the *Salons de la Machine*; for the machine, like those gentlemen the artists, has its annual salons. Go and see the *Salon de l'Automobile, de l'Aviation, la Foire de Paris,* which are the most beautiful displays in the world. Look carefully at the work. Every time the execution is the work of an artisan it is good. Every time it is desecrated by a professional it is bad.

It should never be necessary for manufacturers to leave their own ground and address themselves to professional artists; *that is what causes all the trouble.* These splendid fellows believe that there is a category of demi-gods above them, who make marvellous things, much more beautiful than theirs, and exhibit these immortal *chefs d'oeuvre* annually at the *Salon des Artists Français,* the *Salon de la Nationale,* or elsewhere. They turn up at the private view in morning dress, and they humbly go into raptures in front of these imbeciles who are not worth tuppence in comparison to them.

If they could destroy the stupid prejudice, if they *knew that the most beautiful annual salons of plastic arts are their own,* they would have confidence in those admirable men who surround them, *the artisans,* and they would not go looking elsewhere for pretentious incompetents who massacre their work.

What definitive conclusion can be drawn from all this? That the artisan is everything? No. I think that above him there are a very few men who are capable of elevating their formal ideas to a level which would reach the first rank of Beauty.

Such men must be capable of considering the work of the artisan and that of nature as primary material, to be ordered, absorbed and fused completely in their brains with a perfect balance of the two values: the conscious and the unconscious, objective and subjective.

The life of plastic form is terribly dangerous; it is perpetually ambiguous. No criterion is possible; there is no arbitration panel to distinguish the indifferent from the beautiful.

The Impressionist painter Sisley, confronted with two of his paintings which were not quite identical, could not tell which was the fake. We must live and create in a constant turmoil, in this continual ambiguity. Those who deal in beautiful things are unaware of it. In this connection I will always remember one year when I was hanging pictures at the *Salon d'Automne,* and I had the advantage of being next to the *Salon de l'Aviation* which was about to open. Through the partition I could hear the hammers and the songs of the mechanics. I crossed the barrier and never, in spite of my familiarity with such displays, had I been so impressed. Never had such a stark contrast confronted me. I had left vast gloomy, grey surfaces, pretentiously framed, for beautiful, metallic objects, hard, permanent and useful, in pure local colours. Steel in infinite varieties played against vermilions and blues. The geometrical power of the forms dominated everything.

The mechanics saw me go by. They knew they had artists as neighbours and in their turn they asked my permission to go to the other side. And these good fellows who were decent and fine, brought up amongst beautiful raw materials, and who had never seen an exhibition of paintings in their lives, fell into ecstasies over work which I wouldn't rate.

I will always remember a lad of sixteen, with fiery red hair, with a new blue workjacket, orange trousers, one hand stained with Prussian blue paint, rapturously contemplating nudes in gilded frames.

Without the shadow of a doubt, in his modern workman's outfit, blazing with colour, he killed the whole Salon, leaving nothing more on the walls than vaporous shadows in old frames. This dazzling lad, who gave the impression that he had been fathered by an agricultural machine, was the symbol of the exhibition next door, of the life of tomorrow, when Prejudice will be destroyed.

---

50 Leon Trotsky, *Literature and Revolution, Tatlin's Monument,* 1924

As soon as a surplus will come after the most urgent and acute needs of life are covered, the Soviet state will take up the problem of gigantic constructions that will suitably express the monumental spirit of our epoch. Tatlin is undoubtedly right in discarding from his project national styles, allegorical sculpture, modelled monograms, flourishes and tails, and attempting to subordinate the entire design to a correct constructive use of material. This has been the way that machines, bridges and covered markets have been built, for a long time. But Tatlin has still to prove that he is right in what seems to be his own personal invention, a rotating cube, a pyramid and a cylinder all of glass. For good or bad, circumstances are going to give him plenty of time to find arguments for his side ...

The purpose of the main building is to make glass

headquarters for the meetings of the World Council of People's Commissars, for the Communist International, etc. But the props and the piles which are to support the glass cylinder and the pyramid – and they are there for no other purpose – are so cumbersome and heavy that they look like unremoved scaffolding. One cannot think what they are for. They say: they are there to support the rotating cylinder in which the meetings will take place. But one answers: Meetings are not necessarily held in a cylinder and the cylinder does not necessarily have to rotate. I remember seeing once when a child, a wooden temple built in a beer bottle. This fired my imagination, but I did not ask myself at that time what it was for. Tatlin proceeds by a reverse method; he wants to construct a beer bottle for the World Council of People's Commissars which would sit in a spiral concrete temple. But for the moment, I cannot refrain from the question: What is it for? To be more exact: we would probably accept the cylinder and its rotating, if it were combined with a simplicity and lightness of construction, that is, if the arrangements for its rotating did not depress the aim.

---

51 M. Szczuka and T. Zarnower, *What is Constructivism*? 1924

What is Constructivism?

1. Not any particular portion of art (e.g., a picture or poems) but art as a whole.

2. Not expressing one's personal experiences and moods, but looking for a *practical* application for the creative drive, flowing from the original instinct of art, displayed in every product of human labour.

3. Building of things by all available means, with the practical purpose of those things as the primary consideration.
It does not mean that the constructivist programme cancels disinterested creation in art.

4. A system of methodical collective work, controlled by a self-conscious will, aiming at the perfection of the results of the collectively attained results of work; and also inventiveness.

5. Mechanisation of the means of work.
Hand-made forms contain graphological biases, characteristic for individual artists; a mechanical performance offers an absolute objectivism of form.

6. Economic use of material.
Exactly as much material as is indispensable.

7. The properties of the created thing must *depend* upon the employed material.
Constructional merits of the material – the types of its surface – its colour – its different surface properties as dependent on the finish – its peculiarities when exposed to light etc.
T. van Doesburg said about colour as a property of building materials:

'New architecture uses colour (not painting), throws it into light, displays with it the changes of shapes and space. Without colour we would have no play of shapes. It is only by means of colour that we can attain a clear, optical balance and equilibrated integration of the particular parts in the new architectural style.

'To harmonise the while (in the sense of space and time, and not in the two dimensions) by colour – this is the task for a painter. In the subsequent stage of development, it will be possible to substitute a transformed material for colour (the task of chemistry) . . .

'Colour (it must be made clear to architects – enemies of colour) is not an ornament or embellishment – it is an essential element, organically belonging to architecture like glass and iron.'

8. Building of a thing according with its own principles.

9. Constructivism does not imitate the machine, but it finds its equivalent in the machine's simplicity and logic.

10. The problem of *construction*, rather than the problem of form.

11. Construction determines the form.
Form has its origin in construction.
Application of the achievements of technology to expand the range of opportunities.

12. To focus the creative effort in the first place upon architecture – cinema – printing and the so-called world of fashions.

13. The problems of health and convenience have been often held back by architects for aesthetic reasons – a constructivist constructor takes them up as the problems of primary importance.

To introduce art into life as a factor contributing to the general development and in its turn dependent upon the changes occuring in the other fields of human creative activity, mainly on technology.
The problems of art and the social problems are indivisible.

Constructivism does not aim at creating a style as an unchanging fixed pattern based upon forms once invented and accepted, but it takes up the problem of *construction* that may and must be subject to continuous changes and improvements, under the influence of the ever new and more complex requirements imposed by the general development.

---

52 Hugo Häring, *Approaches to Form,* 1925-6

The form of artefacts can be seen as derived partly from the needs of function and partly from those of expression. Factual demands conflict with aesthetic demands in the material medium as things take shape. The relative contribution and emphasis of these two influences varies according to the objects involved, and also with the materials, the epoch, the country and the culture. Functional demands tend to dominate expressive ones where functional performance is considered of paramount importance, while expressive demands come to the fore where function is less clearly defined. The buildings of everyday life: houses, ships, fortifications, bridges, canals, etc. have always been dominated by function, while our buildings for deities and for the dead have been left almost entirely to expression. The derivation of form from these two concerns explains our whole conflict in the choice of form, as functional forms do not always fulfil expressive needs and vice versa.

Forms which result from functional criteria are created by life, and are therefore of an elementary and natural kind, not originated by men; while forms chosen for the sake of expression derive from laws formed by the human intellect. Thus functionally-based forms, though they are continuously modified by external circumstances, are fundamentally eternal and universal because they are constantly regenerated by life; while forms created for the sake of expression are ephemeral and exposed to changes in human cognition. This means that on the one hand functional forms arise naturally and, so to speak, anonymously, while forms created for the sake of expression originate from a psychological constitution and are therefore to a large extent subjective and indefinable. In other words, functional forms are the same throughout the world and throughout history, while expressive forms are bound to 'Blut und Erkenntnis' (blood and knowledge) and thus dependent on time and place. The history of form is in reality merely the history of variations in expression.

There has been a great change in our attitude towards expression in the past decades. Under and during the reign of the geometrical culture, formal expression was derived from laws which were contrary to life, to the creation of life, to movement and to nature, laws recognised in purely geometrical forms. We have since discovered that purely functional things have forms which can satisfy us in terms of expression, and indeed some forms created solely out of functional necessity become more satisfying in terms of expression as they become functionally purer, and that this kind of expression resulted in a new aesthetic. We acknowledged the expressive qualities found in machines, ships, cars, aircraft and thousands of other objects and instruments. This discovery marks a turning point in the history of form.

We now attempt not to allow our attitudes towards function to conflict with our needs for expression, but to keep them side by side. We try to relate our ideas about expression to life creation, movement and nature, for in our creation of functional forms, we follow in the tracks of nature. In nature, form is the result of the organisation of many distinct parts in space in such a way that life can unfold, fulfilling all its effects both in terms of the single part and in terms of the integrated whole; whereas in the geometrical cultures form is derived from the laws of geometry.

If we prefer to search for shapes rather than to propose them, to discover forms rather than to construct them, we are in harmony with nature and act with her rather than against her. In this we are only asking for an attitude which we have long held in other spheres of life to be applied to the world of objects: so this change in our attitude to objects is not exceptional and confined to a narrow field, but part of a general change in the organisation of our spiritual life. Our change in the process of design and construction can therefore be seen as having its origins in this general change. We no longer take a motif on which we plan to base the form we create out of the geometrical world but take it instead from the world of organic forms, as we have seen that, in order to create for life, we must create as nature does, organically and not geometrically.

The motions of our spiritual life stem from this change in our attitude to organisation, and our new methods of planning are the result of new concepts. We need a plan in order to be able to organise things, and to form and build them. It is our concern to find such a plan, for the needs of what we build according to the plan must have been considered in the planning process. Plants do not grow under the control of circular geometry, but forms that are identical with circular geometry can be found in nature. For in nature all forms, including crystals and other geometrically shaped ones, are generated by specific internal forces, while in geometrical planning form is imposed from the outside, which is in opposition to its creation from within. Creativity in building results from a creative planning approach. If a man works without intellectual preconceptions about planning methods, and this in natural response to the situation, he is bound to act creatively and as nature does. In our geometrical culture, with our thirst for order and limited planning concepts, we are fertile in our planning only while we allow forms to unfold naturally, without the imposition of geometrical laws and without everything being forced into geometrical envelopes. Geometrical planning concepts give results which are economical and efficient, but destructive to life. In the geometrical cultures planned forms are eroded by the life which they contain. Thus triangles or squares give way to circles or rectangles, which further loosen towards the kind of shapes resulting from organic planning. We must realise that the moment we reject our intellectual preconceptions and act in the way that nature plans, we organise things in such a way that they develop a personality and serve life as a whole. This whole is the formal expression of contemporary life.

If we are searching for a means to generate new physical forms, we must first find a means of generating a new consciousness and a new society, since we are unable to determine the significance of a part while we cannot see the whole to which it belongs. If we feel that artefacts should be created in a way which is parallel to nature, society must also be predisposed towards nature and not against her.

We must discover things and let them unfold their own forms. It goes against the grain to impose a form, to determine it from outside, to force it according to abstract laws. We were as wrong in using them for historical demonstrations as we were in making them express our individual moods. And we were also wrong in bringing things back to geometrical or crystalloid basic forms because that is to exert force on them (as

Corbusier does). Basic figures are not original natural shapes for forms, they are abstract and derived from intellectual laws. The kind of unity which we construct on the basis of geometrical figures is for so many things merely a unity of form and not a unity with life, though we want unity with life and in life. A polished metal sphere appeals to us intellectually, but a flower is an emotional experience.

To impose geometrical forms is to make them uniform and mechanical, but we do not want things to be mechanical except in the way they are made. To mechanise things is to give them a mechanical life, a dead life, but to mechanise the process by which they are made is to win life.

The form things take can be identical with geometrical forms as it is in crystals, but in nature one never finds form to be geometrical in origin or in content. We are therefore, against the principles of Corbusier (but not against Corbusier).

We should not try to express our own individuality, but rather the individuality of things; their expression should be what they are.

---

53 Frederick Kiesler, *Manifesto,* 1925

Living buildings – city of space – functional architecture.

The new form of the city arises from necessity:

the country-city, because the separation of country and town is abolished

the time-city, because time is the dimension of its spatial organisation

the space-city, because it hovers freely in space, is decentralised into parts according to the terrain

the automatic city, because the daily routine of life is mechanised.

What more are our houses than stone coffins towering up from the ground into the sky? One storey high, two storeys – three hundred storeys high. Masonry rectangles and decagons? Entrenched coffins of stone, or wood, or clay, or concrete – with air-holes.

Churchyards have more aim for the skeletons of the dead than our cities have for the lungs of the living. Grass grows round each grave, a little greensward, a gravel path separating each from its neighbour. Each grave a green island. Each man his own master; each with his own settlement. Settlers take note!

And our cities? Walls, walls, walls.

Let us have no more walls, no more shutting up body and soul in barracks, this whole barrack-culture with or without decoration. What we want is:

Transformation of global space into cities

To release ourselves from the earth, abandonment of the static axis

No walls, no foundations

A system of tension in open space

The provision of new possibilities of living and thereby of requirements which will transform society.

Have we found a good bit of carrion? All sticking together in one place and sinking our teeth in there, and only there, searching and searching just on this one spot of earth on which this city of London, New York, Paris . . . is built? Piling up on top of one another. And we are afraid; and we all press against one another.

Are those really *your* questions? Whether the walls should be decorated or not? We have no time for such questions! Away with the walls, promoters and rank imitators, breathe in fresh air through your lungs and this question disappears! Bash *your* head against empty spaces! We must have something to laugh at!

Enough architecture has been created. We want no new edition, however cleverly it may be conceived. In place of older designs with one tarted-up front, new models with four smooth fronts; in place of baroque lines, straight lines; in place of rectangular windows, square windows. The expert is bankrupt. What really interests everyone is: how do we live within these straight or crooked walls; in what life – new life – do these quadruple or *x*-tuple fronts originate? In place of decoration, smooth walls; in place of art, architecture – away with all that: I demand *living building, the space-city, functional architecture.*

Building adequate to the elasticity of the functions of life. It is all one whether you put up domes over men, or cubes. Either way they suffocate. And your window-holes do not release them.

We must discover the impulses of the time, just as we discovered electricity, and must invent the new life as we invented the motor. Until then it is a process of material digestion.

The new city will bring the solution of the problem of traffic and hygiene; it will make possible diversity in private life and the freedom of the masses. It is not built just to satisfy, but to provide the greatest possible abundance from the strictest economy of means.

Houses that we put up over men while we tell them: Sleep well, eat well, take plenty of fresh air; houses in this sense will no longer exist, and with their disappearance the narrow streets will dissolve into free dwelling- and work-places.

You have always misunderstood: the riding-school has held up hoops for you, and, *allez-oop*, you have jumped through them; now it is a square. Tomorrow...?

Mind that the old horse you are riding does not bolt with you, so that your scent lies in the dirt.

---

54 Hannes Meyer, *The New World,* 1926

The flight of the *Norge* to the North Pole, the Zeiss planetarium at Jena and Flettner's rotor ship represent the latest stages to be reported in the mechanisation of our planet. Being the outcome of extreme precision in thought, they all provide striking evidence of the way in which science continues to permeate our environment. Thus in the diagram of the present age we find everywhere amidst the sinuous lines of its social and economic fields of force straight lines which are mechanical and scientific in origin. They are cogent evidence of the victory of man the thinker over amorphous nature. This new knowledge undermines and transforms existing values. It gives our new world its shape.

Motor cars dash along our streets. On a traffic island in the Champs Elysées from 6 to 8 p.m. there rages round one metropolitan dynamicism at its most strident. Ford and Rolls-Royce have burst open the core of the town, obliterating distance and effacing the boundaries between town and country. Aircraft slip through the air: Fokker and Farman widen our range of movement and the distance between us and the earth; they disregard national frontiers and bring nation closer to nation.

Illuminated signs twinkle, loud-speakers screech, posters advertise, display windows shine forth. The simultaneity of events enormously extends our concept of 'space and time', it enriches our life. We live faster and therefore longer. We have a keener sense of speed than ever before, and speed records are a direct gain for all. Gliding, parachute descents and music hall acrobatics refine our desire for balance. The precise division into hours of the time we spend working in office and factory and the split-minute timing of railway timetables make us live more consciously. With swimming pools, sanatoria and public lavatories, hygiene appears on the local scene and its water closets, faience washbowls and baths usher in the new line of sanitary fittings in earthenware. Fordson tractors and von Meyenburg cultivators have resulted in a shift of emphasis in land development and speeded up the tilling of the earth and the intensive cultivation of crops. Borrough's calculating machine sets free our brain, the dictaphone our hand, Ford's motor our place-bound senses and Handley Page our earthbound spirits. Radio, Marconigram and prototelegraphy liberate us from our national seclusion and make us part of a world community. The gramophone, microphone, orchestrion and pianola accustom our ears to the sound in impersonal-mechanised rhythms: His Master's Voice, Vox and Brunswick see to the musical needs of millions. Psychoanalysis has burst open the all too narrow dwelling of the soul and graphology has laid bare the character of the individual. Mazdaism, Coué and Die Schönheit are signs of the desire for reform breaking out everywhere. National costume is giving way to fashion and the external masculinisation of woman shows that inwardly the two sexes have equal rights. Biology, psychoanalysis, relativity and entomology are common intellectual property: France, Einstein, Freud and Fabre are the saints of this latterday. Our homes are more mobile than ever. Large blocks of flats, sleeping cars, house yachts and transatlantic lines undermine the local concept of the 'homeland'. The fatherland goes into a decline. We learn Esperanto. We become cosmopolitan.

The steadily increasing perfection attained in printing, photographic and cinematographic processes enables the real world to be reproduced with an ever greater degree of accuracy. The picture the landscape presents to the eye today is more diversified than ever before; hangars and power houses are the cathedrals of the spirit of the age. This picture has the power to influence through the specific shapes, colours and lights of its modern elements: the wireless aerials, the dams, the lattice girders: through the parabola of the airship, the triangle of the traffic signs, the circle of the railway signal, the rectangle of the billboard; through the linear element of transmission lines: telephone wires, overhead tram wires, high-tension cables; through radio towers, concrete posts, flashing lights and filling stations. Our children do not deign to look at a snorting steam locomotive but entrust themselves with cool confidence to the miracle of electric traction. G. Palucca's dances, von Laban's movement choirs and D. Mesendieck's functional gymnastics are driving out the aesthetic eroticism of the nude in painting. The stadium has carried the day against the art museum, and physical reality has taken the place of beautiful illusion. Sport merges the individual into the mass. Sport is becoming the university of collective feeling. Suzanne Lenglen's cancellation of a match disappoints hundreds of thousands, Breitensträter's defeat sends a shiver through hundreds of thousands. Hundreds of thousands follow Nurmi's race over 10,000 metres on the running track. The standardisation of our requirements is shown by: the bowler hat, bobbed hair, the tango, jazz, the Co-op product, the DIN standard size and Liebig's meat extract. The standardisation of mental fare is illustrated by the crowds going to see Harold Lloyd, Douglas Fairbanks and Jackie Coogan. Grock and the three Fratellini weld the masses – irrespective of class and racial differences – into a community with a common fate. Trade union, co-operative, Ltd., inc., cartel, trust and the League of Nations are the forms in which today's social conglomerations find expression, and the radio and the rotary press are their media of communication. Co-operation rules the world. The community rules the individual.

Each age demands its own form. It is our mission to give our new world a new shape with the means of today. But our knowledge of the past is a burden that weighs upon us, and inherent in our advanced education are impediments tragically barring our new paths. The unqualified affirmation of the present age presupposes the ruthless denial of the past. The ancient institutions of the old – the classical grammar schools and the academies – are growing obsolete. The municipal theatres and the museums are deserted. The jittery helplessness of applied arts is proverbial. In their place, unburdened by classical airs and graces, by an artistic confusion of ideas or the trimmings of applied art, the witnesses of a new era are arising: industrial fairs, grain silos, music halls, airports, office chairs, standard goods. All these things are the product of a formula: function multiplied by economics. They are not works of art. Art is composition, purpose is function. The composition of a dock seems to us a nonsensical idea, but the composition of a town plan, a block of flats ...? Building is a technical not an aesthetic process, artistic composition does not rhyme with the function of a house matched to its purpose. Ideally and in its elementary design our house is a living machine. Retention of heat, insulation, natural and artificial lighting, hygiene, weather protection, car maintenance, cooking, radio, maximum possible relief for the housewife, sexual and family life, etc. are the determining lines of force. The house is their component. (Snugness and prestige are not leitmotifs of the dwelling house: the first resides in the human heart and not in the Persian carpet, the second in the attitude of the house-owner and not on the wall of the room!) Today we have new building materials at our disposal for building a house: aluminium and duralium in plates, rods and bars, Euboölith, Ruberoid, Forfoleum, Eternit, rolled glass, Triplex sheets, reinforced concrete, glass bricks, faience, steel frames, concrete frame slabs and pillars, Trolith, Galalith, Cellon Goudron, Ripolin, indanthrene paints, etc. We organise these building elements into a constructive unity in accordance with the purpose of the building and economic principles. Architecture has ceased to be an agency continuing the growth of tradition or an embodiment of emotion.

Individual form, building mass, natural colour of material and surface texture come into being automatically and this functional conception of building in all its aspects leads to pure construction. Pure construction is the characteristic feature of the new world of forms. Constructive form is not peculiar to any country; it is cosmopolitan and the expression of an international philosophy of building. Internationality is a prerogative of our time.

Today every phase of our culture of expression is predominantly constructive. Human inertia being what it is, it is not surprising that such an approach is to be found most clearly at first where the Greeks and Louis XIV have never set foot: in advertising, in typographical mechanical composition, in the cinema, in photographic processes. The modern poster presents lettering and product or trademark conspicuously arranged. It is not a poster work of art but a piece of visual sensationalism. In the display window of today psychological capital is made of the tensions between modern materials with the aid of lighting. It is display window organisation rather than window dressing. It appeals to the finely distinguishing sense of materials found in modern man and covers the gamut of its expressive power: fortissimo = tennis shoes to Havana cigarettes to scouring soap to nut chocolate! Mezzoforte = glass (as a bottle) to wood (as a packing case) to pasteboard (as packing) to tin (as a can)! Pianissimo = silk pyjamas to cambric shirts to Valenciennes lace to 'L'Origan de Coty'!

In Esperanto we construct a supranational language according to the law of least resistance in standard shorthand, a script with no tradition. The constructive mode of thought is most urgently needed in town planning. Unless we approach problems of town planning with the same impartiality as the factory engineer, we shall throttle the social life of the modern city through monument worship and uncritically accepted ideas about street axes and viewing points. The city is the most complex biological agglomeration, and it must be consciously regulated and constructively shaped by man. The demands we make on life today are all of the same nature depending on social stratification. The surest sign of true community is the satisfaction of the same needs by the same means. The upshot of such a collective demand is the standard product. The folding chair, roll-top desk, light bulb, bath tub and portable gramophone are typical standard products manufactured internationally and showing a uniform design. They are apparatus in the mechanisation of our daily life. They are manufactured in quantity as a mass-produced article, as a mass-produced device, as a mass-produced structural element, as a mass-produced house. The standard mental product is called a 'hit'. Because of the standardisation of his needs as regards housing, food and mental sustenance, the semi-nomad of our modern productive system has the benefit of freedom of movement, economies, simplification and relaxation, all of which are vitally important to him. The degree of our standardisation is an index of our communal productive system.

Art has an undisputed right to exist provided the speculative spirit of mankind has need of it after the graphic-coloured, plastic-constructive, musical-kinetic overthrow of its philosophy of life. This new creative work can only be done on the basis of our time and with the means of our time. Yesterday is dead; Bohemia is dead. Dead are atmosphere, colour values, burr, mellow tones and random brush-strokes. Dead the novel: we have neither the suspension of disbelief nor the time to read. Dead picture and sculpture as images of the real world: in the age of films and photos they are a dissipation of effort and the endless 'beautification' of our real world through the interpretations of 'artists' is presumptious. Dead is the work of art as a 'thing in itself' as 'art for art's sake': our communal consciousness will not tolerate any individualistic excesses.

The artist's studio has become a scientific and technical laboratory, and his works are the fruit of incisive thinking and inventive genius. Like any product of its time, the work of art today is subject to the living conditions of our age, and the result of our speculative dialogue with the world can only be set down in a precise form. The new work of art is a totality, not an excerpt, not an impression. The new work of art is an elemental creation made by primary means ... The new work of art is a work for all, not a collector's piece or the privilege of a single individual.

The revolution in our attitude of mind to the reorganisation of our world calls for a change in our media of expression. Today is ousting yesterday in material, form and tools. Instead of the random blow with an axe, we have the chain mortiser. Instead of the scumbled line of the charcoal pencil, we have the clean-cut line produced with the T-square, instead of easel-work, we have the drafting machine. Instead of the French horn, the saxophone. Instead of a copy of light reflections, we use light itself to create with (as a photograph, a light organ, projected cinematography, picture photography). Instead of the sculptural imitation of movement, we have movement itself (the synchronised film, illuminated advertising, gymnastics, eurhythmics, dancing). Instead of lyrics, we have the sound poem. Instead of the novel, the short story. Instead of colour tone, we have value of the colour in luxes. Instead of sculpture, we have construction. Instead of caricature, photosculpture. Instead of drama, the sketch. Instead of opera, the revue. Instead of frescoes, the poster. Instead of painted material, the colour of the material itself.('Painting without a brush' in itself calls for picture construction for manual reasons). The nine muses were long ago abducted by practical men and have stepped down again into life from their high pedestals, more humdrum and more reasonable. Their fields have been expropriated, confused and blurred. The boundaries between painting, mathematics and music can no longer be defined; and between sound and colour there is only the gradual difference of oscillatory frequency. The depreciation of all works of art is indisputable, and there can be no question that the continued utilisation of new and exact knowledge in their place is merely a matter of time. The art of felt imitation is in the process of being dismantled. Art is becoming invention and controlled reality.

And personality? The heart?? The soul??? Our plea is for absolute segregation. Let the three be relegated to their own peculiar fields: the love urge, the enjoyment of nature, and social relations.

---

55 Kasimir Malevich, *Suprematist Architecture,* 1927

The architect looks with regret upon the unavoidable necessity of fulfilling a purpose and ardently seeks to combine within himself the engineer and the artist, in order to unite in every task the 'attractive with the useful' (the engineer would only pay attention to 'usefulness'). This fusion became his primary task. Yes, he is even convinced that architecture free of purpose does not exist. Looking back in history, however, he would realise that his art lives on as a mark of beauty, and that it is pure form. Also, those monuments of architecture which are free of any purpose are held in great esteem. From this I draw the conclusion that architecture is basically a pure art form (architectonic) and that God's Kingdom on Earth resides in this pure form, which we can only observe, but cannot 'use' for any purposes because that which serves a function cannot have originated in God's Kingdom on Earth or in Heaven. And therefore no 'matter-of-factness' (*Sachlichkeit*) can offer us what art does. The most *sachlich* engines, telegraph, and radio apparatuses do not help us to reach the Promised Land.

In my Suprematist architecture I see the beginnings of a new Classic art of building, an art which, since time immemorial, has created 'beauty' solely.

Art always presents the present in all the past and future.

Three

The search for form

Unlike the extracts in Part 1, which emphasised the importance of tradition and reasonable common sense as guide-lines for architects and designers, and unlike those in Part 2 which were so far removed from the actual practice of building that they have to be labelled 'visionary' or 'artistic', the extracts in this section are not only committed to a complete change of direction to what went before, but also linked directly to the actual business of building. The mature aesthetic of the International Style accepted space as the prime creative ingredient for the modern architect and R. M. Schindler was ahead of his time in recognising this quality (56), though Muthesius also showed himself keenly aware of the possibilities of the aesthetic of insubstantial but spatially exciting forms, such as the wire-spoked bicycle wheel (57). Transparency and the opening out of the structure were therefore also crucial (77, 79, 88, 93). There is a good deal of speculation about the relationship between functional efficiency and beauty and it is important to realise how few theorists tried to make a direct equation between the two. On the contrary most writers followed Muthesius (57) in distinguishing between technical efficiency, which may sometimes lead to beautiful forms through the refining process of calculation and resistance to stress, and the extra artistic creativity which has to be added by the artist or architect to turn the efficient into the beautiful. Kurt Ewald describes how the forms of machines themselves develop progressively towards beautiful solutions only after the pioneering stages, of solving the functional problems, are over (72) and Gropius, Taut and Riezler provide different slants of their own (73, 86, 89). Rietveld, Blomfield and Schindler in very different ways, all point to fallacies in the mechanical concept of beauty (83, 91, 93).

Otherwise, there is a surprising cohesion in the views of the main protagonists of the Modern Movement between 1923 and 1932, split mainly by one great divide, that which separated Walter Gropius and Hannes Meyer at the Bauhaus (59, 74, 87). This conflict was really about the rôle of the artist in society, which Meyer felt should be directly related to economic and political awareness, while Gropius wanted to preserve an element of isolation for the artist, in which to create. Thus, despite the general reaction against the crafts, in their Arts and Crafts clothing, there was a continual interest in personal expression whether in art or craft at the Bauhaus and elsewhere (59, 60, 61, 71, 75, 76). A staple of almost all International Style thinking was that all architecture should be aiming towards mass housing, directly related to the new social conditions (58, 59, 60, 64, 65, 81, 83, 87, 89, 92). Part 4 will deal with this kind of material more consistently, but it finds its way into every aspect of the Modern Movement's thinking. There is almost complete agreement, too, that the architect should compose with 'elemental', or 'elementary' forms, that is, those which lie 'objectively' at the basis of all human aesthetic responses, and have the least possible frills or individual eccentricity about them. Of course, to outsiders, these forms looked as romantic and as wilful as the eclectic horrors everyone disliked (62, 91). There is a general belief among the modernists, that standardisation would provide the key to a whole new range of industrial processes and materials within the reach of the architect (58, 65, 66, 68) while still allowing scope for the creation of good forms. There is a pretty widely shared belief in Internationalism as evidence and guarantee of the spread of the Modern Movement and also a strong reaction among the traditionalists (59, 62, 77, 79, 81, 91). As a guide to the material in this section, Breuer (92) gives a retrospective account of the beliefs of the period which is extremely valuable for its measured views and can be compared to the equally exhaustive but more committed analyses of Gropius (59) and Schlemmer (60) who, between them, sum up most of the early views held by the German founders of the International Style. Ginzburg also gives a summary of the progress of the International movement (81). It is interesting to see how many of the ideas in Part 3 are in fact developments from Arts and Crafts principles in Part 1, mixed with the idealism of those in Part 2.

56 R. M. Schindler, *A Manifesto,* 1912

1.

The cave was the original dwelling.
A hollow adobe pile was the first permanent house.
To build meant to gather and mass material, allowing it to form empty cells for human shelter.

This conception provides the basis for understanding all styles of architecture up to the twentieth century.
The aim of all architectural effort was the conquest of structural bulk by man's will for expressive form.

All architectural ideas were conditioned by the use of a plastic structural mass material.
The technique of architect and sculptor were similar.
The vault was not the result of a room conception, but of a structural system of piling masonry to support the mass enclosure. The decoration of the walls was intended to give the structural mass a plastic face.

These old problems have been solved and the styles are dead.

Our efficient way of using materials eliminated the plastic structural mass. The contemporary architect conceives the 'room' and forms it with ceiling and wall slabs.

The architectural design concerns itself with 'space' as its raw material and with the articulated room as its product.

Because of the lack of a plastic mass the shape of the inner room defines the exterior of the building. Therefore the early primitive product of this new development is the 'box-shaped' house.

The architect has finally discovered the medium of his art: *Space.*

A new architectural problem has been born. Its infancy is being shielded as always by emphasising functional advantages.

2.

The first house was a shelter.
Its primary attribute was stability. Therefore its structural features were paramount.
All architectural styles up to the twentieth century were functional.

Architectural forms symbolised the structural functions of the building material.
The final step in this development was the architectural solution of the steel skeleton: its framework is no longer a symbol, it has become form itself.

The twentieth century is the first to abandon construction as a source for architectural form through the introduction of reinforced concrete.

The structural problem has been reduced to an equation. The approved stress diagram eliminates the need to emphasise the stability of the construction.

Modern man pays no attention to structural members.
There are no more columns with base, shaft and cap, no more wall masses with foundation course and cornice.
He sees the daring of the cantilever, the freedom of the wide span, the space-forming surfaces of thin wall screens.

Structural styles are obsolete.
Functionalism is a hollow slogan used to lead the conservative stylist to exploit contemporary techniques.

3.

Monumentality is the mark of power.
The first master was the tyrant.
He symbolised his power over the human mass by his control over matter.
The power symbol of primitive culture was confined to the defeat of two simple resistances of matter: gravity and cohesion.

Monumentality became apparent in proportion to the human mass displacement effort.
Man cowers before an early might.

Today a different power is asking for its monument.
The mind destroyed the power of the tyrant.
The machine has become the ripe symbol for man's control over nature's forces.
Our mathematical victory over structural stresses eliminates them as a source of art forms.
The new monumentality of space will symbolise the limitless power of the human mind.
Man trembles facing the universe.

4.

The feeling of security of our ancestor came in the seclusion and confinement of his cave.

The same feeling of security was the aim of the medieval city plan which crowded the largest possible number of defenders inside the smallest ring of walls and bastions.
The peasant's hut comforts him by an atmosphere in violent contrast to his enemy: the out of doors.

Rooms that are designed to recall such feelings of security out of our past are acclaimed as 'comfortable and cosy'.

The man of the future does not try to escape the elements.
He will rule them.

His home is no more a timid retreat: The earth has become his home.

The concepts 'comfortable' and 'homey' change their meaning.
Atavistic security feelings fail to recommend conventional designs.

The comfort of the dwelling lies in its complete control of: space, climate, light, mood, within its confines.

The modern dwelling will not freeze temporary whims of owner or designer into permanent tiresome features.

It will be a quiet, flexible background for a harmonious life.

57 Hermann Muthesius, *The Problem of Form in Engineering,* 1913

The most recent period of technical design differed from all previous periods in that there was a duality of approach, which depended upon whether a design was to be treated and judged as something 'useful' or as something 'beautiful'. Useful design was the province of the engineer, beautiful that of the architect. No beauty was expected from the useful; on the contrary, it was an established principle that an engineer's constructions must by their very nature be ugly. In cases where it was thought necessary to eliminate this ugliness the architect was called in to devise some sort of masking. The so-called 'aesthetic improvement' of engineering buildings has been with us for a long time, and what was nearly always meant by this was the elevation of an engineering building to the land of art by the application of 'architectonic' or 'ornamental' features.

But for the great majority of engineering buildings the assistance of the architect–embellisher was not called upon. It was considered that they were simply functional buildings, and that was excuse enough for their ugliness. It was also, allegedly, a question of cost, and the money for embellishment was not available in projects working on a tight budget. So workshops and warehouses were built as temporary structures in whatever haphazard form decreed by the cheapest method. Factories got the usual zigzag roof shape; water towers and windmills loomed into the air with grotesque outlines, quite uncriticised from any point of view of taste; iron bridges spanned rivers in hard lines. This was the situation of functional (utilitarian) buildings designed solely by the engineer; and for decades it was regarded as an entirely natural state of affairs.

The history of human technology shows, step by step, that though the invention of new devices proceeds relatively fast and with apparent ease, men have always found it very hard to arrive at the definitive form for these new creations. Dilemma and perplexity constantly arise. Usually the first solution is to clothe it in the familiar form of some earlier similar object. The first railway trains were mail coaches put on rails, the first steamers were sailing ships with steam engines built in, the first gas-jets for chandeliers imitated wax candles.

Consider what a difference there is between the first imitation mail-coach and the express train of today, and what a striking form today's ocean liner has developed, compared with the old sailing ship. But in both cases it has taken the work of generations to get to that form which today we regard as self evident and as expressing the essence of the object.

The Gothic flywheels and the Doric beams of the first machines were only stopgap solutions to a dilemma. Here too the inappropriateness of these forms was soon recognised; people began to phase out these borrowings from old art, and to develop forms inherent in the thing itself. This occurred through the elimination of all ornament and the return to the so-called pure functional form. Perhaps they did not suspect at that time that the fulfilment of pure function by itself does not create a form satisfactory to the eye, nor that it is essential that other factors must contribute to the design, perhaps unconsciously. At any rate, the first product of engineering to develop to a pure style was the machine, which by the beginning of the present century was so perfected that it was customary to admire the so-called beauty of the machine, and to see in it to some degree the most striking representative of the growth of a modern style. In recent thinking about art in the last ten years, the beauty of the machine has played an important rôle, usually coupled with thoughts about pure functional form.

Developments in wrought iron construction have run somewhat differently. At the start decorative ornamentation was attempted; this was soon abandoned, but without such clarified relationships being achieved as was the case in machine construction. The engineer more or less gave up trying to treat common problems of construction from the point of view of tastefully refined form. There was certainly an extraordinary amount of building going on: the railway bridges, viaducts and stations which the new age needed were practically all built of wrought iron; but only in exceptional cases was it considered necessary to do anything about appearances, and in these cases it was usually the abovementioned masking with façade features borrowed from earlier architecture. Aesthetic theory contributed to the strengthening of this prevalent error by condemning wrought iron lattice constructions as an artistic dead end; Gottfried Semper pronounced on iron construction that anyone thinking of taking an interest in it will 'hit upon an infertile ground for art'. There can be no question, he continued, of a monumental wrought and cast iron style, for the ideal of such a style would be invisible architecture; the thinner the metal web, the more perfect it is in its own way. This damning dismissal by Semper has since then been taken up in various guises by many theoreticians. Almost always they come to the conclusion that iron is too thin to create aesthetic effects – a judgement that is based on the assumption that massiveness is a necessary component of aesthetic effect. Clearly there is a false conclusion here, in that an ideal based on customary usage has been taken to be absolute. This has happened because previous generations built in materials that did have massiveness, such as wood and stone; if they had had thin metal bars at their disposal, then slenderness would today probably be taken as the normal and the ideal, and massiveness would be judged unaesthetic. We should not forget that in our aesthetic values custom plays an inordinately large part. Remember how absurd the first bicycle seemed to us with its wire spokes and its pneumatic tyres. Nobody thinks them abnormal today; in fact the very slimness of the spokes gives us an impression of delicacy and elegance. Moreover, it is by no means true that up till now only massiveness has produced aesthetically successful results. In earlier technical construction the relationship of strength to size was determined by the material used. In antiquity beside the compact temples built of stone blocks we find fine-limbed metal constructions, like the most delicate bronze candelabra and metal furnishings from Pompeii.

Some people might maintain that true architecture is concerned with the enclosure of inner spaces, and that as such enclosure demands massive walls, the roof of a hall or large space made of iron with a glass covering could in no way be regarded as aesthetically pleasing. But this too is an historical error. For the ideal of High Gothic was to eliminate wall surfaces almost completely and to give the supports an undreamt-of slenderness. The immense spaces between these thin ribs of the construction were filled with glass, like the modern hall roof; but of course that age which was so rich in artistic potential knew how to produce an aesthetically effective element from those glass walls – the stained glass window.

Appliances and equipment have of course nothing to do with the enclosure of space, but the way they are shaped must also be regarded from the point of view of form, i.e., the effect they will have on the eye. This is principally the province of the engineer, who creates tools and machines to make work easier, and fashions bridges, railways, and vehicles for traffic, and weapons for war. To condemn a delicate and slender form as artistically unworkable for appliances and tools must appear as sheer nonsense. On the contrary, we admire a fine surgical instrument because of its elegance, a vehicle because of its pleasing lightness, a wrought-iron bridge soaring over a river because of its bold use of the material. And we are right to do so, for in the muscularity of those slim parts we confirm the triumph of technology which has risen to the limits of mastery of material. So the slenderness of iron in no way hinders or restricts the aesthetic effects of the engineer's creations. The general direction of aesthetic speculation is therefore quite mistaken here.

In any case, it is not the job of aesthetics to make predictions. Almost whenever it has tried it, it has gone wrong. The task of aesthetics is to record and classify, to draw conclusions *a posteriori*, not *a priori*. It is never in a position to shackle the restless progress (of creativity) by laying down laws about future development. Development advances into the undefined, and the task of aesthetics is merely to trace retrospectively the path it has taken.

All assumptions about the artistic effect of the engineer's work, however, function on the proviso – and here we are getting to the heart of the matter – that artistic feeling is embodied within it. This proposition may sound self evident, but it must be emphasised. The idea that it is quite sufficient for the engineer designing a building, an appliance, a machine, merely to fulfil a purpose, is erroneous; and the recent often-repeated suggestion that if the object fulfils its purpose then it is beautiful as well is even more erroneous. Usefulness has basically nothing to do with beauty. Beauty is a problem of form, and nothing else; usefulness is the plain fulfilment of a purpose. A beautiful object can of course also be useful, and a useful one beautiful. But the determining factor for our object is the principle that beauty need not hamper usefulness. To combine the beautiful with the useful, and indeed to achieve the most complete possible satisfaction of both demands, is, as is known, the essential task of architecture. But it would be quite wrong to assume that this task does not exist outside architecture. On the contrary, one must generalise completely and assert that the whole of mankind's activity, in toolmaking, in building, in construction design, in fact all his visible activities, is subject in a general sense to the same principle that architecture in particular must obey, namely, the combining of the useful and the beautiful.

From this point of view the question whether engineering buildings can, should or must have an aesthetically beautiful effect, can be seen in quite a different light. The demand for an aesthetically acceptable effect becomes a foregone conclusion. Indeed, one must ask oneself in astonishment how there could ever have been a time when one deliberately dared to call good form dispensable. The engineer who did this would be denying one of the fundamental laws of human activity; he would be acting inhumanly and unnaturally. Since they are part of the whole of human creation, the engineer's buildings are subject to those same laws with which other things, some of them far less important, comply. Their great significance in modern architecture, their important part in the shaping of our countryside and towns, their enormous economic value, all these factors make it imperative that the design of such buildings take into account the principle of good form.

The development so far of engineering building, where it has taken place free of the architect's false cosmetic work, shows us, moreover, that a degree of purification in the direction of good form has already taken place. A large number of engineering works, bridges, stations, lighthouses, silos, are aesthetically effective, irrespective of whether the designers' feeling for beauty has played a subconscious part and exerted an influence beyond the slide rule, or whether this or that particular architect has consciously striven for and achieved good form.

---

58 J. J. P. Oud, *Architecture and Standardisation in Mass Construction,* 1918

The nature of architecture is determined not only by factors which may be described as spiritual, but also very much by social and technical factors. More than any other art form, architecture has its roots in human society and depends on social considerations, even in its most individual expression.

The idea of inner balance and perfection is much more meaningful when applied to the art of painting, for instance, than when applied to architecture, which is prevented from achieving this inner balance by its dependence on the dualism of necessity and beauty. Architecture is a balancing of purely architectural and utilitarian factors, and any evaluation of it from an aesthetic point of view must presuppose this compromise ...

This is why the question arises as to whether architecture is a true art-form or not.

It has to be admitted that, on purely aesthetic grounds, architecture is restricted in its possibilities in such a way that the degree of pure expression which can be achieved through it is limited. Purity of expression in architecture can only be increased when the aesthetic and utilitarian factors come to resemble each other as closely as possible, thus making it less necessary to adjust one in relation to the other ...

One thing is certain; the aesthetic of modern buildings will not be based on the buildings of the past: they will be shaped by the essential characteristics of modern society and technology, and will therefore be completely different from those of any previous period.

The modern architect must therefore be technically knowledgeable (or at least have a clear understanding of modern building technique) and have a very broad awareness of social factors ...

Traditionally (or for as long as we can remember), every architect has been allowed to design his own doors and windows for himself – a right which he will not lightly give up. Where the building of private houses is concerned, he can go on enjoying this privilege; but in the case of mass construction the growth of industrial methods in our time demands that the criteria for the building of private dwellings be set aside. The problems of mass construction must be examined with an open mind, avoiding the reinterpretation of existing forms and searching instead for designs based on a real understanding of the task. Architectural possibilities will be opened up in a way which has not happened for a very long time. If aesthetic considerations are also taken into account in the design of standardised buildings, then a truly monumental style of architecture can be evolved.

The design of standard types of buildings will bring back the proportions and rhythms of a town which are so lacking in the present-day townscape. The artist–architect must, however, take great care not to become ruled by his observance of these ideal proportions and types.

Much will depend on how far standardisation goes: whether it will be the mere definition of standard types (trade standards) of doors, windows, etc., or whether it will mean the design of complete standard house types. But however far standardisation goes, it will always be possible to create beauty by the grouping of building blocks, doors, windows or whole houses to create contrasts of proportions and ratios. And this does not even take into account the possibility of introducing (where it is economically possible) decorative materials such as brick, so that textured surfaces can be alternated with plain ones in double or triple strip patterns, while still retaining the total effect of mass. This is the outcome of modern production methods, which have already been accepted unwillingly by their private builder and which have extended their influence to luxury products, such as metal-framed windows and stair-rails. The architect who has had to build blocks of dwellings has also turned to standard trade models for mantel-pieces, wall-coverings, parquet floors, wall-tiles, sanitation installations, etc., out of pure economic expediency.

If the acceptance of the mass-produced product is completely in keeping with the spirit of the present time, as far as architecture is concerned, it comes at exactly the right psychological moment. The anarchy in the construction industry – brought about both by a lack of aestheticism and by too great a concern with aesthetics – will be limited by the truly aesthetic use of the mass-produced product. The architect acts as a theatrical director, stage-managing mass-products into an architectural whole, creating an art of proportions. The lust for aesthetic excess, on the other hand, can be satisfied in the design of private houses.

59 Walter Gropius, *The Theory and organisation of the Bauhaus,* 1923

The dominant spirit of our epoch is already recognisable although its form is not yet clearly defined. The old dualistic world-concept which envisaged the ego in opposition to the universe is rapidly losing ground. In its place is rising the idea of a universal unity in which all opposing forces exist in a state of absolute balance. This dawning recognition of the essential oneness of all things and their appearances endows creative effort with a fundamental inner meaning. No longer can anything exist in isolation. We perceive every form as the embodiment of an idea, every piece of work as a manifestation of our innermost selves. Only work which is the product of inner compulsion can have spiritual meaning. Mechanised work is lifeless, proper only to the lifeless machine. So long, however, as machine-economy remains an end in itself rather than a means of freeing the intellect from the burden of mechanical labour, the individual will remain enslaved and society will remain disordered. The solution depends on a change in the individual's attitude towards his work, not on the betterment of his outward circumstances, and the acceptance of this new principle is of decisive importance for new creative work.

The character of an epoch is epitomised in its buildings. In them, its spiritual and material resources find concrete expression, and, in consequence, the buildings themselves offer irrefutable evidence of inner order or inner confusion. A vital architectural spirit, rooted in the entire life of a people, represents the interrelation of all phases of creative effort, all arts, all techniques. Architecture today has forfeited its status as a unifying art. It has become mere scholarship. Its utter confusion mirrors an uprooted world which has lost the common will necessary for all correlated effort.

New structural elements develop very slowly, for the evolution of architectural form is dependent not only upon an immense expenditure of technical and material resources, but also upon the emergence of new philosophical concepts deriving from a series of intuitive perceptions. The evolution of form, therefore, lags far behind the ideas which engender it.

The art of architecture is dependent upon the co-operation of many individuals, whose work reflects the attitude of the entire community. In contrast, certain other arts reflect only narrow sections of life. The art of architecture and its many branches should be not a luxury, but the life-long preoccupation of a whole people. The widespread view that art is a luxury is a corruption born of the spirit of yesterday, which isolated artistic phenomena (*l'art pour l'art*) and thus deprived them of vitality. At the very outset the new architectural spirit demands new conditions for all creative effort.

The tool of the spirit of yesterday was the 'academy'. It shut off the artist from the world of industry and handicraft, and thus brought about his complete isolation from the community. In vital epochs, on the other hand, the artist enriched all the arts and crafts of a community because he had a part in its vocational life, and because he acquired through actual practice as much adeptness and understanding as any other worker who began at the bottom and worked his way up. But lately the artist has been misled by the fatal and arrogant fallacy, fostered by the state, that art is a profession which can be mastered by study. Schooling alone can never produce art! Whether the finished product is an exercise in ingenuity or a work of art depends on the talent of the individual who creates it. This quality cannot be taught and cannot be learned. On the other hand, manual dexterity and the thorough knowledge which is a necessary foundation for all creative effort, whether the workman's or the artist's, can be taught and learned.

Academic training, however, brought about the development of a great art-proletariat destined to social misery . . .

Since the academy trained a myriad of minor talents in drawing and painting, of whom scarcely one in a thousand became a genuine architect or painter, the great mass of these individuals, fed upon false hopes and trained as one-sided academicians, was condemned to a life of fruitless artistic activity ...

Meanwhile, the crafts – and more especially the industries – began to cast about for artists. A demand arose for products outwardly attractive as well as technically and economically acceptable. The technicians could not satisfy it. So manufacturers started to buy so-called 'artistic designs'. This was an ineffective substitute, for the artist was too much removed from the world about him and too little schooled in technique and handicraft to adjust his conceptions of form to the practical processes of production. At the same time, the merchants and technicians lacked the insight to realise that appearance, efficiency and expense could be simultaneously controlled only by planning and producing the industrial object with the careful cooperation of the artist responsible for its design. Since there was a dearth of artists adequately trained for such work, it was logical to establish the following basic requirements for the future training of all gifted individuals: *a thorough practical, manual training in workshops actively engaged in production, coupled with sound theoretical instruction in the laws of design.*

The objective of all creative effort in the visual arts is to give form to space. But what is space, how can it be understood and given a form?

Although we may achieve an awareness of the infinite we can give form to space only with finite means. We become aware of space through our undivided Ego, through the simultaneous activity of soul, mind and body. A like concentration of all our forces is necessary to give it form. Through his intuition, through his metaphysical powers, man discovers the immaterial space of inward vision and inspiration. This conception of space demands realisation in the material world, a realisation which is accomplished by the brain and the hands.

The brain conceives of mathematical space in terms of numbers and dimensions. *The hand masters matter* through the crafts, and with the help of tools and machinery.

Conception and visualisation are always simultaneous. Only the individual's capacity to feel, to know and to execute varies in degree and in speed. True creative work can be done only by the man whose knowledge and mastery of the physical laws of statics, dynamics, optics and acoustics equip him to give life and shape to his inner vision. In a work of art the laws of the physical world, the intellectual world and the world of the spirit function and are expressed simultaneously.

Every factor that must be considered in an educational system which is to produce actively creative human beings is implicit in such an analysis of the creative process. At the State Bauhaus at Weimar the attempt was made for the first time to incorporate all these factors in a consistent programme ...

The guiding principle of the Bauhaus was therefore the idea of creating a new unity through the welding together of many 'arts' and movements: a unity having

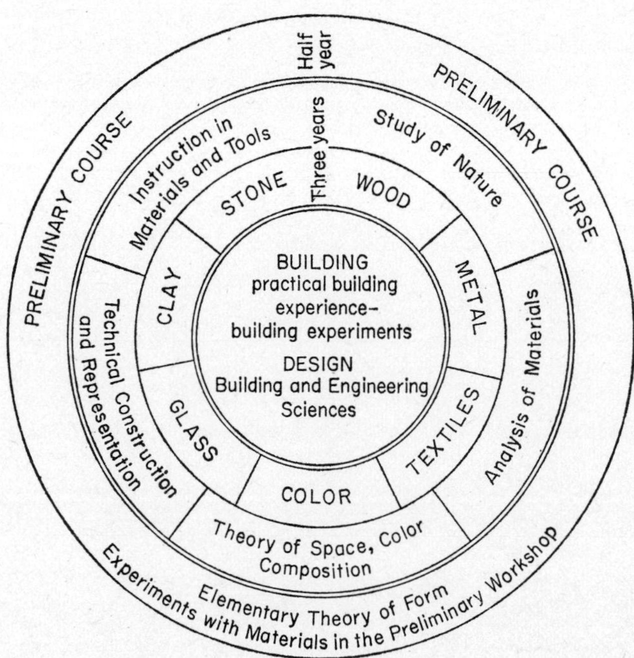

its basis in Man himself and significant only as a living organism.

Human achievement depends on the proper coordination of all the creative faculties. It is not enough to school one or another of them separately: they must all be thoroughly trained at the same time. The character and scope of the Bauhaus teachings derive from the realisation of this.

The curriculum

The course of instruction at the Bauhaus is divided into:

Instruction in crafts (*Werklehre*):

Stone	Wood	Metal	Clay	Glass	Colour	Textiles
Sculpture workshop	Carpentry workshop	Metal workshop	Pottery workshop	Stained glass workshop	Wall-painting workshop	Weaving workshop

Instruction in materials and tools

Elements of book-keeping, estimating, contracting

Instruction in form problems (*Formlehre*):

Observation	Representation	Composition
Study of nature Analysis of materials	Descriptive geometry Technique of construction Drawing of plans and building of models for all kinds of constructions	Theory of space Theory of colour Theory of design

[Gropius then gave details of some of the departments]

The preliminary course (Vorlehre)

Practical and theoretical studies are carried on simultaneously in order to release the creative powers of the student, to help him grasp the physical nature of materials and the basic laws of design. Concentration on any particular stylistic movement is studiously avoided. Observation and representation – with the intention of showing the desired identity of Form and Content – define the limits of the preliminary course. Its chief function is to liberate the individual by breaking down conventional patterns of thought in order to make way for personal experiences and discoveries which will enable him to see his own potentialities and limitations. For this reason collective work is not essential in the preliminary course. Both subjective and objective observation will be cultivated: both the system of abstract laws and the interpretation of objective matter.

Above all else, the discovery and proper valuation of the individual's means of expression shall be sought out. The creative possibilities of individuals vary. One finds his elementary expressions in rhythm, another in light and shade, a third in colour, a fourth in materials, a fifth in sound, a sixth in proportion, a seventh in volumes or abstract space, an eighth in the relations between one and another, or between the two and a third or fourth.

All the work produced in the preliminary course is done under the influence of instructors. It possesses artistic quality only in so far as any direct and logically developed expression of an individual which serves to lay the foundations of creative discipline can be called art.

Instruction in crafts and form problems

In earlier centuries when there was no academic instruction in the crafts or arts, students were taught independently by a master who was a craftsman as well as an artist. Such instruction would still be the best. But, because of the disastrous secession of art from the workaday life of the people, in our time such creative versatility no longer exists and it is therefore impossible for one man to undertake a student's entire art education. Synthesis is the only solution: coordinated instruction by two masters, one a craftsman, the other an artist. Thus, doubly trained, a future generation of creatively gifted workers may once more achieve a new productive coordination, and may gradually become indispensable collaborators in the working life of the people. With this in mind the Bauhaus has ruled (1) that every apprentice and journeyman is taught by two masters, a craftsman and an artist, who work in close cooperation; (2) that instruction in crafts and in the theory of form are fundamental; no apprentice or journeyman can be excused from either.

<table>
<tr><td colspan="2">Production work in the workshop of the preliminary course. Work in all the crafts under the technical supervision of the respective masters.</td><td>Studies in materials. Free creative work in different materials</td><td>Theory of form and colour</td></tr>
<tr><td>Drawing from Nature</td><td>Mathematics Physics Mechanics</td><td>Draughting and technical construction</td><td>Synthetic study of space (Synthetische Raumlehre)</td></tr>
</table>

General coordination (*Harmonisierungslehre*)

Instruction in crafts

Training in a craft is a prerequisite for collective work in architecture. This training purposely combats the dilettantism of previous generations in the applied arts. The teaching of a craft serves solely to train the hand and to ensure technical proficiency; it is by no means an end in itself. Its aim is to add to a many-sided education rather than to develop the specialised craftsman.

The Bauhaus believes the machine to be our modern medium of design and seeks to come to terms with it. But it would be senseless to launch a gifted apprentice into industry without preparation in a craft and hope thereby to reestablish the artist's lost contact with the world of production. He would be stifled by the materialistic and one-sided outlook predominant in factories today. A craft, however, cannot conflict with the feeling for work which, as an artist, he inevitably has, and it is therefore his best opportunity for practical training.

The principal difference between factory production and handicraft lies not in the machine's superiority over more primitive tools as an instrument of technical precision, but in the fact that in the factory each operation involved in manufacturing a product is performed by a different man, whereas the craft product is made entirely by one person. But if industry is to develop, the use of machinery and the division of labour must be maintained. Neither factor is in itself responsible for the loss of creative unity which has resulted from technological development. The root of the evil exists rather in the much too materialistic attitude of our times and in the loss of contact between the individual and the community.

It follows that the Bauhaus does not pretend to be a crafts school. Contact with industry is consciously sought, for the old trades are no longer very vital and a turning back to them would therefore be an atavistic mistake. Craftsmanship and industry are today steadily approaching one another and are destined eventually to merge into one. Such a new productive union will give every individual that understanding of and desire for cooperation which is essential to creative work. In this union the old craft workshops will develop into industrial laboratories: from their experimentation will evolve standards for industrial production.

The teaching of a craft is meant to prepare for designing for mass production. Starting with the simplest tools and least complicated jobs, he gradually acquires ability to master more intricate problems and to work with machinery, while at the same time he keeps in touch with the entire process of production from start to finish, whereas the factory worker never gets beyond the knowledge of one phase of the process. Therefore the Bauhaus is consciously seeking contacts with existing industrial enterprises, for the sake of mutual stimulation. From these contacts with industry the apprentice and, later, the journeyman learn not only to extend their technical experience but also to consider, in carrying out their work, the unavoidable demands which industry makes on the individual to economise on time and means. In the same measure, the academic superciliousness of another day constantly dwindles, and respect for hard realities unites individuals engaged in a common work.

After three years of thorough training, the apprentice undergoes a work-test in the presence of a committee of established craftsmen. Having passed this, he becomes a publicly certified journeyman. Every journeyman at the Bauhaus who is publicly certified is entitled, as soon as he considers himself sufficiently advanced, to a further test as 'Bauhaus journeyman'; the requirements of this test are more severe than the public test, especially in regard to the journeyman's creative ability.

Instruction in form problems

Intellectual education runs parallel to manual training. The apprentice is acquainted with his future stock-in-trade – the elements of form and colour and the laws to which they are subject. Instead of studying the arbitrary individualistic and stylised formulae current at the academies, he is given the mental equipment with which to shape his own ideas of form. This training opens the way for the creative powers of the individual, establishing a basis on which different individuals can cooperate without losing their artistic independence. Collective architectural work becomes possible only when every individual, prepared by proper schooling, is capable of understanding the idea of the whole, and thus has the means harmoniously to coordinate his independent, even if limited, activity with the collective work. Instruction in the theory of form is carried on in close contact with manual training. Drawing and planning, thus losing their purely academic character, gain new significance as auxiliary means of expression. We must know both vocabulary and grammar in order to speak a language; only then can we communicate our thoughts. Man, who creates and constructs, must learn the specific language of construction in order to make others understand his idea. Its vocabulary consists of the elements of form and colour and their structural laws. The mind must know them and control the hand if a creative idea is to be made visible. The musician who wants to make audible a musical idea needs for its rendering not only a musical instrument but also a knowledge of theory. Without this knowledge, his idea will never emerge from chaos.

A corresponding knowledge of theory – which existed in a more vigorous era – must again be established as a basis for practice in the visual arts. The academies, whose task it might have been to cultivate and develop such a theory, completely failed to do so, having lost contact with reality. Theory is not a recipe for the manufacturing of works of art, but the most essential element of collective construction; it provides the common basis on which many individuals are able to create together a superior unit of work; theory is not the achievement of individuals but of generations.

The Bauhaus is consciously formulating a new coordination of the means of construction and expression. Without this, its ultimate aim would be impossible. For collaboration in a group is not to be obtained solely by correlating the abilities and talents of various individuals. Only an apparent unity can be achieved if many helpers carry out the designs of a single person. In fact, the individual's labour within the group should exist as his own independent accomplishment. Real unity can be achieved only by coherent restatement of the formal theme, by repetition of its integral proportions in all parts of the work. Thus everyone engaged in the work must understand the meaning and origin of the principal theme.

Forms and colours gain meaning only as they are related to our inner selves. Used separately or in relation to one another they are the means of expressing different emotions and movements: they have no importance of their own. Red, for instance, evokes in us other emotions than does blue or yellow; round forms speak differently to us than do pointed or jagged forms. The elements which constitute the 'grammar' of creation are its rules of rhythm, of proportion, of light values and full or empty space. Vocabulary and grammar can be learned, but the most important factor of all, the organic life of the created work, originates in the creative powers of the individual.

The practical training which accompanies the studies in form is founded as much on observation, on the exact representation or reproduction of nature, as it is on the creation of individual compositions. These two activities are profoundly different. The academies ceased to discriminate between them, confusing nature and art – though by their very origin they are antithetical. Art wants to triumph over Nature and to resolve the opposition in a new unity, and this process is consummated in the fight of the spirit against the material world. The spirit creates for itself a new life other than the life of nature.

Each of these departments, in the course on the theory of form, functions in close association with the workshops, an association which prevents their wandering off into academicism.

Instruction in architecture

Only the journeyman who has been seasoned by workshop practice and instruction in the study of form is ready to collaborate in building.

The last and most important stage of Bauhaus education is the course in architecture with practical experience in the Research Department as well as on actual buildings under construction. No apprentices are admitted to the Research Department: only certified journeymen capable of working out by themselves technical and formal problems. They have access to the draughting office adjoining the Research Department, as well as to all the workshops, in order to enable them to study other crafts than their own. They are invited to collaborate both on the plans and the actual construction of buildings for which the Bauhaus has been commissioned, so that they may have the experience of cooperating with all the building trades and, at the same time, earn their living.

In so far as the Bauhaus curriculum does not provide advanced courses in engineering – construction in steel and reinforced concrete, statics, mechanics, physics, industrial methods, heating, plumbing, technical chemistry – it is considered desirable for promising architecture students, after consultation with their masters, to complete their education with courses at technical and engineering schools. As a matter of principle, journeymen should have experience (machine work) in manufacturing workshops other than those at the Bauhaus.

The most important condition for fruitful collaboration on architectural problems is a clear understanding of the new approach to architecture. Architecture during the last few generations has become weakly sentimental, aesthetic and decorative. Its chief concern has been with ornamentation, with the formalistic use of motifs, ornaments and mouldings on the exterior of the building – as if upon a dead and superficial mass – not as part of a living organism. In this decadence architecture lost touch with new methods and materials; the architect was engulfed in academic aestheticism, a slave to narrow conventions, and the planning of cities was no longer his job.

This kind of architecture we disown. We want to create a clear, organic architecture, whose inner logic will be radiant and naked, unencumbered by lying façades and trickeries; we want an architecture adapted to our world of machines, radios and fast motor cars, an architecture whose function is clearly recognisable in the relation of its forms.

With the increasing firmness and density of modern materials – steel, concrete, glass – and with the new boldness of engineering, the ponderousness of the old method of building is giving way to a new lightness and airiness. A new aesthetic of the Horizontal is beginning to develop which endeavours to counteract the effect of gravity. At the same time the symmetrical relationship of parts of the building and their orientation towards a central axis is being replaced by a new conception of equilibrium which transmutes this dead symmetry of similar parts into an asymmetrical but rhythmical balance. The spirit of the new architecture wants to overcome inertia, to balance contrasts.

Since architecture is a collective art, its welfare depends on the whole community. As an extreme instance, the monument is only significant when it springs from the will of the whole nation. This will does not yet exist today. But even the construction of absolutely necessary housing is at a standstill thanks to the makeshift economies of our time. Nowhere are the fundamental problems of building studied as such.

Standardisation of units

For this reason the Bauhaus has set itself the task of creating a centre for experimentation where it will try to assemble the achievements of economic, technical and formal research and to apply them to problems of domestic architecture in an effort to combine the greatest possible standardisation with the greatest possible variation of form. Therefore the buildings which are to be thought of as outgrowths of modern technique and design may be conceived as an assembly of prefabricated and standardised parts so applied as to fulfil the varying requirements of those to be housed.

The artist and the technician must collaborate in carrying out this task. Any industrially produced object is the result of countless experiments, of long, systematic research, in which business men, technicians and artists participate to determine a standard type. To an even greater degree, the standardisation of building units for industrial production will require the generous cooperation of all concerned, in business, in engineering, in art. Such cooperation would be a real demonstration of farsightedness. It would, in the end, prove more economical than the use of substitutes.

The Bauhaus has taken the first steps towards such collaboration with the building of an experimental house at its 1923 exhibition, which was an actual demonstration of new conceptions of housing as well as of new technical methods.

Every architect must understand the significance of the city in order to be able to engage activity in city planning; he must recognise *simplicity in multiplicity* as a guiding principle in the shaping of its character. Form elements of typical shape should be repeated in series. All the building parts should be functional limbs of the comprehensive organism which depends simultaneously on building, street and means of transportation.

The investigation of these problems constitutes the final stage of the course in building. A student who has achieved technical perfection and absorbed all that the Bauhaus can teach him can be certified a master.

The goal of the Bauhaus curriculum

Thus the culminating point of the Bauhaus teaching is a demand for a new and powerful working correlation of all the processes of creation. The gifted student must regain a feeling for the interwoven strands of practical and formal work. The joy of building, in the broadest meaning of that word, must replace the paper work of design. Architecture unites in a collective task all creative workers, from the simple artisan to the supreme artist.

For this reason, the basis of collective education must be sufficiently broad to permit the development of every kind of talent. Since a universally applicable method for the discovery of talent does not exist, the individual in the course of his development must find for himself the field of activity best suited to him within the circle of the community. The majority become interested in production; the few extraordinarily gifted ones will suffer no limits to their activity. After they have completed the course of practical and formal instruction, they undertake independent research and experiment.

Modern painting, breaking through old conventions, has released countless suggestions which are still waiting to be used by the practical world. But when, in the future, artists who sense new creative values have had practical training in the industrial world, they will themselves possess the means for realising those values immediately. They will compel industry to serve their idea and industry, will seek out and utilise their comprehensive training.

The Stage

Theatrical performance, which has a kind of orchestral unity, is closely related to architecture. As in architecture the character of each unit is merged into the higher life of the whole, so in the theatre a multitude of artistic problems form a higher unity with a law of its own.

In its origins the theatre grew from a metaphysical longing; consequently it is the realisation of an abstract idea. The power of its effect on the spectator and listener thus depends on the successful translation of the idea into optically and audibly perceptible forms.

This the Bauhaus attempts to do. Its programme consists in a new and clear formulation of all problems peculiar to the stage. The special problems of space, of the body, of movement, of form, light, colour and sound are investigated; training is given in body movements, in the modulation of musical and spoken sounds; the stage space and figures are given form.

The Bauhaus theatre seeks to recover primordial joy for all the senses, instead of mere aesthetic pleasure.

An organisation based on new principles easily becomes isolated if it does not constantly maintain a thorough understanding of all the questions agitating the rest of the world. In spite of all the practical difficult-

Johannes Auerbach and Blüthner (?), First Bauhaus signet, 1919
Bauhaus Archive, Berlin

Oskar Schlemmer, Second Bauhaus signet, 1923
Bauhaus Archive, Berlin

ies, the basis of the growing work of the Bauhaus can never be too broad. Its responsibility is to educate men and women to understand the world in which they live and to invent and create forms symbolising that world. For this reason the educational field must be enlarged on all sides and extended into neighbouring fields, so that the effects of new experiments may be studied.

The education of children when they are young and still unspoiled is of great importance. The new types of schools emphasising practical exercises, such as the Montessori schools, provide an excellent preparation for the constructive programme of the Bauhaus since they develop the entire human organism. The old conservative schools were apt to destroy harmony within the individual by all but exclusive headwork. The Bauhaus keeps in touch with new experiments in education.

During the first four years of constructive work, many ideas and problems have evolved from an original idea of the Bauhaus. They have been tested in the face of fierce opposition. Their fruitfulness and salutary effect on all phases of modern life have been demonstrated.

---

60 Oskar Schlemmer, *The Staatliche Bauhaus in Weimar,* 1923

[Manifesto from the publicity pamphlet *The First Bauhaus Exhibition in Weimar, July to September 1923*.]

The Staatliche Bauhaus in Weimar is the first and so far the only government school in the Reich – if not in the world – which calls upon the creative forces of the fine arts to become influential while they are vital. At the same time it endeavours, through the establishment of the workshops founded upon the crafts, to unite and productively stimulate the arts with the aim of combining them in architecture. The concept of building will restore the unity that perished in debased academicism and in finicky handicraft. It shall reinstate the broad relationship with the whole and, in the deepest sense, make possible the total work of art. The ideal is old, but its rendering always new: the fulfilment is the style, and never was the 'will-to-style' more powerful than today. But confusion about concepts and attitudes caused the conflict and dispute over the nature of this style which will emerge as the 'new beauty' from the clash of ideas. Such a school, animating and animated itself, unintentionally becomes the gauge for the convulsions of the political and intellectual life of the time, and the history of the Bauhaus becomes the history of contemporary art.

The Staatliche Bauhaus founded after the catastrophe of the war, in the chaos of the revolution and in the era of the flowering of an emotion-laden, explosive art, becomes the rallying-point of all those who, with belief in the future and with sky-storming enthusiasm, wish to build the 'cathedral of socialism'. The triumphs of industry and technology before the war and the orgies in the name of destruction during it, called to life that impassioned romanticism that was a flaming protest against materialism and the mechanisation of art and life. The misery of the time was also a spiritual anguish. A cult of the unconscious and of the unexplainable, a propensity for mysticism and sectarianism originated in the quest for those highest things which are in danger of being deprived of their meaning in a world full of doubt and disruption. Breaking the limitations of classical aesthetics reinforced boundlessness of feeling, which found nourishment and verification in the discovery of the East and the art of the Negro, farmers, children, and the insane. The origin of artistic creation was as much sought as its limits were courageously extended. Passionate use of the means of expression developed in altar paintings. But it is in pictures, and always in pictures, where the decisive values take refuge. As the highest achievement of individual exaggeration, free from bonds and unredeemed, they must all, apart from the unity of the picture itself, remain in debt to the proclaimed synthesis. The honest crafts wallowed in the exotic joy of materials, and architecture piled Utopian schemes on paper.

Reversal of values, changes in point of view, name, and concept result in the other view, the next faith, Dada, court jester in this kingdom, plays ball with paradoxes and makes the atmosphere free and easy. Americanisms transferred to Europe, the new wedged into the old world, death to the past, to moonlight, and to the soul, thus the present time strides along with the gestures of a conqueror. Reason and science, 'man's greatest powers', are the regents, and the engineer is the sedate executor of unlimited possibilities. Mathematics, structure and mechanisation are the elements, and power and money are the dictators of these modern phenomena of steel, concrete, glass, and electricity. Velocity of rigid matter, dematerialisation of matter, organisation of inorganic matter, all these produce the miracle of abstraction. Based on the laws of nature, these are the achievements of mind in the conquest of nature, based on the power of capital, the work of man against man. The speed and supertension of commercialism make expediency and utility the measure of all effectiveness, and calculation seizes the trascendent world: art becomes a logarithm. It, long bereft of its name, lives a life after death, in the monument of the cube and in the coloured square. Religion is the precise process of thinking, and God is dead. Man, self-conscious and perfect being, surpassed in accuracy by every puppet, awaits results from the chemist's retort until the formula for 'spirit' is found as well ...

Goethe: 'If the hopes materialise that men, with all their strength, with heart and mind, with understanding and love will join together and become conscious of each other, then what no man can yet imagine will occur – Allah will no longer need to create, we will create his world.' This is the synthesis, the concentration, intensification, and compression of all that is positive to form the powerful mean. The idea of the mean, far from mediocrity and weakness, taken as scale and balance, becomes the idea of German art. Germany, country of the middle, and Weimar, the heart of it, is not for the first time the adopted place of intellectual decision. What matters is the recognition of what is pertinent to us, so that we will not aimlessly wander astray, In balancing the polar contrasts; loving the remotest past as well as the remotest future; averting reaction as much as anarchism; advancing from the end-in-itself and from self-directedness to the typical, from the problematical to the valid and secure – thus we become the bearers of responsibility and the conscience of the world. An idealism of activity that embraces, penetrates and unites art, science, and technology and that influences research, study, and work, will construct the 'art-edifice' of Man, which is but an allegory of the cosmic system. Today we can do no more than to ponder the total plan, lay the foundations, and prepare the building stones.

But, *We exist! We have the will! We are producing!*

---

61 F. H. Ehmcke, *The Bauhaus in Weimar,* 1924

The number of catchwords being used in the Bauhaus nowadays begin to sound like some kind of art journalism. Everything we do lacks conviction, clarity and originality. We have become altogether too scientific and too abstract. After all, an arts and crafts workshop is not a chemistry laboratory where exact research can solve a problem down to the tiniest detail or an operating theatre, where the surgeon's knife reveals each individual nerve fibre indispensable for the proper functioning of a healthy organism. Surely it would be preferable for us to try to reconstruct what was once a living entity and to hand it on to coming generations as a vital whole.

It is precisely because the Bauhaus has run up the

banner of relating the parts to the whole that criticisms can be voiced as to whether it really is working towards its stated goal. This does not always appear to be the case. And if you look closer you will soon see why ... Deprived of all worthier duties, the artist withdraws, powerless and despairing, into the four walls of his studio where he alone is in command, and glues together pieces of blotting-paper, sacking, mother-of-pearl buttons, lamp cylinders and pram-wheels, because this is his only means of expressing his primitive, sincere awareness of the peculiar attraction of materials. This is what accounts for the private drama and the grim 'tear with a smile' humour of the 'Merz' artist. But anyone who undertakes to lay the foundation stone for a new and better 'culture' must not only be able but must feel bounden to restore things to their rightful place ...

Seen in this light, the theories issued by the Bauhaus on what should and should not be studied are to be viewed with the utmost caution. Or perhaps we are wrong to take the playful constructions, however appealing, made up of cane chair-seats, tin cans, buckles and men's braces as 'sour kitsch' compared with the sweeter version of yesterday which gleaned its elements from the values of earlier periods. This is a sore point ...

It is definitely high time we stopped analysing and tried to see just a little more clearly how much of our heritage can still be salvaged in the general process of destruction and can provide a basis for positive work in the future. The slightest effort made in this direction will bring us far nearer to our target than a thousand novelties displayed with noisy trumpetings. No style was ever conceived in flawless purity like Minerva from Jupiter's head. It has always had to rid itself gradually of the dross and residue of an earlier state. It is no more possible today to build a new style entirely in the air than it was before and to begin all over again every five years as if we had to atone for a new Fall. Seen at close quarters, it thus appears that what at first sight seemed like the strength and unity of the Bauhaus, namely the absence of a tradition in persons and ideas, has now proved to be its weakness.

It was not altogether by chance that this association sprang up in the heart of red Thüringia at the time of the Weimar Republic and that it developed during the years from 1919-23. It is a true reflection of the outlook of most people in Germany today. As soon as something seems rotten or disagreeable within, the whole house must be razed to the ground and we must start all over again from scratch. No sooner have tried methods been shown to have their shortcomings than people nervously shun even the most recent achievements in their attempts to forget everything that has ever been.

But the capacity to go beyond one's specific aim has always been a feature of will-power and inner strength. Purely formal accomplishments will not provide the mechanism to steer the intellectual and economic life of Western Europe back into safe waters. But actual conditions always reflect wider cultural implications and the fact that the Weimar Bauhaus has come into being at all is thus extremely impressive. We must take up a position because it is a challenging symbol of our present state of chaos, awaiting the day when a god will cry – Let there be light!

---

62 K. Nonn, *The State Garbage Supplies* (*The Staatliche Bauhaus in Weimar*), 1924

Gropius, (with his programme), is not new; he is not even relevant today. New is merely his crass negation of all ... principles with regard to his own and his students' work – in spite of the [published] programme – for in their performance the Bauhaus people grossly rebuff all precepts of reason. This is the fault of the totally misdirected permeation of concrete reality with an abstract, almost mystical conception of art, which does not deserve the name 'philosophy' claimed for it. Whoever ventures to follow the reasoning set down in writing in the publications of the Staatliche Bauhaus will put down the book – if he has sufficient self-control to read through the entire book – with a feeling of shame that such illogical presentations are being offered to the world, with the sanction of the state, to make a laughing stock of all that is German.

The material results of these 'abstract' art practices – as they are actually being called – are lamentable. Instead of an art with spiritual content, which honours craftsmanship and genuineness of material and which answers to actual needs, we are faced by the results of puttering around with all kinds of 'materials', like briquettes, garters, old chair seats and tin cans, which are labelled compositions and studies. We are offered scribbles lacking content, such as have been laughed at for the past ten or twelve years in futuristic, etc., exhibitions. And comparable to this are the technical–architectural pseudo-philosophical phrases of the 'instruction' on the 'creation of living form through colour, form and sound'. The Bauhaus people have established an 'abstract stage synthesis', and they have 'created' a 'new typography' by having a Japanese write German letters from the top down, instead of from left to right. They have composed a new ballet and for that purpose founded a Bauhaus stage; the Bauhaus kitchen and the Bauhaus housing settlement were the last requisites remaining for the completion of the communal type of living based on a cosmic point of view.

And finally, they organised an international Bauhaus exhibition during the Fall of 1923, corresponding to the mixed make-up of Bauhaus followers, and published the already mentioned Bauhaus book with a programme and the results of their work, in three languages. The scandal was even international. In Germany, the reaction, after a speechless silence of shocked astonishment, was a cry of anger from the specialists at this outrageous extravagance in employing State funds for such oddities. Some former friends hastily tried to disassociate themselves with discomfited stammerings, for what the Bauhaus offered in these first public displays stands so far beyond the pale of any kind of art that it can only be evalued pathologically, even if one is willing to take it for outrageous personal publicity. The clearly recognisable philosophical attitude, which is entirely devoted to negating everything that exists, causes the Bauhaus people to lose all social connection, in the widest sense, with the rest of the world. They are extravagant in their aspirations, and are sterile like all 'artists'. The work of the Bauhaus carries signs of the deepest spiritual isolation and disintegration. The public therefore rightfully objects to the notion that in this manner young artists and craftsmen in Thuringia who still have sober and honest aspirations are simply going to be barred from a thorough education if the Staatliche Bauhaus continues to exist in its present form. A small band of interested persons, who for the most part are foreigners, should not be allowed to suffocate the healthy mass of youthful German art students like a layer of oil on clear water. Moreover, this undertaking was only ostensibly based on artistic endeavours. It was, in reality, intended to be politically partisan from the beginning, for it proclaimed itself the rallying point for the sky-storming socialists who believed in the future and who wanted to build a cathedral of socialism. Well, the reality around us shows what this cathedral looks like.

The Bauhaus in Weimar, too, contributes a fitting artistic note with its 'works of art' that are put together from the ingredients of a junk pile. The blossoms of this direction of art have been amply sufficient to prove the futility of the Mephistophelian spirit of negation, which has been its distinguishing mark since 1919. It was left to Gropius himself to disgrace his art in the manner described. But instead of Faust, why should not his evil ghost have haunted Weimar for a change? The Landtag will exorcise the ghosts of the Blocksberg. Life arises only from the will to positive action and not from negation on principle.

63 Robert Mallet-Stevens, *Architecture and Geometry*, 1924

Architecture is an art which is basically geometrical. The cube is the basis of architecture because the right angle is necessary. In practice, walls are generally vertical, floors are horizontal, columns, pillars and posts are vertical, terraces and the ground are horizontal, stone blocks are parallelepipeds, windows and doors are rectangular, the steps of a staircase consist of vertical and horizontal planes and the corners of rooms are nearly always right angles. We need right angles.

A house, a palace, is composed of a set of cubes. At all stages in the history of art the house has been cubical. Each country, each century, each fashion has made its impression on the cube, with sculptures, mouldings, pediments, capitals, ornamental foliage, scrolls – so many decorative details which are often of no use to the structure but which give the charm of the play of light and shade. Building in stone, in fact, only allowed a block to be made, composed of various elements, to which the decoration was related as if glued on.

Nowadays reinforced concrete has completely transformed the problems which the builder has to solve. A thousand shapes are possible, unexpected silhouettes spring up, often strange, but rational and sincere. Reinforced concrete allows overhangs, the elimination of numerous points of support, and the reduction of the various structural elements to a minimum. So the proportions are profoundly modified and the aesthetic becomes different.

The modern architect can make something other than a compact block of stone, wood, iron, zinc, cast iron, staff, marble, stucco, bricks or lead; he can 'play' with a series of monolithic cubes. Applied decoration is no longer called for. The architect does not need to carve mouldings on to a façade. The material the architect is sculpting is the house itself; the projections and the rectilinear setbacks will form great planes of light and shade. Instead of scrolls or garlands of leaves, there will be smooth surfaces butting up against other smooth surfaces. Architecture has become monumental.

The plans of houses, too, will be transformed. There is no need to place walls directly over each other (for structural reasons). Central heating allows you to glaze huge expanses of window. Reinforced concrete allows you to use very small piers and projecting porch roofs to protect the exterior, with terraces laid out as open-air rooms. Every detail of construction is altered. There are new needs, there are new techniques. The aesthetic is new.

Moreover, ornaments are expensive and these days economy is an important factor for builders. 'Poverty will save architecture', the excellent Belgian architect Victor Bourgeois said recently. It is true, the high cost of living has dealt a very hard blow to useless decoration.

Finally, the reason which must bring the new architecture about is our absolute need to have an aesthetic corresponding to modern life. The machine triumphs. The eye understands the accuracy, the simplicity of machines. We are accustomed to the lines of motor cars, locomotives, aeroplanes, telephones, electric radiators, radio aerials, and we like them. Smooth surfaces, crisp articulation, clean curves, polished materials, right angles; clarity, order. This is the logical and geometrical house of tomorrow.

64 Le Corbusier, *The New Spirit in Architecture,* 1924

Last year I visited the construction site of a huge dam in the Alps; this dam will certainly be one of the finest achievements of modern technology and one of the most awe-inspiring for anyone who feels enthusiasm for such things: the site is imposing, it is true, but the final effect results chiefly from the combined efforts of reason, inventiveness, ingenuity and boldness. I was accompanied by a friend of mine, a poet: we were foolish enough to impart our enthusiasm to the engineers who were showing us round the site; but we only succeeded in arousing their laughter and scorn, and even some misgivings. They did not take us seriously; they thought that we must be slightly mad. We tried to explain that we admired their dam because we could judge what radical transformations might be brought about by having works of similar breadth in our towns for example. And suddenly, these men, who are involved in doing positive, logical, practical things, exclaimed: 'So you want to spoil our cities! You barbarians! You are forgetting the rules of aesthetics!' They were quite different from us by the nature of their thinking: being accustomed to conceiving and executing projects based on pure calculation, they revealed that they were incapable of imagining the consequences of their work in any other field; they remained in the past ...

If people are already tired of all the talk about mechanisation, it is proof of the incredible speed with which ideas are implanted: when we began our search for purification in an area swarming with ideas, in our efforts to construct a coherent system of thought, basing ourselves on the current changes in society, on the social climate, we were being completely original; we were dealing with people who only exclaimed, in pleasure or indignation, at the turmoil created by the machine, at the machine-gun, the power-hammer, at the smoking machine, which devours men; unlike them, we wanted to learn from the machine and then leave it to its simple rôle as our servant. It was not our intention to marvel at it, but to assess it; we would classify our findings so that following this victory of reason, we might find elements to touch our emotions.

I think this classification that we undertook has been useful for a whole series of researches carried out since then. Furthermore, we specified the conditions in which mechanisation developed, the law of economics which governs the way all work is carried out these days. We postulated that mechanisation is based on geometry and established that our lives depend on geometry, that it is our very language, by which I mean that geometry denotes order and that mankind expresses itself only through order.

The first thing a man does is to square up, to arrange, put in order, look plainly at what is before him; he has discovered the way to measure space by using coordinates on three perpendicular axes. The phenomenon is so innate of order that it is surprising that it should even have to be mentioned. But do not forget that we are emerging from a period – the end of the nineteenth century – of reaction, terrible reaction against order, and of fear at the powerful incitement to order brought about by the advent of the machine: people did not want order; the idea of a new way of life based on order dates back only a few years.

I repeat, order is the manifestation of mankind. When you leave Paris by train, what do you see unfolding before your eyes but an immense work of arrangement? A struggle against Nature to conquer her, to sort things out, to make life comfortable and, in brief, to live in a human world which would not be the stronghold of hostile Nature: *our* world of geometrical order? Our work is based on geometry. The rails are absolutely parallel, the embankments are the realisation of geometric designs; bridges, viaducts, locks and canals and all the urban and suburban creation which extends far into the countryside, show that when man acts and gives expression to his will, he inevitably becomes a geometrician and his creations are based on geometry.

His presence is betrayed by the fact that in a natural landscape, human effort is revealed by straight lines, verticles, horizontals, etc.

Thus towns are planned and houses built under the rule of the right angle.

The recognition of the decisive and essential value of this angle is an affirmation of general order which is of great importance and influence in aesthetics and hence in architecture ...

It is customary to study the phenomenon of architecture by looking only at palaces; obviously they do represent a certain achievement. But I intend quite simply to discuss the house and this is certainly sufficient reason to justify the formulation of laws and rules of architecture. Today, architecture is concerned with the house, with the ordinary, everyday house for normal, everyday people. It is no longer preoccupied with palaces. By studying a house designed for ordinary people, *for all and sundry*, we rediscover the *human bases*, the human scale, our typical needs, functions and emotions. A house has to fulfil two purposes. First it is a *machine for living in*, that is, a machine to provide us with efficient help for speed and accuracy in our work, a diligent and helpful machine which should satisfy all our physical needs: comfort. But it should also be a place conducive to meditation, and, lastly, a beautiful place, bringing much-needed tranquillity to the mind. I am not claiming that everyone finds art sustaining: I am merely saying that for some people – certain mentalities – a house must bring a feeling of beauty. Everything concerned with the practical purposes of the house is provided by the *engineer*; everything concerned with meditation, a spirit of beauty, a pervading sense of order (which would be the mainstay of that beauty) depends upon the *architecture*. *Engineering* on the one hand, architecture on the other.

The house is a direct consequence of the phenomenon of anthropocentrism, that is, the notion that everything centres on man. This is simply because the house is of interest to us alone, inevitably and more than anything else. Our house is bound up with our movements like the snail's shell. So it is important that it fits us well.

It is necessary to reduce everything thus to the human scale. It is the only solution to adopt, and it is above all the only means of looking clearly at the present problem facing architecture and of allowing a complete revision of values. Such a revision is indispensable after an era which is in culmination of nearly six centuries of *pre-mechanisation* culture. This brilliant era which has now been shattered by mechanisation was unlike ours in that it concentrated on external display, on palaces for noblemen, on churches for popes.

Now as I have said, we are confronted by a new phenomenon: mechanisation. The methods of building a house on a human scale are so topsy-turvy, so greatly enriched and so different from what we are accustomed to that everything handed down to us from the past is no longer any use, and we are cautiously seeking a new aesthetic. We are on the brink of a new approach which we shall try to give expression to.

Anthropocentrism or the restoration of the human scale, means quite simply that doors and windows must be studied; a house is a box with doors and windows in it; doors and windows are elements of architecture.

People have contrived to put up buildings with doors twelve metres high or three metres high; they are equally unsuitable. Permissible measurements have been stretched and little by little a code of arbitrary measurements has been formed, whilst our height of 1 metre 80 has remained unchanged. We need to revise these measurements, and the elements of architecture.

65 Le Corbusier, *Mass produced Buildings,* 1924

For most people the notion of mass production in art or architecture implies the abandonment of true art, of good workmanship and of dignity. The object made on the production line embodies the growing horror of this machine age. The most strenuous efforts of the various arts are directed against the menace of mass production. Love of beauty and perfection calls for resistance to the conveyor belt product. The love of Louis XIV, Renaissance or Gothic beauty! The perfection of work done by hand. Spherical shapes which are half square, mis-shapen cylinders, bumpy surfaces!

The growing horror of this century is, in fact, beauty based on purity of form and precise execution. Machines are replacing hand work; the spheres are smooth; the cylinders have the kind of precision only attainable in theory: without fuss, the machine produces surfaces which are faultless.

Yes, but the poet has been assassinated. For the poet is a terrestrial creature, displaying his melancholy at the sorrows and failures of this sick world.

That poet has not been assassinated: he dies because the terrestrial age is passed.

No, the poet is reborn.

For the poet is one who loves perfection and wants to make man into God. His joyful vigour exhorts us; it seeks out and finds reasons and ways of making gods. And the poet holds a ball of shining steel in his hand and thinks: and this is proof of the existence of the God whom I seek.

Mass production demands a search for standards. Standards lead to perfection.

When it is decided to make 100,000 items, that item is examined very closely, that one must meet 100, or 1000 requirements, which are the requirements of 100, 1000 or 100,000 individuals. If the requirements of 100,000 individuals are satisfied, it can be said that the human constants have been met and that a being has been created *which is like a son to Man.* The sole underlying principle of art must be the deep satisfaction of human needs. What else is our folklore which has survived over the centuries, if not a focus on the human scale of profoundly unanimous feelings, expressed in forms which have a truly universal effect upon all men? When 100,000 people have formed an opinion about a single issue, then a choice has been made, a positive judgement has been formed and perfection is attained. A standard is the result of a process of selection.

But there is another reason for the enduring quality and beauty of the standard. To create a standard you must satisfy completely economic criteria. You must find the exact, and not the approximate solution. And precision is the essence of beauty. Beauty consists of emotive interactions and only very precise constituents can interact. Economy is the fundamental principle of beauty. Economy is the most elevated sense of the word.

Now, economy in the most brutal sense of the word dictates the methods of mass production. When I make a single object, the wastage of materials, effort and time does not matter. Multiplied by 100,000, such wastage becomes unacceptable. At that moment economy in the brutal, materialistic sense, becomes economy in the most elevated sense.

This century appears full of the richest promise because the law of economics is the key to all our actions. This is because the machine, as inevitable and bewildering as a cataclysm, provides us with the means of carrying out fresh ideas in fresh conditions.

In our hearts, we quibble and cling to memories, we tremble before the uncertainty of the future and only reluctantly follow the impetuous leaps of our minds. We have fears and doubts. Even while we are breaking into vast new fields with our mathematics and with our machines, which direct us and push us powerfully and vigorously along, we nevertheless cast back a regretful glance.

But a new and implacable situation is upon us.

Let there be a new spirit (*esprit nouveau*) to light up our work with gladness!

Little by little this new spirit is forming. The greatest crisis of the present day stems from the conflict between our new situation and our way of thinking which is retarded by adherence to traditional practices and beliefs.

There are positive signs that, faced with the new facts, we are forming a new spirit and approaching harmony; the signs are clear: the demise of the decorative arts, the arrival of a purified, intense, concentrated art, with a strongly poetic content (modern art; cubism in particular is an early example); slowly, construction sites will adapt to industrialisation; the introduction of mechanisation in construction work will lead to the general acceptance of *standard elements*; even the design of houses will alter, under the sway of the new economics; the standard elements will provide unity of detail, and unity of detail is an indispensable requirement of architectural beauty. Then our towns will lose that appearance of chaos which blights them at the moment. Order will reign and new networks of streets, more immense and with a wealth of architectural solutions will present us with magnificent sights.

Thanks to the machine, to the identification of what is typical, to the process of selection, to the establishment of a standard, a style will assert itself. That order which the poet seeks by looking back to past eras, will reign once again; the poet must look forward, holding in his hand a ball of shining steel as a symbol of perfection henceforth attainable; he must be the advocate of order, and must bring to the new order of things, his spirit in its quest for harmony. New patterns will be established; the style of our time . . .

---

66 Le Corbusier, *Appeal to Industrialists,* 1925

If only Renault, Peugeot, Citroën, Le Creusot or one of the big metallurgists could organise the building industry!

The window, considered as a mechanism. Automatically sliding, air-tight fit. Give us the mechanical window!

We architects will be very happy with a fixed module. Once we have that module, *we can start composing with it.*

Here is an example of a module and its derivatives.

These are the natural spaces provided by reinforced concrete.

Take care! The windows must not open inwards, in the rooms they occupy, nor outwards on the façades.

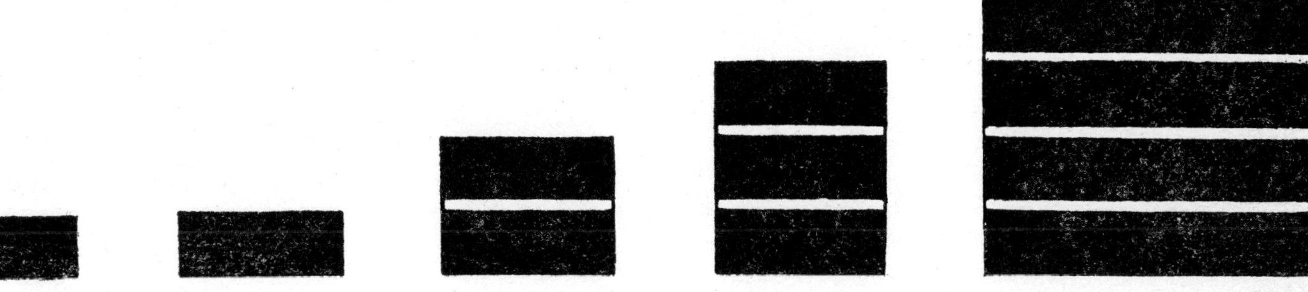

Photo Lucien Hervé

They must glide sideways (only the first one may pivot).

If I have ten windows providing light, three or four will be sufficient for ventilation.

Roneo made some interesting metal doors for us, but their technical division abandoned us and never produced our windows. The Menuiserie Metallique du Sud Est (South East Metal Fabrication) of Grenoble manufacture sheet metal in a very interesting way. Van Hamm of Brussels have left us. Raoul Decourt started off cautiously.

What attempts at persuasion to achieve the result which still evades us!

All our luxury apartments, all our private *hôtels*, all our villas; all our workers' houses, all our blocks of flats, are conceived and executed with the same window, a standard element. In a few years we have got very close to the anthropocentric module.

But ... all we have had up till now has been the work of the locksmith and not the mechanic. The window is the mechanical standard element of the house. You press a switch, or more simply, turn a crank handle and the windows slide quietly open or shut ...

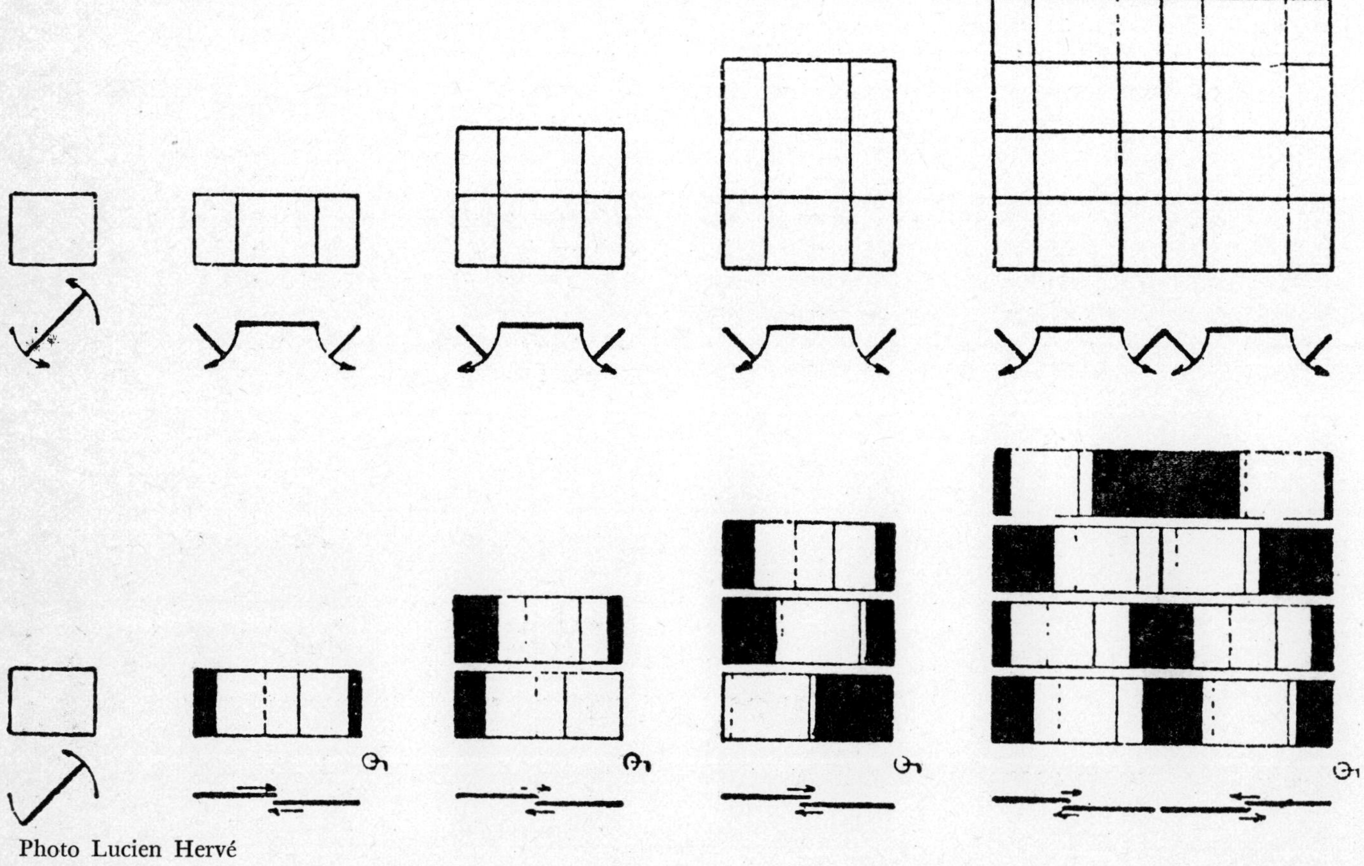

Photo Lucien Hervé

67 Le Corbusier, *A Single Trade,* 1925

Before we had reinforced concrete, all the various trades had to be on the spot to construct a house. After twenty years of using reinforced concrete, we may speculate: a single trade on site: the builder?

The builder constructs the exterior and interior walls, the floor, stairs and roofs (roof-terraces); he puts in the doors and windows. Then it only remains for the joiner to install the cupboards [*casiers*] for the house.

Up till now, the builder has prepared cavities for doors and windows for the joiner; the joiner comes along, takes the measurements, returns to his workshop and makes his doors and windows according to the various measurements; he returns to the site and puts them in place, adjusting them, planing them down and making them a true fit.

It would be possible for the builder to put mass-produced (machine made) doors and windows into place, just like bricks. This is an up-to-date solution that we have already partly introduced on several sites.

Up till now the house fitments have only been roughly designed; they do not occupy a designated place in the house.

However, the kitchen, pantry, dining-room, lounge and bedrooms are places where specific functions are carried out. Each of these rooms requires its own equipment, which must be ready to hand. Since a modern dwelling is planned with a view to saving space, the old expedients (cupboards, cabinets, chests) intended for storing such equipment, are no longer acceptable. 'Each implement in its rightful place', so purpose-built furniture, like office furniture.

Bring office furniture into the apartment, but according to a different aesthetic plan. After all, a house is only fitments on the one hand, and chairs and tables on the other. The rest is clutter ...

The *container* (cabinets) mass-produced, finished in one of the numerous varnishes available, or coated like a car (as we are starting to do in our buildings: coated walls and fitments). The *contents* (fixtures), from the simplest to the most lavish, from the most economical to the most sophisticated, produced by the carpenter, painter, finisher etc.

When mass-produced, these standard fitments, which could be put together in many different combinations, could be sold in a local store (*au* Bazar de l'Hôtel-de-Ville) or on the Champs Elysées: they stand against a wall up to any height, or even form a wall. So, *a single trade*: the joiner no longer has to set foot inside the building and no longer seriously holds up the work. His goods are only brought into the house when it is being furnished, inside dry walls.

The builder is master of the site. He will be entirely the master when the reform of the present method of dividing the land into lots (building plots) permits us to build on regular rather than irregular pieces of land and helps us to fix upon a more precise style of dwelling. Then the shell made by the builder will provide a casing which will house the heating system and sanitary installations. The introduction of standard fitments was heralded long ago by office furniture, by 'Innovation' style furniture and also by the ingenious, bold and elegant designs of Francis Jourdain.

As for us, we can draw up our plans from now on with a few fixed dimensions: doors, windows and standard fitments; it is a pleasure to gradually leave behind arbitrary methods and improvisation. Standard doors, windows or fitments call for the *cooperation of technical experts.* We would do well to consider that it is not us, the architects, who design a radiator, a w.c., a light bulb, a porcelain wash-basin, etc. which form the equipment of a house. The tendency is towards improved equipment; we are lucky to be able to hand over to the technical experts. Our rôle is to arrange and proportion ...

68 Le Corbusier, *Standardisation cannot resolve an architectural difficulty,* 1925

(With a truly philanthropic purpose, Monsieur Henri Frugès is having one hundred and twenty houses built in the New District in Pessac.)

Us: – Each house and group of houses has necessitated a detailed study on the drawing board, using a scale of five centimetres to the metre. Detailed and difficult, critical. All the more detailed, critical and difficult in that at Pessac, we are working *with standard elements only*: the same window everywhere, the same stairs everywhere, the same door, the same heating, the same concrete cell measuring 5 x 5 and 2½ x 5 metres, the same fittings for cooking, washing and sanitation.

Monsieur Henri Frugès: – Well then: does this indicate the failure of standardisation and mass production? It would seem that with everything standardised, systematic instructions, either by numbers or diagrams, should suffice to inform the site foreman about the placing of each house and where the openings to the sky should be.

Us (for a year we have been discussing difficult cases): – In fact it is the failure of standardisation. *Unless it is its redemption.* A work can only affect us emotionally and touch our sensibility if its form has been dictated by a genuine purpose. Monsieur X (unknown to you and us, who will become the owner of one of these houses) will only be aware of this *purpose* if we have put it there.

It is the trouble we shall have taken to coax him to this small piece of ground, by giving him all the light he needs, by providing shelter from harsh winds, by placing his flowers and fruit trees in a sunny position, by thinking about where his kitchen should be, by putting his front door perpendicular to the pathway, his window looking out on a lovely view, his bedroom screened from his neighbour's gaze, etc.

If this well-meaning intention did not figure in each house, we would be guilty of jerry building, and mass production and standardisation would be found wanting, because the dwelling would not be good to live in. The standards are an alphabet. With these letters we must find a way of *writing the names of your future house-owners.*

---

69 Le Corbusier, *A Contemporary City with Three Million Inhabitants,* 1925 (and 1922)

The irregularly shaped building plots which exist now in cities and which must disappear in the face of problems posed by the future, absorb all the creative powers of architecture and wear out the architect. The creation which results is irregular – by definition – a rickety weakling, a water-tight solution only pleasing to someone who knows the background.

We must be able to build freely: inside and out.

Aesthetics of the town

(The town outlined here is a pure play of geometric forces)

It is actuated by a vast new module (400 metres). The regular grid of its streets which intersect at every 400 metres and 200 metres is uniform (easy for the traveller to get his bearings) but none of its aspects are alike. Here the forces of geometry play a fugal symphony.

We enter through the English garden. The fast moving car travels along the raised motorway; a majestic avenue of skyscrapers. We draw nearer; the twenty-four skyscrapers seem to multiply in space; to left and right, set in their squares, stand the administrative buildings; closing up the space, the museums and universities. Suddenly, we are beneath the first skyscrapers. Between them is not the meagre crack of light you see in a distressing city like New York, but a vast space. The parks unfold before us. The terraces rise up in tiers on the lawns and in the groves. Buildings of low, spreading proportions guide the eye far away into the fleecy tree-tops. Where are the petty procurators' palaces? Here stands the City, full of people, in the pure still air, and the noise is quelled beneath the foliage. Chaotic New York is vanquished. In the light stands a modern city.

The car has left behind the flyover and its 60mph

Le Corbusier, A Contemporary City: the parks at the foot of the skyscrapers
Almanach d'Architecture Moderne, Crès, Paris, 1925

(100 km) pace: it drives slowly into the residential areas. The set-backs extend the architectural perspectives far into the distance. Gardens, recreation grounds, playing fields. Everywhere is dominated by the sky, stretching into the distance. The horizontal bands of terraces show up neat flat areas bordered with greenery which are hanging gardens. The regularity of the elements of detail punctuate the bold outline of the large masses. Softened by the blue sky in the distance, the skyscrapers present the large surfaces of their geometric walls made entirely of glass. In the glass which covers their façades from top to bottom, the blue gleams and sky sparkles. Dazzling. Huge, shining prisms.

Everywhere the view is varied; the grid is based on 400 metres, but it is curiously modified by architectural contrivance. (The set-backs provided are in counterpoint with a module of 600 x 400 metres.) The traveller arriving by air from Constantinople or Peking, perhaps, suddenly sees amidst the unruly features of the rivers and forests this clear impression which marks the organised city of men: this pattern which is the attribute of a human brain. At dusk, the glass skyscrapers are ablaze.

It is not the literary dynamite of a dangerous futurism, thrust rowdily into the reader's face. It is a spectacle arranged by Architecture, using the resources of plastic art, which is the play of the forms beneath the light.

---

70 Le Corbusier, *Words,* 1925

Words (1925)
Are our children really destined to spend their lives in this vast geometric barracks, living in mass-produced houses with mass-produced furniture, all propelled at the same hour, by the same trains, to identical offices in identical skyscrapers? Their recreation, their leisure pursuits regimented to the same pattern, everyone will have his small piece of ground; and if they enjoy gardening, there are allotments; notice that private garden sprinklers are banned, being considered out-of-date and not very efficient; even in their smallest amusements, they must never forget what is useful. Poor wretches! What will become of them in the midst of all this appalling speed, organisation and uniformity? So much logic pushed to its ultimate consequences, so much 'science' and 'mechanisation' everywhere, lurking on every page and crowing triumphantly: that is quite enough to put you off 'standardisation' for ever and to fill you with nostalgia for 'disorder'.

This appraisal of *Urbanisme* appeared in *L'Architecte,* the mouthpiece of (amongst others) Messrs. Plumet, Bonnier, Dervaux.* *L'Architecte* is to be found on all architects' desks. The article in question is elsewhere very agreeable and even flattering. The part I have extracted here is in some sense the 'But, nevertheless,' of a whole generation. You would think we were on the barricades; struck by a bullet in the heart, the hero, before collapsing, declares his principles with an eloquence which becomes more animated at every turn. The battles of former days were eloquent and have stereotyped our vocabulary; the words flow, a parliamentary eloquence is kindled; words! The generation of 1870 shares its little drama with us. What am I saying? You would think that Stevenson had not invented his engine yet.

Let us look closely at the words of this very 'standardised' protest:

This vast geometric barracks is proposed in order to bring a completely new variety to the appearance of

---

* Architects in charge of the 1925 Exhibition.

our towns, to replace the 'corridor street' which is the only attribute of towns today, by perspectives of great architectural potency: the redents (set-backs) the honeycombed surfaces, the skyscrapers. If you examine the plan of the 'Contemporary Town' and imagine the layout as built, if you attempt a theoretical walk from one part of the town to another, you would appreciate that the scenes alter with every step, that they are never repeated, and that the 'corridor' town is dead. It is replaced by a town where space, and the views close-to and afar, and numerous architectural combinations are brought into play; the generous scale of the plan is complemented by the elevations: an unbroken succession of different views is unfolded against the sky. Any professional who is not preoccupied with a profession of faith dating from 1870, could easily read this much in the pages of the indicated book.

The houses are mass-produced but of course, as are those houses of every period which correspond to a particular type: the Haussmann style, the Louis XVI style, the Louis X style, etc.

Mass-produced furniture. You forget to mention the manufacture which has for a long time been carried on in the Faubourg Saint-Antoine. You know very well that for centuries they have been producing standard ranges of furniture there: in one yard, chairs' feet, in another, wood for making beds, etc. Could you suggest a percentage, one in a hundred, in a thousand, in ten thousand, of households which for generations has not been using mass-produced furniture? All I ask is that we build modern mass-produced furniture and not affectations of royal styles.

All propelled at the same hour by the same trains to identical skyscrapers. Come now, don't try to persuade us that before the fatal appearance of my book, trains departed at whim, arrived when they chose, and having arrived, were turned into firewood so that the same trains should not be running the next day. The next day, at the end, alas, of this imaginary time, these trains would arrive at a different station, so as not always to be doing the same thing and to preserve in the travellers a sense of the unexpected!

Identical offices! They are all so different at present: the large, panelled lounge for the deputy director – with pink marble fireplace and *Bernot briquettes*; the windowless anteroom for the office boy; the bedrooms for the engineers or accountants, with fireplaces in white marble (standard range) and *Bernot briquettes*; the typists in the kitchen at the back. These are the identical offices which now house the business world of Paris, from the Boulevard Sébasto to the Étoile. And very poor offices they are too!

Leisure pursuits regimented to the same pattern: I beg your pardon! I am suggesting that around the houses (and I will make this possible) people can play football, tennis, basketball and all the traditional sports that can only be played if there is enough room. I make enough room. You know that these days there is no room and the only social activity *regimented to the same pattern* is playing dice [*zanzi sur le zinc* – a kind of dice game played on bar counters] or holding seances at home, neither of which solve the problem of the lungs, legs, biceps or moral well-being of the population.

Everyone will have his small piece of ground. It seems to me that this is the dream that you have all been pursuing for the past thirty years, in your writings. Do you seriously hold it against me that I have provided everyone with a small piece of ground? Private sprinklers are forbidden, because I have contrived by architectural grouping, to introduce automatic watering. A sad loss (if I may say so) for humanity! The sprinkler is an entity: my roof, my sprinkler! A whole life is stretched towards these two symbols of the age of shepherds. Don't take away my sprinkler begs Mimi Pinson through the flowery mouth of M. Saint Granier.

Appalling speed, organisation and uniformity as opposed to appalling delays, disorder and uniformity. If we are talking about the researches or *Urbanisme* then we must replace appalling uniformity by an *ever renewed diversity*. And anyone who cares to look (in Vienna, Berlin and London, even more than in Paris) at city suburbs, at town streets, will find *uniformity*, everywhere and *Urbanisme* which draws attention to these unfortunate results of a lack of organisation, strives to suggest some solutions.

But then, all this logic pushed to its ultimate consequences, all this science and mechanisation everywhere on every page, these are the unpardonable crimes of an architect gone astray. Yes, of course: an architect should not be logical, should be ignorant, and in the twentieth century should scrupulously avoid the machine. Let us take note of this definition of an architect in the very influential mouthpiece of Messrs Plumet, Bonnier and Dervaux.

Lurking on every page and crowing triumphantly: They are triumphant? Thank you. That is the intention.

That's quite enough to fill you with nostalgia for 'disorder'. There! Architecture is requested to lead to disorder. See, M. Paul Valéry, how your *Eupalinos* is received in this year of 1925, and as a conclusion to the Exhibition of Decorative Arts I would certainly say that this echoes M. Léandre Vaillat's profession of faith, if it were not scandalous to mention the names of M. Paul Valéry and M. Léandre Vaillat together in the same sentence. They discuss the same thing, architecture, but it is not at all the same thing, it is two quite different things which have nothing in common. There are levels which cannot communicate with each other.

If I have analysed the review in *L'Architecte* word by word, it is because I considered it a good example of the innumerable clichés (standardised and how!) by which people cling to a dead past and try to stifle the early signs of a new state of mind in public opinion. This article in *L'Architecte* written by professionals in a professional journal, sums up the many indignant feelings aroused during the summer by the Pavillon de l'Esprit Nouveau, and let me know how cutting the press can be.

My analysis reveals word by word, Words! Words! Words are so powerful! You can do a lot with words. The established situation takes refuge behind words.

---

71 Walter Behrendt, *The State of the Arts and Crafts,* 1925-6

Crafsmanship has preserved its high standards of technical skill during the war and the post-war period. In all spheres of industry people will insist on using this skill both knowledgeably and conscientiously, working honestly and with care. The results are of high quality, worthy of great respect. Nevertheless the published word is clear proof that we are unable to relate our lives to this world of craft which is so rich in its forms. We do not know how to begin to come to terms with its colourful, varied creations. Already the term 'craft' is often used with a derogatory undertone of irony. It is also recognised that the stimulating effect of a simple machine made object – the clean-cut lines of a polished nickel-plated steel match-holder or an artless inkbottle made in matt rubber – can make a stronger impact on us than any artistic and technically accomplished piece of modern craftsmanship. The heretics are even saying that the kind of upholstery you find in a modern car is as much a work of craftsmanship as that in the ornamental show coaches of the old dukes in Baroque times.

So-called craftsmanship is now in an extremely precarious and difficult situation. It lacks clear ideological direction which would give meaning and content to its products, to surpass mere decoration and achieve essential form. Unless the crafts adopt a single-minded goal in their creation of form, they will fall prey to the meaningless whims of individual taste ... Taste alone is not sufficient, it cannot substitute for ideological guidance ...

Only architecture can give clear, ideological guidance to the crafts. It alone can liberate craft from its present fruitless position as 'art for art's sake'. Architects create relationships in *space*, which is what produces an integrated theme in their work. The elements are unified, from the ground plan, right through to the ornamental detail, following a single idea based on the articulation of space, which gives it all meaning and substance.

But architecture itself at present is involved in a spiritual change of direction. The climate of contemporary awareness was what stimulated this new direction. This contemporary awareness finds its climax in the passionate admission of the strong creative forces of the time and strives to create a free path for this power by understanding its essence. Instead of prejudice and tradition, it offers reality; instead of theory and dogma, intense concentration. It seeks to replace dead maxims with ideas drawn directly from life and tries 'to understand life through life itself'. Commitment to essentials is the outstanding feature of this new attitude, whose emotional intensity is at its highest when this commitment is met.

In all spheres of creative work that are under the uncompromising influence and power of Art the commitment to essentials is already clear. That is the real reason why the spirit of our time is so aroused by the sight of certain industrial products – by a car or an aeroplane, a sailing boat, a locomotive or a modern toy. All these essential forms are developed organically to suit their functions and reveal a new decisive feature of modern life. That is why they seem so striking to us.

Architecture too, is in the process of rebuilding a new creative direction from first principles, based upon the new contemporary awareness. It is rejecting old formal rules, decorative gestures, pure decoration, and is attempting in many different ways to discover the principle of organic form which has already become the established order in industry. Meanwhile the first successful attempts at realising forms derived from these essential principles exist all over the world.

These important new architectonic ideas do not evolve from the particular problems of relating spatial elements. The deciding factor is not the accentuated horizontal or the renunciation of ornament, but a new attitude towards the process of creativity which is emerging, not only in architecture, but in all creative fields. This new approach operates on an essentially different basis from the old, based on new ideological principles conditioned by the climate of contemporary thought. That is why the design movement gained no active support with its slogan of 'form without ornament'. This seductive slogan, despite the support it received, only concerns inessential superficialities. The core of the new creative problem will not be satisfied with this slogan which offers no ideological direction but only the danger of a new fashionable formula.

Contemporary thought is concerned with the essential. It strives for the purity of form which is the fulfilled expression of organic creation. Our time rejects trivia, no longer appreciates the many-faceted, pleasing charm of individual varieties of form. It scorns ornament and decoration – in one word it is anti-craftsmanship. That is the status of the crafts at present. Although it contains the highest technical skills and a highly developed craftsmanlike dexterity, the applied arts are isolated as an artistic activity. They cannot be self-sufficient and must take the essential step of joining up with architecture. On the one hand, some craftsmen are creating expensive goods for their own sake, against the grain of contemporary demand, for an imaginary, scarcely definable clientele. On the other hand, others are producing work oriented to the new design principles, courageously ahead of their time, for the as yet imaginary spaces of a new architecture. There is no really solid foundation for either group, so that the fate of all the decorative arts at this time hangs in the balance, suspended in a vacuum . . .

72 Kurt Ewald, *The Beauty of Machines,* 1925-6

Beauty is among those conceptions which are apparently easy to explore, but about whose true nature no one will ever be clear. Of course we strive, as our fathers and grandfathers strove from different premises, to attain a perfection answering to the ideal presentation of beauty. Naturally we can never discover whether our own ideal image comes near to absolute beauty; we have to believe it. Kant regards a material object as beautiful if its appearance arouses the feeling of a pleasant emotion – provided that this feeling is not traceable to baser instincts in the beholder. He calls it 'a sensation of a finer sort, so called either because one can enjoy it for a longer time without satiation or exhaustion, or because it as it were presupposes a sensitiveness of the soul making it receptive to virtuous emotions, or because it is evidence of talent and superiority of intellect'. We are not disposed to quarrel with this definition, since we find that our own experience confirms it. We also feel justified in making use of the great philosopher's definition for the aesthetics of technology, and in drawing the following conclusions from it.

To say that the perception of beauty in technical things in general, and in the construction of machines in particular, is something arrived at only in the most recent times is one of those presumptuous and superficial exaggerations in which this hasty, readily forgetful age abounds. Let us see how far such an assertion is founded on fact.

Three stages of development can be clearly distinguished in the history of the construction of machines, each having characteristics which are of decisive significance in the assessment of the concept of beauty. The first period begins with the initial efforts to put into practice the thought processes on which a given machine was to be based; it covers various unsuccessful, but continually improving, experiments until the point is reached at which the inventor is satisfied with the reliable working of his latest model. Watt's steam engine, Fulton's steamship, Stephenson's *Rocket* locomotive can obviously be looked on as goals of that kind, standing at the end of a long, or not so long, series of trials. Once satisfied in principle that the machine will work without trouble, we try to aim further, to produce a perfected model which gives the highest performance with the most economical means; this struggle for mechanical efficiency represents the second stage of development. Efficiency rises steadily, getting nearer and nearer to a theoretically calculable, but never attainable, value; finally it reaches a level near the limits of practical possibility, and can only be improved in the course of a comparatively long period of development work on small details. Broadly speaking, the invention of the machine has been perfected. Now we can think about putting the new-won aids to work on a wider scale. The harvest-time begins, in which we draw profit from the earlier experiments to the greatest possible extent. The purely mechanical–technical, theoretical–constructional processes are eclipsed by aims on a national–economic level. The third, and at present the most recent, period in the history of machine construction is the period of quantity production and standardisation.

Very many kinds of machine construction are undoubtedly already well into this last stage of development. Certainly most modern machines arouse in us that feeling that Kant regards as the criterion of 'beauty'. A good modern machine is thus an object of the highest aesthetic value – we are aware of that. In colloquial speech we may describe such a machine as 'beautiful' – the philosopher weighs up his concept more cautiously and calls it 'sublime', for its appearance does not at all arouse a pleasant sensation as 'joyful and smiling'; it evokes pleasure 'with a shudder'. How it actually makes its effect is something we can only appreciate with our emotions; we get our true view of objects whose outward appearance is displeasing when we accept that those features which account for the lack of harmony are none the less

1 Hector Guimard: Dressing-table mirror in lemonwood and copper, 1897–8 [12]

2 Charles Plumet and Tony Selmersheim: Billiard room, 1899 [13]

3 Emile Gallé: Salon furniture based on the forms of cereals, field poppies, potato flowers and spring wheat, ca. 1900 [14]

4 Emile Gallé: Mouldings based on the stems of the orchis and cow parsnip, ca. 1900 [14]

5 Walter Gropius and Adolf Meyer Fagus: Shoe-last Factory, Alfeld-an-der-Leine: first building phase, 1911–12 [26]

6 Victor Horta: Maison du Peuple, Brussels: auditorium, 1895 [31]

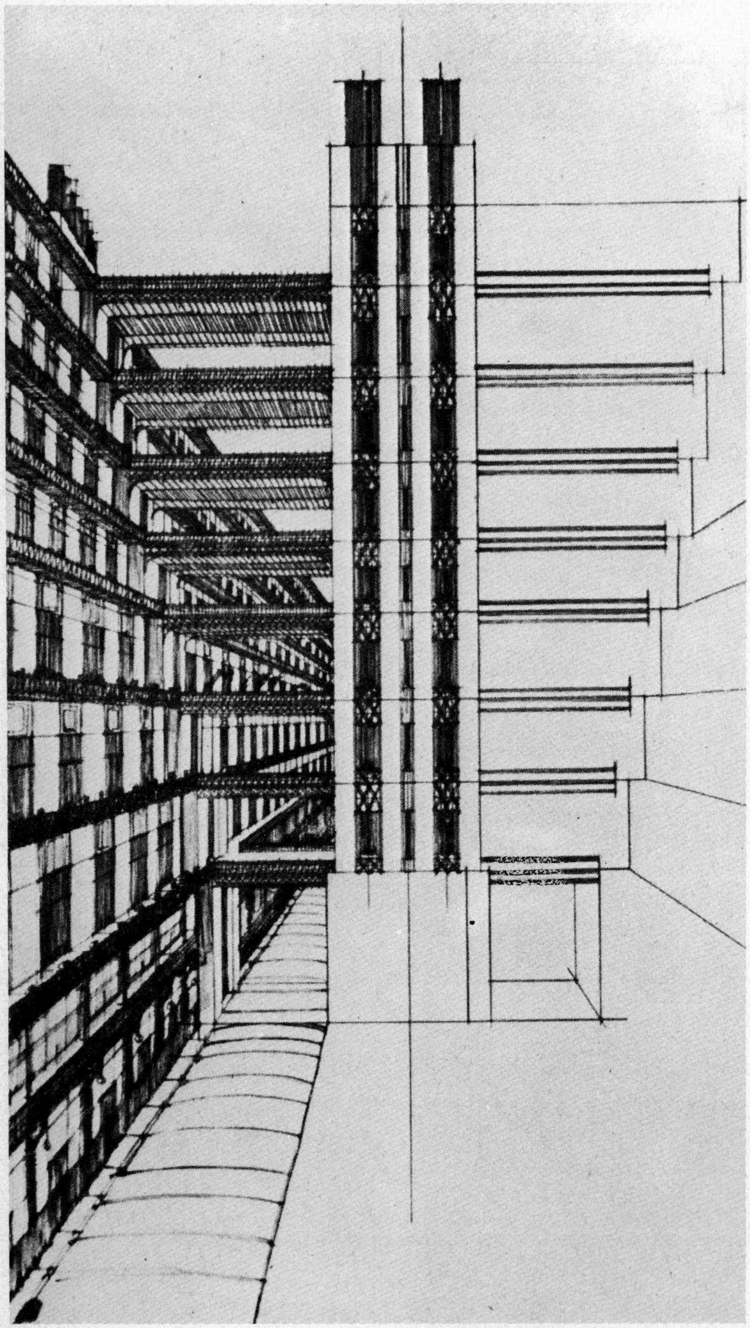

7 Antonio Sant'Elia: Drawing for *La Città Nuova*, 1913–14 [32]

8 V. E. Tatlin: Monument to the Third International, 1919 [40]

9 Frederick Kiesler: Type T display board, Vienna Theatre Exhibition, 1924 [53]

10 Mies van der Rohe: Project for glass skyscraper, 1921 [54]

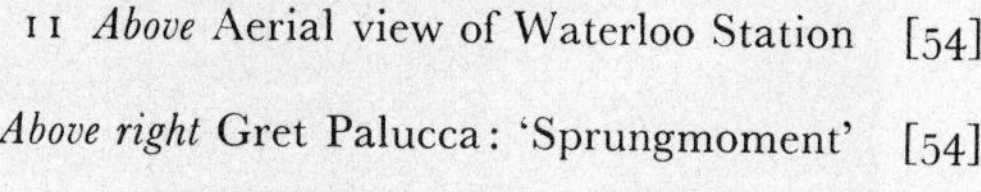

11 *Above* Aerial view of Waterloo Station [54]

12 *Above right* Gret Palucca: 'Sprungmoment' [54]

13 *Right* Co-op dwelling: interior, 1926 [54]

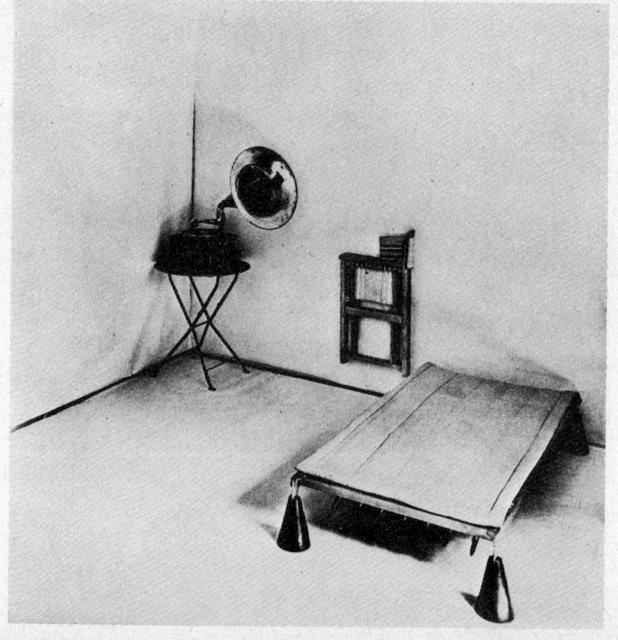

14 *Left* Kasimir Malevich: Architecton, ca. 1923 [55]

15 *Centre* Industrial lathe with hydraulic action: Magdeburger Werkzeugmaschinenfabrik A.-G. [72]

16 *Bottom left* Model of a Junkers metal aeroplane (J/1000) [73]

17 *Bottom right* Metal tube construction of a fuselage, showing splices and joints [73]

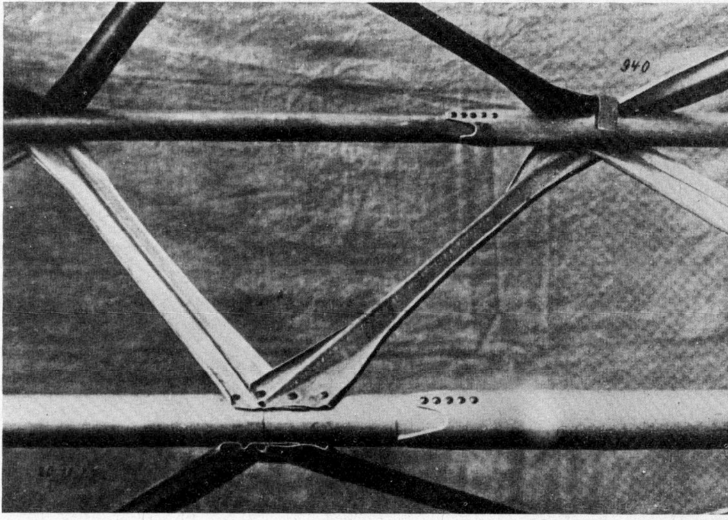

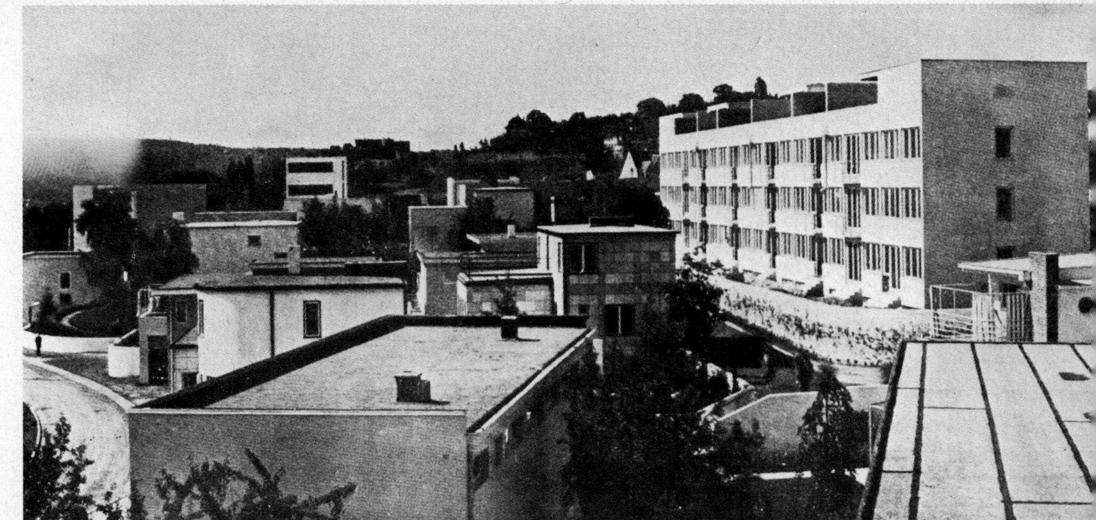

18 *Top* View of Weissenhof Siedlung, Stuttgart, 1927 [77]

19 *Centre left* Chassis of a diesel-engined carriage: Eisenbahn-Verkehrmittel A.-G., Berlin, Waggonfabrik Weimar. [84]

20 *Centre right* Mart Stam: House in the Weissenhof Siedlung: living room, 1927 [100]

21 *Bottom* Mart Stam: House in the Weissenhof Siedlung: study, 1927 [100]

b

d

f

22 Projects for the Reichsbank Competition, 1933 [108]

- a Mies van der Rohe
- b Wilhelm Kreis
- c Emil Fahrenkamp
- d German Bestelmeyer
- e Hans Poelzig
- f Walter Gropius

23 Postcard of the Weissenhof Siedlung as an Arab village.
'In 1927 the Werkbund housing estate at Weissenhof in Stuttgart was opened with flags and fanfares, and the triumph of the New Architecture was jubilantly proclaimed to an astonished world. At the reception on the eve of the opening of this building exhibition, which was directed expressly against the vernacular methods of building championed by the Heimatschutz, the then managing director of the Württemberg Werkbund made fun of the Heimatschutz architecture with its strong traditional ties. But the victors' triumph did not last long. Soon enough the word was: "Ah, how quickly do beauty and stature fade! Yesterday on a proud horse, today shot through the breast." [It rhymes in German.] And now people are making jokes about the products of the Weissenhof estate.
He who laughs last laughs longest!'

Quotation taken from *Schwäbischer Heimatbuch*, 1934

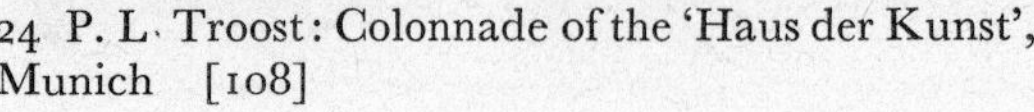

24 P. L. Troost: Colonnade of the 'Haus der Kunst', Munich [108]

25 Zeiss headlamp with hollow tube attachment [114]

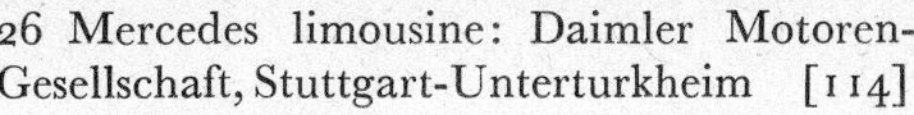

26 Mercedes limousine: Daimler Motoren-Gesellschaft, Stuttgart-Unterturkheim [114]

27 Old bus chassis: Nationale Automobil-Gesellschaft, Berlin Oberschöneweide [114]

28 The new Niederflur chassis for buses [114]

29 Berlin buses [114]

30 *Top left* Marcel Breuer: Wassily chair, 1925 [116]

31 *Top right* Mies van der Rohe: Cantilever chair, 1926 [118]

32 *Middle left* Ferdinand Kramer: Chair designed for production by Thonet in bentwood, ca. 1926 [118]

33 *Middle right* Traditional Thonet bentwood chairs [118]

34 *Lower right* Le Corbusier, Pierre Jeanneret and Charlotte Perriand: Chaise longue, 1929 [120]

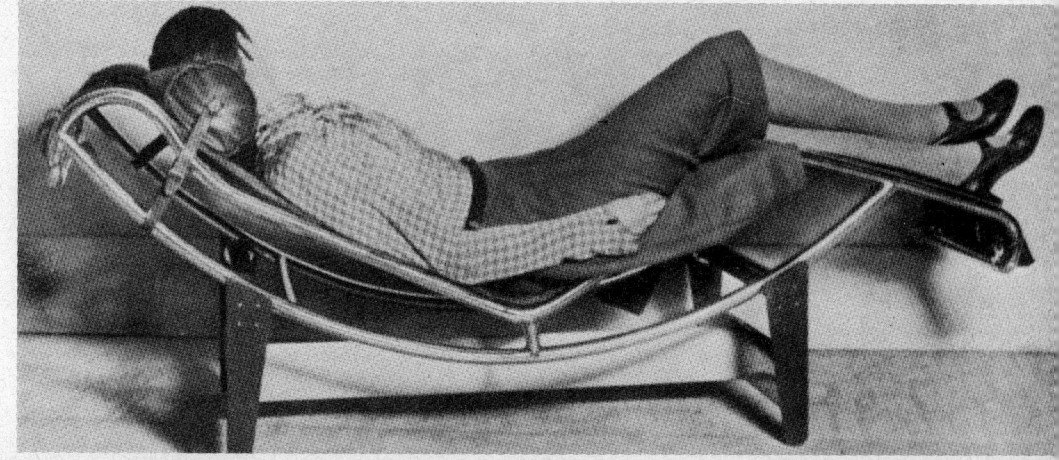

aesthetically necessary. Observations of this kind lead to the following conclusions: the machine makes its effect on the beholder through its working as much as through its form. Its working is always 'sublime', as its aesthetic effect can only be recognisably influenced by its styling. This alone can raise the product of iron and steel to become a thing of artistic worth, or on the other hand cancel out the aesthetic effect of a machine in motion. If we look further into the rules that govern good design, we find that the factors of highest aesthetic value lie precisely in the purely practical, in the sober clarity of the style of construction. Modern machines are built on purely functional lines, with the purpose of achieving a given performance with the most economical – which means the most perfect – means. The more consciously and methodically this aim is pursued, the more practically and functionally the construction of the machine will be conceived and the more satisfying will be its aesthetic effect – and no wonder, for the more clearly will the beholder appreciate the intentions of those who conceived and created the machine. The same threads are being spun here, connecting the creator, his creation and the beholder, which bind us when we look at a work of art: we experience the sensation of beauty or nobility when the work of art fills us with the intellectual and spiritual richness of the master.

Despite all that there is in common, no one will be so bold as to compare even the most perfect machine with a work of representational art. The two belong to different worlds; there are eternally divisive barriers between them.

We are proud of our 'beautiful' machines today, and inclined to look down on the 'tasteless' productions of our ancestors. True, the machines of the past do not at all conform with our ideas of good design. But does that really make them any less beautiful? Unquestionably the machines of the first development period were built entirely functionally. They were thus subject to the same aesthetic rules that we have recognised as correct for the present time. They must have seemed 'sublime' to sympathetic people of the time, insofar as their design followed that time's concepts of the highest technical efficiency. The same is true of the second period of machine construction, which we have called the struggle for efficiency. Here again the target is maximum technical suitability, though this did not always come out quite clearly in the design. We can remember machines of that period which were consciously endowed with elaborate decoration; we are thinking here of the richly ornamented shields on locomotives and ships or of artistically forged fences round steam engines; also the preference for shiny copper and brass components. This may seem to be a secondary aim of a purely aesthetic kind, but in fact such decoration also comes within the concept of the period of what was technically appropriate. Loving attention to detail and artistic decoration belong just as inseparably with good craftsmanship as do precise fits and tolerances with the mass-production techniques of today. Such decoration became false, and consequently inappropriate and aesthetically objectionable, only when it was used to make manufactured parts look as if they were hand-made.

There have been faultless machines in every period, so long as we interpret 'faultless' by the standards of the contemporary technique – that is our conclusion so far. There have also been men in all periods who have understood the beauty of machines; Max Eyth or Max Maria von Weber give eloquent witness of this. If there is still a general idea that the aesthetics of the machine have only been fostered recently, that can be attributed simply to the attitude of laymen towards the essential nature of technique. The first steam engines, which opened up the age of technology and industry, were unwelcome foreign bodies in people's lives; only a few understood and foresaw their blessings; the great mass of people, especially the educated classes, met them with undisguised hostility. Only the disadvantages of the machines were perceived: they destroyed the peacefulness of nature with their noise and their smoke, they led to the building of ugly, dirty factories; only turbulent, uneducated people liked them. We can sympathise with the educated laity of that time if they were wholly unsympathetic with the new phenomenon; given the conditions, they just could not get it into their heads that there could be any connection between the concepts of 'aesthetics' and 'machine'. People stuck to this basically negative attitude for a long, long time, more and more repelled by the unattractive social and industrial effects which the mighty Industrial Revolution brought with it. They coined the catchword of factory-work, which degraded men to the level of slaves of the machine. They obviously never thought about the unfortunates who must have built the pyramids they admired so much, or the galley-slaves who served as prime mover for the proud fleets of the Romans. Only quite recently has a real feeling for machines penetrated to wider circles and with it a general sense of the machine's aesthetic effect. And what caused this conversion? The machine had long ceased to be a foreign body in a man's life; it had not only become a part of the general life-style, it had become an indispensable object of the daily life of every individual, even every layman. Only that can explain how it was that such early mechanical inventions as water-wheels, windmills, bells, guns, mail-coaches and ships had for a long time been accepted and utilised by poets, thus being valued at their true aesthetic worth; they had been among mankind's valuable aids for many years when the first steamship made its appearance. It is only fair to say that the road to an understanding of technical beauty was made more difficult for the layman by examples of ill-designed machines, not to mention those monstrous efforts to create a technical style with artistic means. Everyone knows that there is no single solution to any technical problem; even with the best of systems there will always be a number of constructive possibilities to reach the same end. To work out the harmonious solution calls for a delicate feeling for design, for the management of lines and surfaces. We can safely say that this feeling for form is generally richly developed. (Our illustrations give examples from the most widely differing branches of modern machine construction, which beyond doubt can be described as aesthetic.) What rôle individual surfaces and lines play in the total effect, what means are employed, or have to be avoided, in the achievement of a good form, what the engineer can himself consciously contribute to a shapely design, all this must be sorted out in detail when opportunity arises.

How our views on the beauty of machines will develop in future can be forecast with some certainty on the basis of our reasoning up to date. We know that every machine has gone through the three prescribed development periods; the aesthetic effect alters with technical progress. Development proceeds as a rule more peacefully as the machine advances nearer to perfection; accordingly the styling also changes more steadily and more slowly. We can show this by reference to examples from everyday life. Motor-locomotives, which at present have reached the transition from the first to the second stage, cannot yet be said to be technically perfect and so aesthetically unobjectionable; but their technical improvement, and with it the perfection of their styling, is progressing rapidly. The steam locomotive, in contrast, has already reached the third stage; after the end of the second stage, technical improvement is generally reckoned to have come to an end, apart from details; thereafter the exterior form will change only slowly, and not in a striking way. Thus the fact that the steam locomotive has hardly undergone any improvement in technical beauty in the past decade is in no way surprising; it is a logical conclusion from the relationship between the aesthetic and the technical, which has been more closely laid down here. Standardisation and normalisation ought to represent the climax of technical development. It follows that machines which have already reached the final stage will not in future experience any essential or sudden change. That is not to say that particular types of machine have come to the end of their development. The steam locomotive – to stay with our earlier example – is renewing itself in the turbine engine or the high-pressure engine; but both of these are mechanically separate forms of the earlier types, to such an extent that they in their turn will have to go through the three development stages on their own account, both technically and aesthetically.

73 Walter Gropius, *Where artists and technicians meet,* 1925-6

We have gradually become accustomed to the fact that the artistic creator must attend the same school as the technical designer and constructor. It was a blessing when the anti-decorative movement was at last able to break through, penetrate into industrial workshops and listen in on how to manufacture modern utility articles; but the campaign against formalism has been going on for twenty years now and its pioneers have still achieved only minor successes. It is precisely the most clear-cut and obvious ideas which are always the ones which take the longest to be realised. They are radical, that is to say rooted, in origin which allows them to be effective not in a narrow, easily comprehensible sphere of influence, but instead in all spheres of life.

An entire generation of artists thus threw itself into trying to discover the first principles of formal creativity, making use of all methods of anatomical analysis and global synthesis. It proclaimed its results loudly, and doggedly, and in every possible key, to make the sluggish and half-deaf general public aware that art is not an abstract luxury but a vital human affair and as such can only be understood in reference to Man's elementary physiological qualities and his natural environment. It has nothing whatsoever to do with national considerations, aesthetic formalism, or other restricting factors of a material nature. This revolution in artistic attitudes has brought us an *elementary insight* into new modes of creativity and technical transformations have provided the *tool.* Every effort must now be made to allow the two forces to prevail, to draw the artist from his pathological seclusion by bringing him into contact with the therapeutic realities of the working-world and at the same time broaden the rigid, narrow and almost *exclusively* material outlook of the leaders of our economy.

The artist's more all-embracing view will enable him to preserve the intellectual lead he has won, but only protracted acquaintance with production methods in the widest sense will allow him to survey the entire creative network. His interest centres on the way technical articles are put together and on the organic unfolding of the manufacturing process because, as far as his work is concerned, he has recognised that his principles and those of the engineer are basically the same. A thing is determined by its nature and if it is to be fashioned so as to work properly, its essence must be investigated and fully grasped. A thing must answer its purpose in every way, that is fulfil its function in a practical sense, and must thus be serviceable, reliable and cheap. Evidently 'the greatest result with the smallest means' must be achieved if such conditions are to be met. The value of this old rule was soon recognised by our technological age for solving material questions, as it governs the engineer's activity, but in intellectual matters the laws of economics take longer to penetrate as more knowledge and careful thought are needed for their appreciation. This is the focal-point of culture and civilisation which illuminates the fundamental difference between the technological product made by a sober mathematical mind and the 'work of art' created by passion. The one is the objective sum of the work of countless individuals while the other – beyond that – is a unique result, a self-contained subjective microcosm, which will grow in significance with the fame of its creator.

But the 'work of art' is always simultaneously a technical achievement. What attracts the artistic creator to the completely rational realisation of his technique? His creative materials! Since their intrinsic honesty, the neat undemonstrative fusing of the parts into a single organism according to function and the bold use of new materials and methods are also the obvious first principles for *artistic* creativity. The 'work of art' must be made to 'function' in the spiritual as well as the material sense, exactly like the engineer's design, such as an aeroplane whose inescapable purpose is to fly.

In this sense the technical product provides the artist with a model and he will find that by immersing himself in its processes of manufacture he will gain invaluable incentive for his own work.

---

74 Walter Gropius, *Bauhaus Dessau—Principles of Bauhaus Production,* 1926

The Bauhaus wants to serve in the development of present-day housing, from the simplest household appliances to the finished dwelling.

In the conviction that household appliances and furnishings must be rationally related to each other, the Bauhaus is seeking – by systematic practical and theoretical research into formal, technical, and economic fields – to derive the design of an object from its natural functions and relationships.

Modern man, who no longer dresses in historical garments but wears modern clothes, also needs a modern home appropriate to him and his time, equipped with all the modern devices of daily use.

An object is defined by its nature. In order, then, to design it to function correctly – a container, a chair, or a house – one must first of all study its nature, for it must serve its purpose perfectly, that is, it must fulfil its function usefully, be durable, economical, and 'beautiful'. This research into the nature of objects leads to the conclusion that by resolute consideration of modern production methods, constructions, and materials, forms will evolve that are often unusual and surprising, since they deviate from the conventional (consider, for example, the changes in the design of heating and lighting fixtures). It is only through constant contact with newly evolving techniques, with the discovery of new materials, and with the new ways of putting things together, that the creative individual can learn to bring the design of objects into a living relationship with tradition and from that point to develop a new attitude towards design, which is:

A resolute affirmation of the living environment of machines and vehicles.

The organic design of things based on their own present-day laws, without romantic gloss and wasteful frivolity.

The limitation to characteristic, primary forms and colours, readily accessible to everyone.

Simplicity in multiplicity, economical utilisation of space, material, time, and money.

The creation of standard types for all practical commodities of everyday use is a social necessity.

On the whole, the necessities of life are the same for the majority of people. The home and its furnishings are mass consumer goods, and their design is more a matter of reason than a matter of passion. The machine – capable of producing standardised products – is an effective device, which, by means of mechanical aids – steam and electricity – can free the individual from working manually for the satisfaction of his daily needs and can provide him with mass-produced products that are cheaper and better than those manufactured by hand. There is no danger that standardisation will force a choice upon the individual, since due to natural competition the number of available types of each object will always be ample to provide the individual with a choice of design that suits him best. The Bauhaus workshops are essentially laboratories in which prototypes of products suitable for mass production and typical of our time are carefully developed and constantly improved.

In these laboratories the Bauhaus wants to train a new kind of collaborator for industry and the crafts, who has an equal command of both technology and form. To reach the objective of creating a set of standard prototypes which meet all the demands of economy, technology, and form, requires the selection of the best, most versatile, and most thoroughly educated men who are well grounded in workshop experience and who are imbued with an exact knowledge of the design elements of form and mechanics and their underlying laws.

The Bauhaus represents the opinion that the contrast between industry and the crafts is much less marked by the difference in the tools they use than by the division of labour in industry and the unity of the work in the crafts. But the two are constantly getting closer to each other. The crafts of the past have changed, and future crafts will be merged in a new productive unity in which they will carry out the experimental work for industrial production. Speculative experiments in laboratory workshops will yield models and prototypes for productive implementation in factories.

The prototypes that have been completed in the Bauhaus workshops are being reproduced by outside firms with whom the workshops are closely related. The production of the Bauhaus thus does not represent any kind of competition for either industry or crafts but rather provides them with impetus for their development. The Bauhaus does this by bringing creatively talented people with ample practical experience into the actual course of production, to take over the preparatory work for production, from industry and the crafts.

The products reproduced from prototypes that have been developed by the Bauhaus can be offered at a reasonable price only by utilisation of all the modern, economical methods of standardisation (mass production by industry) and by large-scale sales. The dangers of a decline in the quality of the product by comparison to the prototype, in regard to quality of material and workmanship, as a result of mechanical reproduction will be countered by all available means. The Bauhaus fights against the cheap substitute, inferior workmanship, and the dilettantism of the handicrafts, for a new standard of quality work.

---

75 Wassily Kandinsky, *The Value of the Teaching of Theory in Painting,* 1926

Various methods can be used for instruction in painting; nevertheless, these methods remain divided into no more than two main groups:

1. Painting is dealt with as an end in itself, that is, the student is trained to become a painter; the student acquires the necessary knowledge of painting at a school – as far as this is possible by instruction – and does not necessarily have to go beyond the limits of painting.

2. Painting is regarded as a force participating in the process of synthesising, that is, the student is guided, beyond the limits of painting but by way of its own principles, to the work of synthesis.

This second point of view is the basis for the instruction in painting at the Bauhaus. Of course, different methods may be used here too. Concerning my own guidelines specifically, my opinion is that the following aspects must direct these guidelines as their main purpose and eventually as their final purpose:

(i) Analysis of the elements of painting as to their intrinsic and extrinsic values
(ii) Relationships of these elements to those of the arts and to nature
(iii) Composition of these elements of painting in thematic form (solutions to systematic thematical problems) and in relation to painting itself
(iv) Relationship of this composition to the other arts and to Nature
(v) Recognition of laws and purpose

At this point I must be content with a general outline ... but even this brief, schematic explanation indicates what I have in mind. Up until now, there has in fact not been any systematic analytical thinking in problems of art, and to be able to think analytically means to be able to think logically ...

The young and particularly the beginning artist must from the outset become accustomed to objective, that is, scientific, thinking. He should learn to avoid the 'isms' that generally do not lead to the point, but rather misconstrue transient details as being fundamental problems. The capability of being objective towards the work of others does not exclude subjectivity in one's own work, which is only natural and completely healthy: the artist is allowed to (or rather 'must') be single-minded in his own work ...

By studying the elements of painting thoroughly to see which are the building blocks of art, the student develops – aside from a capability of thinking logically – the necessary 'feel' for the artistic means. This simple statement should not be underestimated: the means are determined by the end – hence, the end is understood by way of the means. The inner, deeply involved understanding of the means and the simultaneously conscious and unconscious activity with these means discards all those purposes alien to art which, thus, appear unnatural and repulsive. In this case the means, in fact, serve the end.

The feeling of kinship with the elements of one field of art increases ... with the study of the relationship of these elements to those of other fields of art ... The relationships of the elements of art as such to those of nature put this whole problem on a much broader philosophical base ... Thus the search for synthesis in art becomes the search for synthesis in general ...

In practice, extreme specialisation represents a heavy wall that separates us from the efforts to achieve a synthesis. I hope I need not prove a number of facts generally known today: for example, the recognition of laws in the composition of paintings. Yet, for the student to acknowledge this basic fact is not in itself sufficient – it must be implanted inside the student and it must be done with such thoroughness that the knowledge of this fact enters into his fingertips all by itself. The most moderate or the most powerful 'dream' of the artist has actually little or no value as long as his fingertips are incapable of following the 'dictates' of this dream with the utmost precision. In order to develop this capacity, the teaching of theory must be combined with practical (thematic) exercises ... The laws of nature are alive, since they embrace everything that is static and dynamic; in that sense they are equivalent to the laws of art ... [Thus] an understanding of the laws of nature is absolutely necessary for the artist. But this simple fact is still entirely unknown to the art academies.

[Schematic outline: means and purpose of teaching]

Means

Analysis of the elements of painting
Relationship to the other arts and to nature
Composition of the elements of painting in the form of themes and in painting itself
Relationship to the other arts and to nature
Recognition of laws and purpose

Purpose

Analytical (universal logical) thinking.
Thinking in terms of synthesis. Ability to unite separate parts. Theoretical and actual lawfulness and their relative value in practice.
Synthetic creativity and work, understanding of the creative principles in nature, and Nature's intrinsic kinship to art.
Training of fingertip sensitivity and education of the individual.

It is obvious that the other arts can serve this educational goal just as well as painting does. But it is equally obvious that painting is especially well suited for this educational rôle at the Bauhaus:

1. Colour and its application have a place in all the workshops where, therefore, the method described

can serve purely practical purposes as well.

2. Painting has been the art form which for decades led every one of the movements in art and has provided stimulus for all the other arts – especially architecture.

76 Georg Muche, *Fine Art and Industrial Form*, 1926

After an extraordinarily significant period of creative interchange between two fields that are intellectually at opposite poles, it appears that the close contact between modern art – especially painting – and the technological development of the twentieth century must lead inevitably and with surprising consequence to mutual rejection. The illusion that fine art must be absorbed in the creative types of industrial design is destroyed as soon as it comes face to face with concrete reality. Abstract painting, which has been led with convincingly unambiguous intentions from its artistic Utopia into the promising field of industrial design, seems quite suddenly to lose its predicted significance as a form-determining element, since the formal design of industrial products that are manufactured by mechanical means follows laws that cannot be derived from the fine arts. It becomes evident that technological and industrial development is of a completely characteristic nature, even in regard to design.

The attempt to penetrate industrial production with the laws of design in accordance with the findings of abstract art has led to the creation of a new style that rejects ornamentation as an old-fashioned mode of expression of past craft cultures, but that nevertheless remains decorative. But it was considered possible to avoid this merely decorative style, just because the characteristic way in which the fundamental laws of form had been creatively investigated by means of abstract painting appeared to have uncovered that these laws do not pertain just to the fine arts but are particularly significant in their general validity.

The enthusiasm for technology took on such proportions that the artist, with his epistemological arguments – often all too logical ones – disproved his own existence. The square became the ultimate picture element for the superfluous – for the dying – field of painting. It became an ingenious and effective document of faith in functional form in the sense of purely constructive design. It became the evil eye against the ghosts of the past, who had enjoyed art for art's sake. The renunciation of art seemed to be the only way to protect oneself from the fate of being an artist in an age that needed nothing but engineers. This led to a new aesthetic from which, in the ecstasy of enthusiasm for modern design, a broad theory was developed which is extraordinarily intolerant towards art. This intolerance resulted from the need for the theory to set a concrete aim evoking the semblance of practical usefulness. But it seems that art, even after it has been broken down into its actually quite art-free elements, cannot evolve where it is considered irresponsibly wasteful to violate the laws of utility by such an abundance of riches as art provides. Such is the case in industry and technology. As long as the engineer was bogged down in the style of past craft cultures, the industrial product remained of inferior quality with respect to its design. The ornamental trimming by the handicrafts did nothing to improve this short-coming. But also design in accordance with constructivist principles that were derived from abstract painting in such an extraordinarily imaginative and consistent manner, can rarely be justified except in cases where the process of production has not, or not completely, been modernised: in architecture and a few other peripheral areas.

Hence an architecture came about which used forms that looked surprisingly modern – despite the fact that its technology must remain old-fashioned as long as the engineer does not accept the entire problem of constructing dwellings as his own. This architecture, which appears to be more than applied art, is actually nothing more than the expression of a new will-to-style in the traditional sense of the fine arts. Modern architecture is not yet part of the creativity of modern production which, already in its design theme, reflects the methods of industrialised production. The straight line became the formal idiom of the modern architect – especially the straight line in its horizontal-vertical relationship and its versatility for static–dynamic applications in designs for spaces. This highly intense contrast appeared to be at the same time both the expression of the new attitude towards style and the appropriate basic form for the mechanical process of production. This was an error!

The forms of industrial products, in contrast to the forms of art, are super-individual in that they come about as a result of an objective investigation into a problem. Functional considerations and those of technological, economic, and organisational feasibility, become the factors determining the forms of a concept of beauty that in this manner is unprecedented. Inventive genius and the spirit of commercial competition become factors of creativity. An age – the 'age of the machine' – wants to emerge.

The preceding interpenetration of art and technology represented a moment of great significance. That moment freed technology from its last ties to an aesthetic that had become old-fashioned and in which art was taken to absurd lengths, and now it was able to go beyond this stage to find itself anew in the limitless sphere of its own reality. Art cannot be tied to a purpose. Art and technology are not a new unity; their creative values are different by nature. The limits of technology are determined by reality, but art can only attain heights if it sets its aims in the realm of the ideal. In that realm opposites coincide. Art has no ties to technology; it comes about in the Utopia of its own reality. The artistic element of form is a foreign body in an industrial product. The restrictions of technology make art into a useless something – art, which alone can transcend the limits of thought and give an idea of the immensity of creative freedom.

---

77 Werner Gräff, *'The Dwelling', Weissenhof Exhibition,* 1927

The aim

According to its most significant pronouncements, the new architecture is striving towards a new way of living, and towards a more rational use of new materials and new constructional methods. These are more important than the creation of a new form or style.

We say 'according to its most significant pronouncements' advisedly, since inevitably the mass of its fellow-travellers has fallen a prey to the seductions of formalism, without making the slightest contribution to the essential process of change. This must be emphasised all the more because it is naturally the unusual form which first hits the eye, and resistance to new developments in architecture is always directed primarily against the external appearance.

If the opposition were to seek some clarification of what is meant by a reform of living standards and rationalisation of construction methods, the dispute would no doubt be more fruitful.

It cannot be denied that during the course of the last decade the way of life not only of an intellectual élite but also of the large mass of the population, and especially the younger generation, has undergone extensive changes. The more obvious factors in themselves – an increased appreciation of fresh air, colour and mechanical aids, the upsurge in sporting activity, social mobility and economic needs – are bound to cause radical changes in our way of living in the long run. But it has hitherto been impossible to create decisive new forms for domestic architecture, since the process of transformation is still in full swing. Indeed the customary dwelling which has served us for centuries seems unbearably ill-suited to the new generation – almost as if they were given frock coats to wear. Yet we have absolutely no idea of their wishes, not even a tolerably clear indication of the direction they wish to take. What is worse, neither have most of the modern architects. Only a few of them have the necessary frankness, freedom and visionary strength – the rest, in this present and decisive moment, must content themselves with the rôle of fellow-travellers.

Frank Lloyd Wright had the necessary qualities twenty years ago. He knew the way to a new kind of living. But his compatriots have so far been unwilling to follow him, and he will have to be patient for another ten years.

Even the vanguard in Europe see that they must have patience for some time yet (although the fellow-travellers in particular have an unfortunate tendency to run ahead of the pack). Obviously a new domestic culture cannot be forced on people. But if the majority of the population are as yet unclear as to the direction they wish to take, one can at least try to sharpen their senses, break down prejudices, awaken instincts and carefully observe their impulses.

Perhaps the new generation do not know how they want to live purely because they have no idea that they have a choice. In that case they must be shown the new technical postulates of domestic architecture, they must be acquainted with the most practical domestic equipment and machines; they must be made aware of the fact that the most talented architects throughout the world are striving after something new, even if their schemes prove merely fanciful. And so long as one gives practical examples of the different types of dwelling, it is preferable to fix things as little as possible, to show on the contrary that everything has yet to be given its final shape, which will be developed out of the way it is used. *This* is the reason for the variable ground plans in the skeleton building of Mies van der Rohe, Le Corbusier, and Mart Stam. In this way we can help to discover people's preferences in their domestic arrangements.

And this, in outline, is the aim of the Werkbund 'Dwelling' exhibition, Stuttgart, 1927.

---

78 Le Corbusier and Pierre Jeanneret, *Five Points of a New Architecture,* 1927

Several years of practical application on the building site form the foundation for the theoretical ideas which follow.

Theory requires precise formulation. We are totally uninterested in aesthetic fantasies or attempts at fashionable gimmicks. We are dealing here with architectural facts which point to an absolutely new kind of building, from the dwelling to the Palace.

Supports

In order to solve a problem scientifically, you first have to identify the separate elements. In a building, therefore, you can immediately distinguish between the supporting and non-supporting members. Instead of the earlier kind of foundations, on which the building rested without calculating the stresses, we install individual pile foundations, and instead of walls, individual supports. The supports and their foundations are worked out exactly to meet the loads imposed on them. These supports are spaced out evenly and deliberately, without taking the internal arrangement of the house into account. They rise directly from the ground by 3, 4, 6 etc., metres and raise up the ground floor. So the rooms are lifted clear of rising damp; they have light and air; the building plot is left to the garden, which is consequently able to come right in under the house. The same site area is won again on the flat roof.

Roof-gardens

The flat roof requires us, first of all, to use it logically for living purposes: roof terrace, roof garden. On the

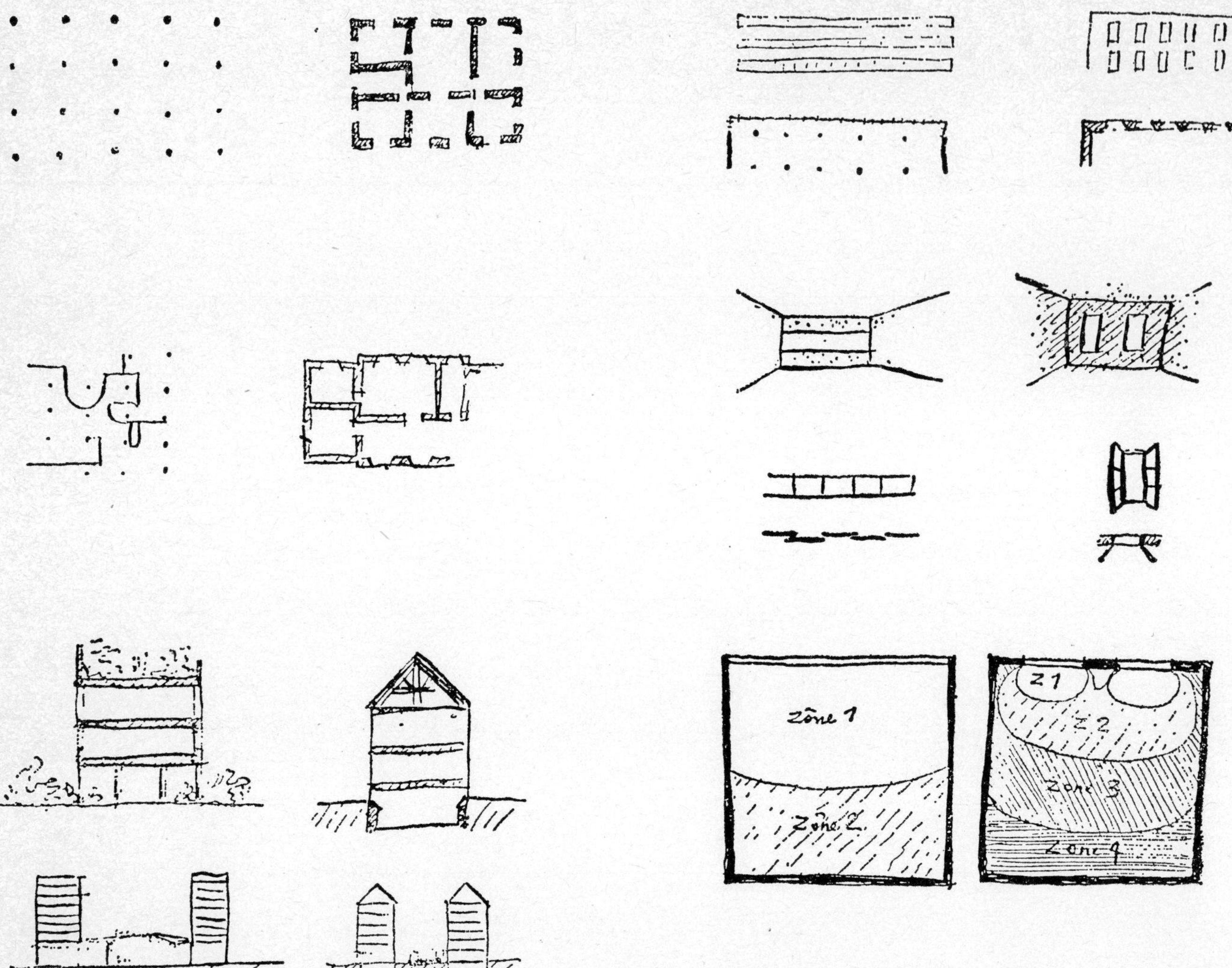

Le Corbusier Comparative sketches to show the advantages of the 'Five Points'
Photo Lucien Hervé

other hand, reinforced concrete needs protecting from changes in temperature. Too much contraction and expansion of the reinforced concrete can be controlled by maintaining constant humidity on the concrete roof slab. The roof terrace meets both requirements: a layer of sand kept moist by rain, and covered with concrete flagstones, with grass growing in the cracks, and flower beds in which the earth is in direct contact with the sand. In this way, the rainwater will drain away quite slowly, through down pipes inside the house, and we can keep the roof slab continually moist. The roof gardens will boast highly luxurious vegetation. You can plant shrubs and even small trees up to 3 or 4 metres in height quite easily.

In this way the roof garden will become the favourite part of the house. In general, the roof garden means that a city can win back for itself the whole built-up area.

Free Plan

The system of supports rises from the ground to the roof, carrying the floor slabs. The partition walls can be situated wherever they are needed, at will, since each storey is completely independent of all the others. There are no more bearing walls, only membranes of whatever thickness is required. What results from this is the complete freedom to arrange the plan as you wish, freely deploying the means at your disposal, which easily compensates for the rather high cost of reinforced concrete construction.

The Long Window

Together with the floor slabs, the supports create rectangular openings in the façade, through which light and air can come flooding in. The window stretches from support to support, and thus becomes a long window. Awkward vertical windows are therefore redundant and with them the ugly window mullions and supports. Consequently, rooms are lit evenly from wall to wall. Experimental research has proved that a room illuminated in this way is eight times higher in light intensity than a similar one with the same area of vertical windows.

The whole history of architecture turns precisely on this question of wall apertures. All at once, reinforced concrete produces the possibility of having maximum illumination.

The Free Façade

By cantilevering the floor slab out over the supports like a balcony, all round the house, you move the whole façade away from the supporting structure. You take away the load-bearing nature of the façade and are able to extend the windows as far as you like, without any direct connection with the internal divisions. A window for a house can perfectly well be 10 metres long, or 200 metres for a Palace (our project for the League of Nations in Geneva). So, we have freedom in the creation of the façade.

The five basic points laid out above involve a fundamentally new aesthetic. Just as we can get very little from the literary and historical instruction meted out at school, so nothing remains for us any more of the architecture of earlier epochs.

---

79 W. Lotz, *Weissenhof Exhibition,* 1927

The main part of the exhibition is formed by the Weissenhof residential site. It sticks out strangely amid the traditional architecture of the suburban approach from Stuttgart. But when seen by itself it spreads across the slope with surprising naturalness. Such a natural grouping and layout is otherwise only to be found in medieval town quarters and tropical villages. There are no fancy arrangements. The landscape, variations of terrain, sun, light and air, form an ensemble of living forces into which Mies van der Rohe's overall plan and the individual houses are sympathetically inserted. Thus the development seems almost like a living organism; everything is naturally interrelated. Indeed, this seems to us the most important and beneficial aspect of the Stuttgart site: that the exponents of the current architectural revolution are not attached to dogmatic principles, they do not stick mindlessly to slogans, but modestly subordinate their ideas to the demands of human life and needs. Yet they also go further than this, not in formal terms, but in the desire to point the way to a new form of living, which will come to terms with the contemporary forces so often regarded even now as the enemies of all human culture: technology, industry and rationalisation.

No doubt much of what is shown can and will be criticised. Errors of detail will appear, but this is why the development was built. It is an experiment and without experiments there are no results, and no progress. In many of the speeches which were made, there were constant and anxious reassurances that this was not an end but a beginning. If these assurances were intended to forestall criticism they seem misguided. The development is bound to become a whetstone for critical opinion. But we should wholeheartedly support the attitudes which have led to the creation of these buildings, for surely no forward-looking human being can doubt that the experiment will bring results of great importance, or that it is an event of great cultural significance.

The exhibition of plans and models should complement the development itself and draw attention to the generation of architects who in every country are standing up openly and sincerely in support of the new architecture. Here one has an overwhelming impression that these developments are not the expression of a style in the old-fashioned sense, based on and embodying a specific formal language, but that they are grounded in the structure of our times, answering to the specific demands of the task in question. And as Mies van der Rohe emphasised in his opening speech, this part of the exhibition shows that the Weissenhof site is not just an example of contemporary fashion in this country but part of a movement which is spreading throughout the world. And we may count ourselves lucky that we are able to examine the designs and plans of this group from all over the world, gathered together here in one place.

---

80 Mies van der Rohe, *Remarks on my block of flats,* 1927

In the building of rented apartment blocks today, economic considerations demand a rationalisation and standardisation of construction. But, on the other hand, the increasing variety of our housing needs demands the greatest freedom of methods of utilisation. In the future it will be necessary to satisfy both these tendencies. For this, skeleton construction is the most suitable system. It permits rational manufacture while leaving free the organisation of interior space. If one limits oneself to designing only the kitchen and bathroom as permanent rooms, on account of their installations, and if one resolves to divide up the remaining living space with movable walls, then I believe that by these means we will be able to satisfy every reasonable domestic requirement.

---

81 M. Ginzburg, *Results and prospects,* 1927

One of the principles spawned by the October Revolution which has proved most potent for modern artistic labour is undoubtedly *constructivism*. The struggle for the new tenets of constructivism began in the Soviet Union in 1920. The 'ideological content' of constructivism consisted in a departure from the metaphysical essence of idealistic aesthetics and a move towards consistent artistic materialism. The constructivists at that time set themselves the task of destroying the abstract forms and old aspects of art, and of rationalising artistic labour.

However, the vital principles of constructivism have

now been adopted by theatrical producers and designers, leftist painters, constructivist poets and so on, who have transformed what are often essentially revolutionary principles into an individual 'constructive-aesthetic style'. Constructivism has been on a host of occasions not only distorted and vulgarised but also used in what is its absolute antithesis – a purely formal and aesthetic basis. As a result, to this day the general public has not managed to differentiate fully the artistic methods of this 'pseudo-constructivism' from the true vital principles of constructivism. Essentially, the majority of the polemics, attacks and difficulties which constructivism has had to experience, have to a large extent resulted from this confusion, which explains the inability or reluctance amongst our critics to understand these two, as it were diametrically opposed concepts.

Aleksei Gan's propaganda book *Constructivism* which was issued in Moscow in 1922, represents the first attempt to formulate and disseminate in print the vital ideas of constructivism.

The constructivists' declaration and programme, presented in 1920 to the plenary session of the Institute of Artistic Culture (Inkhuk), and the above-mentioned book, represent, so to speak, the first signposts to the future development of constructivism. In one of the extracts from this book which at that time appeared in our periodical press, we read, amongst other things:

> But attacks against Marxists being 'hurt by aesthetics' will be sterile after constructivism has made the transition from the realm of *theory* to *action* and has shown *in action* its connection with the Marxist conception of life ...

Since that time five years have elapsed. During those five years much has been done by Soviet architecture in the realm of *action*. The following lines will endeavour to trace the results of this action, and to outline the prospects for the further development of constructivism in one of the most important realms of artistic labour and production – architecture.

In 1923 we have a landmark for constructivism in its first concrete architectural action – the Vesnins' project for a 'Palace of Labour' completed for a competition which the Moscow Architectural Society was commissioned to announce by the Moscow Soviet.

For the first time we see embodied in this work the vital principles of the new approach to the resolution of architectural problems. This work is uniquely important and valuable for its *new plan*. Instead of an intricate, involved configuration, with many courtyards and passages, giving a better or worse, but almost always a stereotyped symmetrical and purely ornamental impression; instead of, in other words, an old-style specific plan, the Vesnin brothers alone, for all the defects and shortcomings of their work, nevertheless provided in this competition a new approach to the same assignment, concentrating all the locations in a new way, rejecting all internal courtyards, attempting the creation of a new social organism, whose inner life flowed as a whole not from the stereotypes of the past, but from the novelty of the job itself. The whole of its further development was subordinate to and anticipated by an elliptical hall for 8,000 people, joined by a sliding wall to another hall for 2,500 people, providing in this case a colossal meeting-place for the representatives of the working people of the whole world – an architectural conception of grandiose proportions. Such is the simple, monolithic three-dimensional expression of the 'palace' from the outside, flowing logically from its internal conception, and interrupted rhythmically only by the few horizontal and vertical lines of a reinforced concrete framework as well as some utilitarian additions, such as a radio mast, a clock, and so on.

There is a curious comparison between the Vesnins' palace and Walter Gropius's project of a building for the *Chicago Tribune*, which was also completed in 1923, and which – in the laconic simplicity of the same framework of horizontal and vertical lines – in fact has close parallels with the palace.

But these two almost simultaneous projects, which arrived at a single system of external partition as a function of a single construction, clearly highlight the difference between the tasks confronting each other.

At a time when Gropius's *Chicago Tribune*, a brilliantly executed, radically constructed object designed with a new simplicity, has for its inner content the typical American conception of the 'Business House', the Vesnins' 'palace' originates from a new social conception of the organism of a building, so establishing a fundamental characteristic of constructivism.

Although the Vesnins' next work – the joint-stock company ARCOS building – is on the surface completely unlike the *Chicago Tribune* building, it comes far closer to it in its essence for the simple reason that by dint of the peculiarities of the job and the site, it represents the typical planned conception of comparable banks, and reduces all the revolutionary achievements of the authors to a mere external design.

Accordingly, only the Palace of Labour can be regarded as the first landmark of genuine constructivism, for while the ARCOS building, with its system of vertical and horizontal planes, with the clarity of its proportions, the restrained simplicity of the whole and its details – is a beautifully executed object, it lacks the authentically revolutionary stamp of constructivism. Nevertheless, the Palace of Labour did not receive the appreciation it deserved, and the ARCOS building made an immense impact in the broader circles of modern architects and on our student youth. The explanation of this phenomenon is extremely simple. The Palace of Labour was the first realisation of the method of constructivism. It cannot be imitated. It can only be followed – along the thorny path of independent, thoughtful and creative work. The ARCOS building is a new formulation of the 'conception of façades'. It is externally revolutionary and internally inoffensive. It is the line of least resistance, which the majority takes.

This was the way that the first stages of the 'new style' was created; its unique characteristic consisted in a framework of horizontal and vertical lines, filled either by the body of a wall or by continuous fenestration. In this way the so-called 'glass-mania' arose – it was the easiest and most irresponsible means of filling the framework, the amount (of filling) being determined not by the actual need for light, but by the spaces formed by the partitions in the framework. It required a deal of time for the transition to be made from this initial period, which advanced the construction framework of a wall to the exclusion of everything else, to a more penetrating conception and interpretation of an external wall, not only as an elementary quantity in construction, but also as an isolated plane, behind which is concealed definite social content.

During this period the work of Soviet architects proceeded in almost complete isolation from Western Europe and America, and the similarity between certain of our concepts and those of our comrades abroad can be explained as the natural outcome of the same preconditions in construction. Starting from 1924-25 a series of Western European magazines began to come through to us, acquainting us with the achievements of foreign architects, and at the same time exercising considerable influence on our everyday work. It should, however, be pointed out that the achievements of our Western comrades have in the same way been subject to the influence, on the one hand, of the vital principles of constructivism, exported to the West in 1922 by Lissitsky and Ehrenburg, and on the other, to the influence of the Suprematist compositions of Malevich, whose architectonics of planes, volume and space bore an extraordinary resemblance to the three-dimensional architectural compositions of the Dutchmen Doesburg and van Esteren.

Be that as it may, with the help of a whole series of magazines and books, above all with the help of the Czechoslovakian magazine *Stavba,* the French *Esprit Nouveau,* the Dutch *De Stijl* and the Polish *Blok,* Soviet architects are recognising that behind the customs barriers in almost every European country there is a group, however large or small, of revolutionary innovators, whose paths intersect our own at some point. Just now we are learning to value and respect Walter Gropius's many years of persistent and obdurate revolutionary work, we admire Le Corbusier–Saugnier's acute mind and rational inventiveness, in a series of projects and theoretical books which have reappraised all the old architectural values.

But in connection with this acquaintance with our Western comrades' achievements, there is another phase of the 'latest new style', which has borrowed from Le Corbusier only the formal attributes of his work, only his treatment of the external wall, the horizontally extended window, or some of the other design details. Within the broader circles of our architects and youth there has grown a fashionable new veneer of this style which has replaced the previous one without at any point approaching a fundamental solution of an architectural problem. While giving our Western comrades' achievements their due, constructivist architects wish to obtain from them not such and such formal elements but those vital principles and working methods which actually are of great assistance to our work, in some instances reinforcing it, in others enabling a clear understanding of those divergences and disagreements which result from the completely different social and economic conditions of our existence ...

We increasingly face an awful danger – the danger of the appearance of a canonic new style, the danger of the appearance of a stereotyped new design, which disregards the organism of the assignment, and which acquires its own independent aesthetic existence.

In other words, what is at issue is the substitution of the truly revolutionary principles of constructivism which go to the very essence of each task and compel its reappraisal, starting from the plan and the construction, and finishing with the design flowing organically from them – the substitution of these principles by the external stereotypes of the new style, under which is concealed an atavistic planned conception or an archaic construction method.

It is extremely important and necessary that we recognise this danger in time, and warn ourselves against this easier path, but one alien to us ...

Constructivism is the most up-to-date working method of this day. The constructivist is working today for the sake of tomorrow. Therefore he must banish all of yesterday's stereotypes and canons, and any danger of utopianism as well. He must not forget that while working for tomorrow, he is nevertheless building today ...

The attempt at the reconciliation in the new dwelling of the workers' completely individualised family life within our view of the growing need for a social–collective life, for the emancipation of women from unnecessary household burdens – this is a manifestation of the will of the architect to take his place in the building of a new life, in the creation of a new organism – the social capacitor of our time. This ... represents the basic feature with which we should characterise the work of the Soviet constructivist architect ...

* * *

With our desire at all costs to put our principles to effect not on paper, but in the real construction of life, we must at all costs make our work conform to the possibilities of its realisation ...

Thus, summing up the results of our first social survey not from the point of view of the individual success of one or other of our comrades, but from the point of view of the collective advancement of constructivism's practical working methods, we can formulate with much greater precision our most urgent problems.

(i) We must first of all place on the basis of our work, the careful and persistent working out of this task: *work on the creation of the social capacitors of the epoch, which represent the true aim of constructivism in architecture.* The work on the creation of a new type of dwelling should be continued at a deeper level, and in exactly the same way comparable work should be started on the other urgent problems of the day – particularly the problem of the standardisation of the basic and most widespread social buildings, and the still most neglected question of the principles of new town planning.

The maximum public attention needs to be drawn to this work, and it should in every way possible be joined with the work of our comrades who are directly at the sources of the new existential and productive interrelationships.

(ii) Our activity must be intensified in the sphere of the elaboration and popularisation of the most appropriate constructional methods and constructional materials in relation to our economic and technical potential. The struggle must be intensified for the right to build a new architecture with new constructional methods and new constructional materials.

(iii) *Questions of architectural design within the terms of constructivism must at all costs be raised and analysed under laboratory conditions.*

We must study and examine in every possible way the architect's material which is formed in the very process of the utilitarian construction of an object: plan, volume, space, colour, texture and so on.

We must study it so that we master it and subordinate it in the process of the resolution of an architectural problem.

We must with more than usual application and thoroughness clarify all these questions of architectural design, not, of course, in order that they should acquire a self-satisfying independent existence, but only so that they should be used in the best possible way, subject always to the utilitarian constructional essence of the organism.

It is necessary to raise questions of architectural design as questions of the level of skill of an artist's work, as questions of purely architectural culture. We must grasp that a conception perfect in its architectural expression is achieved in the process of utilitarian constructional development *not mechanically, not of its own accord,* but on the basis of the architect's higher level of skill, on the basis of his architectural culture, which is the result of the greatest possible mastery of architectural material, the result of the ability to utilise and subordinate to oneself all the peculiarities and properties of plane, volume and space.

And in addition it is necessary to approach these problems with great caution, in order to avoid all the dangers of abstract aesthetic interpretations of objects, which lead inevitably to the alienation of form from content, the primordial evil of pre-revolutionary architectural dualism.

The formulation and resolution of all these most important problems of form within the terms of constructivism must become one of the OSA's [Association of Contemporary Architects] immediate tasks, and must receive exhaustive coverage in the pages of our journal.

---

82 Gustav Platz, *Elements in the creation of a new style,* 1927

Seen from a historical standpoint a style is the outcome and expression of the life of a given cultural group, of a given age. Whether dealing with houses, clothing, customs, the fine arts, music or literature, an immense wealth of distinct characteristics is visible in a complete picture of the outward forms of a period and their combined orchestration appears to us to sound like a great symphony of life.

From the orderly appearance of this general view we can scarcely sense that the beginnings of some tumultuous development plus the variety of powerful personalities concerned produced strident discordant notes and deadly conflicts, traces of which we can detect in all transitional periods of style. How otherwise would it be possible for early Christian art to present itself as a continuation of Roman art, or for rounded and pointed arches to live side by side, peacefully, in many cathedrals, or for the appearance in the same place and at the same time of the daring and delicately vaulted arches of the Foundling Hospital in Florence and the grim weight of the Palazzo Pitti?

Does this not mean that the traditional concept of style is a pious deception? Given that arranging things in an orderly fashion is the concern of the man who wishes to find out and understand things, yet he must not forget that everything that has life is fluid, that history can only be understood as eternal change, that nothing is stable except for the Ideal.

Only when grasped from this point of view is it possible to find a satisfactory aesthetic definition of style for the fine arts. Then all fighting over the superiority of a specific conception of the essence of the developing style will die away. For in the historical context it will be immaterial whether a theoretician gives his concept of style a materialist or an idealist tinge.

Gottfried Semper, in his large scale work of 1860, *Style in the technical and constructive arts*, regards 'the finished work, first of all, as the result of the material uses for which it is intended, whether this is in fact the case, or merely presumed and understood on a higher symbolic level; and secondly, as the result of the material needed in its production, as well as the result of the tools used and methods applied'.

Progress on the road to the goal of a more elevated, idealist conception can be seen in Alois Riegl's firm statement (in *Late Roman Art Industry*):

In contrast to Semper's mechanistic interpretation of the nature of a work of art I have advocated a teleological one in 'Questions of Style'. This is because I see in the work of art the outcome of a definite and purposeful artistic intention, which won through in the struggle with practical purpose, raw materials and techniques.

In our age, which needed a world cataclysm to overcome the dangers of materialism, it is principally due to Behrens that the concept of style was cleansed of the scab of materialism. For the practising artist it is the sovereign, conscious artistic intention which is the driving force behind any structure.

In the end, for the philosopher it is the whole of the shifting circle of ideas of an era, the mood and feel for life, the soul of the nation which is the most powerful impulse in any development in style.

If we were to concentrate on architectural style and if we tried to express the concept in a generally acceptable way, then architectural style seems to us to be the symbolic, artistic crystallisation and expression of every aspect of life in a social community at a given period, comprising the following elements:

The total culture, its religion and philosophy of life, race and landscape, habits and customs, politics and economics.

Material considerations (intended purpose, raw materials, design principles, construction methods, climate).

The artistic intention of the individual.

'All changes and periods of growth in the cultural soul show themselves in architecture: the awakening of a new feeling in the world means the birth of a new architectural style.' (Fritz Zadow)

[Platz believes the 'new civilisation will come if all productive forces want it and firmly believe in it'.]

Fighting between opposed philosophies of life and economic systems still rages: materialism and idealism, capitalism and socialism; we have not the least intimation when clarity will return. The two opposite poles of humanity, the individual and the collective, are engaged in the most bitter struggles for power. The world has been split into national camps and power groups. Mankind today lacks nothing so much as unity. And yet the spirit of the age, however chaotic it looks to those perplexed, is busy crystallising new forms. It is stronger than all political and economic ties, stronger than the artistic genius who cannot break free from the pressures of the age. From amidst the hardest struggles an architectural style will arise which bears the stamp of the new age; for above everything that has happened stands the historical meaning of the new facts, ensuing from the victories of technology over matter and the power of nature.

This new technology rules and changes the world. It has given birth to new Promethean consciousness towards the world, which could be described as the conquest of gravity and the conquest of space. Technology works the miracles of chemistry, transportation and telephony; it demands a rhythm of life which was unknown to all earlier ages. Technology creates new conditions for existence and at the same time new objectives in building.

Every style is imposed on an age like fate; it is the manifestation of the era's metaphysical significance, 'a mysterious imperative'. The decisive factor in the developing style of our age is the immediate material influence of the technical revolution. We can lay claims that this style is a primary one. For every primary style is of a constructive nature (compare Gothic).

Our new world is building itself up with new stones and in a new way. Today the new building method is the naturally formative power: elastic structures using large spans and wide projections determine the look of today's architectural designs. We are witnessing today a repetition of what happened in imperial Rome, when its best architectural work was produced in providing things for common use. The artist, who understands the signs of the time, adapts himself to this fate drawing from it the joy of creating and the courage to affirm it. The strongest personality becomes just another useful link in a chain of phenomena, which receive their inspiration from the laws of nature. The mathematical and physical sciences (the theories of elasticity, statics and dynamics), technical discoveries (sheet iron, cement, reinforced concrete) have become the motive power in an upheaval which is changing our concepts of statics and architectural beauty.

We are standing at the beginning of a process of development which demands our greatest interest. Can we not see in the mirror of our surroundings how the traits of our own soul are imprinted on them and immortalised? The new designs of our age are developing, the home and dress of the new mankind is rising out of chaotic unrest in a formative process, whose decisive moments we are living through and whose result will be a new style.

In the labyrinth of shapes, in a world of ugly buildings, only clarity and purity of form can point the way forward for an enquiring mind. Today a new primary form is taking shape. It is our duty to recognise it amidst the mass of faces, and as far as the great distance from it allows, to evaluate it. For it is only with propriety and rhythm that this form gains dignity as they raise it up as a monument to the spirit and soul of our age.

---

83 Gerrit Rietveld, *Utility, Construction:* (*Beauty, Art*), 1927

In my opinion, there is no reason why anyone should provide a justification for making something; on the contrary, the need for concrete expression is removed if one has been able to express that need in words first. And there is no need to explain work which has already been carried out.

Efforts are now being made by a great number of people to determine the direction in which architecture is going.

Some artists want to do away with art, replacing it by pure, economical construction; yet, at the same time, they are seeking to achieve particular forms. They consider the straight line and the right angle as truly universal, while the acute angle is arbitrary, and therefore individual.

Their admiration for the products of modern technology – railway bridges (the biggest), locomotives (the fastest), aeroplanes and cars (the latest) – and of most mechanical products is so great that they describe the ideal house as a machine for living in . . .

I want to try to determine the relationship between beauty and art, as well as the relationship between these two and utility and construction.

It seems just as wrong to me to accept or reject constructional forms for aesthetic reasons as to accept or reject aesthetic elements on constructional or economic grounds. It is frequently difficult to decide whether an element introduced on apparently aesthetic grounds does in fact offend against the more essentially constructional aspect. This explains why the uninitiated sometimes find it difficult to understand why decorative elements are the result of purely technical considerations current at the time of manufacture; in chairs dating from the time of Louis XV, for instance, the curvature of the wood is explained by the fact that it was cut with a bow-saw, which tended to produce a slightly curved line rather than a completely straight one, and by the fact that the grain of most wood is slightly askew. A leg or length of wood which was slightly curved was more easily smoothed and hollowed with a gouge (a concave-bladed chisel), than with a file or scraper. The hollow profile of the leg was often best interrupted at the joints by a little ornamental work, because of the different directions of the grain of the various sections; the addition of a little scroll or rosette in the context of the sober curving lines of the chair give an effect of gracefulness which looks as though it had been dictated by totally aesthetic considerations, rather than by a necessary constructional consideration. This is why the so-called cushion-panels and hollow profiles on the doors of Dutch Renaissance cupboards are in fact quite necessary – to protect its half-inch thick panels against warping.

Art and beauty are quite different. In the first place, art is not concerned with beauty. It is unavoidable that even the most prosaic construction should have more to it than mere outward appearance. Things become real (perceptible) to us through their appearance (form, colour, sound, smell and hardness or softness).

Whether we find this reality beautiful or ugly is a question of attitude and opinion; it is, in any case, a matter of personal preference and dislike. Art makes visible the individual characteristics of each object as they are perceived by the various senses; it takes the idea of beauty to a more general level. Art is creative, by its very nature, because it makes reality and recognises it.

Tagore says: 'By the limitation of the limitless the truth becomes reality.' When construction goes against physical and chemical laws, it becomes unacceptable; but does it follow from this, that construction must become entirely 'natural'? After all, it is essentially anti-natural in the sense that it implies the willing of things into existence. In so far as the appearance of a building is against the rules of building, it is unacceptable, but does it follow from this that the most well-built building is the most significant one? A solidly-built artifact will sometimes have an insignificant appearance.

Is the sound of the life of a large city, for instance, the finest music or the most meaningful sound-expression of contemporary life? I do not think so. It is, however, quite possible for such a phenomenon to be made to appear beautiful. The same goes for carefully calculated constructions, which in their positive correctness, display a kind of unified efficiency which excludes contradiction. The object can only appear true if its form expresses unity. This unity can be expressed through decorative elements, through form, through colour arrangements, or through the interpretation of the object's function in its form. Regardless of the aesthetic value of these arguments, I find them objectionable as far as art is concerned. A work of art is a free and creative act. By the same token, all that we can create is a delimitation of space, and *no more* (even the materials which are used take on more significance by virtue of their position in space, than by their individual form). The precise need to protect oneself against nature gives practical validation to the creation of such space artifacts. In other words, the practical application of art (applied art, functional art, etc.) does not exist.

Bolland says: 'Being is essentially only appearance.' Tagore says: 'Art has no other explanation except that it appears to be what it is.'

A few works of art are sufficient to convey the essence of things for centuries; no one can escape from this. The meaning of art is an unspecific quality; constructions which are meant to be objective often appear in a pure form. Because art expresses the essence of things, it will often be found surprisingly to provide for unrecognised needs.

84 W. Lotz, *Space in Transport Vehicles*, 1928

Nothing is so well calculated to entirely change our old conception of space – a clearly defined volume cut out of the atmosphere – as the fact that today there are rooms being built that move with immense speed, travel over the sea and are borne through the air. Conditioned as we were by technical and constructional methods, what we used to talk of as space was a piece of the atmosphere whose bounding planes had been 'built', and built indeed in the old sense by using materials which had first to be firmly sunk into the ground and then extended upwards. But even with these methods earlier periods produced some irrational forms – which in this sense we should take to mean forms which, going beyond the conception of the materially recognisable and measureable, cannot be measured and only reveal themselves to the artistic perception. Thus in a Gothic cathedral the space-element, from an artistic point of view, consists not of a section bounded by pillars and windows but of a fluid, unbounded space which is shaped more by the element of light, of tone and colour, and particularly by the greater or lesser modulation of these, than by definite material limits.

Today people are making rooms enclosed in a suspended framework of light metal and supported in the air by wings or by a gas-filled envelope. Or they are making rooms which are built into the hull of a ship, actually suspended inside it, or attached by springs to a chassis to run over roads and rails. Suspended space is a form that can be found today even in fixed architecture, where for instance a radio tower restaurant is suspended, towering far above its point of support and giving the impression that it has no point of connection with the ground. There are certainly attempts in modern architecture to make us see that space should no longer be looked on as something stable, fixed and self-contained, but as something coextensive with the surroundings. The space contained in the new coaches on the Berlin tramways, with their central side entrances and huge window panes broken only by narrow metal strips, has long ceased to be a space in the old sense. You travel through the streets protected from wind and weather, yet you are fully conscious of being in the street.

It is, of course, not an artistic idea but a purely functional one, one that suits our age, which gives us fresh ideas simply because they are nothing more than technical form. Dr Riezler once developed the idea in *Die Form* that it is wrong to simulate hotel rooms in designing ships' saloons and cabins, because it is disagreeable to be reminded by the rolling of the ship that you are actually supported on a high column of water. Fortunately the present shape of aircraft prevents the cabin being designed too much like a drawing-room. It would perhaps be a good thing if the passenger accommodation in aircraft could be designed even less along lines that suggest the old enclosed compartment of the railway train or tram and more in a way that gives the passengers the feeling of being in a space that flies and hovers, in which they would not feel so depressingly claustrophobic.

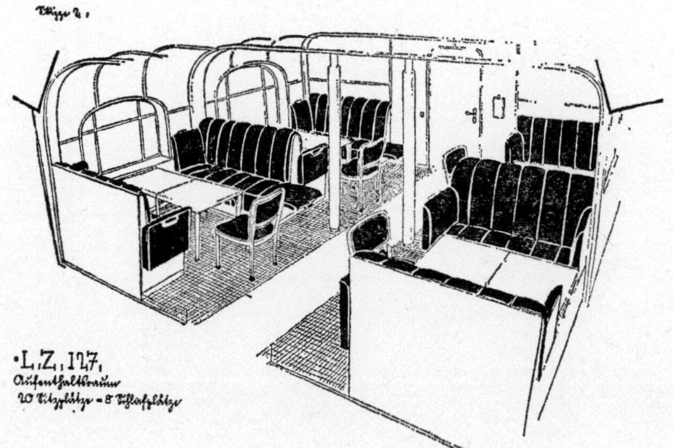

Paul Griesser, Design for cabin for the L.Z.127 airship
Die Form, vol. III, 1928

We illustrate here a proposed design for the cabin of the Zeppelin which Professor Paul Griesser prepared for the firm of Bernhard Stadler of Paderborn, and which was submitted to the Zeppelin works as a sketch before the cabin was constructed. We understand that the carrying out of this project did not fail during the trials; unfortunately the works did not choose to take the project any further. That is a great pity, because Professor Griesser's suggestion, which is of course to be looked on as no more than a preliminary idea, is at least logical in conception. The sloping side-panels of the exterior are retained in the inner walls, and the cabin would not have given the impression, as the cabin actually built does, of being a room in the old sense of the word.

85 Mies van der Rohe, *On the subject of exhibitions,* 1928

Exhibitions are the tools of commercial and cultural effort. They need to be handled with proper thought.

Both the style and effect of an exhibition are determined by the underlying problems it poses. The history of the great exhibitions shows clearly that the only exhibitions to have achieved significant success were those which demonstrated topical problems, and whose presentation was appropriate to their aims.

The era of imposing exhibitions which show an immense profit is gone. The significance for our age lies in the achievement of an exhibition, whose value can be shown only by its cultural effectiveness.

Commercial, technological and cultural presuppositions have changed radically; technology and commerce are confronted by completely new problems. It is extremely important to recognise these fully and to find a meaningful solution, not merely for commerce and technology, but for our whole social and cultural existence.

If the German economy – and, in addition, the European economy – wishes to stand its ground, then it must recognise its specific duty and perform it. The path leads from quantity to quality, from extensivity to intensivity.

That is the way for commerce and technology to join with the significant forces of spiritual and cultural life.

We stand in the midst of great changes, changes that will alter the world.

The duty of all future exhibitions is to show these changes and promote them. Only if they succeed in bringing these changes sharply into focus, will they manage to have a positive effect. Only if the central problem of our age – the intensified pace of living – becomes the substance of exhibitions, will they be able to find a meaning and a justification.

They must be demonstrations of the driving forces, and lead the way to a revolutionary manner of thinking.

86 Walter Riezler, *The Purpose and Concept of Technical Beauty,* 1928

Nowadays no further words need be wasted on showing that there is such a concept as 'technical beauty'. What principles lie behind it, that is to say, following what aesthetic laws would a design give rise to this concept, is a question which has been occupying numerous serious scholars for years. But even if we have to admit that very many fine and profound thoughts have already been expressed about the general nature of engineering and the importance of this new emerging discipline field, yet we still know precious little about the aesthetic side of the problem. Perhaps it is precisely this which demonstrates that this new world of design has in fact emerged from the depths of the unconscious. If it were the work of the human intellect alone, then the latter would not have missed the opportunity right from the beginning of laying down rules on how to produce this form correctly. But in practice development was such that an abundance of new forms had come into existence before men even became aware of them . . .

These days the only commonly accepted principle of a technical aesthetic is this: 'that only in pursuing the function required is a formally beautiful configuration to be reached' (Kurt Ewald).

Now in the case of the railway carriage, which is used as part of the passenger service, we scarcely need any further discussion on what this purpose is. Obviously the more efficiently a coach fulfils this purpose, the better the coach is. The only question is whether it unequivocally follows from this that the form is also beautiful. Let us take an illustration of the passenger coach's steel chassis, which must form the basis of whatever shape is finally produced, and compare it with completed carriages. And then we are bound to discover, over and over again, with every separate part – whether it is the design of the external or internal walls, or the shape of the window and the door frames, or the luggage racks and door handles – that there are hundreds of different design possibilities, between which there is more or less freedom of choice. For the time being we will disregard completely the more decorative rôle of the final internal furnishings of, say, the restaurant car or the Pullman coach. The person who carefully studies these illustrations should already be able to identify a wealth of different formal solutions to the problem of the carraige. A practical reason can also be found for many of these variations: windows with a flush finish are certainly more economic than bow-shaped ones and a carriage. A practical reason can also be found for many cleaned much more easily than one with profiled surfaces. But is this really enough to explain why the smooth coach with rectangular windows seems to us to be more 'beautiful' than the other one?

Perhaps we can answer this question more easily if we examine closely yet another case: this time it is the design of the motor car, the latest examples of which can, at this very moment, be more closely studied at the Berlin Motor Show. Here it becomes even clearer how much of a free choice is available to the designer. Judging from the external appearance there is scarcely anything which has been unequivocally dictated by technical considerations. There was a time once when it was thought that the external design must be dictated by purely technical considerations, that is, by the most effective possible reduction of wind resistance. This point of view may still be of some value today for racing cars; but for the rest 'streamlining' and 'drop-shape' designs vanished years ago, essentially because it has been realised that any advantages gained thereby were too insignificant. Today the shape of the saloon car, leaving aside purely practical things needed for comfort, is determined solely by aesthetic considerations. Thus the car has already become a genuine 'form-problem', without it being possible, on the other hand, to discover the rules governing these shapes by enlisting the help of the usual aesthetic concepts. It scarcely needs saying that any kind of ornamental design is not only superfluous but downright senseless: the two ornamental American cars at the Motor Show – one in a Louis XVI style, the other covered with 'modern' ornaments – are a grotesque absurdity. But neither has any other form, whether it is the curving of a surface of a line, or the relationship of one part to another, anything at all to do with any earlier forms. In fact the designs have been developed wholly by bearing in mind the nature of a car. But, for all that, the forms have not been dictated unequivocally by the car's nature; they are not real examples of 'functional form', rather they are the visible implementation of the technical vitality of the motor car, and the more incisive the implementation is, the more complete is the effect produced. And as the essence of the car is to travel as fast as possible, then the shape evolved cannot be a peaceful one, but must somehow relate to this movement. It is in this relationship that the inner meaning of the design lies and for this reason it would be totally incomprehensible to a man from an earlier age as he would have no conception of extreme speeds which, moreover, appeared to be achieved without any outwardly visible driving force. It is astonishing what perfection has already been attained by some models of cars and how impressively powerful they are. But these achievements are by no means dependent on a straightforward refinement or improvement of the individual model, but depend entirely on how well the impression of speed has been realised. For us the most important thing in this seems to be that the line of movement running along the entire car should be unbroken, whether it takes the form of a simple straight surface, which preferably should dip down a little towards the rear, or a regular harmonious curve – very beautifully done in some of the exhibited Roadster models. This is the law of 'functional form' in the purest sense of the word which in this case prevails right down to the smallest detail.

Now the railway carriage is also subject to this law of 'functional form'. Its form, too, only satisfies us when it takes the fact of motion into consideration and not when its form has been thought out as if it were a stationary container, carefully finished and with a feel for correct proportions. It is for this reason and not to make it easier to clean that it is important to keep the surfaces as smooth as possible and to divide them up as little as possible. Above all every vertical division disturbs the impression of motion – as a comparison between the exterior of an English restaurant car and that of the new Rheingold express clearly shows. And the curved window fittings of the Chilean Pullman carriage are not inappropriate because technically they are more trouble to produce, but solely because they disturb the uniform horizontal design and because every window has the appearance of being something resting peacefully within itself, like bow windows in a house. For this reason it is also better if the windows can be made broader than they are tall, as this has further advantages for those inside as it affords a wider field of vision.

As we have just tried to indicate in the broadest outline, the problem of the external shape of an automobile or a railway carriage is undoubtedly not to be seen as a 'form problem' of a purely technical nature because we are not just dealing with purely technical matters but with vehicles, and to a certain degree these vehicles look after human comforts; in other words they also have another job to do, to please. This of course involves the risk that matters of 'taste' will be taken into consideration when designing. This feature can be seen here and there in railway carriages, even more with motor cars and once again most of all in the distinctive Pullman car, where the greatest care has been spent on the design. Here a certain affectation in the design is quite often met with, having grown out of a striving for the greatest elegance and the most individualistic shape possible. And you will always be able to point out how, through this striving, the demands of a purely functional design have been neglected, and although this design principle can easily stand a great degree of refinement it can never stand any thoroughgoing individualisation. Obviously the danger lies closest at hand, when, following the very commendable desire to meet all the requirements of taste and in attempting seriously to achieve the greatest beauty, the task of doing the design work has been handed over to an artist – in fact most likely an interior designer or an industrial artist. Certainly there are some first-rate men amongst them who are competent enough successfully to perform such a task – but not until they have freed themselves from everything they need for their usual work; for technical design is autonomous – a subject, about which more will be said at the end of the article.

This conflict in design will naturally be most strikingly apparent above all in the designing of the interior of the railway coach. This would appear to be a task which is very akin to the design of other interiors and therefore could be accomplished by using very similar methods. Our pictures [in Kurt Ewald's paper, *The Beauty of Machines*] give very significant examples. The English restaurant cars especially are truly model examples of a bad arty-crafty solution. The walls are decorated as though we were dealing with living-rooms circa 1800 and all the sliding doors must, because it is the right thing to do, stand in the middle surrounded by a sumptuous framework, although the corridor is placed to one side; this means that one door can't be opened at all! If, once again, we were to compare this with the interior of the carriages of the Rheingold express, then we would find a solution in complete harmony with the exterior of the coach (discussed more fully above), which nevertheless is not the slightest bit less elegant or comfortable. The same is also true of the very good Swedish corridor carriage, and of the new Mitropa sleeping compartments, examples of which are given in this issue. None of these examples could have been executed successfully without an interior designer, but a successful solution can only be achieved when the artist has the strength and flexibility to rid himself of everything he has become familiar with in his other jobs and to immerse himself totally in the peculiarities of this work.

Clearly it is not easy for an artist, as he consequently comes into direct contact with a totally new sphere of design, to which no bridges lead from art: technical design is autonomous. It springs directly from that power which is either motion itself or else produces motion. For this reason it cannot be so well grasped and produced by anyone else as by him who has this power at his command, namely the engineer. He would appear to be taken up by totally different matters than those concerning design. But clearly formative powers are alive in him too, totally subconscious, as they are everywhere where something excluding vitality is taking place: the formal developments in machinery, even in those parts which are clearly determined by their function, prove this. The speed of this development is astonishing, the wealth of ever-new, excellent designs carry us away in admiration; and that this formative process is still proceeding almost subconsciously or at the most is left to one's feeling for form, is merely a guarantee of the physical necessity of these new designs. And the taste for this new concept of beauty – which is already commonly felt today amongst the general public, and which, above all, has become almost a matter of course for the rising generation – coupled with a delicacy of feeling for the smallest differences, should prove to us that this is a matter which concerns us all and whose solution is therefore a decisive factor in the development of human civilisation. This is how it stands: there is a new realm on the rise and we would misunderstand it if we thought that in this realm questions of 'function' alone would be dominant. These functions themselves will later be ruled by a new spirit of life – of whose essence we have today hardly an inkling but whose rise is believed in by the most committed.

---

87 Hannes Meyer, *Address to the Student Representatives at the Bauhaus,* 1928

... You speak of chaos and I admit that this term is not entirely false. But chaos is not only to be found here in the Bauhaus; the whole world is full of unresolved problems. I am convinced that we, as human beings, are living for no other reason than to solve the problems posed by life. There is absolutely no reason, then, for us to hang our heads low. Concerning internal affairs, I concede that it was a mistake to present you with a *fait accompli* with respect to the change of Directors. But this was only a mistake in theory. Please try to imagine the practical consequences, particularly in respect to external policy, which would have resulted from prior discussions of such a proposition. Nothing would have changed in fact, but the matter would have been exploited to the utmost by the opposition press. Before the decision could be published, a successor had to be chosen. The Bauhaus stood or fell on this point.

The organisation of the Bauhaus, if it is to be viable,

must be guided by the given facts. It is not possible to reorganise the Bauhaus completely, neither today nor later, nor is this intended. First of all, the organisation is going to be geared to the budget. It is impossible to convert the Bauhaus into a scientific school for the simple reason that the small budget does not provide any means for appointing the needed scientifically trained faculty. Moreover, it is not up to the Director of an institute to give it his personal stamp. He is merely the man who is supposed to coordinate all the paths that converge in him and form one constructive entity.

Let us compare the Bauhaus with a factory. The Director is merely an employee, and a change of employees does not disturb the entire set-up. What is the Bauhaus supposed to be and what has it been up to now? It is supposed to be a combination of workshop activity, independent art, and science. The workshop does not merely provide practical training but is meant to develop design ability. Independent art is self-explanatory, and as far as science is concerned, I think that it too is a purely mental activity having nothing to do with dull school methods and red tape.

Why are there conflicts within the Bauhaus about matters of theory and practice? These conflicts are actually identical with those we have with people outside, and they are rooted in a lack of mutual understanding, in the absence of personal communication between human beings. We must approach everything with a little better grasp of psychology. Psychology is everything. But the primary factor we have to deal with is the activity of the mind. I intend to establish a close personal relationship with the students. I admit that this has not been the case so far. I am also sorry to have to confess that I know some of the workshops by their names only. From now on all this is going to change. But this mutual getting to know each other should not just be something for me to work on; it is of vital necessity for all *Bauhäusler*, Masters as well as students. If you should get into a situation that leads to misunderstandings, I ask you to approach the matter from a psychological point of view, and then the situation will clear itself.

I have various reasons for wanting to make a few more remarks on the years in Weimar. It was the postwar period of revolution and romanticism. All those who participated, feeling like the 'children of their time' were right to do so. It would not have been merely unnatural but indeed wrong not to have been moved in such stirring times. But now the conflict for these people [which makes it difficult for them] in finding their way to us is [this]: They have not been aware that a new age has begun. They should, for once, open their eyes and look around in their environment; then they would notice that conditions have changed radically. Today, as yesterday, the only correct thing is to be 'children of [one's own] time' ...

Our work at the Bauhaus is also linked to this problem. Is our labour going to be determined by internal or by external factors? Do we want to be guided by the requirements of the world around us, do we want to help in the shaping of new forms of life, or do we want to be an island which [promotes the development of the individual] but whose positive productivity, [on the other hand] is questionable? I think that much of the discontent in the Bauhaus can be traced to such difficulties. At least in my architecture department I have observed that work there is suffering somewhat, that people do not know what they are working for because their work is not yet in as close a relationship with the outside world as would be desirable. These people were [almost] in a state of neurosis ... Long before the negotiations on the budget began and long before there was any mention of a change in Directors I have revised the curriculum thoroughly.

The draft which you see here is the work of the summer, not that of the conferences of the Masters. I ask you to take this whole thing as nothing more than a draft that will require many changes and improvements. Only a few sections – such as the special section on the architecture department – have been more thoroughly worked out. Hence, I would like to ask you to check these sections, particularly carefully and to tell me if they are acceptable. The other sections above all the departments of painting, are virtually not worked out at all. There I lacked the cooperation of the ... professors. I would now like to ask [particularly] the students of these departments to give me ... practical suggestions.

---

88 Arthur Korn, *Glass in Modern Architecture,* 1929

[...] A new glass age has begun, which is equal in beauty to the old one of Gothic windows.

Up to the present time glass has been a secondary building material, which remained subservient in spite of all its intrinsic ornamental strength, in spite of its crucial position in the interplay of structural forces, in spite of its underlining contrast with the masonry of the walls. The contribution of the present age is that it is now possible to have an independent wall of glass, a skin of glass around a building; no longer a solid wall with windows. Even though the window might be the dominant part – this window is the wall itself, or in other words, this wall is itself the window. And with this we have come to a turning point. It is something quite new compared to the achievements through the centuries ... it is the disappearance of the outside wall – the wall, which for thousands of years had to be made of solid materials such as stone or timber or clay products. But in the situation now, the outside wall is no longer the first impression one gets of a building. It is the interior, the spaces in depth and the structural frame which delineates them, that one begins to notice through the glass wall. This wall is barely visible, and can only be seen when there are reflected lights distortions or mirror effects.

Thus the peculiar characteristic of glass as compared to all materials hitherto in use becomes apparent: glass is noticeable yet not quite visible. It is the great membrane, full of mystery, delicate yet tough. It can enclose and open up spaces in more than one direction. Its peculiar advantage is in the diversity of the impression it creates ...

Glass has an extraordinary quality which enables it to render an outside wall practically non-existent, when one compares such a wall to those made of other materials – stone, wood, metal or marble – all of which form solid barriers.

Obviously, the opening up and perforation of a wall has been an aim and a problem for a considerable time and in some instances solutions were found which made the interior of a building visible from without, but never before did man succeed in enclosing and dividing up space by a single membrane. It is this membrane which really encloses a building, but only with certain qualities of a solid wall, such as defence against temperature variation and noise, as well as the provision of safety. This is not a purely imaginary wall as it is in the case of the regular rhythm of columns around a classical temple.

It is evident that a material of such qualities requires the building itself to be remodelled, conceived in a revolutionary way ...

The window as the structural element of the large glass surface has to be redesigned from the basic principles. This was done not only because of the general tendency to reconsider and redesign each of the few basic elements of the modern building, but also because the window is the most exposed element in an outside wall, and furthermore, because a window has to be movable with a frame as thin as possible. This is the reason why quite a number of new window constructions appeared on the market – both casement and sliding windows ...

With the advance of glass as a building material its use for other purposes also increased. Apart from its extensive use for light fittings, it is being used for the sake of its intrinsic beauty, its hygienic, hard and protective surface in conjunction with furniture of various kinds ... But glass is also used for the manufacture of cooking utensils in the form of fire-proof dishes and other glassware, including intensely refined test tubes and complicated laboratory glass vessels, and these show the wide scope of its use and its form. It is in just these admirable shapes and forms that we see how much we can still expect if one day men are to succeed in extending these creations into the realm and dimension of large buildings with suspended pipes in spirals and glass tubes to take staircases and escalators.

---

89 Bruno Taut, *Five Points,* 1929

What is, therefore, the new movement?

(i) The first and foremost point at issue in any building should be how to attain the uttermost utility.

(ii) The material employed and the construction adopted should be entirely subservient to the first principle.

(iii) Beauty originates from the direct relationship between building and purpose, from the natural qualities of the material and from elegance of construction.

(iv) The aesthetics of modern architecture recognise no demarcations between façade and ground plan, road and courtyard or between the back or front of a building. Nor does any detail exist for its own purpose alone, but should be designed to serve as a necessary part in the general plan. Everything that functions well, looks well. We simply do not believe that anything can look unsightly and yet function well.

(v) The house, as a whole as well as in detail, forfeits both demarcation and isolation. In the same way that the details depend on their common interplay, so does the house depend on its comrades. It is the result of collective and social ideas. Thus repetition is not undesirable – on the contrary it is the most important factor in art. The same constructions for the same requirements, for which exceptions should only be made in the case of exceptional requirements. Special requirements, for which exceptions in repetitions of style would be made, we admit only, or principally, in a building of collective, that is to say, social significance.

This somewhat theoretical principle might possibly be summarised in a single sentence:

If everything is founded on sound efficiency, this efficiency itself, or rather its utility will form its own aesthetic law. A building must be beautiful when seen from outside if it reflects all these qualities. But we do not only see the exterior of the building. We go indoors and look to see whether the same conformity is shown throughout. We can discover, therefore, from the ground plan whether the building is beautiful rather than from the exterior, that is to say, whether it is good and nicely adapted for use. If this is the case, it will not only fulfil our needs, but organise them into a superior and better order than previously experienced. The architect who achieves this task becomes a creator of an ethical and social character; the people who use the building for any purpose, will, through the structure of the house, be brought to a better behaviour in their mutual dealings and relationship with each other. Thus, architecture becomes the creator of new social observances.

The simple thesis for the new aesthetic ought to be the following:

The aim of Architecture is the creation of the perfect, and therefore also beautiful, efficiency.

90 Ernst Kallai, *Ten Years of Bauhaus,* 1930

It was ten years ago that Walter Gropius reorganised the Weimar School of Arts and Crafts and named the new school 'Bauhaus'. The success of his creation is well known. What, during the early twenties at Weimar, used to be the vehemently disputed activity of a few outsiders has now become a big business boom. Houses and even whole housing settlements are being built everywhere; all with smooth white walls, horizontal rows of windows, spacious terraces, and flat roofs. The public accepts them, if not always with great enthusiasm, at least without opposition, as the products of an already familiar 'Bauhaus style'. But in reality the initiative for this kind of architecture originated by no means at the Bauhaus alone. The Bauhaus is just one part of an international movement that developed quite a while ago, particularly in Holland. But the Bauhaus became the first school of this movement. It has been highly effective in disseminating its ideas and has been extraordinarily successful as a place for experimentation. The reputation of the institute has quickly spread and reached even the remotest corners of the country. Today everybody knows about it. Houses with lots of glass and shining metal: Bauhaus style. The same is true of home hygiene without home atmosphere: Bauhaus style. Tubular steel armchair frames: Bauhaus style. Lamp with nickel-coated body and a disc of opaque glass as a lamp shade: Bauhaus style. Wallpaper patterned in cubes: Bauhaus style. No painting on the wall: Bauhaus style. Incomprehensible painting on the wall: Bauhaus style. Printing with sans-serif letters and bold rules: Bauhaus style. Everything written in small letters: bauhaus style.

EVERYTHING EXPRESSED IN BIG CAPITALS: BAUHAUS STYLE.

Bauhaus style: one word for everything. Wertheim sets up a new department for modern-style furniture and appliances, an arts-and-crafts salon with functionally trimmed high-fashioned trash. The special attraction is the name 'Bauhaus'. A fashion magazine in Vienna recommends that ladies' underwear no longer be decorated with little flowers, but with more contemporary Bauhaus-style geometrical designs. Such embarrassing and amusing misuses in the fashion hustle of our wonderful modern age cannot be prevented. His Majesty the snob would like something new. Very well. There are enough architects making the Bauhaus style into a new decorative attraction. The exhibition of cold splendour is back again. It has just been rejuvenated, has exchanged the historical robe for a sort of pseudo-technological raciness. But it is just as bad as before ... The new Berlin despises the swollen marble and stucco showiness of the 'Wilhelmian' public buildings and churches, but it revels in the hokus-pokus of megalomaniac motion-picture palaces, department stores, automobile 'salons' and gourmets' paradises with their shrieking advertisements. This new architecture, the slender nakedness of its structure shining far and wide and bathed in an orgy of lights at night, is by no means, so we are told, ostentatious; it is rather 'constructive and functional'. Hence, once more: Bauhaus style. But let us take heart. For small home owners, workers, civil servants, and employees the Bauhaus style also has its social application. They are serially packaged into minimum standard housing. Everything is very functional and economical. Furniture and household articles are within easy reach and, according to Westheim: the suicidal gas main is in their mouth ...

Let us keep the slogan 'Bauhaus style', since it has already become a household word even where it is no more than a cover for a corruption of originally more sincere intentions. With all due respect to the difference between these intentions and the commercialisation of the Berlin Broadway. It cannot be denied, however, that the work of the Bauhaus itself is in no way free of aesthetic overcultivation and of dangerous formalism. It is true that discarding all ornamentation and banning each and every curved plane and line in the design of houses, furniture, and appliances has led to the creation of very interesting, new and simple forms. But whatever was obvious about these new functional forms has by no means always made as much sense. Rather, the products which were to be expedient and functional, technical and constructive, and economically necessary were for the most part conceived out of a taste-oriented arbitrariness decked out in new clothes, and out of a *bel-esprit* propensity for elementary geometric configurations and for the formal characteristics of technical contrivances. Art and technology, the new unity – this is what it was theoretically called and accordingly practised – interested in technology, but art-directed. This is a critical 'but'. Priority was given to the art-directedness. There was the new formalistic wilfulness, the desire to create a style at all costs, and technology had to yield to this conviction. This is the way those Bauhaus products originated: houses, furniture, and lamps which wrested attention primarily by their obtrusively impressive form and which, as a logical result of this characteristic, were accepted or rejected by the public and the press as being the products of a new style, namely the Bauhaus style. But they were not accepted or rejected for being the products of a new technical development in the building or furniture industries. Of course the Bauhaus, in numerous programmatical and propagandistic publications, affirmed time and time again that the formal characteristics of its products were no more than the inevitable results of a 'strictly relevant' fulfilment of function, rather than an intention to create a style. Yet a few years of practice were already enough even for the eyes of the younger Bauhaus generation to recognise that these products were outdated handicraft. This may be less florid than customary handicraft. But it is instead inhibited, prejudiced by a doctrinaire mock asceticism, stiff, without charm, and yet pretentious to the point of arrogance. Fellow-travellers who are smarter businessmen and are more unscrupulous have not hesitated to make frankly shoddy handicraft out of this somewhat clumsy trouble-child of the new functional design. Where is the dividing line between genuine and false Bauhaus style? The Bauhaus started things rolling with its aesthetic ambition; it must now accept the fact that others are going to add all the rest right up to the bitter end. Why is it that a similar fate does not threaten a swivel chair or the 'Zeiss' lamp? The reason is that these products are not born of the unity of art and technology but are genuine constructions evolved from industrial technology: they are creations of engineering. It would be revealing to ask one of the 'Zeiss' engineers for his opinion on the technical and illumination properties of the Bauhaus lamps.

Gropius established, among others, the following guide lines for the Bauhaus programme:

> The Bauhaus wants to assist in the development of present-day housing, from the simplest household appliances to the finished dwelling ... The Bauhaus workshops are essentially laboratories in which prototypes of products suitable for mass production and typical of our time are carefully developed and constantly improved ... The prototypes that have been completed in the Bauhaus workshops are reproduced by outside firms with whom the workshops are closely related ... The Bauhaus brings creatively talented people with ample practical experience into the actual course of production, people who have mastered both technical and formal problems, and who are to take over the preparation of models for production in industry and the crafts ...
>
> Particularly with respect to building: the mass prefabrication of houses should be attempted and units should be kept in stock which would be manufactured not on the site but in permanent workshops, to be easily assembled later. These would include ceilings, roofs, and walls. Thus it would be like a children's box of blocks on a larger scale and on the basis of standardisation and production of types.

This programme is extraordinarily up to date and very 'social'. Modern industry and business have attracted a tremendous number of people to their places of production and distribution. This has caused a social need in the area of housing which can only be overcome by mass production. The industrialisation of the building and the home-appliance industry is an urgent socio-economic and socio-political requirement. Industrial production methods, by way of a process of mechanical elimination, inexorably cast off any discrepancies with respect to form which might interfere with the impersonal neutrality and complete fulfilment of the function of the articles. To put Bauhaus production into the service of such standardising elimination and to train, at the Bauhaus, the leaders of a modern construction and home-building industry is admittedly a highly important and productive idea. But this idea must be followed in reality and not, as has many times been the case in practice at the Bauhaus, deviate into formalism.

It is not enough to force industrial mass production and in so doing, in the design of these products, to allow artistry – despite schematic simplification it is still aesthetically wilful – to triumph over the engineer. Architecture must strive resolutely to accomplish 'social, technological, economic, and psychological organisation' (Hannes Meyer). Otherwise architecture will remain – Bauhaus style, a hybrid solution, indecisive about form, neither emotional and free like art, nor straightforward, accurate, and necessary like technology. The result of this ambiguity of the Bauhaus style is the strange and inhibited situation of free art at the Bauhaus, especially that of painting. This inhibition stems from the secret or open hostility between most of the architectural and workshop members. These semi-artists and semi-technicians find arguments to present themselves as superior to the painters with respect to their usefulness and their powers of reasoning. No engineer would ever dare take such a position. It is clear that this hostility is no more than their way of protecting themselves against their own artistic drives which have been repressed by the fact of their association with technology. Bad conscience with respect to the demands of form is thus anaesthetised.

Yet, painting is avidly carried on at the Bauhaus, right next door to the imposing reinforced concrete structures and the huge glass planes, in the shadow of these strutting, rationally cold, expedient, and industrially aesthetic three-dimensional structures, so to speak. Whoever was to find a chance to peek into the rooms and studios of the Bauhaus people at night would be surprised to see how many painters are standing in front of their easels, painting away at their canvases – some of them secretly, like high-school students who furtively write poems, with a bad conscience perhaps, because instead of sweating over functional modern buildings or folding tables or lamps, they remember just that part of the famous Gropius phrase about 'art and technology, a new unity' that deals with art, leaving technology to the technologists. These painters are transcending all rationalised expediency and the principle of aesthetic usefulness the Bauhaus preaches, with an indifference as if they were living on some fantastic planet of art where everything is in a state of surrealism. The more the efforts of the Bauhaus workshops and the practice of the building industry focus on the achievement of the kind of straightforwardness that is functionally and structurally directed and mass production and standardisation oriented, the more the Bauhaus painting falls into the other extreme. Either it revels in dreams, visions, and blunt confessions of the soul or in paradoxical juggler's tricks between tangible reality and its conversion into metaphysics. It is interesting and curious to note that such art, concerned with psychic introspection and with the sceptical and playful enjoyment of contradictions, was able to develop, particularly in such close contact with the modern, daily practice of the purpose-minded Bauhaus. This development is curious and yet characteristic, for it is to be interpreted as a natural relaxation and compensation. The overemphasis on industrial technology and rational organisation, on the other hand, is bound to activate all the powers of the spirit. In this respect the Bauhaus can well be considered a proving ground in the sense of intellectual, cultural activities. The discrepancies between the soul and technology which today exist at the centres of the Euro-American civilisation are put to their toughest test at the Bauhaus, where close human contact and close associations in practical work have developed under one roof. Daring balance, cerebral and soul equilibristics: Bauhaus style.

Or is it simply a case of the left hand not knowing, or not wanting to know, what the right hand is doing, and vice versa? Is it a case of not knowing that architecture and art are going separate ways, as husband and wife do in a modern companionate marriage? Antiseptically clean separations are basically very well liked at the Bauhaus. One separates painting from representation. The painting has to be abstract. In Kandinsky's paintings a tree or a face may not even accidentally sneak in. They are immediately contorted past recognition or are expunged altogether and assigned to photography. Everything representational belongs to the realm of photography. Violators of this principle are making punishable reversions into an epoch of art that has been discredited. Still, there are painters at the Bauhaus who dare look at nature. Feininger, Klee, and a good number of younger painters. But they don their visionary protective goggles in order not to shield their spiritual eyes from the crude materialism of reality.

Hence once more: clean separation. Just as between soul and belly! 'Eros' has very little influence at the Bauhaus. People are either reserved, straightforward, and cerebral, or they are simply sexual in an unsublimated way. People either pray according to German industrial standards or listen to phonograph records of American jazz hits twanging about sentimental voluptuousness. People are balancing out antitheses: Bauhaus style. There is little human fulfilment, little that is vigorous, genuine, and whole. There is far too much theory, over-exaggeration, and abstraction. What is urgently needed is reform ...

---

91 Reginald Blomfield, *Modernismus,* 1934

I do not myself believe that such a great and permanent art as Architecture can be finally lost in the quicksands of Bolshevism, unless all our civilisation goes down in the ruck, but it is well to be watchful and critical, it is well to try to understand what this new movement means to forecast, so far as possible, the direction in which it is tending, to sift what is good in it from what is rubbish and imposture, and to make wise use of whatever good element there may be in it for the advancement of the living art of Architecture.

Art of course cannot stand still. The conditions of life and its demands inevitably change, and the extraordinary developments of applied science in the last fifty years have introduced elements that have to be reckoned with in the design of buildings. In addition to this, the cataclysm of the war has thrown everything into the melting-pot – literature, art, and music. People are obsessed with the idea that the war has permanently changed all the conditions of life; they forget that there have been great wars before, and probably will be again; and to insist that there must be a violent change all round, before a stable equilibrium can be restored, seems to me to be only the outcry of panic.

It is forgotten that, unlike those countries in which the new movement is most popular, ours is a very old civilisation, with a character of its own, unique in its way, and we are not to abandon lightly instincts and traditions which are ingrained in our people even if not consciously realised. It is significant that the wildest efforts of the New Architecture are being perpetrated today in Finland, and of course in Russia. At Moscow there is a 'House of Labour', deliberately designed by M. Golosov on the model of a dynamo; and the largest and most dominant part of this building is designed as an enormous cog-wheel. Then there is that notorious observatory at Potsdam, by Herr Eric Mendelssohn,* which looks like the gun-turret of some nightmare battleship, with the lower part of it shaped like a ram, and windows designed to resemble the embrasures of eight-inch guns ...

In an international exhibition of modern architecture held at Milan (1933) there was shown 'a rest-room in a steel tenement house' in the Modernist manner. This 'rest-room' was a long, very narrow room with the whole of one side filled in with glass. The designer seems to have thought that he must be all right if the whole of one side of his room was glazed, but a well-lit room is neither all light nor all shade, but the result of the balanced adjustment of both. Any place more utterly unsuitable for rest and quiet than this room I

---

* Although I dissent from his views entirely I should like to take this opportunity of expressing my sympathy with Herr Mendelssohn. He has been driven out of his country by the Nazis and had to take refuge in England and start again in a strange land. May one hope that observation of an old and deeply rooted civilisation may lead him to modify his outlook on art?

cannot imagine. These apostles of efficiency are so amazingly inefficient. The result of a continuous line of windows (a favourite trick of the new manner much affected by Herr Mendelssohn) must be that the partition walls of the rooms run out into the windows, without any returns, with no place where you can keep out of the draught, or if necessary out of the light. What happens when summer heat is at 80°F and in winter when it is 20°F below freezing-point? If 'modern people think and do and want these things' they must be a strange race, resembling those famous spinsters of whom it was said:

Miss Buss and Miss Beale
Cupid's darts do not feel:
How different from us,
Miss Beale and Miss Buss.

Moreover, to borrow a useful phrase of Mr Trystan Edwards – there is such a thing as good manners in architecture – and what might be endurable in a suburb of Paris or Berlin is quite intolerable on the Chilterns and the English countryside ...

By the 'New Architecture' I do not mean contemporary architecture that moves freely and boldly on more or less traditional lines; such, for example, as the work of Westmann, Tengbom, and Ostberg in Sweden, and several very able colleagues of my own in England, young as well as old. The New Architecture that I refer to is that movement now widely recognised on the Continent as such, and widely prevalent in Europe and America, a conscious and deliberate change in the whole orientation of architecture. It has entirely superseded the 'Pompier manner' of the Opera House at Paris, with its unconvincing parade of magnificence, and a very good thing too. But it has dashed off into the opposite extreme of crude and unabashed brutality, and total disregard of the amenities of town and country ...

I must confess that in these extravagant forms it makes little appeal to me; yet one must admit that in its effort at simplification, its dismissal of meaningless ornament and contempt for prettiness, its anxiety to do everything with a purpose, however wrongly that purpose may be conceived, the New Architecture is right in principle as far as it goes, and in its origin it had a real justification in the misconception of architecture that made the nineteenth century so futile. There can be little doubt that the sentimentalism of that century has much to answer for ...

The demand for fakes met with an immediate response in the supply of large and costly volumes of photographs illustrating the domestic architecture of the past, seldom accompanied by measured drawings or any critical letterpress worthy of the name. These furnished the amateur with a standard and a measuring-rod; and the architect had to comply.

But Architecture is a living art, and all this mummery of revivalism held it up, till architects themselves began to see that at this rate the art would get nowhere, and from sheer exasperation some of them turned anarchists. Indeed I sometimes think that the illustrations of old buildings in our weekly journals are largely responsible for the revolt of the New Architecture. By the beginning of this century, people who really thought about architecture were getting tired of all this beating the air, and the more headstrong and reckless said there was nothing for it but to clear out the lot, forget the past, and begin again with a clean slate. To those who have not entirely lost their head and retain some affection for the past, they say that they are just mouldering among the graves. The Modernist will have none of it, and they picture to themselves a new world in which collectivism is to take the place of individualism, and architecture will grow of itself, because form will no longer be a matter of considered design so much as a spontaneous development from what is supposed to be the purpose of the building and the nature of the materials employed. It follows from this, so the Modernist argues, that the less one's mind is stored with knowledge of antiquity, the better the prospects of the New Architecture. Thus a mind quite empty of such knowledge will be all the more ready to accept any form that presents itself, good or bad, beautiful or ugly according to old-fashioned ideas, terms which of course have no sort of meaning in a system in which one thing is held to be as good as another. Indeed it might seem that the mind of the designer, instead of being active and creative, will have to be passive and receptive, waiting for the impress of purely external conditions. If this is really so, architecture will be a very easy affair, because the design will come of itself, and the long years of critical study of the Art, hitherto supposed to be necessary for its mastery, will be dispensed with as a mischievous waste of time. It is a regrettable fact that thoughtless and badly trained students are already adopting this ridiculous view as a convenient short-cut to the practice of Modernist architecture. It appears that this is also the view of the Modernist painters and sculptors – who seem to think that geometrical diagrams are all that are necessary to make a picture, and a lump of clay put together anyhow all that is requisite for works of sculpture. The study of anatomy and the actual appearances of Nature are clearly superfluous.

It is a cardinal point with the New Architecture that, as Herr Taut puts it, 'fulfilment of purpose (Functionalism) is the task of the architect', and that the aim of architecture is the creation of 'perfect, and therefore also beautiful, efficiency' – words which beg the whole question of architectural design. Among the instances given of this efficiency are a hangar for an airship in France, a silo for cement, grain elevators at Buffalo, U.S.A., and a refuse destructor at Cologne. This at once raises the vital questions of purpose, efficiency, and beauty. The underlying assumption is that anything which answers the immediate purpose for which it is created must *ipso facto* be beautiful. M. Le Corbusier has much to say about the beauty of liners and motor-cars, and M. Golosov – as I have already said – was so impressed with the beauty of a dynamo that he designed his building as a cog-wheel. But there is a dangerous confusion of ideas in this conversion of efficiency into terms of beauty. As thoughtful persons we undoubtedly derive satisfaction from machinery that fulfils the purpose for which it has been constructed, but this is an entirely different feeling from the thrill that we feel instantaneously and spontaneously from beauty in any shape, beauty of the human form, of the sea and the land, of cloud and sunshine, of noble buildings and great works of art. As a French writer once said, these alone set ringing within us that little bell of emotion which is different in kind from the conscious intellectual satisfaction we derive from efficient machinery. That some forms of mechanical construction have an accidental beauty of their own under certain conditions, one may readily admit; a great liner, for example, coming towards one on a sunlit sea, or the fine thin lines of steel construction, such as cranes or electric towers and the like; but change the mechanical object and the argument falls to pieces. Big Bertha, for example, could drop a shell into Paris from a range of thirty miles, undoubtedly efficient but unspeakably ugly. The engine of a French express can do its seventy or eighty miles an hour, or whatever is asked of it in the way of traction, but is about as unsightly and squalid an object as it would be possible to find. Efficiency may be perfect and yet the result very far from beautiful; and it seems to me that this most mischievous fallacy, which is based on a very inadequate view of what constitutes efficiency in architecture, lies at the root of the New Architecture and confuses that Art with the applied science of Engineering, the scope of which is wholly utilitarian. The architect is concerned with something more than the plain facts of construction, and whereas the engineer is concerned with construction and little else, the architect starts further back with a plan and ends further on with what he puts on it. The New Architects ignore this vital distinction. It will be found that among the illustrations of the New Architecture most of the buildings, particularly in Germany, are factories and workshops, no doubt admirably efficient, but destitute of any aesthetic appeal, and not intended to make any. I maintain, on the contrary, that though the architect, like the engineer, begins with the facts of plan and construction, unlike the engineer he has to carry his thoughts and invention further, and out of those facts evolve forms and combinations of forms which definitely appeal to our aesthetic sense, and this involves such time-honoured considerations as rhythm and proportion, scale, silhouette, mass composition, and all that is implied in the old French term *ordonnance* ...

Another claim made by the New Architects is that they alone recognise material as the determining factor in design ...

I have heard that the new façade of Olympia is much admired as an example of design in concrete, but the company who supplied the bricks for this building issued an advertisement on which was shown the façade of Olympia with the superscription 'This is *not* a concrete building at all'. So it is not a concrete building at all, but a brick and steel building with a thin skin in another material, apparently synthetic stone. So far as I can see the New Architects make sedulous efforts to conceal their material – and their claim that they allow them to develop a style of their own has no foundation in fact. I have seen, in the outskirts of London, large factories in which glass and steel and presumably reinforced concrete are combined with good effect, but the fact is that concrete, whether reinforced or not, is a material of rather doubtful value for public and domestic buildings. It is unhandy, and results in the monotony of standardised forms, in which the individual touch of the artist disappears, and, unlike brick and stone, becomes more and more ugly every year of its life. In cities its surface soon becomes intolerable. If it is smooth, the effect is greasy, and if rough, indescribably squalid. Used on a great scale, out in the open country where the rain and the wind beat on it, or where the sea washes it, these things may not matter, but on a small scale for domestic buildings, and in towns in any building, concrete is inferior as a building material to brick and stone, and more particularly to brick. The Germans, in places such as Hamburg, have wisely adhered to the brick architecture of North Germany. Admirable use of brick is being made in modern buildings in Sweden, Denmark, and England, and one is glad to note that in some of the largest blocks of buildings recently erected in London, brick has recovered its rightful place. Brick is still the best, most permanent, and economical building material that has ever been invented by man.

---

92 Marcel Breuer, *Where do we Stand?* 1934

In the past I have been opposed to much of this theorising about the New Architecture, believing that our job was to build, and that our buildings sufficed, since they speak plainly enough for themselves. I was, moreover, not a little startled when I realised how often there was a considerable discrepancy between the theories and the personalities who advanced them. The danger of all theorising is that, by carrying one's arguments too far, one is apt to leave the world of reality behind. Some of the principles of the Modern Movement have been widely adopted, but they have been compromised by being used separately without any co-ordinating relation to the aims of that Movement as a whole. A closer examination of the ideology of the New Architecture has therefore become a pressing necessity.

The protagonists of the Modern Movement have been occupied with the classification and development of their individual designs. This meant that further propaganda was left to chance, industrial advertisements, and the technical press. As a result much has been distorted, much overlooked.

Modern terminology is fond of snappy slogans: and each of these slogans serves only some isolated detail. A correlation of these heterogeneous parts to their unifying whole is still lacking. Whereas the pioneers of the Modern Movement have now succeeded in establishing a very broad intellectual basis, which is in harmony with their own work, the younger generation still confines itself to rigid formalisation. Architecture is an alarmingly many-sided complex, and as soon as one leaves the technical sphere, all conceptions tend to become vague and overlapping.

What, then, are the basic impulses and methods of the New Architecture, leading to that overall and balanced improvement in the first place, an absence of preconception of any kind, especially the traditional preconception.

Secondly, an ability to place oneself in immediate objective contact with a given task, problem, or form in a clear, transparent way.

Thirdly, to create aesthetic satisfaction by contrast and use of elemental forms.

(1) Let those who prefer respectful transition from the principles of one school or style to those of another, adopt them if they will.

What we believe is what we have perceived, experienced, thought, proved, and calculated for ourselves.

At this point, I should like to consider traditionalism for a moment. And by tradition I do not mean the unconscious dependence on the immediate past. That the type of men who are described as modern architects have the sincerest admiration and love for genuine national art, for old peasant houses and for the masterpieces of the great epochs in art, is a point which needs to be stressed. What interests us most when travelling, for instance, is to find places where the daily activity of the population has remained unchanged. Nothing is such a relief as to discover a creative craftsmanship that has been developed and handed down for generations from father to son, and that is free of the pretentious pomp and empty vanity of the architecture of the last century. Here is something from which we can learn, though not with a view to imitation. For us the attempt to build in a national tradition or an old-world style would be inadequate and insincere. The modern world has no tradition for its eight-hour day, its electric light, its central heating, its water supply, its liners, or for any of its technical methods. One can roundly damn the whole of our age; one can commiserate with, or dissociate oneself from, or hope to transform the men and women who have lost their mental equilibrium in the vortex of modern life – but I do not believe that to decorate their homes with traditional gables and dormers helps them in the least. On the contrary, this only widens the gulf between appearance and reality and removes them still further from that ideal equilibrium which is, or should be, the ultimate object of all thought and action.

It may, perhaps, seem paradoxical to establish a parallel between certain aspects of vernacular architecture, or national art, and the Modern Movement. All the same, it is interesting to see that these two diametrically opposed tendencies have two characteristics in common: the impersonal character of their forms; and a tendency to develop along typical, rational lines that are unaffected by passing fashions. It is probably these traits that make genuine peasant art so sympathetic to us – though the sympathy it arouses is a purely platonic one. If we ask ourselves what is the source of the solid, unselfconscious beauty, the convincing quality and reasonableness of peasant work, we find that the explanation lies in its unconsciously, and therefore genuinely, traditional nature. A given region has only a few traditional crafts and uses a few definite colours.

Roughly speaking, the same things, or variants of the same things, have always been made there. And even these variations follow a regular and recurrent rhythm. It is their uninterrupted transmission through local and family associations which conditions their development and ultimately standardises them as type-forms.

In one direction at least our modern efforts offer a parallel: we seek what is typical, the norm; not the accidental but the definite ad hoc form. These norms are designed to meet the needs, not of a former age, but of our own age. Therefore we realise them naturally, not only with craftsmen's tools, but with modern industrial machinery.

If one examines industrial standardisation, one cannot fail to perceive that it is representative of an 'art', of traditional development which is the result of exploring the same problem over and over again. What has changed is our method: instead of family traditions and force of habit we employ scientific principles and logical analysis.

I want to avoid misunderstanding. I do not for a moment mean that peasant art and the Modern Movement have any connection in fact with one another. All I wanted to do was to bring out the similarity between certain tendencies which have led, or can lead, to relative perfection in each. In any case, we can all admit that there are numbers of old peasant farmsteads that we find far more stimulating than many so-called 'modern' houses.

To sum up: it is quite untrue to say that the Modern Movement is contemptuous of traditional or national art. It is simply that the sympathy we feel for each does not take the form of making us want to use either as a medium for the utterly different purposes of the present day.

I should like to divorce the 'unbiased' aspect of the New Architecture from association with terms like 'new', 'original', 'individual', 'imaginative', and 'revolutionary'. We are all susceptible to the persuasion of that word 'new'. Society pays its meed of respect to anything new by granting it a patent. International patent law is based on two principles: 'technical improvement' and 'newness'. Thus novelty becomes a powerful commercial weapon. But what is the Modern Movement's real attitude to this business of 'newness'? Are we for what is new, unexpected, and a change at any price, in the same way that we are for an unbiased view at any price? I think we can answer this question with an emphatic negative. We are not out to create something new, but something suitable, right, and as relatively perfect as may be.

The new in the Modern Movement must be considered simply a means to an end, not an end in itself, as in women's fashions. What we aim at and believe to be possible is that the solutions embodied in the forms of the New Architecture should endure for ten, twenty or a hundred years as circumstances may demand – a thing unthinkable in the world of fashion as long as modes are modes. It follows that, though we have no fear of what is new, novelty is not our aim. We seek what is definite and real, whether old or new.

We have tired of everything in architecture which is a matter of fashion; we find all intentionally new forms wearisome, and all those based on personal predilections or tendencies equally pointless. To this can be added the simple consideration that we cannot hope to change our buildings or furniture as often as we change, for example, our ties.

If by 'original', 'individual', or 'imaginative' artistic caprice, a happy thought or an isolated flash of genius is meant, then I must answer that the New Architecture does not aim at being original, individual, or imaginative. Here, too, there has been a transformation in the meaning of terms. According to our ideas, modern architecture is 'original' when it provides a complete solution of the difficulty concerned. By 'individual' we understand the degree of intensity or application with which the most various or directly interconnected problems are disposed of. 'Imagination' is no longer expressed in remote intellectual adventures, but in the tenacity with which formal order is imposed upon the world of realities.

The ability to face a problem objectively brings us to the so-called 'revolutionary' side of the Modern Movement. I have considerable hesitation in using the word at all, since it has recently been annexed by various political parties, and in some countries it is actually inculcated into school children as an elementary civic virtue. In fact, revolution is now almost becoming a permanent institution. I believe that what was originally revolutionary in the Movement was simply the unheard of principle of putting its own objective views into practice. Our revolutionary attitude was neither self-complacency nor propagandist bravura but the inward and – as far as possible – outward echo of the independence of our work. Although to be revolutionary has received the sanction of respectability, this causes us considerable qualms: the word inevitably has a political flavour.

Politics, of course, play an immensely important part in architecture, as in life, but it is a mistake to identify that part with any one of its different functions. To come down from the general to the particular:

The technical and economic potentiality of architecture is independent of the political views of its exponents. It follows that the aesthetic potentiality of architecture is also independent of their political views; and likewise the intensity with which particular architects may apply themselves to the solution of particular functional problems.

Politics and architecture overlap, first, in the nature of the problems presented to the latter; and, secondly, in the means that are available for their solutions. But even this connection is by no means a definite one. For instance, how does it help us to know that Stalin and the promoters of the Palace of the Soviets competition are communists? Their arguments are very much the same as those of any primitive-minded capitalistic, or democratic, or Fascist, or merely conservative motor-car manufacturer with a hankering for the cruder forms of symbolism. In spite of life and thought, no one can deny that each of these spheres has a highly important non-political side to it, and that that side determines its nature. The architect, as such, is content to confine himself to analysing and solving the various questions of architecture and town-planning which arise from their several psychophysical, coordinating, and technical–economic aspects. And I believe that work of this kind leads to material advances which have nothing to do with politics.

(2) The second dominant impulse of the Modern Movement is a striving after clarity, or, if you prefer it, directness. No romantic tendencies are implied in either of these terms. They do not mean that we wear our hearts on our sleeves, or on our long horizontal windows.

This particular exemplification of 'clarity' has caused a great deal of harm – in the same way that the desire to show construction openly has often led to the violation of structural principles or to their naïvely childish over-emphasis. Clarity interpreted in this spirit has been responsible for a decidedly uncomfortable world full of screwheads and intellectual exhibitionism. With a little naïve good-will, the famous principle of inside-out 'exteriorisation' can be relied upon to conjure up a perfect wilderness.

The principle of clarity, as we understand it, expresses itself in the technical and economic fields of architecture, through emphasis on structural laws and practical functions; and in the aesthetic field by simplicity and a renunciation of all irrational forms.

The New Architecture might be compared to a crystalline structure in the process of formation. Its forms correspond to human laws and functions, which differ from those of nature or organic bodies. In its more immediate conception this New Architecture of ours is the 'container' of men's domiciles, the orbit of their lives. Are our buildings identifiable with descriptions such as 'cold', 'hard', 'empty-looking', 'ultra-logical', 'unimaginative and mechanistic in every detail'? Is it our aim to trump the mechanisation of offices and factories with the mechanisation of home life? Whoever thinks so has either seen only the worst examples of modern architecture, or has had no opportunity to live in or make a closer inspection of the best. There may also be some confusion in his ideas. Does he perhaps mean pompous when he says 'human'? a brown sauce of wallpaper when he invokes cosiness? empty pretence when he demands 'peacefulness'? Anyhow, he attributes intentions to us which we have never had.

The origin of the Modern Movement was not technological, for technology had been developed long before it was thought of. What the New Architecture did was to civilise technology. Its real genesis was a growing consciousness of the spirit of our age. However, it proved far harder to formulate the intellectual basis and the aesthetic of the New Architecture intelligibly than to establish its logic in practical use. One has experienced all too often that something like a functional kitchen equipment has made hypercritical people far more accessible to our ideas; and that as a result they have not infrequently become reconciled to our aesthetic. The ease of this method of approach led certain modern architects to outbid each other in broadcasting technical progress, and to rely on theoretical deductions supported by columns of figures. A deliberately statistical attitude to architecture ensued, which degenerated into a competition as to who could go furthest in denying it any sort of aesthetic moment. The engineer was proclaimed the true designer, and everything was declared beautiful that was technically efficient.

I think we can take it that this tendency has nearly

seen its day. Engineering structures are by no means necessarily beautiful because they are engineering structures, though they may often be beautiful either because their builders had a marked talent for form, or as a result of that scientific tradition which in time evolves a satisfactory industrial form for everything – the norm, the standard. Also, there is, of course, a great deal to be said for the practical objectivity of engineering methods in facing technical problems. The engineer has been responsible for several things which, in contrast to many architectural designs of the last century, were at least useful.

To call things by their proper names, let us not bamboozle ourselves into believing that the achievements of engineering are *ipso facto* beautiful.

To sum up: to us clarity means the definite expression of the purpose of a building and a sincere expression of its structure. One can regard this sincerity as a sort of moral duty, but I feel that for the designer it is above all a trial of strength that sets the seal of success on his achievement; and the sense of achievement is a very basic instinct. Nor do I see any puritanism in our cult of simplicity, but rather a zest for obtaining greater effect with less expenditure; the satisfaction of fashioning something out of nothing with intelligence and arrangement of one's main resources. By this I mean winning colour, plasticity, and animation from a flat white wall.

Where does rationalism end and art begin in the New Architecture? Where is the dividing line between them, and how is it fixed? I could not trace that border if I tried. Architecture seems worthy of notice only in proportion as it produces an effect on our senses, and our senses are strangers to rationalising processes. It is the same whether this effect, which we can, if you like, call 'beauty', has been created by an engineer or an artist: whether it is the result of what is called speculative research, or what is called intuition. I care nothing for any differentiation between these methods, but I care a great deal whether I feel at ease in the finished building.

We have no use for beauty in the form of a foreign body, of ornament, or of titivating undesigned structural elements; not even as an arbitrary magnification of certain dimensions, a purely transient vogue. We have no use for architecture that is labelled symbolist, cubist, neoplastic, or 'constructivist'. We know that the essential and determining elements of a building can be wholly rational without this rationalism in any way affecting the question of whether it is beautiful or ugly. Everyone who has planned, designed, and constructed, knows:

(a) That in spite of the logical volition, the decisive impulse towards coordination very often occurs through uncontrollable reflexes.

(b) That even in the most objective exploration of a given problem by the logical method of procedure, in nearly every case a final – one might almost say illogical – choice between different combinations has to be made.

(c) That the commanding and convincing impressiveness of really inspired construction is the outcome of an inflexible tenacity which is almost passionate, and that that passion transcends mere logic.

(3) I now come to the third dominant impulse of the Modern Movement: the relation of unbroken elements to one another – contrast. What is aimed at is *un*schematic design. Whoever supposes that our preference for flat roofs inclines us to adopt flat tops for our coffee-pots; that the cubic forms of our buildings will be echoed in our lighting fixtures; or that our guiding principle of establishing unity and a certain harmonious relation between all these things can be labelled as a 'style', has entirely misunderstood our objectives. There is no hard and fast formula for doing this or that in the New Architecture. Wherever you find identical forms in different places, you can be sure it was due to the adoption of a similar solution for a similar problem. But when a cupboard begins to look like a house, a house like the pattern of a carpet, and the pattern of a carpet like a bedside lamp, you can be certain that it is not modern work in the sense that 'modern' is used in this talk. We strive to achieve a definite design for all different elements, and we arrange them side by side without dressing them artificially for the purpose. The elements

receive different forms as a natural consequence of their different structure. Their complete individuality is intended to establish a kind of balance which seems to me a far more vital one than the purely superficial 'harmony' which can be realised by adopting either a formal or a structural common denominator. We reject the traditional conception of 'style', first, because it gainsays sincere and appropriate design; and secondly, because the link between quite justifiable differences in appearance produces the sort of contrast we consider characteristic of modern life. Contrasts like building and nature, a man's working life and his home life, voids and solids, shining metal and soft materials, living organisms like plants against the stark plain surfaces of a wall; also in the polarities of the discipline of standardisation to the freedom of experiment. Such contrasts have become a necessity of life. They are guarantees of the reality of the direction we have chosen to adopt. The power to preserve these extremes without modification (that is to say, the extent of their contrast) is the real gauge of our strength.

---

93 R. M. Schindler, *Space Architecture,* 1934

Anybody who reads about modern architecture in current publications comes constantly upon the reiteration of how important it is for the modern architect to deal with 'space'. However, if one analyses the various pronunciamentos issued by the groups or individuals who want to lead the modern architectural movement, one does not find any real grasp of the space problem.

In the summer of 1911, sitting in one of the earthbound peasant cottages on top of a mountain pass in Styria, a sudden realisation of the meaning of space in architecture came to me. Here was the house, its heavy walls built of the stone of the mountain, plastered over by groping hands – in feeling and material nothing but an artificial reproduction of one of the many caverns in the mountain-side. I saw that essentially all architecture of the past, whether Egyptian or Roman, was nothing but the work of a sculptor dealing with abstract forms. The architect's attempt really was – to gather and pile up masses of building material, leaving empty hollows for human use. His many efforts at form-giving resolved themselves continuously into carving and decorating the surface layers of his mass-pile. The room itself was a byproduct. The vault was not invented as a room-form, but as primarily a scheme to keep the masses hovering. The architectural treatment of the inner room confined itself to the sculptural carving of the four walls and ceiling, shaping them into separate faces of the surrounding pile of sculptural mass. And although improved technique has constantly reduced the actual bulk of this structural pile, essentially the architect was still concerned with its sculptural treatment. All conventional architecture of the occident, including all historical styles, was nothing but sculpture.

And, stooping through the doorway of the bulky, spreading house, I looked up into the sunny sky. Here I saw the real medium of architecture – *space*. A new medium as far as human history goes. Only primitive uncertain gropings for its possibilities can be found in historical buildings. Even the Gothic builder merely caught it between his sculptured pillars without attempting to use it consciously as a medium of his art.

'Architecture' is being born in our time. In all really modern buildings the attitude of the architect is fundamentally different from the one of the sculptor and the one of his brother, the conventional architect. He is not primarily concerned with the body of the structure and its sculptural possibilities. His one concern is the creation of space forms – dealing with a new medium as rich and unlimited in possibilities of expression as any of the other media of art: colour, sound, mass, etc.

This gives us a new understanding of the task of modern architecture. Its experiments serve to develop a new language, a vocabulary and syntax of space. Only as far as the various schools help us in that direction can they be considered significant.

Shortly after my revelation in the mountains, a librarian in Vienna handed me a portfolio – the work of Frank Lloyd Wright. Immediately I realised – here was a man who had taken hold of this new medium. Here was 'space architecture'. It was not any more the questions of mouldings, caps and finials – here was space forms in meaningful shapes and relations. Here was the first architect. And the timeless importance of Wright lies especially in these first houses. I feel that in his later work he has again become sculptural. He tries to weave his buildings into the character of the locality through sculptural forms. The hotel in Tokio seems the play of a virtuoso with traditional oriental motives, rather than the product of a direct impregnation by the nature of the locale. And although as an artist far above most of his contemporaries, this somewhat relates his later work to the 'Modernistic School'.

In the main the work which is generally called 'modernistic' is an architectural backwash of the several movements of modern art in Europe, such as futurism, cubism, etc. These buildings try to achieve an up-to-date city character by a play with highly-conventionalised contrasting sculptural forms. Instead of conceiving the building as a frame which will help to create the life of the future, they limit themselves, like a painting or a piece of music, to an expression of the present with all its interesting short-comings. And it is in this way that the buildings of the World's Fair in Chicago have to be understood. Architecturally they are the last outcry of the chaos of the recent past, unfortunately without any attempt at opening a way towards a better architectural future.

The sub-conscious realisation that architecture in its old sculptural form has died as an art, leads to an attitude characteristic of our age. Blind to the growth of a new art dealing with a new medium (space) in their midst, the 'Functionalists' ask us to dismiss architecture as an art altogether. They want to build as the engineer does, producing 'types' without other meaning but that of function. They limit themselves entirely to the problems of civilisation – that is the struggle to adapt our surroundings to our limitations. They forget that architecture as an art may have the much more important meaning of serving as a cultural agent – stimulating and fulfilling the urge for growth and extension of our own selves.

To make matters worse and public attention more concentrated, a group of functionalists have given their breed a name: International Style. Problems of form as such are completely dismissed. The manufacturer (influenced by considerations of available equipment, competition, labour rules, profit, and personal inertia, etc.) is the god who furnishes 'form' ready-made. The classical code of set forms for columns, architraves and cornices, is replaced by [a] stereotyped vocabulary of steel columns, horizontal parapets, and corner windows, all to be used equally both in the jungles and on the glaciers.

The ideal of perfection of the new sloganists is the machine – without regard for the fact that the present machine is a crude collection of working parts, far from being an organism. Endlessly we are being shown photographs of the present automobiles as an example of formal machine perfection, forgetting that what we see in looking at a modern automobile is not a 'machine'. The sheet-metal hood with which its designer covers the working parts is only slightly functional. It is very definitely nationally characterised, subject to fashion, and bound by a tradition as relentless as the one which defines our clothes. What is still more important, the automobile, and for that matter all machines, are essentially one-dimensional, whereas the house as an *organism* in direct relation with our lives must be of four dimensions.

Most of the buildings which Corbusier and his followers offer us as 'machines to live in', equipped with various 'machines to sit and sleep on', have not even reached the state of development of our present machines. They are crude 'contraptions' to serve a purpose.

The man who brings such machines into his living-room is on the same level of primitive development as the farmer who keeps cows and pigs in his house. Mere instruments of production can never serve as a frame for life. Especially the creaks and jags of our crude machine age must necessarily force us to protect our human qualities in homes contrasting most intensely with the factory.

The factory must remain our servant. And if a 'Machine-Made House' shall ever emerge from it, it will have to meet the requirements of our imagination and not be merely a result of present production methods. The work of Mr Buckminster-Fuller in propagating the tremendous possibilities which the use of our technique of production may have for building construction, is invaluable. If he creates his Dymaxion house, however, entirely from the viewpoint of facile manufacture, letting all considerations of 'what' take care of themselves, he is putting the cart before the horse. The space architect has primarily a vision of a future life in a future house. And with the clearing of that vision the necessary technique for its realisation will undoubtedly develop. Although Mr Buckminster-Fuller realises the coming importance of space-considerations in architecture, his Dymaxion house is not a 'space creation'. However 'ephemeral', to use his own term, it may be, it is born of a sculptural conception. Its structural scheme is akin to the one of the tree, and although its branches and members may try to wed it to space by the tenderest interlockings, the 'room' they enclose is not an aimful space conception but a by-product without architectural meaning.

Modern architecture can not be developed by changing slogans. It is not in the hands of the engineer, the efficiency expert, the machinist or the economist. It is developing in the minds of the artists who can grasp 'space' and 'space forms' as a new medium for human expression. The development of this new language is going on amongst us, unconsciously in most cases, partly realised in some. It is not merely the birth of a new style, or a new version of the old play with sculptural forms, but the subjection of a new medium to serve as a vehicle for human expression.

Four

Housing and the wider political context

The interface between architecture and politics in the 1920s and 1930s, as in most periods of modern history, was housing. Housing was the dominant need between the wars and a private battlefield for political expression. As we have seen in Part 3, the social factor was one of the cardinal points in the aesthetic of the Modern Movement, to the extent that modern architecture was almost universally condemned as bolshevist in traditionalist and conservative circles. Similarly the Nazis in Germany were able to extract political capital from the general prejudices against high density urban housing which the Modern Movement architects appeared to be putting forward as the answer to all housing ills. Put at its simplest, the main polarisation in all these extracts can be seen to be between the International Style belief in the possibilities of standardisation, mass-production and industrialisation of the components of housing, which were felt to be the only way to guarantee the basic values of minimum healthy accommodation, privacy, services, heat and light, and the appeal to the traditional virtues of 'homely' domestic architecture, reassuring in its materials, forms and racial homogeneity. The issue of industrialised mass housing (94, 99, 100, 103, 105, 106, 109, 114) can be set against the principle of preserving and extending the best of the old (98, 102, 110). Most people recognised the need to build for the masses at a price they could afford and advocated rationalisation and a concentration on essentials (98), but most English critics were convinced that 'good' and 'cheap' were necessarily opposed (95, 96, 97). The Arts and Crafts conviction that 'good' form was necessarily linked to craftsmanship and 'good' materials, persisted throughout the period. In the 1930s, however, in Germany, it took on altogether more disturbingly nationalist and racialist overtones. The political confrontation in Germany is well expressed by Walter Riezler (107), and, from the outside, by Philip Johnson (108). The Weissenhof Siedlung built as a Werkbund housing exhibition in 1927 was one of the key battlegrounds, set in the centre of conservative Württemburg, where men like Schmitthenner and Schuster (110, 112) drew on reserves of popular feeling which stigmatised the International Movement as foreign, oriental, Jewish and bolshevist. The traditionalist group, Der Block, was founded as a direct reaction to the Weissenhof Siedlung Exhibition. Modern Movement architects were also keen propagandists, and it is interesting to compare the way the Weissenhof Siedlung (director, Mies van der Rohe) emerges from their accounts (99, 100, 101, 105). It is a critically important commentary on the period that housing, the most essential task facing all architects, and recognised universally as such, was subjected to such fiercely partisan debate which tended partly to draw attention away from the most important elements in the problems of modern housing. No one today can accept universally every aspect of either the International Style or the traditional dogmas on housing.

---

94 Walter Gropius, *Programme for the establishment of a Company for the Provision of housing on Aesthetically Consistent Principles,* 1910

Underlying Idea

The Company which is to be established regards the industrialisation of housing as its aim, in order to provide for the building of houses the incontestable advantages of industrial production, i.e., best materials and workmanship and a cheap price . . .

The fundamental principle of industry is subdivision of labour. The creator concentrates all his energies on making his idea, his creation, come to life, the manufacturer concentrates his on durable and cheap production, the merchant on well organised distribution of the product. This use of specialists is the only way by which essential, i.e., spiritual, creation can be made to work economically and the public can be supplied with products of aesthetically and technically good quality.

It is true also of the building of houses. To a certain extent industrial production has already entered this field, but the types introduced by entrepreneurs for the sake of making profits are immature and technically as well as aesthetically bad and therefore inferior in quality to houses whose parts are still produced by hand . . .

The new Company is to draw the consequences from this situation and combine by means of industrialisation the aesthetic activity of the architect and the economic activity of the entrepreneur ...

Thus a happy union would be established between art and technics and a large public enabled to possess mature works of architecture and reliable and durable products.

The reason why careful detailing in all respects can, even where a simple house is concerned, be of such high cultural significance lies much deeper. It lies in the concept of the *Zeitstil* (style of the time).

The way private houses are built today, the tendency deliberately to stress uniqueness i.e., the opposite of the principles of modern industry, cannot possibly create a type of housing characteristic of our age. Methods based on craftsmanship are antiquated and must be replaced by the acceptance of a modern concept of industry. The search for the odd, the wish to be different from one's neighbour, makes unity of style impossible. It is a search for what is novel, not for the perfect type. The example of all styles of the past shows that they all worked to established formal principles with variations only to fit special cases ...

The necessity for conventions can also be demonstrated from their practical advantages. The more an individual ground plan differs from what is based on the needs of an age and has been worked out by generations, the more will its own qualities suffer. What is true of the plan, is true of the whole house. Past periods respected traditions. The Dutch brick house, the French apartment block of the eighteenth century, the Biedermeier house of about 1800 were all repeated in series. In England this desire for conventional identity, based on a firm power to organise, led to terrace housing exactly identical, continued without a break throughout whole districts. The result was great economies and at the same time (admittedly unintentionally), aesthetic consistency. However because the English builders did not intend to produce works of art, their single-minded pursuit of economic advantages produced in the elevations a drab uniformity.

The Realisation of the Idea

Use of the same parts and materials for all houses

The idea of industrialisation in housing can be translated into reality by repeating individual parts in all the designs promoted by the Company. This makes mass production possible and promotes low costs and high rentability. Only by mass producing can really good products be provided. With the present methods of building houses it is a matter of luck whether one finds efficient and reliable craftsmen. Mass production in a factory guarantees identity of products. Nearly all parts of a house can be produced in factories, such as:

Building – staircases, railings, windows, doors, cornices, doorways, balconies, bay windows, verandas, dormer windows, and grilles

Decorating and furnishing – furniture, panelling, ceiling panels, floors, wallpapers, door furniture, handles, key-holes, etc., linoleum, lincrusta, light fittings, textiles, ceramics and cutlery

Given the trend of our age to eliminate the craftsman more and more, yet greater savings by means of industrialisation can be foretold, though in our country they may for the time being still appear utopian. In America Edison casts in variable iron forms whole houses with walls, ceilings, staircases, plumbing, etc., and can thereby dispense even with the bricklayer and joiner*.

For all essential parts the best dimensions have to be decided first of all. These standard dimensions form the basis for the designs and are to be kept in future designs. Only by this means can mass sales be guaranteed and special fitting in the case of replacements and repairs be avoided.

Of each item there are available a number of designs of different execution and price, but the same size.

All questions of form, colour, material and internal equipment are put down and catalogued as variants. All parts fit exactly, as they are made by machine to

* This was reported in *Building News* 91, 249 (1906) and cited in P. Collins (1959) *Concrete*, p. 90

the same standard dimensions. For the same reason they are interchangeable.

Furnishings promise to be an important field ...

In the same way all technical and sanitary installations, i.e. hot and cold water, bathroom equipment, electrically operated ventilation, electric lighting and cooking apparatus will be ready-made and offered according to whatever arrangement and price are suitable ...

Multiple use of designs

The guiding idea of the Company is to be that comfort is not obtained by overdone bogus splendours, but by clear spatial arrangements, and by the conjunction and selection of tested materials and reliable techniques. It is in this field that higher excellency will be offered and confirmed by guarantees granted over several years. For it is exactly here that the Company believes itself able to establish and maintain its reputation ...

The houses as designed are independent, coherent organisms not tied to any site, devised to fit the needs of modern civilised man in any country, not only Germany. Interchanges between civilised nations are growing with the growing facilities of traffic. The result of this is the establishment of new international needs and a unified direction in all vital questions. National costumes tend to disappear and fashion is becoming a common factor in all civilised countries. In the same way, there is bound to be a common convention in housing transcending national frontiers ...

To satisfy the changing needs of the public, the Company has prepared detached houses of different types and sizes from the working-class house to the upper-class villa. They will be put into operation according to demand. The advantages of detached houses need not be reiterated. Everybody wishes to own property. The strength of this wish even among the poorer classes is demonstrated by the allotments round our cities ...

It is likely that the Society will make sufficient profit from the sale of such detached houses. However, it will also be desirable, taking into consideration the appearance of a town as a whole and also higher profits, to lay out and build coherently larger estates inside and outside a town. This could be done under contracts with entrepreneurs ...

The principle of creating coherent streets out of rows of identical houses can also be applied to blocks of flats in cities ...

In the case of the largest types of such blocks of flats one could again, where opportunity arises, think of simplifying the running by means of centralisation of services.

---

95 Anon, *Good and Cheap,* 1918

Without further apology we propose to deal with a question which naturally and obviously is exercising thoughtful minds. Put succinctly this question is why should good furniture, good pottery, good stuffs and so forth be so expensive as to be within the grasp only of the relatively few, who as affecting the large real issue hardly matter. The small wealthy class hardly matters from this point of view, which must after all be the D.I.A. Design and Industry Association view, because their need of better things is negligible compared with the need of the great majority of people, who are positively or comparatively poor ...

To become true to our reiterated aims, to justify our position as genuine reformers, to show ourselves alive to present and future needs, we have to drop pious protestations and vague ethics, and cleave to the necessity for providing good, cheap things ...

At one of our recent luncheon meetings Mrs Ernestine Mills broached the same question. After the war, she said, we were to have thousands of new houses built for work-people. How did the Government propose that these cottages were to be furnished? Beautiful cottage furniture had been produced for a long time, but at a price impossible for the people who would inhabit these houses. We can conceive nothing more farcical or discouraging than this idea of beautiful 'cottage' furniture exclusively designed for the pseudo, week-end cottager, who motors down from Mayfair, while the real cottager disfigures his dwelling with hideous shoddy because good so-called cottage furniture is not for poor purses.

One speaker, it is true, gave the impression that the D.I.A. had contemplated producing standardised cottage furniture, a project nipped by war conditions. If that were in fact the case we have much to thank the war for. But a more accurate statement of what the D.I.A. really had projected in this matter is that a *typical* set of good and cheap cottage furniture already made, should be made available to the public – a very different thing. The last thing we should father is this idea of standardisation, which would surely kill all local individuality and expression. Too well we know the horrid effects of this fatal result of bureaucratic minds. For we have seen standard elementary school buildings, purple bricks, glazed tiles and all, the perfect model of those gloomy prisons that numb young minds in Limehouse or Halifax, dumped ready made into the mountain villages of Wales ...

The D.I.A. knows that its high ideals have no chance of fructifying unless they strike down to a real and permanent subsoil. The vacillating vogues and taste of the cultured rich do not help, save to swell balance sheets. Our only hope of recreating design and industry, in the condition we demand, is to set a standard that will form a solid popular taste for simplicity and right design. To effect this we must prove our case that design is fitness. And this we shall never do while we postulate that poor people need not apply for the benefits of our scheme. Fitness, if it have any meaning, must signify ability to answer common needs, not special cases ...

Will anyone deny that for sheer hard wear and practical efficiency the ordinary kitchen table and chair are admirable? We cite a kitchen table as a type of simple straightforward construction that has never been complicated by the question of super-added decoration ...

If it be conceded that a well designed table and chair, no more expensive than and as durable as the ordinary kitchen furniture, can be produced as cottage 'living-room' furniture, the rest seems to us to follow. Then we could say: 'We can give you good cheap ware and chairs and tables, but you mustn't expect them to be mahogany or Chinese porcelain; we guarantee the strength and fitness of their substance and the rightness and fine lines of their design. As we have spent nothing on trimmings we charge you nothing but for quality.' And there we find ourselves repeating our favourite aphorism.

The conclusion of the whole matter is this. The essential condition is cheapness; are we, the D.I.A., to solve the problem of making good cheap things a social and commercial success, or shall we leave it to more enterprising and 'live' people? Just as the essential qualification for an aeroplane is that it should fly, and just as all plans and estimates for it must be primarily directed to that end, so to answer the needs of a world in which most people are and always will be poor (to say nothing of the immediate consequences of this devastating war) out of fitness furniture must have cheapness for its conditioning consideration. For us the added task of making goodness compatible with that first essential. Our immediate problem is not the rich man and what he can buy; our more pressing duty is to satisfy the requirements of the great majority. As Sedding says: 'Art can never live a wholesome life or prosper, that is not related to the people at large, nor exercised for their pleasure. Art that is not common to the people has failed in its mission, as it deserves to fail' ...

96 Alfred P. Simon, *Good and Cheap,* 1918

Sir,

Tempted by the invitation posted on the first page of the D.I.A. current issue, one ventures to offer an analysis of the points raised by the article, 'Good and Cheap.'

With no wish to carp, and accepting its tenets in the main, it is, unfortunately, apparent that the formula – 'D.I.A. must cleave to the necessity of providing good, cheap things' – is nearly akin to 'unpractical sentimentalism', and that it lays itself open to the very reproach which itself levels. For what, exactly, does the word 'cheap' stand? It is but a relative term and so is the definition 'within the purchasing power of the positively or comparatively poor'. The real definition of cheapness as set up by the general tenor of the essay, is the ability to compete successfully in terms of *£ s. d.* with the badly-made object, and it is on this interpretation that the writer has evidently evolved his arguments.

But how will these arguments work out in practice? Can good workmanship, with the necessary corollaries of good material, good working conditions, and reasonable hours of labour, compete with the shoddy object of practical commerce, made with no thought as to durability, but all concentration upon its selling qualities; not to appeal to the reason but solely to attract the eye of the purchaser? The care and precision required in the workmanship, and the quality of the material necessarily employed in the simply-made object, as opposed to the one whose defects are covered by ornament, all make for greater expense in extra labour, and for less showy results. Careful thought and satisfactory answers must be given to these questions if D.I.A. is to establish a firm hold upon industry and if it is to avoid being classed as a body of unpractical idealists.

But to bring the argument further: what reason is there to suppose that the 'positively or comparatively poor', as a class, have any desire to possess the good and cheap of D.I.A. standard?

It may be taken as a fact that the average class of positively and comparatively poor have no desire to do anything but to copy as closely as possible the prevailing fashion, and to furnish their 10 by 12 feet parlour on lines laid down by their neighbour or, where there are evidences of imagination working, to imitate the sumptuous surroundings of some Lady Clare Vere de Vere. The poorest living-room has some pretensions to taste, and black indeed is the day when the treasures, i.e., horrors, of the mantelpiece have to suffer a temporary eclipse; but as the greater imaginative powers are shown (manifesting themselves in a superabundance of unnecessary objects), the more they are guided by the realms of romance of the penny novelette and the 'Family Herald'. Once the aforesaid Lady Clare makes a practice of refusing or accepting the noble duke's advances from a background of austere simplicity, without the adjuncts of gilded ornaments and exotic plants, then, and then only, will our parlours discard their present furnishings, decorations, and aspidistras. Then will it be possible for such purses to have the few necessary and beautiful objects of D.I.A. standards at a not greater cost than the many useless and ill-made objects which the present standards deem necessary.

We are, therefore, not entirely wasting our efforts if we cannot produce our furniture in competition with that which is made solely for trade purposes, nor is it a waste of effort to educate the wealthy patrons so long as human nature remains what it is. Fashion, if harnessed to our needs, will effect much more than any high-souled discourse, and we shall have travelled a long way in the direction most desired if we succeed in imposing our standards on those who, merely by wealth, are prominently in the public eye. For through them shall we create naturally the demand for our wares, which demand will itself remove their economic disabilities ...

97 M. H. Baillie Scott, *Good and Cheap,* 1918

Sir,

I venture to assert that Mr Simon is quite right in his estimate of the depraved tastes of the poor, both in the dwellings they live in, and all the appointments of their daily lives. But I think we may well go further than that, and include in his general indictment the public as a whole – those who live in villas expensively furnished as well as those humbler folk, whose conception of the ideal house centres in a bay window adorned with lace curtains, and fenced from the road, say with a cast iron railing picked out in blue and gold ...

As long as people can get cheap and flashy smart-looking things to put in their houses they will choose such things. And this is probably equally true of the old days too. Only in those days *such things were not made.* If it is beyond our powers to educate the public to apprciate good work, is it beyond our powers to prevent the production of bad work? The average human being is a strange compound of good and bad. Given a social state which panders to what is bad, and bad will be accepted in following the line of least resistance. If then we leave the question of educating the public taste, and consider the matter of production, how it may be asked, can good work only be produced? ...

As long as our detestable commercial system of labour and capital pulling in opposite directions persists, so long will it be impossible to produce good work. What we require as a fundamental condition for good work is the grouping of our industries in associated bands of workers, giving to the worker that security and protection which he once enjoyed in the old Guilds. In such association no alien and autocratic power must exist to degrade his labour for the purposes of profit. Good work will then automatically follow, because every workman has a natural instinct to do good work if he has a chance – just as in playing a game ...

In a properly constituted world I should enter the Guild of carpenters, and after due initiation into the mysteries I should become one of a great company with its own traditions, ideals, and *espirit de corps,* which would make itself responsible for all my needs, and secure me against all risks.

If this is Utopian, it is at any rate a Utopia which once existed in England before the Midas curse fell upon us, under which fell enchantment no good work can be produced, or ever will.

---

98 W. R. Lethaby, *Housing and Furnishing,* 1920

There is much talk of Housing at the present time, valuable and necessary talk, but yet up to the present it is a case of much talk and little house. Still it is necessary to try to stir up general interest, even enthusiasm and passion, in the hope that a real beginning may soon be made.

Housing, of course, is not merely a cottage question; it is an immense national question and also an immediately individual question in which we should all be decidedly interested. Housing is health and temper and a large part of living. It must be one of a very few greatest of all questions. Pride of home is pride of country. Housing is the necessary preliminary 'plant' and 'capital' for our national life. We have to accumulate force for renewal. We need to clear our general aims and to consider our policy as a whole. Our aim should be to develop a fine tradition of living in houses. It is a matter for experiment, like flying. We should seek to improve in detail point by point. There are enough sketch designs; now we want solids. Exquisite living on a small scale is the ideal. 'House-like' should express as much as 'ship-shape'. Our airplanes and motors and even bicycles are in their way perfect. We need to bring this ambition for perfect solutions into housing of all sorts and scales.

The chief obstruction to our having better houses has been the superstition that they should be built in a style ...

We have to put an *efficiency style* in the place of this trivial, sketchy picturesqueness. Even leaving out the style trimmings would be something. If you cut away disease and surplusage, you strengthen and consolidate. There are many cases in which the half is greater than the whole. We have to prune our building forms as we prune a fruit-tree and sternly cut away the dead wood. Whenever we concentrate on some directing datum, some reality like health, serviceableness or even perfect cheapness, true style will certainly arise as the expression of this and the other human qualities embodied. To design in 'a style' is to design a seeming which stands in the place of style proper. This style superstition is a much greater evil than I could persuade you to believe. It filters down to lower and lower strata, and the poor man is at last persuaded that nightmares of vulgarity and discomfort are necessary offerings to 'style'.

The dwelling-house should be sound, dry, light, warm, and sweet. We should save in all thoughtless extravagances, and concentrate on the conquest of dirt, disorder, and waste. Houses must be built for living rather than for letting ...

Science is what you know; art is what you do. The best art is founded on the best science in every given matter. The art of shipbuilding is the science of shipbuilding in operation. The notion that there are special 'art forms' or 'art colours' has led to all sorts of pretences and sham picturesquenesses. Art is high competence in doing what is worthy to be done. Very occasionally there is in art a sort of poetry over and above: such addition of feeling can be expressed by giving it an *h* and calling it *heart* ...

Other things being equal, so far as may be, preference should be given to local materials and to traditional ways of using them. This traditional use is embodied experience. On the other hand, we should beware of supposing that any reasonable materials such as concrete, cast-iron or plastering are necessarily inartistic. It is the business of art to use the materials given to us by Nature so that they will look well; and when they are well used they will look well ... Concrete should be frankly used. If blocks are better for constructive reasons than a continuous mass, then use blocks by all means, but do not imitate stone. The surfaces should be finished with white or colour wash.

Frankness is the great thing; disguises and subterfuge are always repulsive in building. Bungling, pretence, and compromise are the enemies to be feared ...

Besides the problem of building new cottages there is the very serious problem of repairing old ones. To destroy all the old cottages of the land which are not up to a living standard would so alter our countryside and villages that much of England would be destroyed with them – the 'Old England' we talk about so plentifully. To destroy these cottages would be like a preliminary step to asphalting the country all over. These dear cottages vary from district to district as the soil varies – they are dialects of building, and hold history and emotions which we cannot plan and specify and contract for. Of timber, stone, flint, granite, cob, brick; roofed with thatch, tiles, and stone slabs, they grew out of the ground and are as natural as rabbits' burrows and birds' nests – they are men's nests. Yet the aggregate number of the unfit must be enormous, for they have been terribly let down and each one is a special problem.

Most of them, I am confident, could be mended by reasonable expenditure if we cared to care for them. What is needed is that the various local authorities should at once consider and set about experimenting. Putting in concrete floors, lining the damp walls and relaying the roofs would often do all that is required without any injury to the old buildings which show that the British people had grandfathers. I may say here that I believe that the Society for the Preservation of Ancient Buildings are giving attention to this tremendously urgent matter, and I know that from their long experience in caring for old and frail buildings their help would be worth having ...

99 Walter Gropius, *How can we build cheaper, better, more attractive houses?*, 1927

The provision of housing for people is concerned with mass needs. It would no longer occur to 90 per cent of the population today to have their shoes specially made to measure. Instead, they buy *standard products* off-the-peg, which, thanks to much improved production methods, satisfy the requirements of most individuals. Similarly, in the future the individual will be able to order a house *from stocks* which suits his needs. The fundamental transformation in the whole of the construction industry from the industrialised point of view means there is an urgent necessity for a solution to this problem, appropriate to the age. Preconditions for a rational construction industry which would produce better and cheaper housing are:

(i) Mass production of off-the-peg prefabricated housing, the housing no longer being produced on the actual building site but in special factories which make individual parts (including ceilings, roofs and walls), capable of later reassembly. The *wholesale manufacture* of these building block units is based on standardisation.

(ii) Utilisation of new techniques and raw materials which economise on space and bricks and mortar.

(iii) Rationalised management of the building on the actual site. Assembly line dry building methods following an exact timetable with the greatest possible elimination of wastage.

(iv) Rationalised building plans which will be thoroughly studied down to the last detail on large scale models before building actually begins – as with plans for assembling machines.

(v) Farsighted monetary policies from building financiers, aiming to avoid any raising of interest rates on building capital by the elimination of unproductive intermediate stages.

The introduction, industrially, of assembly line dry building methods helps avoid the numerous hitches, contingencies and unavoidable consequences of the old building methods. Fittings which do not fit due to inaccurate wall measurements or due to the effects of dampness in the building, unforeseen jobs which must be paid for on a day to day basis (such as caulking and plastering), loss of time and money due to protracted 'drying out' periods and other results of the generally hasty planning of 'made-to-measure' housing schemes.

Instead of this: independence from the time of year and the weather, exclusion of dampness in building, guaranteed fitting together of the mechanically produced sections of the building, fixed price and a short, firmly stipulated, guaranteed construction time. Legitimate demands from individuals are safeguarded as only sections and not whole houses will be standardised, and from these sections different housing units can be put together: a combination of the greatest variety possible and the greatest standardisation possible.

The architect's task. To establish an overall plan of 'how we want to live'. This to be based on sociological investigation into housing needs.

To draw up exact house plans for assembling different kinds and variously sized house designs in cooperation with engineers and financiers.

The engineer's task. To discover new building materials from special processes on cheap raw materials available everywhere. The aim will be to conserve space and materials and to improve load-bearing capacity.

To devise new building designs:

(a) for the skeleton construction (non-loadbearing curtain walls in a load-bearing frame).

(b) for the construction of the main body of the house from homogeneous materials (without a load-bearing frame).

To devise individual designs for windows, doors, fitments, fixtures.

The financier's task. To establish, on an economic footing, places to produce all the normalised and standardised building elements.

To achieve constant lowering of prices through continuous production and by extending market outlets.

To procure cheap money for building.

The assumption that industrialisation would make building forms more ugly is wrong. On the contrary standardisation of building elements will produce the fruitful result of creating new houses and towns bearing a common character.

Monotony as in the English suburban house is not to be feared as long as it is insisted that only the *parts* of buildings are standardised, that the *whole* building assembled from them remains variable. Standardisation of parts places no restrictions on the individual design. Their recurrence in differently shaped buildings will have an orderly and soothing effect as does the uniformity of our clothes. And by the same token there will be enough scope for an individual's or a nation's character to express itself.

Pre-prepared variable housing obtainable from stocks will in the coming decades be one of the main products of industry.

The realisation of this comprehensive problem demands concerted action from state and local authorities; from specialists and laymen. It is the job of the large building organisations, state and local government, big business (who will benefit in the long term from any reductions in building costs) to provide the finance for experimentation: what is urgently required is the setting up, with help from public funds, of sites for experimenting with buildings.

Just as industry subjects every article it produces to countless systematic preparatory tests and studies in which financiers, technicians and artists are all equally involved, before its standard form is arrived at, so the manufacture of standardised building parts demands systematic experimental work resulting from a bold combination of industrial, economic and artistic forces.

The Werkbund estate in Stuttgart of 1927 was the first step taken along this path.

100 Mart Stam, *The Stam Houses,* 1927

Because thousands of people are looking for houses, and in many cases have been looking for years; because thousands of young married couples are having to spend the best years of their lives in rented accommodation, in the worst possible conditions, without a home of their own; because present-day housing conditions are having a demoralising effect on the coming generation; because of all these things, the authorities and the architects who advise them have a duty to show the way towards relieving the current housing shortage in as short a time as possible.

The only way of doing this is to establish a standard type of dwelling. The individual, detached house will have to be dispensed with; in its place a type of dwelling will have to be created which, although perhaps taking less account of individual preferences, will still express the generality of human needs, the requirements of every housewife and every family.

In the buildings I have designed for the Weissenhof Exhibition, I have tried to create a standard type which will be mass-produced and highly economical.

But it is important to note that, just like the wheel, the 'new dwelling-house' will require many improvements and development over many years before the standard type is refined to its utmost practicality.

101 W. F. Crittall, *Silver End,* 1928

To those interested in modern development, Silver End Garden Village is often quoted as an outstanding example. The Village was founded by the Crittal Manufacturing Company in 1926. The nucleus of the Village was the factory for the making of the fittings, handles, stays, screws, gearing, hinges, etc., used on the window products of the Company in their larger factories at Braintree and Witham, each about four miles away.

The nature of the work was such that transport was not a serious difficulty; there being no railway, these small parts could easily be transported by light lorries, and, further, the work was suitable for the numerous disabled ex-service men for whom the firm wished to find employment.

In neither Braintree nor Witham was there sufficient housing facilities to provide for the rapidly increasing number of employees which the firm's business demanded, so it appeared that the only way was for the firm to provide its own houses. A large area of agricultural land was purchased, and on it was laid out a town, which, when fully developed, would have 1,000 houses, of which 500 are already built and occupied. Different architects were employed for the various kinds of buildings – the Factory itself, the Village Hall, the Shop, the Hotel and the Houses.

Amongst the latter, the work which has attracted most attention is that built to the design of Sir John Burnet and partner – Mr T. S. Tait. He was given a free hand, inside the limitations of cost, and the result is a pleasing and successful experiment in what can be done with the severely limited problem of the artisan's dwelling. These houses have had a great deal of publicity, and are generally supposed to represent a definite step towards modern architecture in Great Britain.

Beyond the facts, however, that the roofs are flat and the window-panes have a horizontal proportion, instead of the traditional 'diagonal of the width equals the height', there is nothing really fundamentally modern or unusual about them. The walls are of ordinary brick, whitewashed, the other materials are much the same as are usually used in this type of house. The plan, though certainly convenient and generous, is not revolutionary. They are, in fact, a very pleasing new dress on a rather humdrum old body, demonstrating that it is not necessary to be eccentric in order to be interesting.

The County Council have built a large modern school. In the middle of the village is a playing field, the counterpart of the village green. There are churches of three denominations, one of which is a converted barn, in which the original thatching and beams have been preserved. The Village Hall has a seating capacity of six hundred, with a stage, in addition to which it contains billiard and reading-rooms, picture gallery, library, and women's welfare rooms. The hotel is a model of comfort, rarely met with in England, and might almost be described as the 'model pub'.

Of course, the idea is not new. From the earliest days of the Industrial Era, manufacturers have built houses around their factories, mills, or mines, mostly very badly, and with little real desire to do the best thing for their employees. Later examples are schemes built by such as Cadbury's, Rowntree's, Lever's, Reckitt's, and others, which are achievements in the right direction of decentralised development. Silver End is among the latest and most up to date of the endeavours of industrialists to establish a decent standard of living amongst its employees, and the results show, even at this early stage, that the experiment has been justified, as the birth- and death-rate figures testify.

But willy-nilly there must be progress and development, and we must be prepared for power poles, or anything else that our progress demands. No, we must even go farther and seek out new ways and means to fit in with the new age in which we are already well advanced.

It is not easy, of course. Most of us would prefer to live in an old Georgian house to running the risk of being thought 'funny' for preferring one designed by Le

Corbusier, which certainly would call attention to itself if erected at Wimbledon or Hampstead.

Even if the new age seems to be an ugly one, it is up to all of us to make the best of it.

---

102 'Der Block', *Manifesto,* 1928

'The Block' has brought together a group of architects who feel united by their common cultural views and wish to express these in their work.

They agree that the task of modern architecture is to discover a mode of expression suited to the times, but also believe that a nation's individuality and each country's specific circumstances should likewise be taken into account. They follow all new experiments and new opportunities for using modern materials and forms with keen attention but not to the extent of neglecting their heritage and losing sight of known methods.

They refuse to join in the chase for novelty for its own sake, which can only endanger sound and steady development.

[Signatories]
Bestelmeyer, Blunck, Bonatz, Gessner, Schmitthenner, Schultze-Naumburg, Seek, Stoffregen.

---

103 C.I.A.M., *Declaration of Aims,* 1928

On Architecture: ... We particularly emphasise the fact that to build is an elementary activity in man, intimately associated with the evolution and development of human life ...

It is only out of the present that our architectural works should be derived ...

The intention which brings us together is that of attaining a harmony of existing elements – a harmony indispensable to the present – *by putting architecture back on its real plane, the economic and sociological plane*; therefore architecture should be freed from the sterile influence of Academies and of antiquated formulas ...

Animated by this conviction, we affirm our association and our mutual assistance towards the end that our aspirations may be achieved ...

To us, another important point of view is that of economics in general, since it is one of the material bases of our society ...

The conception of modern architecture associates the phenomenon of architecture with that of the general economy ...

The most efficacious production is derived from rationalisation and standardisation. Rationalisation and standardisation directly affect labour methods, as much in modern architecture (its conception) as in the building industry (its achievement).

Town Planning: Town planning is the organisation of the functions of collective life; it applies just as well to rural places as to urban agglomerations.

It cannot be conditioned by the pretensions of an established aestheticism; its essence is of a functional nature.

The functions it embraces are four in number: (i)

dwelling, (ii) work, (iii) recreation and (iv) transportation (which connects the first three functions with one another).

The chaotic subdivision of urban land, as a result of real estate speculation, should be corrected.

Present technical means, which multiply ceaselessly, are the very key to town planning. They imply and propose a complete change in existing legislation; this change should be commensurate with technical progress ...

The following paragraphs are from the byelaws formulated during the congress held at Frankfort-on-the-Main, October 26, 1929:

The aims of this Association are:

(a) To state the contemporary architectural problem.

(b) To re-state the idea of modern architecture.

(c) To disseminate this idea throughout the technical, economic, and social strata of contemporary life.

(d) To be vigilant of the solution of the problems of architecture.

---

104 Alexei Gan, *What is Constructivism?*, 1928

Constructivism, as a materialistic school of artistic labour, as a creative working method, originated, developed and is continuing its social–productive existence under the banner of dialectical materialism.

The methodology of constructivism is inextricably linked with the proletarian revolution and with the socialist building of the Soviet order.

Despite the misrepresentations, distortions and vulgarisation which constructivism has undergone and is undergoing, it has managed to enter into the material–cultural construction of a young society and to introduce authentic realism, the pathos of intelligent proletarian utilitarianism and rationalism, into new aspects of contemporary artistic labour, and also to create an artistic expression of the social–collective purposefulness of a class.

But constructivism did not attain to the latter all at once. Its artistic, creative phase was preceded by a period of stormy conflicts. Constructivism declared an uncompromising war on art, insisted on the disinheritance of the artistic culture of the past, and unlike any other school fought resolutely and consistently against aestheticism.

At the present time, in constructivism's period of practical activity we must expound – not in a polemical, but a positive way – the essence of the destructive and creative tendencies of constructivism, and examine these phenomena as a product of society.

But we should first give a brief historical account of its origins.

The ideological essence of this new social–artistic trend in the building of Soviet culture was already being worked out during the first years of the revolution. By this time the constructivists were to bring the struggle into the open at the First All-Russian Congress of the Workers' and Peasants' Theatre in 1919 ...

Within a year the same fierce struggle between the 'producers from the Left' and the constructivists on one side, and the so-called 'pure' and 'applied' groups on the other, was taking place in the Institute of Artistic Culture (Inkhuk). In the heat of this battle, the constructivists came out with an independent programme, resolutely dissociating themselves from the 'producers of the Left' and finally breaking off all relations with the representatives of idealist aesthetics.

We have already noted that the materialistic tendencies of constructivism first became apparent and were realised by the constructivists during the struggle in the theatrical area of the general artistic cultural front of the proletarian revolution.

Starting from the victorious proletarian class's strivings towards mass activity, constructivism attempted to find in this natural and spontaneous phenomenon the class roots of 'Mass Action', and to reach a formal resolution of this problem within the terms of historical concreteness.

The essence of this mass activity is contained not in *play*, but in the serious purpose of a class in *action*, considered as the active medium of a vast collective, reaching to the current political moment – emotionally.

The opponents of constructivism evaluated this phenomenon quite differently. They were convinced 'that the chief artistic product of *every* revolution always was and always will be *popular* celebrations, since true democracy presupposes the free life of the masses – and in order to be conscious of themselves, the masses must outwardly display themselves, and this is only possible – in the words of Robespierre – "when they themselves are a spectacle for themselves"'.

Against this sentimental, utopian nonsense, constructivism puts forward the vital class viewpoint of 'Mass Action' ...

This is not the place to dwell on the extremely complex problem of 'Mass Action'. We shall discuss this at another time and another place. This new form of artistic labour in the conditions of a collectivist society undoubtedly awaits a great and serious resolution. Constructivism is a school which is examining the artistic culture of a class in its totality and in all its unity in connection with the development of social life and its structure as a whole.

105 Karel Teige, *Contemporary International Architecture,* 1928

The most modern and consistent solutions achieved by contemporary architects are still confined within the bourgeois way of living. All contemporary buildings, even the most modern 'separate mansions' (villas, palaces) as well as housing estates for the exploited poorer classes use the most modern building materials and techniques promoting a rational daily family life and improving hygienic standards. All this activity is still based nevertheless on the bourgeois concept of a family, in particular on the concept: one family, one home, one kitchen. Also the individual whims of the owners are excessively respected. Luxury, diverse equipment, unnecessary artistic furniture, splendour and abundance for the rich and only certain facilities available for the poor ...

Men who try to create a new architecture, a free architecture for a free people, anticipate the creation of a new social order in which private ownership, family and nationality will be unknown. Anticipation is now, however, the tactics of a revolutionary. It is now necessary to prepare the community, to accustom it to new ideas, to revolutionise architecture, architectural production and include the hypotheses of a new organisation of a new world. This statement applies especially to architecture since architecture is the creation of organisation.

The revolutionary liberation of architecture will produce the concept of housing for people not burdened by family or nationality, where a companionship and a collective way of life will exist replacing sumptuous drawing-rooms and private gardens by social district clubs and public parks. Housing will no longer be 'home, sweet home' or 'my castle' ...

The balance of present achievements in the field of housing is not yet clear and the standards for modern living not yet formulated. The Weissenhof estate does not provide any final solutions; its achievements are at present subordinate to the ideas of a bourgeois society within whose boundaries all aims cannot be achieved. In the Weissenhof estate for example, in spite of all technical progress, separate kitchens are provided in each flat and only one bedroom for both husband and wife. In the present economic conditions of a divided class society, it is impossible to hope for a final solution to the housing problem for equality and a new way of life of a new free people. In housing economic and financial class interests still predominate. Nevertheless the experience gained in the construction of contemporary buildings may be used to attempt a theoretical investigation and a determination of hypothetical standards for socialist housing. In order to outline a hypothesis for socialist housing it is first necessary to analyse the means actually available and to examine the needs of modern man in relation to housing. The examination of a building involves the following questions: might the dwelling be smaller? should it consist of only one room which simultaneously serves as a boudoir, study, living-room? Is it actually admissible to reduce the dwelling to only one room which is adapted to complex ends? Do we require the separation into particular premises for particular needs? If so, then what premises and what purposes? Another problem: what degree of comfort can be provided by a socialist community for the disposal of an individual and what comforts shall be reserved for the collective?

The hypothesis of socialist housing must profess that freedom consists of leaving the home. Socialist architecture must reject the concept of rented family houses which must disappear together with ownership (rented accommodation) and family. Our idea is based on present achievements and on the critical assessment of present forms; it outlines modern housing for socialist citizens as an open-plan construction. Recent socialist inventions are dwellings without imprisoning walls, providing a living space which is deprived of furniture rather than encumbered by it, which is full of light and bright colours with free access of sunlight. Even the sun is a desirable commodity. Diogenes, who lived in a tub and renounced everything that he considered superfluous, said to Alexander the Great, 'Move away from the sunlight'. Well then, out with the unnecessary paraphernalia of our daily life but let us have the sun . . .

The housing complex in socialist towns should be composed of single cells designed to fit the people (husbands or wives) but never in accordance with the concept of a family. Its 'standards' depend upon a very extensive change of living habits which must be brought about by social revolution. The new society will no doubt be compelled to reform its customs which already begin to oppress the modern man.

The contemporary concepts of reformed life shown to the public at the Werkbund exhibition by Le Corbusier, Mart Stam, Mies van der Rohe, J. J. P. Oud (especially the equipment, not the design of houses) and W. Gropius must not be considered as the final achievement but merely as a transitory stage. The most far reaching solution of the housing problem is still on paper and cannot yet be realised. Le Corbusier's plan of *'immeubles villas'* represent a collective cooperative complex composed of single units – villas or cottages. It seems that from now the future development will follow a different road: a cooperative complex elimination of kitchens, hotel-like organisation of living providing restaurants, canteen, flats for single persons and a collective comfort: cafeterias, restaurants, festival hall, dancing, baths, playgrounds, reading room and library for the disposal of the collective. Modern architects who build up a socialist community are not satisfied with orders and limitations imposed by the means available at present. Using explicit methods they prepare theories and hypothetical solutions for the architecture of the future. An ideal design for housing is not yet attained; it is said that utopia and ideal are the same thing and both can never be reached. (We would like to say that they can be reached but the way is very hard.) The setting up of an ideal standard for new housing and new architecture must encourage us towards the utopian goal. At present not the utopia but a hypothetical architecture, is important. Changes in architecture cannot be effected without changes in the organisation of production and society, in other words without a social revolution. The theories and hypotheses of the new architecture are the 'battle for tomorrow'. According to Saldow the endeavours in the study of housing are still the 'dreams of a happy future' but these dreams are supported by a number of historical probabilities. Here the renaissance of architecture begins.

106 Ernst May, *Flats for subsistence living,* 1929

Do we need flats for subsistence living?

Objections against the building of smaller flats are frequently raised. The usual arguments are trotted out; the smaller the living space, the more expensive each unit of this space becomes; flats built below a certain size are later impossible to let. Questions of hygiene and mental health are raised and contribute to the final recommendation that larger flats, of about fifty square metres living area, should be built. The old ones would then be passed down to the lower paid.

Who makes these recommendations?

Are they voiced by the hundreds and thousands of homeless who lead a wretched existence in attics and cellars or lodge with friends and relations? No, these are the recommendations of complacent householders who cannot begin to understand the problems of the homeless. So we do not take their recommendations seriously. If the host of rejected workers who hope and strive for adequate shelter were asked to choose whether a small minority of them should have large flats whilst the majority continued to live in misery for years and dec-

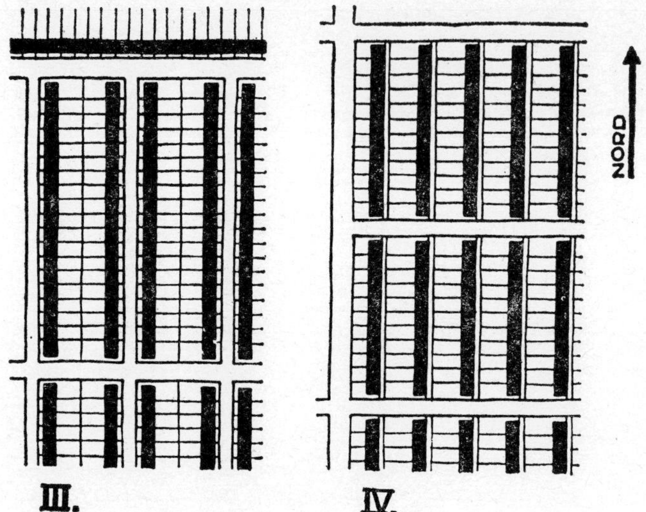

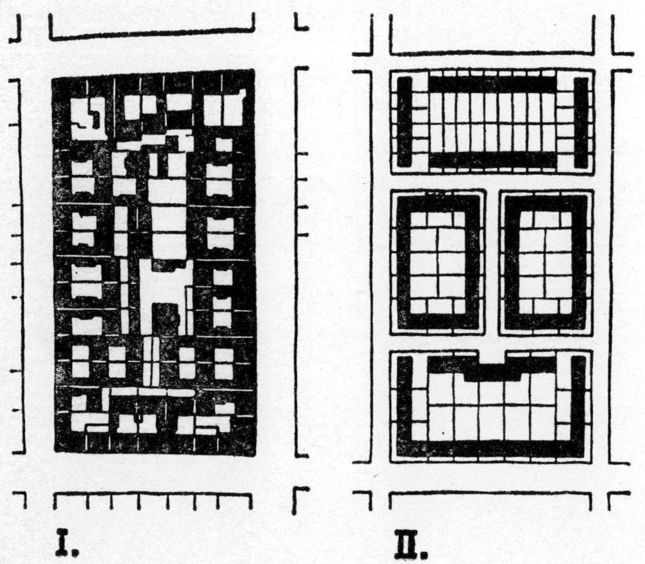

Ernst May, Comparative housing layouts
1 Nineteenth-century chaos
2 The courtyard plan
3 Terrace housing
4 Oriented terraces
Das Neue Frankfurt, 2-3, 1930

ades, or alternatively that the evil of homelessness should be quickly removed by their taking smaller flats (which in spite of being compact provide adequate facilities for modern life) we know that the unanimous response would be: Build us flats which although small, are still healthy and comfortable to live in. Above all, offer them at reasonable rents.

Before the war hundreds of thousands of city flats were built well below the standards laid down by the building regulations. The poor quality of this housing was one of the main causes of deterioration in the health of city dwellers. Flats built since the war are generally of a higher standard but are usually let at a rent that lower paid workers cannot afford. So we need enough flats of sufficient quality to meet the needs of the poor and homeless. *We need flats for subsistence living.*

Who should build flats for subsistence living?

The state of the building index in relation to the average interest rate on loans is one of the major factors which can hinder any adequate building programme in different countries. In Germany at present comparison is unfavourable. For with the building index at 192.8 the interest on loans has risen from a level of 4.51% before the war, to 11.15% in 1929. This means that a worker's flat of 50 square metres living area which would have cost him 30 reichsmark before the war, has risen to a level of 118 reichsmark. So even if we make use of all available resources we shall not be in a position to lower the rents of newly built flats to a reasonable level without a simultaneous reduction of interest rates on loans. That is why the public authority must organise the building of flats for the lower paid workers. Otherwise there is no guarantee that the financial assistance provided by the State reaches those for whom it is intended intact. For the monies which have been set aside to subsidise lower rents are for the use of the general public and should only be employed to aid the building of non-profitmaking flats for the people or to help prospective owner-occupiers. On no account should they be used to stimulate speculative flat building.

How shall these flats for the lower paid be built?

It is still almost impossible to give a positive answer to this question: a negative response is easier. They should be designed to avoid all the past misery that flats for lower paid workers have inflicted on their inhabitants. Whilst the far-reaching field of engineering technology has been developed through exact scientific methods, until now, building has usually developed along intuitive lines.

Even today many architects find it extraordinarily difficult to realise that the core of the problem in designing a block of flats is not its shape and the design of the façade, but the integral structure of each living cell based on the principles inherent in modern living. He must also think as a town planner and integrate the sum of these living cells into the town plan in such a way that suitable amenities are provided for each new community. If this general requirement is only met slowly, then the technical isolation of each flat is more deeply felt. Even if a large number of rooms in a normal building are ranged above each other in rows, correct insight into the numerous individual problems is of immense significance to the community as a whole. In the case of flats for the lower paid workers, a more or less successful solution to each technical problem will help decide whether, and to what extent, the living space can be further reduced. The architect alone cannot be solely responsible for solving the hundreds of issues relevant to this problem. Especially, as so frequently occurs, if he abuses the umbrella of science and resorts to more subjective aesthetic judgements, and tries to utilise every available opportunity to impose his own life style and priorities on the numerous families of lower paid workers who are his clients.

So much unnecessary paper work and so many failures would be avoided if every architect involved in building small flats were obliged to spend a few weeks in a working class family before he began to plan and build. If flats for the lower paid workers are going to be realised we will not be able to do without the help of hygiene experts, engineers and physicists.

In this case man himself is the measure of the importance of this issue. Otherwise the difficulties ahead would seem almost insurmountable. Only respect for the biological and social status of the man which is threatened by the problem of flats for the lower paid workers keeps us from fruitless theorisation and draws us nearer to our goal. We shall build flats which, although let at reasonable rents, will satisfy the material and spiritual needs of their inhabitants.

The exhibition mounted together by the International Congress of Modern Architecture and the Architect in Chief of the city of Frankfurt am Main could contribute. It offers the possibility of furthering the cause of this eminently important task of peacefully uniting the people of the world, encouraging them to aim for the desired goal.

---

107 Walter Riezler, *The Fight for German Culture,* 1932

It seems odd, today, to look back to 1908, when Theodor Fischer made that fine selfless remark, that the true aim of the Deutscher Werkbund was to make itself superfluous. The ten years' limit he gave it has long since passed and no one nowadays – apart from our enemies of course, who pursue us as vindictively as ever – would dream of calling the Werkbund superfluous, unless he were so fainthearted as to believe that all our work had been in vain and that our fight to put across our ideas had been doomed to failure. We have certainly no intention of taking such a cowardly view of things, even if at the outset none of us imagined that the way would be so long and the achievements so few.

As far as 'raising the level of work' is concerned, many of the claims the Werkbund stood for and repeatedly insisted on have unquestionably been realised in the meantime. And there is no need to go into detail to prove it. But on the other hand we have only to think of the industrial fairs to see how common rubbish still is. No doubt the economic upheavals brought about by the war hindered the progress of 'quality work', but this circumstance alone was not wholly responsible. Quite a wide sector of the public is evidently still disinclined to take a serious interest in real quality and reliability. And against the weight of this opinion the Werkbund can visibly do nothing, or lamentably little.

But nothing would be farther from the truth or more dangerous then to suppose that the Werkbund intends to abdicate on account of these difficulties and simply entrust things to time. It began as a militant movement and is well aware that it will always be called upon to fight. Its personal struggle has always had a very special nature, however, not so much against a foe as for a cause. And the Werkbund has turned on the enemy only in self-defence, when it knew that its ideas were being directly threatened, and has shrewdly limited its target, well aware that it lacks the strength to destroy so much that seems different and 'inferior' in its eyes. Whenever it dared to engage in single combat it was invariably defeated, but when it enlisted such means as exhibitions, advertising and personal persuasion to support its ideas, it gained considerable ground because it was able to play upon forces which were already working in its favour. And no one can say that the potentialities for this type of warfare have been exhausted.

On the contrary, a fight is needed more urgently nowadays than ever and will have to be conducted more vigorously than for some time. The immediacy of the danger has become only too clear with the annihilation of the Dessau Bauhaus (though fortunately it has just been resuscitated in Berlin as a private undertaking) and if more blows are to be dealt then much of what we have already achieved may have to be given up, and the most worthwhile creative talent Germany possesses in arts and crafts could be permanently crippled. The Werkbund must marshal all its forces to prevent such a thing from happening.

But it would perhaps be worth finding out exactly who levelled the blow and against whom. The motives were almost certainly political. All the parties in the municipal council concurred in agreeing that the Bauhaus should be closed, but they based their arguments on theories which are considerably older than the Party, infusing them with a passion and a force of propaganda hitherto unknown in Germany. The well-thumbed, somewhat outmoded bourgeois–reactionary views thus acquired an unsuspected impact which, for better or worse, obliges us to come to grips once more with arguments which we thought had been settled for ever.

This is not going to be an easy task, not because the theories are particularly convincing, but because they have been refuted so often. Do we really have to assure people for the hundredth time that modern architecture has nothing to do with Bolshevism? It has repeatedly been pointed out that the present style of building was introduced before the Russian revolution and originally sprang up in die-hard capitalist countries – even though it expressed a new social attitude as well as a new artistic trend. The great historical importance of this is that it was the first time in the history of architecture that a style had been so strongly influenced by social thinking. This could be taken as a sign that social thinking had shown proof of creativity at a time when its influence was only just beginning to spread, but to see this as marking a dangerous revolutionary trend is to show a very strange turn of mind. Anyone who feels uneasy about the fact that the new architecture is 'international' forgets that social preoccupations found expression in highly different places, and also that, technically speaking, modern building principles are more or less the same everywhere, and the national idiom consequently seems less apparent. This is a reality which cannot just be wiped from the face of the earth and any attempt to use artificial means to conceal the gulf dividing the present from the past can only cause harm. Earlier epochs never bothered unduly about how the new fitted on to the old; they simply built as suited the times. And today just as before, the national idiom preserves its mysterious power even without our realising it. The first sign of national characteristics in modern trends can easily be distinguished by the experienced eye (anyone who has been able to take a look at Alberto Sartoris's very useful collection of modern construction from twenty-six countries entitled *Gli Elementi dell Architettura Funzionale,* published by Ulrico Hoepli in Milan, will see this at once). Nor should it be forgotten that the designs which have appeared so far are the very early specimens of the new manner, though such constructions as the much-revered Tugendhat house clearly show the type of intellectual expression that is available. It is the duty of the Werkbund to develop the new possibilities to the full. There is no longer any choice. The question of whether or not such architecture is no more than a passing fancy has long since been settled and even Herr Schultze-Namburg can do nothing more about that.

It is important to mention Herr Schultze-Namburg. whose name was previously respected in perfectly serious circles, at this point because he has not only played a decisive rôle in annihilating the Bauhaus but is also becoming the most vigorous opponent of everything the Werkbund represents. Admittedly it is seven years since his book, *Art and Race,* was published and the lecture entitled *A fight for art,* which he gave a few years ago in several cities, generally aroused more enmity than approval even among very 'conservative' circles. Even so, the fact that the essay is still on sale in booklet form means that it must be regarded as presenting a very influential point of view. The superficial 'grounds' Schultze-Namburg claims for some very popular opinions makes it difficult to analyse the content objectively, especially as the racial question has now developed into a thorny political struggle, like a kind of creed justified by feeling and dilettante 'research'. There is no alternative but to speak of 'race' when the fate of Germany allegedly hangs on this issue. If we point out that even fascist Italy has lately opted for the so-called international Bolshevist style of building, we hear the reply that Italy has no racial problem and that in Germany things are different.

'Race' is certainly a decisive factor whenever it is a question of achievement and as such very definitely concerns the Werkbund. Unfortunately, however, it is difficult to reach an agreement as to what we actually mean by 'race'. Obviously there are not only different races, but 'good', 'bad', 'strong', 'weak', and this or that type of race, in life as in art. Perhaps a relatively 'pure' race does still exist here and there to please the eye by its beauty and firmness of stature. But this is where things begin to get difficult, because the members of the pure and beautiful race by no means always distinguish themselves by their nobler achievements from those who are racially 'inferior'. The not-so German inhabitants of south-west Germany are undoubtedly more gifted than the racially purer peoples in the north-west. Likewise, there are many representatives of 'inferior' races among the greatest minds, whereas quite a number of more pedestrian figures belong to allegedly 'good' German stock. Achievement seems to stem from other factors and will probably never be possible to explain away with the accuracy which race-theorists very unjustifiably claim. Race is absolutely no guarantee whatsoever of what we commonly call 'character' in its broadest and most significant sense.

The notion of strength of character is the only one that is applicable to cultural work, because cultural activities only prosper when vigorous creative forces find a means of developing to the full. This becomes quite plain if we dare to compare Schultze-Naumburg, the epigone of feeble ancestry, with Mies van der Rohe, a man of the hardiest stock in everything he says and creates ...

A particular period cannot determine exactly what type of art it will produce. Sometimes, deliberate attempts are made to veil the genuinely dreadful aspects which encumber all periods with a form of beauty. This happened in the Renaissance, which was fraught with violence, but not at the time of Gothic art. Other periods have felt the need to escape from their nightmares by giving them concrete expression in plastic form, and possibly this tendency has never been so strong as it is today. The wealth of talented persons who work in this direction, simply because they cannot do otherwise, proves that the trend is genuine and that it corresponds to an inner necessity. Anyone who believes that such forms of expression can be avoided simply lacks a sense of history ... There have been decadent elements of different descriptions in all periods, and only a very elementary view of history could regard 'decadence' as a sign of inferiority. In the history of culture, symptoms of decadence are continually being singled out which seem ominous under certain circumstances for a while, but which soon disappear again and can only be detected in the future by social historians. (It is perfectly easy to trace the portrait of an utterly inferior hopelessly decadent society, in the now forgotten but once highly respected and widely-read novels of Goethe's day.) It is harmful to pay too much attention to such phenomena, because they take on larger proportions than they deserve.

The campaign which the greater majority of the people have now engaged in against the new creative trends and all that they stand for is certainly nothing Germany can be proud of, because its origin lies in fear. When people no longer feel strong enough to deal with a challenge alone, they call in the police. Everyone is so conscious of the current of insecurity running through the world that they shrink back into the snail-shell of intellectual autocracy. And 'autocracy' today more than ever means self-sufficiency, in other words a form of spiritual death. This is all the more significant nowadays, because the way we have chosen requires an open mind. Open-mindedness was always one of our qualities – even the cathedral-builders and the sculptors of Bamberg and Nauburg were open-minded – and if something can still be done for culture today it can only bear fruit if it fights the constrictive tendencies which are closing in from all sides. This is the fight the Deutscher Werkbund must lead, not to serve some International, but with the sole aim of allowing national creative forces the utmost freedom to develop. Germany's culture should not aspire to a backward-looking ideal, no matter how fine it may seem; it should be the product of vital forces in the present which must be allowed to grow according to their nature – it is not given to man to do more.

---

108 Philip Johnson, *Architecture in the Third Reich,* 1933

It would be false to speak of the architectural situation in nationalist socialist Germany. The new state is faced with such tremendous problems of reorganisation that a programme of art and architecture has not been worked out. Only a few points are certain. First *Die Neue Sachlichkeit* (The New Objectivity) is over. Houses that look like hospitals and factories are taboo. But also the row houses which have become almost the distinguishing feature of German cities are doomed. They all look too much alike, stifling individualism. Second, architecture will be monumental, that is, instead of bath-houses, *Siedlungen,* employment offices and the like, there will be official railroad stations, memorial museums, monuments. The present regime is more intent on leaving a visible mark of its greatness than in providing sanitary equipment for workers.

But what these new buildings will look like is as yet completely unknown. Germany as the birthplace of modern architecture can hardly go back to Revivalism since there exist no architects who could or would design in styles. Nor is it possible that they will adopt the Bauhaus style. It is not monumental enough and it has irretrievably the stamp of Communism and Marxism, Internationalism, all the 'isms' not in vogue in Germany today. Somewhere between the extremes is the key; and within the Party are three distinct movements each of which may win out.

First and up till recently the strongest are the forces of reaction, with Paul Schulze-Naumburg at the head. He is the enemy of anything which has happened in the last thirty years. His book *Art and Race,* contains the most stupid attacks on modern art which he considers mere interest in the abnormal, a point of view which he defends by showing juxtaposed clinical photographs of physical abnormalities and modern paintings. In architecture, he approves of nothing since the War, and is himself the architect of many simplified but Baroque country houses including the Crown Prince's palace in Potsdam. As a personal friend of the leaders of the party he is strongly entrenched.

Paul Erwin Troost, best known to Americans as the designer of the interiors on the S.S. *Europa,* is a friend of Hitler's and is also a strong conservative. (That some Americans might consider the *Europa* modern merely shows that 'modern' with us has hardly caught up with reaction in Germany.) The strongest single factor in favour of this group in the new state is that Hitler himself is an amateur architect. Before he entered politics he earned his living as a draughtsman and renderer in Vienna and Munich. This fact, combined with the tradition in Prussia from Frederick the Great to Wilhelm II, that the ruler be his own architect, makes the outlook depressing.

The second group and at present the strongest is that represented by the Kampfbund für Deutsche Kultur, an inner party organisation for the purification of German culture. Their architectural hero is the newly appointed director of the Prussian state art schools, Paul Schmitthenner. Though an outspoken enemy of *Die Neue Sachlichkeit* he claims modernity. His houses are sound, well-proportioned but uninspired adaptations of the vernacular of the early 19th century, much in the same feeling as the best adaptations of the Cape Cod farmhouses in America. His larger buildings are in a half-modern tasteful style, better really than much work in Germany, more modern in intention. It is notorious that official architecture is conservative and Schmitthenner occupies the position formerly held under the social democratic regime by Hans Pelzig and Bruno Paul. He is as competent an architect as either of them.

The third group is composed of the young men in able German artists, Noble and Barlach who are ready to fight for modern art. The most powerful of these is the new director of the National Gallery, Alois Schardt. So far the battle has been fought in the field of painting and mainly around the names of those venerable German artists, Nolde and Barlache who are especially hated by Schulze-Naumburg. In architecture there is only one man whom even the young men can defend and that is Mies van der Rohe. Mies has always kept out of politics and has always taken his stand against functionalism. No one can accuse Mies's houses of looking like factories. Two factors especially make Mies's acceptance as the new architect possible. First Mies is respected by the conservatives. Even the Kampfbund für Deutsche Kultur has nothing against him. Secondly Mies has just won (with four others) a competition for the new building of the Reichsbank. The Jury were older architects and representatives of the bank. If (and it may long be if) Mies should build this building it would clinch his position. A good modern Reichsbank would satisfy the new craving for monumentality, but above all it would prove to the German intellectuals and to foreign countries that the new Germany is not bent on destroying all the splendid modern arts which have been built up in recent years. All revolutions, seemingly against everything of the past, really build on the positive achievements of the preceding decades. Germany cannot deny her progress. If in the arts she sets the clock back now, it will run all the faster in the future.

---

109 Jiři Krohá, *Ideology of Architecture,* 1933

Architectural formalism was always symbolic. It maintained and increased the esteem felt by the largest social class for the laws imposed by the ruling class. The activity of architects was always subject to the social class structure, the beauty of Venus is a formal artistic expression of an architectural workmanship; it is dialectally related to the discrepancy resulting from utilitarian needs. In historical architecture the discrepancy between the utilitarian needs and of an individual and the utilitarian aims of the people is obvious. It cannot be denied that the work of architects was always dictated by the ruling class; it was a class symbol and class instrument to show to the lower classes the way of life and the laws of the ruling class. Thus changes of architectural styles indicate to some extent that changes of architectural symbolism were related to the social and economical transformations. Historical styles vary and originate in close dependence upon the economical and cultural structure of society. The clashes and discrepancies involved in these social and economical changes are also reflected in architecture. In historical architecture these difficulties are overcome to a large extent by an almost planned formalism. The splendour of Roman buildings, its resurrection in the Romanesque style, and the horribly complicated Gothic style appear as symbols of the ideology of the master's material and spiritual might ...

After a further disorientation at the end of the last century and at the beginning of the present century, modern architecture rejected the obsolete servitude to historical conceptions and turned to serve the entire collective community. Formalistic architectural activity was terminated. In liberal middle class communities an architectural movement was developed which dispensed with excessive ornamentation, a characteristic feature of the old symbolic designs. Symbols are superfluous for the new working man, who grows under the influence of modern science, the modern world and modern ideas. Liberal citizens do not require these symbols, as they are able to correctly evaluate their social, clerical and policing purpose, and it is only the conservatives who need them to preserve clannish traditions and emotional self-esteem. The elimination of elements of visual ornamentation in modern architecture is entirely of social and ideological origin; it is not an expression of a lasting repudiation of architectural beauty ...

New construction and production methods, new technical discoveries and new industries provided architecture with new possibilities, which suggested new kinds of projects. The new architecture thus began to turn to planning of specially designed premises for a determined social, collective or individual purpose. A stupendous advance was accomplished by the ideological work of creative contemporary architects, who repudiated the symbols of life and sought instead its real elements. It is quite natural that in this work the architects drew conclusions which did not always conform with official opinion and which were not universally acceptable. It is also natural that among those who wanted to find the basic elements of life some simultaneously became the judges and critics of various aspects of everyday life, of its needs and of social relations. In the study of modern life these architects, whom we now call the vanguard architects, repeatedly pondered about the official false social and moral conventions. Analytical studies always led these pioneers towards the necessity of a new philosophical and political culture. They considered architectural space as a community space which should be arranged in a new way, and applied to this purpose all available technical contrivances, replacing symbols and other fancies with a respect for the positive needs of an individual or of a collective community. The possibility of achieving these aims was provided for by modern techniques and modern products, i.e. by material factors, and under this influence the majority of architects turned towards scientific socialism, especially as they clearly understood that the aim of constructions of a higher cultural and spiritual value is easily achieved by the right control and use of materials. The majority of vanguard architects in contemporary architecture are convinced that their service to the community must be socially fair, i.e. it must be socialist. Thus we can say that the thesis of scientific marxism is reflected in the architectural vanguard of the entire world ...

When we examine contemporary architecture in the world we find that in some countries governed by reactionary political systems, e.g., Germany and Italy, architecture was virtually forced by political and not formal reasons to abandon the vanguard position. In other countries the crisis of social organisations is reflected in architectural retrogression, and only in a few cases is it possible to concede that this particular contemporary architecture follows and continues to develop without interruption the principles of the vanguard movement. Czechoslovak architecture belongs to the latter group and we see here a stupendous progress as compared with the past ...

---

110 Paul Schmitthenner, *Tradition and New Buildings,* 1933

The history of a Race celebrates its fortunes and from this history springs binding tradition. Whoever offends this deep sense of tradition, wrongs history and, by so doing, the very fibres of the nation. The age just past thought in narrow limits only of itself, instead of thinking in terms of generations. A race which does not respect the work of earlier generations and neither protects nor strengthens its foundations, destroys architecture and itself. Seen in this way tradition is eternally new, a growing living reality; it carries the soul, the basic will of the Race from one century to the next. Through the buildings of centuries runs that feature which can quite simply be called 'German'. As different as the countryside and the families in the North and South of the Reich are, as different as every house, village and town is, they are only as different as brothers and sisters of the same blood. This can only be felt by someone who has his roots in the Nationhood, and, for this reason, anything of a foreign nature, if it reaches an influential position, quickly becomes a destroyer of tradition, the tradition which takes care of and increases characteristic qualities and is quite simply the basis of every national culture, born from the maternal womb of the Race. The danger for the whole Nation and its culture in abandoning meaningful tradition is to be seen best in architecture as this is always the ultimate expression of the whole culture of any period. The decline of German architecture began with the abandoning of tradition and collapsed at the beginning of the technological age, which at the same time marked the end of the last integrated cultural and architectural epoch, which we can sum up in the name 'Gothean' ...

The glorious old German towns, which have been built over centuries, form one harmonious whole. It is the spirit of the German Nation in all its glorious variations, from North to South, from East to West, which forms the main melody in the symphony of the beautiful German town. The German spirit in architecture broke with tradition in the suburbs in the years after 1870. The apartment house, the tenement blocks in a pompous and deceitful style, the unrestrained entrepreneurial mentality, all these features of social poverty resulted in faceless and soulless towns. Here can be seen no desire to shape the face of the age and what arose was distorted, a caricature.

Karl Friedrich Schinkel said once:

> The useful and the necessary, however good they are in themselves, become repulsive if they appear without propriety and dignity, and only beauty helps achieve this, which is why beauty is so essential and always deserves to be taken into consideration with the others.

The interpretation of the concepts, beauty, propriety and dignity, characterises the individual and the nation and is of crucial importance for their culture.

Beauty, propriety and dignity are useless things which do not spring from the brain or reason, but solely from the heart. Our way of thinking has been too strongly influenced by the all-calculating intellectual philosophy of the age. All too easily propriety and dignity have been sacrificed to it and not merely in the field of architecture. We can see similar phenomena in literature, the theatre and politics. Whatever yielded profits was allowable and socially acceptable. This calculating intellect left man out of its calculations. This new way of thinking, this exaggerated intellect revealed itself most strikingly in the so-called *Neue Sachlichkeit* (New Objectivity) style of architecture. There is no 'New Objectivity' but only Reason and the concept New Objectivity is itself already an Un-Objectivity ...

The more senseless architectural design became at this time, the more sensible the structure of the machine became. Here we see designs brought to the ultimate simplest form, of the highest quality and with a natural beauty. Around 1900 a conscious move towards healthy architectural design set in, and gained ground slowly but surely. The paths of this new architectural design trodden then were various but shared the same goal – purifying our buildings of empty and therefore un-German pathos. The will to create a German architectural style can be clearly seen in the desire to resume the ties with tradition which were broken earlier, thus precluding any further development. This healthy development in architecture, which for all its progressiveness was closely linked to tradition and was thus German, was disturbed and obstructed by the so-called 'New Objectivity' movement. Whereas during the period of the architectural 'style without style' machines had, within the contexts of the style, been authentically decorated and factories done up to look Medieval or Baroque, now, under the 'New Objectivity', the characteristic features of machine engineering and construction were carried over to church, school and house building. The clearest expression of the moving spirit behind this design style was the coining of the term 'machine for living in'. If it was difficult in 1890 to distinguish law courts from breweries, now many churches were erected which could be mistaken for silos, whilst there was scarcely any difference between schools and shoe factories. The deeper reason behind the 'New Objectivity' way of thinking lay in that 'intellect, refined at the expense of the heart', about which Schiller said nothing was more sacred to him. All obligations to tradition, the countryside, heaven and earth were forgotten. One need only think of those housing estates where this 'Objectivity' was practised: Weissenhof – Stuttgart, Dammerstock – Karlsruhe, Buerlam and others. It will be beyond the comprehension of future generations, but at the same time it will be a sign of the confusion of the post-war years, especially when it is remembered that they dared to speak of these creations as housing reforms. These buildings are nothing other than examples of objectivity, raped and diluted by internationalism. The same irrelevant pomposity of the post-1870 architectural style which proclaimed itself a national art style, appears with the symptoms reversed as an international art style. The spirit is the same, only the form is different. These phenomena of the new unsung spirit in architecture were readily described as part of the new temper of the age. This spirit, the spirit of the 1918 revolution, found its permanent expression in the buildings of the 'New Objectivity'.

The national government under the leadership of Adolf Hitler has undertaken the task of purifying all areas of life of the spirit of 1918. What shall come into being is the German corporate state. But then all 'estates in the Reich' must work together as one community of workmen in the great construction programme, formerly undermined by party politics ...

Every structure small or big, can no longer be regarded first and foremost as part of German national wealth, but as part of German cultural property ...

Following the words of the Reich's chancellor only those trustworthy men should play a decisive leading rôle who have proved their attitude during the years of decadence. Victory is not yet ours. The struggle for German culture is only just beginning. For this reason leadership of the building industry belongs in the hands of those upright architects, who have been in the vanguard of the fight against internationalism and the un-German spirit and who have proved their attitude in deeds as well. An architect's achievement is his work and his character should be recognisable in his work. The Fighting League for German Culture has the important job amongst others of leading the organisation representing the profession.

---

111 F. Schuster, *Five Years of the Weissenhof Siedlung in Stuttgart,* 1933

During the past year the estate which in its time caused such a sensation, all over Stuttgart and beyond the borders of the province, the estate on which so many people pinned so many hopes and expectations, completed the first five years of its existence. Five years is a short enough period for a building, which has got to last anyway until the costs of its erection are paid off. And we were told so much, were promised so much when these examples of the 'new building', the 'Neue Sachlichkeit', were put up, about economical, cheap, rational building, about industrialisation of building methods, standardisation, the living machine, and so on and so forth. When the Bund für Heimatschutz, as in duty bound, then expressed its opinion on the new movement and its manifestations, it was very badly received in a number of quarters, including some where it might have been least expected, and the League was to some extent reproved from higher up. There were those who prophesied that if the League were to begin, or even to think about, ignoring or looking with distrust (!) on the new trends of the age, it would mean the end of its influence and its effectiveness. The League ought to have kept its mouth shut, or at least shown a benevolent interest, in the face of this great innovation that was being prepared. From the opposite quarter it was objected that the main point at issue was that the building exhibition had raised, and illustrated in a practical way, fundamental questions of big city housing. But just what has the exhibition really done for that? The answer lies in the building costs and rents! * The quite possibly cheaper construction of the 'model houses' by mass production was more than wiped out in the context of the national economy by the damage done to the other sides of the industry through growing unemployment, a result of the 'new style'. For the needs of the big city, steadily growing more international in character (especially in the business and industrial quarters), where the concept of the new style is quite appropriate, the exhibition has done least to live up to its claims; only the two big apartment blocks of van der Rohe and Behrens come into the picture. The little one-family houses are quite meaningless for the housing problems of the masses in the big towns; they can only be considered for the sparsely settled outer districts. But even there, if – as in Stuttgart – they cover areas of scenic beauty, exactly the same is true as was said once by the Provincial Commission for Public Monuments about the villages and the threat to them from the 'new building style': 'What matters now is to take all possible care that the village and the hamlet are protected against a thoughtless and tasteless invasion by the unthinking adherents of this concept which is really only adapted for the needs of the big towns; that the lamentable appearance of the period after 1870, which grafted a bogus urban character on our villages, should not be allowed to return'. That is just what the League, which at the time was widely criticised for its opinions, was anxious for.

The experience of the past five years has proved the League right. How many of the promises so loudly proclaimed have been realised, and how much they have cost the city of Stuttgart (and many other German towns) in this short time, is gradually and progressively becoming apparent. Certainly you cannot find a trace now of the 'restless enthusiasm' that was so widely expressed then. There were those then who pointed out that our children and grandchildren, by virtue of their greatly changed attitude to the world generally and of the even greater changes that will have taken place in their economic conditions will live quite fundamentally differently from the way we live now. These changed conditions have made themselves felt in an unexpectedly short time; but the result has been, not the 'living-machine' they were boasting of then, but a return to what is old, tried and trusted. A look at practically all the suburban estates in Germany, the final result of the great age of 'new building' between 1918 and 1931, confirms this.

'Mad, mad, everywhere mad, where'er I turn my gaze.' Was it not mad a few years ago to put up a great new hospital of iron skeleton construction, without a pitched roof, in one of our provincial towns which could draw on a first-class bed of clay and one of our best-equipped brickworks and which bordered one of our richest wooded areas? Isn't it mad to choose the international, so-called cubic architectural style for the new building of a youth hostel on the banks of the 'Swabian Lake', with no objection from the authorities? Nothing can illustrate the inward condition of a people more clearly than the outward appearance of their buildings, and especially of their dwelling-houses. How alike our towns and villages used to look, without any pressure from outside; and what a different picture is presented now. Today we see everything all mixed up together indiscriminately, higgledly-piggledy, the outward expression of our inner carelessness and confusion. The committee tried to get over this by the external motif of rooflessness. But real help is not to be sought in external forms, but only from within, through the awakening and creation of a truly national sentiment and culture such as used formerly to exist and can once again be fostered by the National Socialist movement. It will never again happen then that (as occurred recently) we had, in an idyllic rural village, to battle with the plans for one of these modern-minded architects who wanted to distinguish himself by putting

* Building costs and rents for the Weissenhof Siedlung dwellings were roughly double the general level of Stuttgart municipal housing (treble in some cases), partly because the small number prohibited mass production methods [Editor's note].

up a foursquare, 'sophisticated' cube-house on a beautiful hillside facing the village, in the middle of country houses with traditional local roofs. How ugly, how disruptive, such a group of foreign-looking cubic buildings looks for example in the Hauptmannsreute in Stuttgart. Anyone in future who does not want to make the 'sacrifice' of lining up with the national movement will find himself locked out. To be or not to be, to be national or international, that is the question now.

Meanwhile the Würtemberg working-party of the German Werkbund has met its fate on account of its prejudiced attitude, against which it had been warned long ago from several quarters. In view of the town's unfortunate experiences with the Weissenhof estate, the Reichskommissar for the town of Stuttgart banned them from the new building exhibition with the slogan 'German wood' in the Kochenhof in Stuttgart, which they themselves had originally planned and launched. It is regrettable that things had to go so far which might have been avoided by the exercise of timely judgment by the leadership of the Werkbund. But for some time the committee had become unfaithful to itself. Originally they laid primary emphasis on quality, on excellence and good workmanship, restoring individual craftsmanship to its former pride of place. However, after the upheaval of 1918 they concerned themselves more and more with the search for novelty and experiment, always with one eye on international recognition. Novelty and the rule of the machine were paramount. Even the 'form without decoration', vigorously advocated by the committee, may have had its role as a transitional state after an era of degeneration and barbarism. But regarded as an aim in itself it implies, not superiority, but a decided absence of that. Man is not a machine that can only do one job in one way; there are many capabilities in him. Everyone else cannot be dragged down for the sake of a few. The exaggerated importance given to technology, driven to giant proportions by the unprecedented efforts of wartime, has led to an overlooking of the human element never before experienced, and had led the whole world into an unprecedented crisis which can never be resolved by external means, but only by a basic inner conversion. Man himself, not his creature, the machine, must be restored again to the centre of events. Man's arrogance and presumption have led to another Tower of Babel, another fall of the Titans ... The sense of quality and beauty must be newly awakened and strengthened in all levels of the people, so that good craftsmanship will once more find its markets and all the cheap and nasty rubbish, with its one-price stores and so on, will vanish from the scene. That too is what our countryman, for instance, the founder and director of the Werkhaus, Albrecht Merz in Stuttgart, has been aiming at for years and to some extent has tried to put into practice: to liberate and put to profitable work again the forces asleep in the people, lying fallow under the form of economy we have known until now.

Thus the Bund für Heimatschutz has known all along that in its basic efforts and aims it was at one with the new leadership of Germany, aims to which both aspire like the knight in Dürer's picture or our newborn racial consciousness, the valiant Swabian: 'Step by step, though the whole world were full of devils.'

---

112 F. R. Yerbury, *In Germany Now,* 1933

Modernism as we have known it in Germany is dead. Anyone who wishes to be up-to-date next year and go 'all continental' or German in their London buildings had better go straight away to Germany and study Potsdam or the Seigers Alle, for the Nazis have decreed that Germany shall be German.

The writer has always felt that there has been a sneaking dislike on the part of the German masses to what the architect in Germany regards as a modern building. Now it appears that the Nazis, who represent in the main what we call 'the man in the street', are really going to revolt and get what they want rather than what the architect wishes to give them.

The good old German beer hall, with its naturalistic decorations of mountains and cows, with artificial flowers hanging from the roof, and with enormous brass bands blaring out good soul-stirring, sentimental tunes from the Rhineland, is much to the taste of the average person who finds a spiritual home in the Nazi party. 'This is the real Germany, and it is the sort of thing we want to get back to in Germany,' the writer was told by a member of the Nazis (a Steel-helmet friend said much the same), and, as for the flat-roof type of building, 'No thank you,' he said. 'I like the pointed tile roofs, and I will bet you 100 marks that in future we will have them back again.' Fancy the new German housing schemes, when they start building again, with the old, high-pitched Bavarian gables, with façades made elaborate with concrete 'timber'. One can understand, up to a point, the revolt from some of the scientific machines in which the German people have been told they ought to live. There is one at Liepzig, laid out in a circular plan which, from above and on paper, looks interesting; but the people inhabiting the houses which form a part of the pretty pattern unfortunately do not see it from above, but from the ground. Nothing could be more depressing than a walk round the circles, and one can quite understand the average German, who is essentially a sentimental and kindly fellow, seizing the present régime as a means of escaping from the hands of the makers of the scientific home.

'This internationalism in architecture and art,' said one, 'is not for us. We must go back to our own German traditions and have something for ourselves which will bring happiness to the German people.'

Herr Göring has recently had an apartment decorated in his own taste, which apparently will set a standard for fashionable 'party' people. This strikes a note which is hardly in the taste, shall we say, of Mendelsohn. The Bauhaus at Dessau was closed some time ago. It was here, of course, that Gropius and Mies van der Rohe were bringing up a band of disciples on lines well known from the German architectural papers, and representing possibly the most extreme school of the moderns in Germany; and a short time ago they started up again in Berlin. They, however, received a visit from a party of Nazis, to see exactly what they were doing, and certain posters and other suggestions with a bias to the left were removed; it has now been closed down.

Berlin on Hitler's birthday, was almost like a Boy Scouts' Jamboree. The extreme popularity of Hitler must be recognised, as also must the sincerity of the average Nazi. They are definitely out to do something in which they believe, which, in the main, is a rejuvenation and cleaning-up of Germany. The position is much as in Russia; indeed, the writer found many things which corresponded completely. One is either a member of the 'Party' or not; Hitler is almost as great a hero as Lenin. Hardly a shop window is to be found without postcards, photographs, oil-paintings, or oleographs of the adored leader. The only thing missing is the shop-loads of plaster busts which one finds in Russia of Lenin, but no doubt those of Hitler will come in time.

---

113 Wells Coates, *The Conditions for an Architecture for today*, 1938

For the last four hundred years, Western thought has been directed towards the discovery of the material world, and today it has advanced to a real turning point in the history of world-culture. Will modern science be able to carry through the process of the neutralisation, for man's freedom and happiness, of the blind forces of Nature? Or will it destroy (with the same processes) the defences it has built against these forces? We cannot answer such questions, but, as architects, we must be concerned with the conditions which make us ask them. Considering the present state of architecture and the present state of society, is it indeed possible for architecture to exist at all today? It will be found, I think, that very few architectures *have* existed as individual wholes: and that in each case a true architecture is the direct and most complete expression of a particular mode of society: an expression of that society when it has become stable and conventionalised, when everyday manners and customs have been well accepted by all classes; and, lastly, when the art of ruling and of being ruled has been well founded.

Do these conditions exist today? Let us repeat them: A society with a firm structure in being and manifest in stable form freely accepted by all classes of the people; and a society where the art of governing and being governed exists on firm foundations. The answer is that these conditions do not exist today, and the conclusion is that architecture does not, and indeed cannot, exist until these conditions are fulfilled.

At first sight this appears to be a rather startling conclusion. Do we not see all about us signs of a renaissance in architecture, and, more certainly, in building? This is so, and gives us our second conclusion, which is that society today is in a real state of transition, of reformation, and that therefore we are living in an age when a new architecture is not only possible, but necessary. It is a curious thing that, although human conditions and possibilities have altered more in the last hundred years than they had in the previous ten thousand, customs and habits of life change more slowly than conditions. You have then, today, a true state of transition, of comparative formlessness, a state in which the technical power to do new things is almost everywhere in advance of creative technique to control that technical power for the freedom and happiness of mankind. The time-lag is most pronounced in countries which invented that technical power. Such a country is England.

We (the English) are the inventors of this bareness and hardness, the Romance people are its defenders: with their discovery of sport, their futuristic gush over machines, aeroplanes, etc., they are the most sentimental and romantic moderns to be found. Once a conscious sense of the new possibilities of expression in present life has developed, it will be more the legitimate property of your Englishmen than of any other people in Europe. It should also, as it is by origin yours, inspire you more forcibly and directly. (Wyndham Lewis, 1914)

... Now it is the obstructions and barriers placed over against the development of an architecture for today which I think it most important to analyse and recognise, and I would propose to devote the remainder of this talk to an examination of them. Some discipline must be introduced, to control the vastness of our material. We shall examine what people want, what they can call their own; we shall be frank in stating the effects on architecture of current principles of ownership of property; a concrete example will be given of the possible effect on architecture of modern principles of production; and we shall, I hope, arrive at some conclusions about the conditions for an architecture today.

The requirements of the society we live in must determine the things we make and live with. Our society is above all determined to be free. The love of travel and change, the mobility of the worker himself, grows with every opportunity to indulge it. The 'home' is no longer a permanent place from one generation to another. The old phrase about a man's 'appointed place' meant a real territorial limit: now the limits of our experience are expanding with every invention of science. We move after work, easily, at least within national frontiers; we move for holidays across frontiers; we move away from the old home and family; we get rid of our belongings, and make for a new, an exciting freedom.

What do we mean when we say 'That's mine, that's my property'? For most of us, it must be agreed, it does not mean very much, and for a large majority of the people it must be acknowledged that it represents nothing at all, although it may still mean a very great deal to them. The rise of the industrial machine-age and its techniques of production and of living; the consequent dislocation of adherences, loyalties and direct economic connection to 'home' and 'community' has left vast numbers of our fellow beings without any real property at all, whether private, material, or spiritual. And this, or so it seems to me, from the point of view of the establishment of a stable society, is an entity of obstruction of the most serious order.

Now I would like to make it quite clear that I am not attempting to make a political speech, and I refuse to be misunderstood in this. I have reached these conclusions as an architect attempting to analyse our present society, and to find out the requirements of it, in order that the new society which I believe is a creative necessity if society itself is to survive, may be given that ordered shelter, that aspect and significance, which it is the proper function of architecture to provide. Any obstruction to this goal must be faced, and contrary to the popular fallacy that facts speak for themselves, I believe they do not and cannot, because facts are dumb and must have their spokesmen. The European poor are getting poorer every day, what are we going to do about it? ...

The economics of the new ownership create what I call 'programme' planning, the conditions for the operation of which are simple. Let us take an example. A small site is selected, because you must not tie up too much money in any given scheme. It does not matter whether it is for housing or factory development or whatever it may be. No large-scale replanning of never-been-planned areas is permissible. It is one picture – about the relative size of the picture on a postage stamp – you are asked to exhibit in that street; not a galleryful, by the same artist, in a given area. The maximum coverage of site, number of floors and height, carefully specified for you by the authorities, the estate owner, or the client, are to be achieved. The result is more often than not a bewildering geometrical diagram of rooms dimensioned not too strictly in accordance with their function, and often inadequately equipped. Proper orientation is replaced by the questionable advantages of a 'view' on to a noisy street or a sordid backyard. On the cash side, the result is to be ten per cent.: produced often enough by rigid reduction estimates during the process of construction, so that the architect's careful attention to detail is reduced outside his control to the minimum requirements of a shoddy building technique, the results of which he can and does prophesy in advance. And when the final product is criticised it is the defenceless architect and not the financial operator, who is made the scapegoat. Financial-programme technique of building will produce neither homes nor architecture until people refuse to live with that kind of arithmetic ...

Until the arithmetic changes, what can architects do with this programme?

Let me digress for a moment to examine how some of these new owners of property lived, in their own homes, during the last generation. What values are to be derived by them from the statement 'That's mine!' We must remember that the intimacies of the homes, and so of the lives, whether in work or in play, of our fathers was a museum-type intimacy, and one of the chief occupations of our mothers was that of curator and guide. How barbaric their habit of overloading was! How rarely they were aware that a room exists for the man, and not man for the room, that he and not the bric-a-brac is to be given the best possible setting! ...

The proper place for a museum-piece is in a museum available to everybody at the proper time. A new idea of personal possession is the idea of opportunity and rights to modern civilisation. That is what we should mean when we say: 'It's mine, it's my property.' Modern life demands more freedom, and it is the freedom given by simple order and significance in relation to everything that happens during the day ...

On this score almost the whole of contemporary building is damned: the conditions for an architecture hardly exist at all. The 'museum-pieces' of big business flaunt their vulgarities from plinth to sky-scraping cornice. These cornices! – if we could but see them from the narrow, unlit corridor street below – would be found, no doubt, to be bravely enriched with a 'small pair of Koodoo horns and a skull.'

What I have called the museum-like effect caused by laissez-faire postage-stamp programme building can best be seen by flying over the land as I had the occasion to do myself only this last weekend: across three national frontiers. And it occurs to me to suggest here, if I may, an addition to the curriculum of architectural schools. I would ask that some of the money at your disposal be spent in flying your students over the land, and allowing them to see on plan, what has happened, is happening to it. The first thing you would notice is how very accurate and beautiful is the draughtsmanship of the agricultural worker; how his geometry of use and necessity has impressed itself on the face of the land. Then you will notice the beauty of the natural curves and configurations of the rivers and the still waters, flashing up to you the reflection of the sun in a blinding, miraculous moving line, as you fly across them; these forms, too, follow an ineluctable principle, and give up by their conjunction with the strict geometry of the ploughed fields and planted forests, new values in contrasts. Then you will be noticing the grandeur of the arrangement and planting of the great parks and surrounds to the great houses, where art has followed nature, and nature in turn follows art. Over all the land you will see the pattern of roadways and communications, but on studying these Euclidian diagrams you will not always be able to end with a Q.E.D. Man's geometry begins to show faults. As the roads converge and you pass over the plan of a town, the diagram becomes unnecessarily confused, unreadable; even ugly. And alas! some of the most glaring faults are to be seen in the newest sections of the plan. There is no congruity between this collection of museum-pieces for building and the fine land, trees and rivers beyond. I think you would do well to see ugliness from the air as well as from the land: for when ugliness is seen, beauty can at once be defined.

It is possible that as architects we can quarrel about styles and details whilst all around us illiterate building is being created, even encouraged, by the lack of co-ordinative laws and principles of land utilisation? Unless, as architects, we set the pace, deliver up the principles for large-scale planning and legislation, we shall not have a chance to create the conditions for an architecture. And you, who are about to become architects, do you remember it is your right to demand that you should also be the geometers of the new land ...

As architects of a new order, we should be concerned with an architectural solution of social and economic problems, for the tradition of architecture is to seek the response that leads to freedom and fullness of life. How are we to begin to outline the possibilities, for the future, of our art? Can you combine the possibilities of a vast extension of human leisure and activity and the consequent enrichment of human values, with an order of life which is set against this basic directive? What are the *material* obstructions here? My time allows me to give you one concrete example or contrast, to illustrate a technical hindrance to the solution of our problem. I sum it up in one statement:

Building costs too much.

Why? Because it has never been properly related to the forms, processes and economies of modern large-scale power production. In its elements, yes: but not as a whole, nor even in units comprising many elements, units of a size suited to the scale of the job. This is so because no one has seriously tackled the job of converting the building industry into a modern industry, in the way, for instance, that the carriage works of yesterday finally produced the modern motor-car.

Let us take an example from this industry. The main essentials of the internal-combustion engined car were fully determined about thirty years ago and a car was produced at that time in small quantities at a cost for a given design of, say £600. This machine possessed a multi-cylinder engine burning petrol mixed with air and ignited by an electric spark; a flywheel, clutch, gears and a transmission system to the back axle; front-wheel steering; elliptical springing; pneumatic tyres. Lamps, instruments, even the hood, were extras, and you could choose these and other 'accessories' from a long and expensive list. It was a noisy, unreliable, uncomfortable, and costly car. But it was new, and gave promise of new enjoyments, new freedoms. The modern motor-car differs in no essential way from the old 'crock' of thirty years ago, so far as its principal elements go: but it is produced today in vast quantities at an actual cost of about £60. It is less noisy than you are when you run down the stairs of your own house; it is reliable (more reliable than most domestic hot-water systems!); it is more comfortable in its seating than most of the chairs you crowd into your tiny living-room; and, in spite of heavy taxes, it is cheap to run, or, at any rate, always worth the money you spend on it. There are no 'accessories' to buy as extras: these are all incorporated, built-in to the standard models. Yet it costs only one-tenth the cost of its predecessor, because modern production methods have been perfected in its making. In spite of the lack of modern road systems (the road industry lags behind, with the building industry, in planning and in method), the modern motor-car is less dangerous to human life than is the modern house, as statistics in all countries prove: more people are killed in 'domestic' accidents, in the home, than on the roads, each year.

The design and construction of dwellings today could be said to be at a stage strictly comparable to the design and production of the motor-car thirty years ago. We know what a modern dwelling should include, could include, if it did not cost so much. Yet a home is more important than a motor-car: every living person is qualified, by right, to possess a decent home. Why do we not then begin to build them? The first mass-production car probably cost £500,000 to produce. The first mass-production home would doubtless cost much more than that, and it would take a number of years to produce. And it would include, as a matter of course, all those 'accessories' which today are by the way of being luxuries. It would not be produced for one-tenth the cost of the existing ill-equipped house, because in building there are always processes which are not amenable to one-line production; but it would cost only a half, or perhaps a third, of current costs, and would include everything that was needed, everything that every person has a right to possess; and everything would be of the best for its purpose, designed to last a generation or two, or, in certain circumstances, less time than that. For the conditions of modern life determine that we are not persons of 'fixed abode' in the old sense: we go to the work and the life we want, and that might not be near 'home'. And, besides, modern inventions produce new necessities and appetites: do we dare saddle an unborn generation with too solid, too 'valuable' a property? This description of a new type of mass-produced dwelling would apply to both individual dwellings and to group-dwellings – flats or apartments. (I hope no 'semi-detached' designs would come off the production line!) The essential characteristics of the planning, amenities, equipment and finishes would be the same. Only in the group-dwellings you would have certain 'extras' on account of insulation between dwelling-units, for instance; matched by certain deductions on account of centralised services, and other economies. And you would plan a large number of standard units capable of assembly in a large variety of forms and finishes and colours. And you would assume (you would have to) that your mass-production methods would be matched by mass-planning methods in siting the new dwellings in new group formations, bearing some ordered relation to your work, your play, your entertainment, and to the systems of communications which link these into a community. And to assume this you would also have to assume a mass-intention towards an ordered and stable society. Given those conditions, you could begin to create an architecture for today.

To this attainment there are requisite Science – the science of the inside of things; science, the identifier, measurer, and calculator; and also Art – the science of the outside of things; art the differentiator, selector and maker. For architecture is both a science and an art.

If we are to consider architecture in the grandest sense as the surest and completest art (and I see no reason why we should not think of it in that way) we know that it simply is not even beginning to be created, and cannot be, because the basic principles of a social plan, an economic plan, of a plan for the division of areas for Work, for Habitation and for Leisure, have nowhere been properly thought out or applied. A great deal of analytical work has been done, but the central problem, the problem of the barriers in the mind of the people and their rulers, is not beginning to be solved.

Five

The object in use

Since the Arts and Crafts period, design was assumed to fall within the general area of responsibility of the architect, however little he might actually achieve in the way of practical production. What is interesting in most extracts collected here is the extent to which many architects and designers quickly dropped the language of functionalism whenever faced with real design problems, preferring to relate all questions to the over-riding matter of form (114, 115, 116, 118, 119, 120, 122, 123, 124). Le Corbusier is rare in the extent to which he follows through the Modern Movement catchwords of standardisation and functionalism, seeking to develop his interior 'fittings' and 'equipment' from a rigorous process of analysis and investigation of needs (121). Needless to say, the results are clearly consistent with his aesthetic. Van Doren gives perhaps the clearest exposition of the way in which forms are borrowed from one technical sphere, to decorate and 'stylise' another. Stam was unusual in attacking the whole principle of providing the housewife with ever more gadgetry and domestic machinery (117). In general, the movement during the period was towards using electric and mechanical aids of every kind as an incentive and palliative to compensate the middle class household for the loss, or presumed loss, of its servants and large houses. As in International Style architecture, we find modern materials and techniques assuming potent symbolic forms (115, 116, 118, 120). The industrial designers were in fact least able or willing to dispense with the notion of style, to the extent that advanced industrialisation between the wars probably increased rather than decreased the obsession with novelty, change and forms intended to catch the eye rather than satisfy one's reason or pocket. Whatever else happened during the period covered by this book, the Arts and Crafts principles of honesty, integrity and quality were no more generally in evidence at the end of the period than at the beginning. What was generally accepted was that objects had to be 'modern', 'in keeping with the age' and to look as if they belonged in a world of mass production, machines and limitless power.

---

114 Werner Gräff, *On the Form of the Motor Car,* 1925-6

We Europeans rather pride ourselves on the fact that we disappointed Henry Ford by not adopting his motor car as widely as he expected, in spite of its extraordinary cheapness and reliability. We are also rather pleased that as a result he has recently decided to concern himself with its form. We know that he has hardly altered his motor car since 1907, in fact for eighteen years. It was tasteless even then, but now it appears completely antiquated as well. Ford himself admits, or rather boasts, that he has never attached any importance to the appearance of his vehicle, only to making it cheaper and better from a technical point of view. And his fellow Americans agreed with him, for they bought Fords by the million. Now, however, the European Ford models for 1926 are incomparably more attractive and more comfortable than the old familiar American ones, and this is a significant change.

Certainly, in Europe as in America, a motor car is primarily a means of transport, not an ornament. And if there were no alternative, we would happily sit in the ugliest car imaginable so long as it provided adequate transport. But we have known for the past fifteen years that there *is* an alternative, that a handsome motor car does not go any worse than an ugly one. And even more important, that the cost of manufacturing a pleasantly shaped motor car need not in theory be any higher than that of a tasteless-looking one. We can demand a little intelligence and taste from the manufacturer in return for our money, and expect to pay no more for his hard work than for his negligence.

Thus we dispose of Ford. We need not have said so much about him were it not for his deliberate indifference, which for a long time made him the most obstinate enemy of good styling. But we must be careful not to take Ford for the whole of America – or indeed Germany for the whole of Europe. America (apart from Ford) has been building the most attractive as well as the cheapest and most practical motor cars for a number of years. American colour schemes are full of bold ideas, carried out with such confidence that often one can only wonder at the way in which even really risky colour combinations are successfully resolved. So let us forget Ford and follow our own judgment, and curse the dismal, muddy colours which have predominated in our own motor cars for so many years – that frightful olive green is undoubtedly the worst. Let us observe how much better on average the Americans understand the relationship between polished metal and black, and deplore the fact that one of our most productive motor car factories has sent out tens of thousands of its small mass-produced cars cloaked in a hideous green which no sensitive person can bear the sight of. Could not the manufacturer have taken the trouble to ask a man of taste to select a more refined tone? If he had done so he would surely have also been advised that he had chosen a most unfortunate design for his radiator. The plated metal pressing which covers the radiator frame is nothing less than a disaster.

And since example is more convincing than argument, our man of taste would no doubt have shown him the radiator of the Horch motor car, which is so much simpler, so much more practical and attractive, or a headlamp made by the firm of Zeiss, which is an example of plain and practical beauty, and of a good relationship between polished and matt metal pressings and glass. At automobile exhibitions we are glad to see that engines are becoming plainer and cleaner, while the chassis looks ever stronger and more unified. In these areas, almost all the manufacturers have managed to produce designs which appeal even to the layman, and the latter is certainly better equipped to express an opinion on the bodywork. Now he can find a small car which not only has an exceptionally sleek and restful shape, but is also equipped with roomy, low and comfortable seats; and if he likes speed, then the sports model will especially attract him.

Sedate ladies and elderly gentlemen, on the other hand, will be more attracted by, let us say, the Mercedes limousine; yet handsome though it is, it shows more clearly than any of the other body shapes illustrated here that motor car bodies even today are still a product of the coach-builder's art. And some of us will be disturbed by the feeling that all our present motor car bodies are marked by this division between the craftsmanlike spirit of their design and the industrial methods of their production. The beginnings of an improvement in this direction are already to be seen, but there is no sign of a generally valid solution to the problem.

And now for our largest passenger vehicles. The postal service has suddenly remembered its old privilege and is once again providing transport for passengers. Lemon yellow vehicles speed through the provincial towns as they did many years ago. And grandmothers who still remember the rattling and jingling of the old post coaches now climb into the new omnibuses in wonderment, admiring their broad, soft cushions, their silent progress, the clean and crystal-clear windows which afford such a favourable view. And however much they may be against the automobile in other respects, as far as post buses are concerned, they are all in favour of progress.

The omnibuses are becoming handsomer from year to year, too. Two or three years ago, the bodywork was simply mounted on a lorry chassis. The unmodified frame resulted in a high centre of gravity, and not all companies were able to produce such respectable body shapes as Hansa-Lloyd.

But how much more attractive is the same firm's new express omnibus with its low entrance and numerous doors. Such splendid shapes can only be obtained with the new Niederflur chassis which is now being built for general use in omnibuses. It has finally been recognised that an omnibus need not be any less comfortable than any other form of passenger vehicle.

We are not so far advanced as America, where giant motor buses have recently been introduced for long-distance journeys, approximately 12 metres long, with two double-axled sets of wheels, and seats for 96 people. But we have already recognised the superiority of automobiles over railed vehicles in many cases, and tramway companies are themselves beginning to run motor buses. The increased attention which this form of transport has been given in recent years has done a great deal for its appearance.

But what about the large Berlin motor buses? The chassis builders have made great efforts in this direction and their progress has been brilliant. The firm which manufactures their bodywork is also beyond reproach, and yet, when we see these monsters travelling through Berlin, something disturbs us, spoiling their overall shape.

And then we realise that the shape of a vehicle must be preserved above all *when it is in motion.* That the smoothest line is completely ruined when the bus goes jolting over uneven road surfaces on solid rubber tyres, while the ear-splitting racket produced by the latter detracts most annoyingly from our aesthetic enjoyment. The mechanically minded will also feel that the amount of vibration inflicted on the engine cannot do it any good. In fact the overall repair costs of pneumatic tyres are considerably lower than those for solid rubber. But even before this, we should consider the nerves of the harassed Berliners. At the moment nobody seems to care a jot for them, and we could do with the advertisements of a French tyre manufacturer in which the words 'Parisians! A scandal!' are followed by two pictures, one showing a packed omnibus running on solid rubber and the other lorryload of pigs riding on fat pneumatic tyres. Yes, the French are right! Up, Berliners, to the Central Livestock Market, and you'll see that pigs have a better time than you do, at least while they are alive. Should you only have comfortable transport once you are dead? Get up a demonstration. Off to the offices of the ABOAG! Let the signwriters prepare their placards with the slogan:

OUR NERVES demand PNEUMATIC TYRES

And we will paint one for ourselves which adds: 'And our aesthetic sense too.'

---

115 Johannes Molzahn, *Economics of the Advertising Mechanism,* 1925-6

The heart and nerve of industry are the natural forces of water, wind and fire, or more precisely their conversion into mechanical energy, steam and electricity; that alone gives its meaning and its potential to the whole mechanism of production. Without those productive forces our machines would stand dead and abandoned in the factories. But just as the natural forces of water, wind and fire can only be harnessed to industrial use by interposing some form of resistance to them (turbines, windmills and so on), to convert the forces into mechanical energy, in the same way the productive forces that we find in industrial production only become expressive when similar conditions are fulfilled and the production-psyche is successfully converted into acceptance by the consumer. The comparisons of the functions can be illustrated in parallel tables:

Industry		*Advertising*
Natural forces: water, fire etc.	=	production, materials
Converter: turbine, windmill	=	propaganda machinery
Effective power: mechanical energy	=	consumption, sales

As we have now set out the production-psyche of the natural forces, that which drives the production-machinery through a process of conversion and keeps it going, and appears in the Table as effective power, similarly we have found the converter in the propaganda-machinery, which drives the consumption-mechanism and keeps that moving. We now have to find out the means employed in the propaganda-machinery, to find a converter serving the same purpose in our field as the turbine does in the field of industrial production. Our first problem will be to recognise the psyche of consumption, or acceptance, with its organs and functions, and to deduce from that the means of affecting them. It is not difficult to perceive this acceptance-mechanism in the spirit of the people or its expression in the spirit of the age, which takes material form through an optical-acoustic appeal to the senses ... The propaganda of production must therefore rely primarily on optical functions. But propaganda is in essence information in graphic presentation; the question is, then, to determine which elements of graphic presentation have the greatest optical capacity to make a lasting impression on the psyche ...

We can demonstrate the conversion effect of the symbol presentation in yet another example. Let us

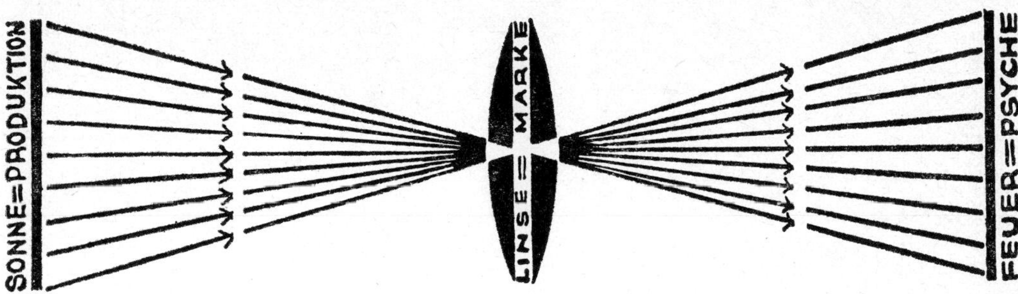

Johannes Molzahn, 'Fire–Psyche' diagram
Die Form, vol. I, 1925-6

take a magnifying glass and hold it between the sun and a piece of paper so that the paper is at the focal point of the lens, and catches fire. In thus creating fire we have converted the sun's energy into active energy. The conception of a symbol-effect is convincing if we show this same experiment to a primitive tribe; the impact would be absolutely shattering and express itself in wild flight from this 'magic', which has so shaken and impressed the whole psyche of the primitive man. The lens has become a symbol of the sun, the unknown function of the lens has engraved itself on the subconscious, a mystery. In this example we have established the principle that the industrial symbol has to construct if it is to produce its effect. The trade-mark has the function of the lens, it stands for the lens as the lens stood for the sun to the primitive people. At the focal point, which corresponds to the concentration-point of the industrial symbol, the same process of conversion has taken place: the production-force becomes effective in the psyche of the consumer, perhaps in the manner indicated schematically

Thus the trade-mark is always the most elementary means, the link between *production* and *consumption*. No organisation can exist and expand for long unless it uses such a device as a token to represent it. If that is the purpose of the emblem, then it must do it without a lot of written backing, building exclusively on optical means, i.e. those means which in the briefest period of time produce the best and most profound impression and preserve the psyche. The significance of the emblem is absolute, its shape is determined purely according to optical-mechanical laws; the function determines the form just as it does in the construction of a machine. The question of the emblem is in fact not an artistic question but a technical–scientific, a kinetic–psychic question; the aesthetic form here, just as in the machine, is only the result of perfect construction in the sense of the greatest possible efficiency ...

But the swift, ever-increasing tempo of life, the rushing traffic, the colossal demands of every second, the age of the cinema and the air-liner, these have not only reshaped our thinking, they have also, and in quite a special way, changed our eyes in their capacity for adjustment and economy, for there is a limit to the amount that can be taken in ...

Pictorial representation, the half-tone block in combination with the industrial symbol, will govern the future of the advertisement and of the street, as well as offices and places of business. For the fantastic expenditure of energy in our times is going to enforce

the most stringent economy in the media of organisation and trade.

Advertising is the dynamic means of exchange, but it cannot be said that that idea has been put into practice yet, albeit the time is ripe.

Johannes Molzahn, Signet for the periodical *Der Strom Die Form*, vol. I, 1925-6

---

116 Marcel Breuer, *Metal Furniture,* 1927

Two years ago, when I saw the finished version of my first steel club armchair, I thought that this out of all my work would bring me the most criticism. It is my most extreme work both in its outward appearance and in the use of materials; it is the least artistic, the most logical, the least 'cosy' and the most mechanical.

What happened was precisely the opposite of what I had expected. The interest shown in both modernist and non-modernist circles showed me clearly that contemporary attitudes were undergoing a change, abandoning the whimsical in favour of the rational. We no longer need to betray reality by creating or at least showing reverence for fantastic but transitory caprices of taste and style (even when this style is the 'modern' one). We have had enough of the everlasting and arbitrary changes of form, colour and style, and so we are seeking clear and logical forms, based on rational principles.

Our work is unrelenting and unretrospective; it despises tradition and established custom. A frequent criticism of steel furniture is that it is cold, clinical, reminiscent of an operating theatre. But these are concepts which flourish from one day to the next. They are the product of habit, soon destroyed by another habit.

Against the changing habits of human utterance there stand the powerful movements of human physical and psychic development.

The mainspring of this development, the basic elements of the current situation, lie in the work which we are now doing.

Let me pick out a special area of present-day production – tubular metal furniture – and deal with its special properties in relation to my own designs . . .

I first experimented with duralumin, but because of its high price I went over to using precision steel tubing.

Steel is lighter than wood. This paradox is simply explained if one considers the static properties of the two materials. Even soft steel, though weighing nine times as much as beechwood, is 13 to 100 times stronger according to the type of load imposed upon it. In addition, steel is a relatively homogeneous material which can be much more easily formed into stress-resistant shapes (e.g. a tubular cross-section) than wood, whose mechanical properties are limited by its tendency to splinter and its non-homogeneous nature.

Basically, a well-constructed steel chair will be better able to cope with static loads than an equally well constructed wooden chair, which means that for the same static loads, a steel chair can be substantially lighter. A chair made of high-grade steel tubing (a highly elastic material) with tightly stretched fabric in the appropriate places, makes a light, completely self-sprung seat which is as comfortable as an upholstered chair, but is many times lighter, handier and more hygienic, and therefore many times more practical in use.

Tubular chairs with wooden seating are also light, manageable and durable.

The severe rationalisation of components – the use of the same components in different types of furniture, the possibility of reducing them to two-dimensional parts (over fifty club armchairs can be packed into a space of one cubic metre, with obvious advantages for transport), and a full regard for industrial and manufacturing considerations all contributed to the social yardstick of a price which could be paid by the broadest possible mass of the population. And I might say that without meeting this yardstick, I could not have found the project particularly satisfactory.

117 Mart Stam, *Away with the Furniture Artists,* 1927

It is nonsense to talk about interior furnishings which issue from the hands of interior designers and furniture artists, just as it is nonsense to suggest a trip to the Riviera to a worker. It is nonsense because 99% of these furnishings are beyond the means of 99% of the population. It goes without saying that it is precisely these worthless furnishings which attract general interest. They are all designs basically for the well-to-do, and the public sees in them the ideal of prosperity. Just as the worker and the petty official long for their own house and garden, and must then be satisfied with a diminutive villa and a diminutive sitting and dining-room, so they desire to see expressed in their furniture this same ideal of prosperity. The result is the appearance of furniture which, although manufactured on a mass scale, is intended to create a false impression of prosperity. In the situation of today, at a time when everyone is engaged in a battle for existence, when the majority of the population can scarcely even satisfy their most immediate needs, it is necessary that:

(i) A standard minimal dwelling should be established.

(ii) In the furnishing of this minimal dwelling, account should be taken not of existing life-styles, but of modern standards of living.

(iii) Instead of corresponding to the bourgeois ideal of prosperity, these furnishings should satisfy the actual needs of the people to the utmost.

In the course of the next few years these demands will be met, on the one hand because the economic circumstances are so unrelenting that the minimal dwelling will become an inevitable necessity, and, on the other hand, because industry has begun to withdraw furniture from the influence of the aesthetes.

The creation of a minimal dwelling is a task which should also be of great importance to the Werkbund exhibition in Stuttgart. For it is necessary that it be made clear how much is superfluous in our houses. Industry is here much to blame. Spurred on by competition it has produced a string of novelties, without there always being a need for these 'inventions'. It is obvious that we are pleased that technology should advance; but the man who considers every technical refinement to be indispensable to his house gives the impression of being a parvenu.

And in the last analysis, what is the point of all these inventions? Is the consumer market really big? Who are these customers? A very large percentage cannot afford to own these things; they remain luxuries.

So it is better to forgo the ideal house with its ideal furnishings; the first thing to do is to devote our energies to the minimal dwelling, to furnish it at a minimal cost, so that the primary demands (sleeping, sitting, eating, cooking) are satisfied in the best, and hence least complicated, manner, and the daily chores can be accomplished quickly and unobtrusively. In this, the furniture and the whole interior arrangement play a more important part than the tools needed for cleaning and maintenance: simple furniture, no matter whether beautiful or not, and simple tools.

The minimal dwelling is of course primarily and predominantly a requirement for those without property, but it is also of value for every modern creative man. By simplifying his demands on his home and his life style, he solves his living problems for himself; instead of creating new demands he jettisons the obsolete ones. The simpler and quicker he can finish the work necessary for the maintenance of life, the more pleasant it is for him. He doesn't need a cellar for storage (a relic of the medieval city) when today's communications make centralised warehousing possible. He does not need wash-houses since machines can take over the washing and drying and do more work in less time. Does his laundry get worn more quickly? Too bad, but all the same, better than that his wife should get worn down.

And why should people eat home-made preserves? If the minimal dwelling has no attic, where every kind of rubbish is kept, so much the better. Then people will not cling on to everything: neither Grandmama's furniture nor memories of their youth. And wives will not collect incomplete dinner sets or outdated clothes. The minimal dwelling is not a miniature villa, nor is it for people who would like to live in a villa. It is a house for people with fewer demands than villa-people make, for people with a different attitude to life, who are not upset at not having the latest technical inventions. If pushed they can live without machines to cut their bread and make macaroni or clean their boots, however beautiful these inventions may be.

We are making a mistake with all these inventions in household equipment. These do not make life simpler. Housework is not being reduced to a minimum. On the contrary, they are causing housekeeping to make fuller demands on our attention, and that must not be the aim. Housekeeping should remain the smallest possible part of our existence.

Living does not mean to modern man in the first place 'setting up house', and 'setting up house' does not mean to the modern woman in the first place 'to do the housekeeping'.

The matter becomes clearer if for a moment we take the dwelling back to its original function: the dwelling is needed for shelter from the weather.

The dwelling has become for us more than shelter, but it should remain predominantly that. It must be able to be cleaned quickly and thoroughly. Household appointments and technology already make that possible; but these techniques and inventions must never be placed in the foreground, for that will result in an empty aimless state of being driven ever onwards. Then we would be turning the peripheral into an essential, and our lives would lose that indispensable simplicity and clarity which each of us needs if we are to accomplish our proper work in our proper place.

118 Willi Lotz, *Suites of Furniture and Standard Furniture Designs,* 1928

The furnishing of the houses on the Weissenhof estate in Stuttgart represented an attempt to replace matching sets of furniture, designed to go together in a room, by an assembly of individual pieces chosen from good, existing standard designs. Instead of suites of matching furniture of a similar design and made of similar materials, the idea was to present *the* chair, *the* table, *the* bed. And, moreover, only those examples were to be chosen which had evolved a standard design from being manufactured to functional specifications. Next to a plywood cupboard was to stand a chair by Thonet, made from lengths of beech curved into shape, and next to this a white painted iron bed. What the things look like standing next to each other is unimportant, if each individual object is simply a typical expression of its nature.

So it came about that the Thonet chair, until then generally used mainly in hotels, became suitable for domestic use. Similarly, the iron bedstead. But those were about the only standard designs to come from industry, and even then it was only the principle that was agreed to – the iron bedstead for instance had its proportions altered ...

The furniture industry manufactures a vast number of suites for different rooms. Every range must be distinguishable from the next and from time to time new ranges must be brought out. The newer ones are only different from the older ones in that in place of an acanthus leaf some modern jagged ornament has been added. This is the fashion, particularly with furniture. More expensive furniture adopts 'cubist' shapes. Dealers always sell their furniture in suites, or 'Rooms', with selected pieces sold all together. The crucial factor for every range is a common style. Naturally this leads the furniture industry astray into crass formalism, as in every industry relying on 'ranges'. The result is that you cannot buy a chair on its own, whose shape has simply developed from its function and its method of manufacture, without it being at the same time part of a specific room-furnishing. The draughtsman has always had to design it. Similarly with wardrobes, in fact with absolutely every piece of furniture ...

But this turning away from furnishing is also dependent on the new conception of space, which in turn is an expression of the new awareness. Furniture, artistically designed and arranged in space – I am thinking here of the best examples and not the vast number of diluted versions turned out by the furniture draughtsmen – is a product independent in its form. It is the first thing to give a space a specific quality, just as the shape of a flight of stairs in a baroque entrance hall is the first thing to really bring the space to life. It is an organic component of those elements whose function is to give shape to a specific space. It belongs in the same company as the wall, the niche, the floor and the ceiling. But the kind of space on view in the Stuttgart estate, although in its early stages of development only, is more impressive than any other and completely different ... This impression is strongest perhaps in Le Corbusier's work. Were one to put heavy, formally pretentious furniture in there, the space would be killed. In Le Corbusier's case all the furniture must be such that it takes nothing away from the space, that the space flows freely with no check to its dynamic.

Quite naturally it follows from this that the furniture to be designed should, in proportion to its use-value, take up as little room as possible and use as little material as necessary. This accounts for the preference for plywood boards and steel tubing. In its appearance, the new furniture, whether it is a cupboard or a seat, must, whenever possible, be self-sufficient and should not seek to relate to the floor, walls, or other pieces of furniture, either through any additions or deviations from the basic shape. 'Must' and 'should not'? – if it has been designed in a consistent manner. It is an organism in itself, because it has to serve a function.

This can clearly be seen in the almost crystalline conciseness of the very latest furniture. Because of this, the cubism of these new pieces, when standing in space, is not decorative but organic ... In general when we think of containers, boxes or cupboards we always think about the shape of the sides or walls, not about the space, just as we think of walls, roofs, doors and window panes when thinking about houses and *not* about the space, which after all is the reason for building all the rest. Even with a chair we think of legs, arms and back, of the visual image of the chair, whereas what is the essential feature is the profile of the seat ...

Objects which are designed not for the sake of appearance, but to fulfil their function as well as possible, will arrive at that form which most clearly expresses that function. The aim set by our generation is to make form an expression of function, not the expression of a self-justifying aesthetic. But things which have sprung from a similar rationale will be able to be seen together without needing to be specifically matched up. The houses built for the Weissenhof estate are a clear proof of this ...

But no one would maintain that *the* chair or *the* bed could ever be finally constructed or that it will actually emerge from a process of natural selection. For if there were such a thing as *the* definitive form, it could only be for a specific period of time and in a specific material ... The German army's mess tin looks different to that of other armies, but they had been just as competently made in each case, and from just as sound a rationale. Personal opinions as well are and always will remain different ... The different shapes of modern chairs show how the same materials can lead to quite different results. The chair designed by Mies van der Rohe differs considerably from the tubular steel Bahaus chair, since he used a structural feature of steel, its elasticity, as a major element of the design. The solution is a brilliant one because the tube serves a unique purpose, but it is not the definitive chair any more than the Thonet or Kramer chair is.

119 John Gloag, *Wood or Metal?*, 1929

The use of metal for furniture is not a new idea. The nineteenth century was distinguished by an enormous output of metal bedsteads, and two thousand years before that era of misused machinery, bronze tables, couches, stools and chairs were contributing to the furnishing of town and country houses in Italy and the Roman provinces. But, until the advent of the metal bedstead, the special properties of the material did not inspire form. The bronze furniture from Pompeii in the Naples Museum, for example, merely illustrates the imposition of various Roman conventions of ornament: we find cabriole legs, claws and hooves terminating those legs, the sphinx, honeysuckle and acanthus motifs. We realise that all the pages of that familiar pattern book of classic decoration have given something to form, and the ductile material, the bronze itself, has only brought rich colour to the furniture. Established conventional forms were used alike for bronze or stone by the Roman craftsmen.

The metal bedstead which appeared so many centuries later was not the product of craftsmanship. It came into the world during the untidy childhood of industrial production, and it lacked conscious design even as an amoeba lacks conscious intelligence. With the cage as their model and iron and brass tubing as their means, hundreds of manufacturers produced and sold these monstrous crudities, garnishing them with knobs and finials and stamped brass twirls and twiddles, and never attempting to use metal graciously. Such was the contribution of nineteenth-century industry to the development of metal furniture.

The New Art* movement produced some experiments

* Art Nouveau

in this field, but it was all drawing-board stuff, unrelated to the material and its sinuous, floreated lines could have been expressed equally well in butter. Except for such starkly utilitarian articles as filing cabinets and other office equipment, there were few serious attempts to create metal furniture until, in the years immediately following the war, this branch of design became associated with what may be called Robot modernism. Germany, released in matters of taste from the heavy carving and rich gilding that the artistic guidance of Wilhelm II had imposed, began to lead Europe in the expression of mechanical art. Dramatic possibilities of design in metal were discovered. Nickelled steel and polished aluminium came into alliance with yielding upholstery of leather and rubber, and chairs and couches appeared which were strictly metallic in character, and were as efficient and about as interesting as modern sanitary fittings.

The metal furniture of the Robot modernist school can claim fitness for purpose, and it exemplifies a just and original use of material. It expresses the harsh limitations of the movement to which it belongs, even as Le Corbusier, who might almost be regarded as the voice of that movement, expresses with lucidity and relentless logic its utter inhumanity.

At the opposite pole of aesthetic aspiration is the metal furniture that mass-production American minds have given to the United and uncritical States. Thin sheets of metal are stamped out to form bed heads and ends, and the sides, backs and doors of cupboards. These sheets are 'assembled', their edges and joints protected by strips of beading and the proportions of wooden prototypes are followed. The result is a simple article of furniture which can be turned out by the million. Painted in plain colours, such things would, at least, earn the description of 'blameless', but treated as they nearly always are to imitate wood (something richly figured as a rule), they become under the dull hands of their makers just so many more unpleasant objects in a world already overcrowded with doleful rubbish. The hero of Sinclair Lewis's depressing book, *The Man who knew Coolidge*, is in the office equipment business and he sings the song of metal furniture made to look like any real rich wood you fancy with the nauseating conviction that he is singing one of the finest songs in the world.

Office equipment is a legitimate field for the employment of metal furniture, and the durability of metal justifies its use in such directions. Honestly designed beds and cupboards, that frankly proclaimed themselves to be metal under a coat of preserving lacquer or nickel or paint, would be preferable to the gummy brown things of wood that hide their poverty of design by some pretentious label such as 'Jacobean' and their weakness of construction by a tangle of ornament that covers gaping joints. But if wood furniture is intelligently designed for mechanical production, then it is very doubtful whether metal furniture could claim any advantage economic or aesthetic.

Although metal equipment may be satisfying to the standards of commercial life, and may adequately resist the wear and tear of an office, there does not appear to be any case for substituting metal for wood in furniture that is designed to give convenience and harmony to a home. A desire for novelty for its own sake may be the excuse for dramatic experiments in mechanistic design, and this may conceivably masquerade under some such high-sounding title as 'a return to basic line', and although such excursions into engineering may demand the use of metal rather than wood they do not afford any evidence of the aesthetic superiority of metal.

The designer may devise an interior in which chairs of shining aluminium are an essential part of the composition; but in such schemes human beings appear intrusive; there is no sympathy between them and the setting.

Metal is cold and brutally hard, and whether it is used for a mid-Victorian brass bedstead or a chair that is formed by simple loops of polished steel tubing and leather cushions, it gives no comfort to the eye.

'The house is a machine for living in' writes Le Corbusier. The implications of that creed can become too austere, and the word *machine* can be grimly misleading. It can even lead some designers to believe that human beings are merely machines for living with the masterful and dramatic things they create in their studios.

---

120 Charlotte Perriand, *Wood or Metal? A Reply,* 1929

Metal plays the same part in furniture as cement has done in architecture.

It is a Revolution
The Future will favour materials which best solve the problems propounded by the new man:
I understand by the New Man the type of individual who keeps pace with scientific thought, who understands his age and lives it: the Aeroplane, the Ocean Liner and the Motor are at his service; Sport gives him health; His House is his resting place.

What is his house to be?
Hygiene must be considered first: soap and water. Tidiness: standard cupboards with partitions for these. Rest: resting machines for ease and pleasant repose. Beds: armchairs: chaises longues: Office chairs and tables: Stools, some high and some low: Folding chairs. The French word for furniture, *meubles* comes from the Latin *mobilis*: meaning things that can be moved about. The only things that come into this category are chairs and tables.

We have stated the problem; now we must solve it . . .

Material now in use and material that ought to be used
Wood: a vegetable substance, in its very nature bound to decay, it is susceptible to the action of damp in the air. 'Central heating dries the air and warps wood.' Since the war, we do not get dry wood any more: it is dried by artificial means, and inadequately.
Plywood: Composition wood:
These should be used for panels, mounted on a metal framework, and allowing for 'play'.
Metal: a homogeneous material of which certain alloys are liable to be affected by acids in the air:
In that case protection is afforded by oxidising, or by application of paint, Duco, etc. . . .
Cupboards of beaten sheet iron:
For chairs, metal 'bicycle' tubes:
A bicycle weighs only 10 to 12 kilograms. The minimum of weight, the maximum of strength.
Autogenous welding = △
This process opens a vast field of practical possibilities.

The ratio between the weight necessary to ensure against breakage and the conditions of construction, in other words, the coefficient of security, would be about 6 in the case of metal, 10 in the case of wood. To be of the same solidity the wood would have to be 14 times as thick as metal:

Thrust
Compression } 14 times more in wood than in steel
Flexion

Technical conclusions:
The Eiffel Tower could never have been made of Wood.
Metal is superior to wood; reasons?
The power of resistance in metal itself;
Because it allows of mass production in the factory (lessens amount of labour required);
Because by means of the different methods of manufacture it opens out new vistas; new opportunities of design;
Because the protective coatings against toxic agencies not only lower the cost of upkeep, but have a considerable *Aesthetic* value.
Metal plays the same part in furniture as cement has done in architecture.

It is a revolution

Aesthetics of metal

Aluminium varnish, Duco, Parkerisation, Paint, all provide variety in the treatment of metal.

If we use metal in conjunction with leather for chairs, with marble slabs, glass and india-rubber for tables, floor coverings, cement,
vegetable substances,
we get a range of wonderful combinations and new aesthetic effects.
Unity in Architecture and yet again *Poetry*

A new lyric beauty, regenerated by mathematical science; Has produced a new kind of man who can love with fervour; Orly's 'Avion Voisin', a photograph of the Mediterranean, and 'Ombres Blanches'.

Even Mont Cervin is restored to a place of honour.

As for the Public:
Operation Theatres: Clinics, Hospitals:
Improve physical and moral health, Nothing extraneous.

Fashion: Look at the shops (which serve the public taste).
They make metallised wood;
They make imitation oak of metal;
They have even planned a chair made of plywood, metal and india-rubber to imitate marble.
Long Live Commerce
The Man of the XXth Century:
An Intruder? Yes, he is, when surrounded by antique furniture, and No, in the setting of the new Interior.
Sport, indispensable for a healthy life in a mechanical age.
Modern mentality also suggests:
Transparency, reds, blues,
The brilliance of coloured paint,
That chairs are for sitting on,
That cupboards are for holding our belongings,
Space, light,
The Joy of creating and of living ...
in this century of ours.
Brightness Loyalty Liberty in thinking and acting.
WE MUST KEEP MORALLY AND PHYSICALLY FIT
Bad luck for those who do not.

---

121 Le Corbusier, *The Furniture Adventure*, 1929

Renewal of the plan of the modern house cannot be undertaken effectively without examining the question of furniture. This is the Gordian knot. It must be cut, otherwise any pursuit of the modern idea is in vain. We are about to change tack: a machinist age has followed the pre-machinist age; a new spirit has replaced the old spirit ...

Woman has got there before us. She has brought about the reform of her dress. She found herself in this dilemma: to follow fashion and by so doing give up what modern technology – modern life – had to offer. To give up sport and, more materially, the chance of employment which has given her a productive rôle in modern life and enabled her to earn her living. By following fashion she could have had nothing to do with the motor car, she would not have been able to take the underground or the bus, nor rush around in the office or in the shops. To carry out the daily *construction* of her toilet: hair-do, boots, buttoning her dress, she would have had to give up sleeping.

So woman cut off her hair and her skirts and her sleeves. She goes around bare headed, bare armed, with her legs free, and she can dress in five minutes. Moreover she is beautiful; she enchants us with the grace of her figure, which dress designers admit to have turned to their advantage.

The courage, the enterprise, the inventive spirit with which woman has revolutionised her dress are a miracle of modern times. Thank you!

What about us men? A dismal state of affairs! In our clothes, we look like generals of the Grand Army and we wear starched collars! We are uncomfortable in our working clothes. We need to carry about us an arsenal of papers and small utensils. The pocket – pockets should be the key to modern dress. If you try to equip yourself with what you need you destroy the line of your clothes; you are no longer well dressed. You have to choose between working or being elegant.

The English costume which we wear has nevertheless achieved one important thing. It has *neutralised* us. It is useful to cultivate a neutral appearance in the city. The main means of expression is no longer in the ostrich plumes of the hat, it is in the face. This is enough. Monsieur Waleffe, in Paris, disgusted with the English, preached a gigantic crusade: silk breeches and silk stockings, buckled shoes and suspenders, 'French' elegance, Latin spirit! and display of calves everywhere! This misfired; everyone just laughed.

At St Moritz, in the snow, modern man comes into his own. At Levallois-Perret, the headquarters of the motor car industry, the mechanic is a pioneer. We, office men, have been beaten by a considerable length by women.

The spirit of reform, then, has made an appearance, but no more. It still has to make its impact on every aspect of life ...

So, what do we mean by furniture?

'The means by which we make our social rank known.'

This, very precisely, is the way kings think: Louis XIV was a brilliant exponent of this mentality. Shall we be Louis XIVs? How about that! If there are millions of Louis XIVs on the earth, there will no longer be a Sun King.

Seriously, are we determined to be Sun Kings?

Furniture consists of:

Tables for working and eating. Chairs for dining and for working. Armchairs of various shapes for resting in various ways and boxes in which to stack the objects we use.

Furniture consists of tools, and servants, too. Furniture serves our needs.

Our needs are everyday ones, regular, always the same; yes, always the same.

Our furniture fulfils constant, daily, regular functions.

All men have the same needs, at the same times, every day, all their lives.

The tools which would fulfil these functions are easy to define, and progress, which brings us new techniques (tubular steel, pliable metal sheeting, autogenous welding) provides us with means of production which are infinitely more perfect and more effective than before.

The insides of houses will no longer look like those of the time of Louis XIV. Hence the adventure.

Our needs are human needs. We all have the same number of limbs, with the same shape and the same dimensions. If there are differences on the latter point, an average measurement is easy to find.

Standard functions. Standard needs. Standard objects. Standard dimensions.

The idea of the *standard* is already well advanced. It is as old as the hills and it has established the form of every civilisation ... The question of the modern standard is already well advanced, but we take no notice of it.

The whole world has agreed on the format and dimensions of writing paper. Office furniture throughout the world is adjusted to the format of writing paper.

The spirit of the machine age has used its ingenuity. What we have done for the motor car we have done for office furniture. A revolution has taken place: the cabinet makers' workshops have been closed and in other parts of the town we have created the steel furniture industry.

Accuracy, efficiency, purity of shapes and lines have arisen ...

I am going to maintain that apart from chairs and tables, furniture is in fact nothing more than pigeon-hole boxes.* Now for the most part, these pigeon-holes

* The French word, *casier*, is untranslatable, combining the idea of a pigeon-hole in an office with an actual box or fitment [Editor's note]

at the moment are badly dimensioned and of doubtful utility: at this point I denounce waste. I will push the enemy back into his trenches, and find out what this furniture is really for. I will make certain that, with the new wood and metal industries, it is possible to construct accurate pigeon-hole fitments with an admirable functionality, of a size which is not approximate but definite and I will be led to conclude that the traditional furniture of the cabinet maker and the salesman does not serve us well at all, that it is a cumbersome relic, which opposes the economical and efficient solution, since it obliges us to build houses which are too large, and it complicates existence by preventing rational administration of the household. Finally, its only purpose is an aesthetic one. Now when an object of utility no longer fulfils a function, when its rationale is aesthetic, it has become a parasite and must be rejected. We will seek a kind of aesthetics which will suit us better; we will look for something which will conquer the heart and the sensibility of a modern man. Let us play the game:

I draw a shelf with glasses on it; a shelf with plates, soup dishes, etc; a shelf with bottles, decanters, etc. Drawers with an automatic arrangement of cutlery. This is the end of the chapter so far as eating utensils are concerned.

I draw a shelf with household linen, sheets, table napkins, etc., a shelf with personal linen, drawers with underclothes, stockings, etc.

I draw a shelf with shoes, a shelf with hats.

I draw a garment hanging on a coathanger; a dress. That is all.

I have just made an inventory of the objects in our daily use.

These objects are all in proportion to our limbs, adapted to our gestures. They have a *common scale*, they obey a standard. If I study the question – and for twenty years I have been obsessed by the anomaly of furniture (I formerly earned my living by fitting out various apartment houses) – I find a common measurement. I find the pigeon-hole which effectively contains all these objects.

I draw this pigeon-hole. It measures 75 cm for the sides and $37\frac{1}{2}$ to 50 cm depth or 150 × 75 at the front and $37\frac{1}{2}$ to 75 for the depth. The variability of the depth measurement results from the various methods of the interior arrangement of this pigeon-hole fitment.

In 1913, when I had to design collapsible equipment for a travelling exhibition for decorative art (and decorative art meant the whole bag of tricks from the office to the drawing-room or the sitting-room), I

Le Corbusier, Layout of standard pigeon-holes
Précisions, Vincent Fréal, Paris, 1920

Le Corbusier, Modular pigeon-holes
Précisions, Vincent Fréal, Paris, 1920

discovered this standard format of 75 cm and 150 cm. And I proceeded to forget about it.

In 1924, we were preparing our Esprit Nouveau Pavilion – in which we wished to solve once and for all both the problem of furniture and that of the aesthetic content of the home. After a rigorous analysis, we then came up with the same dimensions again.

In 1925, the Esprit Nouveau Pavilion seemed to shed light, thought by many to be a pretty glaring light – on this question.

Finally in 1928, our expert in domestic interior design, Mme. Charlotte Perriand, also arrived at the same dimensions. While I am talking to you now, in Buenos Aires, we should have a vast stand at the Salon d'Automne in Paris demonstrating in peremptory fashion the principle of the 'Equipment of a modern dwelling' by standard pigeon-hole fitments.

This has constructural, architectural, economic and industrial implications: it would be sensible to make pigeon-holes industrially: containers in large scale production, which could be sold both to the individual who is doing his own furnishing and to the architect at the planning stage. The former will deploy his pigeon-hole fitment against the walls of his rooms or will use them to establish either full-height or half-height partitions (see the Esprit Nouveau Pavilion, 1925); the latter will build the pigeon-holes into the walls.

All that remains is to fit out the inside of these pigeon-holes. These 'fittings' can range from the most simple, like available office furniture, to the greatest possible refinement. These 'fittings', to be installed later in the standard pigeon-hole boxes, can be sold at the Bazar de l'Hotel-de-Ville* or in the Champs-Elysées.

When the house is completed, while the painters are putting on the final coat, the day before the occupier moves in his books and his cases, the appropriate fittings for the different functions are slotted into the pigeon-holes. The doors will be added – sliding panels in sheet steel, in plywood, marble, glass, aluminium, etc.; a taste for simplicity or opulence can be displayed according to wish.

And if the house is built by dry assembly, you can see how simple it all is.

Try to imagine the new dwelling. Each room is reduced to the adequate minimum and its source of light (a long window or a wall of glass) is perfect. Its shape is suited to its purpose; the doors open in such a way as to guarantee easy circulation. In the bedroom, the library, the drawing-room, the office, the kitchen, shutters are raised or lowered and screens are slid at arm's reach. Behind these appear compartments suitable for what they should contain. Every object is

* One of the large, cheap department stores in Paris. [Editor's note]

arranged as in a jewel casket; certain fittings can be brought forward smoothly on ball bearings; your clothes are spread out before your eyes, etc.

Hence there is no longer any cabinet makers' furniture in the house! I am grieved to think about so many good craftsmen, but I feel that there is a need to adapt ourselves to the new conditions of modern life.

The reduction of furniture to the state of pigeonholes which, if necessary, form the wall itself, can also be obtained by basic methods of construction in reinforced concrete ...

In the office or drawing-room, sewing-room or boudoir; always and everywhere, standard and accurate functions are accomplished and fulfilled; objects of human dimensions, of standard measurements are put in order. Farewell, treasure-chests of yesteryear! ...

Seats?

Let us present a new heresy: *seats are for relaxing in.*

I have omitted to mention the 'style' *in* which – or *according* to which – we have to relax!

On the contrary, I have noticed that, according to the hours of the day, the nature of our preoccupations, the posture we adopt in a drawing-room (and which we change 3 to 4 times during an evening), there are several ways of being seated. You sit 'actively' for working. The chair is an instrument of torture which keeps you admirably wide awake. I need a chair when I am working.

I sit down to chat: a certain armchair gives me a decent and polite position. I sit down 'actively' to deliver a speech, to propound a thesis, to outline my point of view: how suitable this high stool is for my posture! I sit blissfully and I am relaxed: this Turkish stool of the *cavedjis* of Constantinople, 35 cm high and 30 cm in diameter is a marvel; I could sit on it for hours without tiring, just sitting on my backside! And if there are 15 of us in the small drawing-room of our little house, and we want to sit and do nothing, the lady of the house takes from a cupboard the 15 stools stacked one inside the other. I incline towards a more complete *kief*; I remember that Noel, the head of the Voisin (Automobile Company) coachwork department, equipped his 14-horsepower sports model with a spring cushion arranged on the floor; and I travelled 500 km at a stretch on it without feeling tired; I bear it in mind when I furnish my drawing-room. Here we have the machine at rest. We built it with bicycle frame tubes and we covered it with a magnificent pony skin; it is so light that it can be pushed with the foot, it can be moved by a child. I thought of the cowboy from the Wild West, smoking his pipe, his feet in the air higher than his head, against the chimney piece: complete rest. Our reclining chair can be put into any position; my weight alone is enough to keep it in the position chosen: no mechanics. This is the real machine for rest, etc.

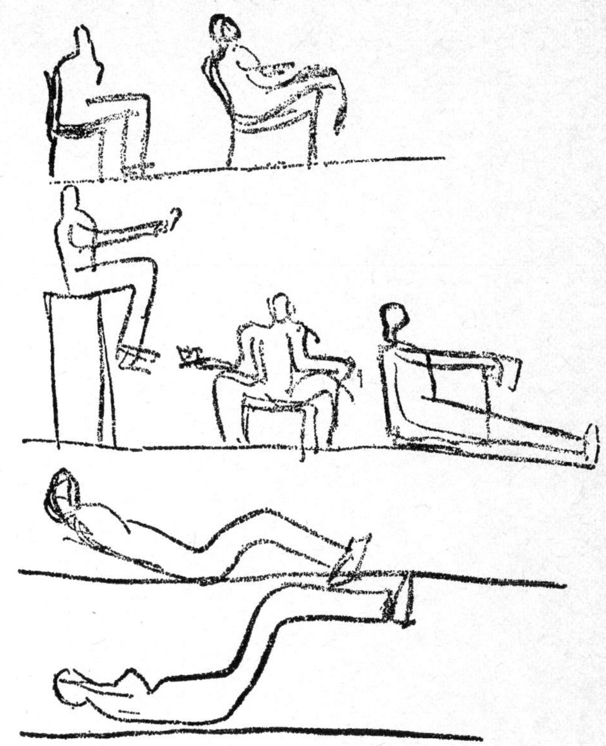

Le Corbusier, Seven ways of sitting
Précisions, Vincent Fréal, Paris, 1920

Modern woman has cut her hair. Our eyes have become acquainted with the shape of her legs. The corset has gone. Etiquette has fallen from favour. Etiquette was born in the Court. Only certain people had the right to sit down and then only in a certain way. Then in the nineteenth century, the bourgeois became king and ordered for himself armchairs infinitely more sculptured and gilded than any the princes of the blood had ever had. 'Good manners' were taught at the convent. Nowadays this is nothing but a bore! A person of distinction never loses his distinction, even at the Carnival. This reassures us!

And, above all, we are about to sit down better!
And the house has been stripped of its furniture.
Space and light abound.
We move about, we act quickly.

And perhaps we will take pleasure in contemplation, during this hour of rest, this hour of relaxation at home?

This is the root of the matter, having a think.

About the harmony of proportions,
or about some poem of mechanics, about the life of ancient or modern peoples, even a poem in verse.
or some music
a piece of sculpture, a painting
or a diagram,
or about such and such a photograph of a simple, sublime, fundamental or exceptional phenomenon.

Life is full of opportunities for collecting ornaments which can serve to promote thought:

This pebble from the seaside
this admirable pine cone
these butterflies, these beetles
this polished steel machine component
or this piece of ore.

The Gods? It is the mind which creates them out of things of the earth.

The adventure? Ah, yes, the furniture adventure! Events are moving forward: the concept of furniture has disappeared. It has been replaced by a new word 'domestic equipment'.*

122 Ernst May, *Town Planning and Illuminated Advertisements,* 1929

The significance for the urban environment of new techniques of illumination is growing rapidly. We are slowly coming to realise the design possibilities which advertising is developing for itself through this new tool. At first our reactions are those of builders faced with new materials and techniques: we are bowled over by all the thousands of innovations; but we gradually begin to control them, so that our works begin to throw off their self-conscious character as they develop signs of a mature mastery of means.

Strong coloured flashing lights attract one's attention. Some American statistics produced evidence that shop-windows lit with an intensity of 180 candlepower stopped only 12 of 100 passers-by; while raising the intensity to 1,200 candlepower had the required effect on 70 per cent. This fact shows us that the nerves of modern urban man need strong stimuli, and so in recent years illuminated advertising has in fact gone over to the use of the strongest possible light-sources. Of course the first result was that the chaotic use of this new advertising medium in every imaginable form and colour increased to a considerable extent the effect of illuminated advertising. In the advertising lights of New York's Broadway we have a classic contrary example. Here the eye can read no words, distinguish no forms, for it is simply blinded by an excess of glittering lights, a plethora of lamps which cancel out each other's effect. The design freedom so often claimed by ad-

* Phrase introduced in *Cahiers d'Art*, 1926, no. 3. [Author's note]

vertising experts can hardly ever have been more clearly taken to absurd extremes than here. Scarcely any other example shows more clearly how large sums of money can be thrown away uselessly on nothing time after time. Of course advertisements must attract attention if they are to fulfil their purpose; but when they all try to surpass each other, scream louder than their neighbour, then advertising loses its sense and becomes merely overbright street-lighting.

In daylight advertising we cannot manage without strict regulations if we do not want to let the destructive work of the last 80 years continue on its course. In brutal tastelessness it has ruthlessly strewn advertising panels and lettering over windows, balustrades, pilasters, columns, gables and dormer windows. So we must make the effort to *regulate advertising*, even if initially there seems to be a contradiction in such a plan. We will only get nearer to a solution to the advertising problem when illuminated advertisements are taken into consideration right at the beginning of the designs for single buildings, for whole streets, for squares. Otherwise, all sorts of patchwork will continue to be stuck up, usually as afterthoughts, on finished buildings which lack all provisions for the mounting of effective advertisements. Any attempt at organising these media from a town-planning point of view must aim to set these light-masses in some order and to increase the effect of these illuminated windows, letter-boards, house-walls, etc., by placing them in contrast to unlit or dimly lit parts of the town's composition.

The *floodlighting* of whole buildings or parts of them for advertising purposes has recently been tried, occasionally with great success; but this will always fail if the surroundings of such buildings are lit by other advertisements of varying kinds. This method is particularly effective when the buildings to be flood-lit are ones which project above the city streets' sea of light, i.e. predominantly towers and high-rise buildings.

Among the numerous sorts of illuminated publicity one should mention *roof advertisements* as being particularly effective. Unfortunately when faced with this proposition most publicity designers seem rather at a loss. The architecture of existing buildings often makes the harmonious installation of such advertisements very difficult. Even where a favourable effect is achieved at night, by day the upper silhouettes of our shopping streets are disfigured by scaffolding, letter-frames and hoardings. It must be a fundamental requirement of all illuminated advertisements on roofs that they fit the architecture of the building harmoniously both by day and by night. The arrangement of rows of free-standing letters, the topping of a building façade with bands of writing silhouetted against the sky, both these methods will in many cases allow the problem to be solved in a satisfactory manner.

Luminous letters in unaccentuated form are relatively easy to integrate into the architecture, providing the buildings have sufficient flat surfaces for the mounting of such letters. Single letters and other forms always need unobtrusive surfaces for their background. They can easily be installed on parapets and on the wall surfaces between the rows of windows. For night effects alone ruthless treatment of the architecture of the building would not matter; but by day designs which disregard architectural features spoil the buildings to a considerable extent.

Illuminated panels are therefore to be preferred, which have a clear-cut shape both day and night, and which, attached to the face of the buildings, can be arranged effectively both in a horizontal and a vertical format. Panels also make it possible to have a rhythmical arrangement of similar or related elements repeated in a systematic fashion. One should not object that such repetition is contrary to the principles of advertising, for the bazaar streets of Chinese and Japanese towns prove the opposite.

It is often possible to use the lamp posts of the street lighting to echo the rhythmical arrangement of such banners. This was tried successfully in the Kaiserstrasse in Frankfurt am Main. A brightly coloured vertical panel without writing served to attract the public's attention, while a second horizontal one carried the advertising message.

Recently the 'cornice light' has been coming more

into fashion. Above the rows of shops in important streets, and repeated at each storey level, bands of lights are fixed; i.e., projecting ledges of varying widths with light sources fixed to the under sides which by means of floodlights illuminate the writing on the wall immediately below them. This form of advertising with light is discreet and has an excellent artistic effect.

More expensive but most effective are the luminous façades recently come into favour. In front of the building, attached to the structural skeleton, a glass façade is fixed, which is illuminated from behind, either over its whole area, or along the sill lines. This luminous façade offers the greatest development potential for night-time advertising, and from an artistic point of view achieves its most splendid effect especially when a very broad space is left around the writing so that the text of the advertisement makes the greatest impact.

A relatively new method is the neon tube, which produces an extraordinarily bright light which is particularly effective for advertising. Neon tubes are most used in the form of letters of trade marks, and signs. Everyone knows the Odol bottle, from which drop pearls of flashing light. In many towns neon tubes have been used successfully, partially in conjunction with writing, for the architectonic enhancement of whole portions of façade.

Besides these various, as it were direct, methods of illuminated advertising, I could mention a great number of indirect systems. I am thinking here in particular of the brilliantly lit shop-windows in cities, whose displays can be enhanced most effectively by means of publicity lighting of the most varied kind. Among the possibilities of indirect lighting I also include the glass walls of lift shafts for office blocks and hotels which have recently and speedily come into use in modern architecture. At night these offer the fascinating sight of brightly lit lifts gliding up and down, and thereby create a strong advertising effect for the firm concerned.

---

123 Maurice Dufrêne, *A Survey of Modern Tendencies in Decorative Art,* 1931

The one aim, of course, of social, scientific and mechanical progress is the material improvement of the human lot by increasing knowledge and developing means of power and speed.

Only . . . this is the result, that in proportion as progress develops knowledge of and intercourse and fusion between men, it diminishes the attraction they feel towards each other and narrows the field of interest.

What is gained materially is lost spiritually.

When men are all alike, they will have no curiosity about each other; when they are no longer curious they will have no emotion, and when there is no more emotion, there will be no more art.

The steamship, the aeroplane, the motor car, the cinema and the wireless bring to our homes an acquaintance with the unknown which has already weakened the temptation to go and explore for ourselves. We are familiar with almost everything which exists and which occurs in the remotest corners of the globe.

Thirty years ago, one could still, a few steps from home, have the satisfaction of meeting, if not the totally unknown, at least something out of the ordinary.

At the present day it would be necessary to go hundreds of miles to experience this pleasure. Travelling is quicker, but the same amount of time is required to have experiences far afield which used to be found next door. Thus progress makes us lose in one way what we gain in another.

Does this mean that progress is harmful to art? No, on the contrary, progress can be useful to art, but artists should only profit by it as a means of renewing their strength; they must not allow it to dominate them.

It is inevitable that communion between men leads to community of ideas, but if of the fraternity and equality of men is born also unity of taste, that is to say, similarity of expression and formulas, it will be all up with poetry, life and art. There will be an end to liberty, to personality, imagination, beauty and to genius. The flame will die out ...

They will lose everything, and the world will be no better off.

Internationalism in art would be a decline in art because the true artist must be an exception. Talent is the expression of an individual, it cannot be standardised.

These melancholy thoughts are inspired by finding ... so many designs under the same influence and of the same kind.

The same chair, mechanical and tubular, is to be found in almost every country – Austria, America, Germany, Sweden, France, etc. It is the anonymous, neutral universal chair.

Only thirty years ago, one could safely say, if confronted by a similar collection of works, that they were *characteristic* of their countries of origin. Today it can only be said of most of them that they are *representative without being characteristic* ...

And this is the root cause of the great Dullness.

What are the causes, arising from progress, of this tendency towards the uniformity and simplicity of international art?

From the material aspect: the need for economy, industrial production, universal use of raw materials which has been made possible through improved facility of export and import, ease of assimilation, the diffusion of new techniques and materials, practical considerations and commonsense, hygiene and familiarity with current fashion.

From the spiritual aspect: a sounder understanding of aesthetic, the commonsense of rationalism, the need for adaptation to new customs, especially since 1914, the inevitable influence of an epoch in which science and the machine are supreme, money is power and speed rules the world.

As the epoch is, so is its art.

Uniformity of life, uniformity in art ...

Decorators now therefore aim at quality in their work rather than ornamental or rich effects, which were formerly in vogue. Instead of employing precious materials and adding artistic and, too often, pretentious decorations to the indispensible form, so as to make the useful ornamental, they aim at making the useful beautiful in itself.

Beauty is not attained by means of additions and complicated arrangement, but by balance, volume, form, material and practicability.

This reliance on truth implies simplicity, as does truth itself.

The more easily a decorated object can be 'placed', the more quickly it goes out of fashion. The pattern, often original and good when first conceived, is all the more liable to be copied and spread if it finds favour. Once it has been repeated it is no longer a novelty. It goes out of fashion, 'dates'. To prevent it dating so quickly, the decoration is omitted: an easy solution for all concerned, since to invent beautiful ornament and apply it in the right place calls for more qualities of every kind than to invent nothing.

In these days when many enrol themselves in the decorative arts, it is a simpler matter to succeed by employing super-simple rather than complex formulas, and this too contributes to the universal cult of 'nothing'.

But ... but ... 'nothing' is a fashion itself, and like all fashions the fashion for 'nothing' will pass.

What will the 'something' be which succeeds it? Let us hope that there will not be an excess of 'something' by way of reaction. Excess in everything – or nothing – is wrong ...

Science has inevitably a powerful influence on art, although there is so great a difference in their origin and purpose that any fusion, or replacement of one by the other, is unimaginable.

Science benefits by its own progress; its triumphs multiply rapidly. Positive and mathematical, it absorbs its own increasing strength. Each achievement of its disciples – engineers, chemists, physicians – is a springboard for those who accompany or follow after. Art on the contrary does not progress.

Every formula, every emotion, every work is limited to the artist who is responsible for it. The conclusion of the work of one scientist may be the departure point for that of another. Not so the work of an artist. Science progresses, art does not.

Science can only invent new material means of expression for art, but contributes nothing spiritual, and it is this last quality alone which is art itself.

The machine has beauty, but this beauty only exists in the movement which animates it, in the practical force it generates. The beauty of the machine is not actually present, it is a potential beauty.

Everything mechanical has a certain material beauty, for without technical perfection nothing in this domain could function and endure. If the form of the machine is beautiful it is because it consists solely of the essential. But to demand of the machine, in whole or in part, the same emotions as are aroused by a work of art which comes from the soul and heart with their message to other souls and hearts, is nonsensical.

A motor car is beautiful only in proportion to the speed of which it is capable, a dynamo in proportion to the power it generates.

The machine flatters man's weakness. Art raises him to its own level.

The logical, unswerving rationalism of the machine which is arid and brutal, is not appropriate in the domestic arts.

To construct a bed according to the same aesthetic as a suspension bridge, or to construct a house like a factory, to design a dining-room as chilly as a laboratory, shows a total lack of psychology.

And so reappears the need for variety, for imagination and contrast which is innate in man.

On coming home from the office or from a motor race it is restful, bodily and mentally, to find something different. It is no relaxation to leave the driver's seat in the car only to sit down in another exactly like it, although motionless.

After a dismal walk in the damp woods or the exhilaration of a ski run, how pleasant it is to find a wood fire and pile carpets, how soothing the easy chair, 'deep as a tomb'. After the cosmopolitan hotel, anonymous and levelling, how delicious it feels to come back to the home, where we keep our memories, and our 'I', among the dear and friendly things which are ours alone.

One day perhaps science will cause the downfall of art, but it will never replace it. Matter will reign over mind, force over feeling, utility over poetry. As far as one can judge by its beginnings that reign will not make men either happier or better.

The moral of all these remarks is that it is necessary and urgent for artists in every country to buckle to ...

Architecture, houses, manners, customs, colours, poetry, music, flowers, ribbons and songs, may all men carefully preserve you and serve you according to his heart and his heaven, if the earth is not to be without joy.

---

124 Harold Van Doren, *Streamlining,* 1940

The scene is the office of the vice-president and sales manager of the Peerless Laundry Equipment Corporation. The vice-president is speaking.

'Gentlemen, this is Mr Blank. He has been engaged by our company to streamline our line of laundry tubs.'

Mr Blank is one of that mysterious yet over-publicised fraternity of industrial designers. He is being introduced to other members of the company: the vice-president in charge of production, the chief engineer, the plant superintendent.

Streamlined laundry tubs! What is poor Blank to say? He knows that the substitution of a few radii or soft curves for angles and sharp edges bears about as much relation to genuine streamlining as knitting sweaters does to the science of hydraulics. But the client calls it streamlining.

Streamlining has taken the modern world by storm. We live in a maelstrom of streamlined trains, refrigerators, and furnaces; streamlined bathing beauties, soda crackers, and facial massages.

True streamlining is not nearly so important, nor so frequently met with in problems of industrial design, as the general public probably thinks. But it is a phenomenon no designer can ignore and no modern book on design can afford not to discuss.

The manufacturer who wants his laundry tubs, his typewriters, or his furnaces streamlined is in reality

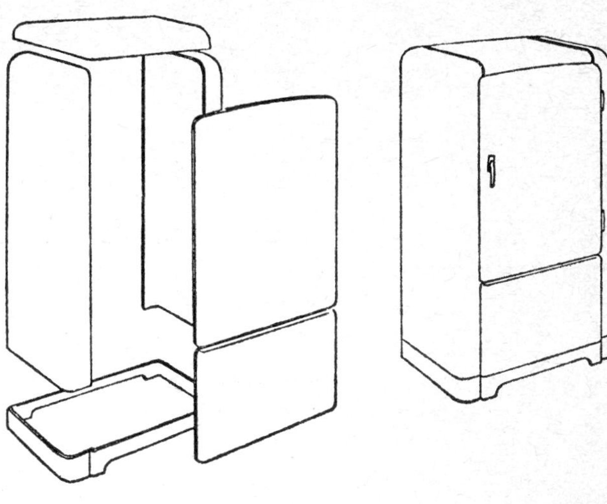

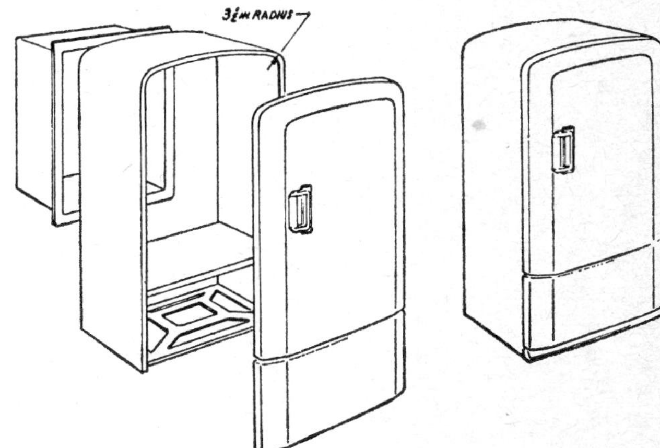

Norge Division of Borg Warner Corporation,
Two designs for streamline pressed steel refrigerators for mass production, 1933
Industrial Design, McGraw-Hill, New York, 1940

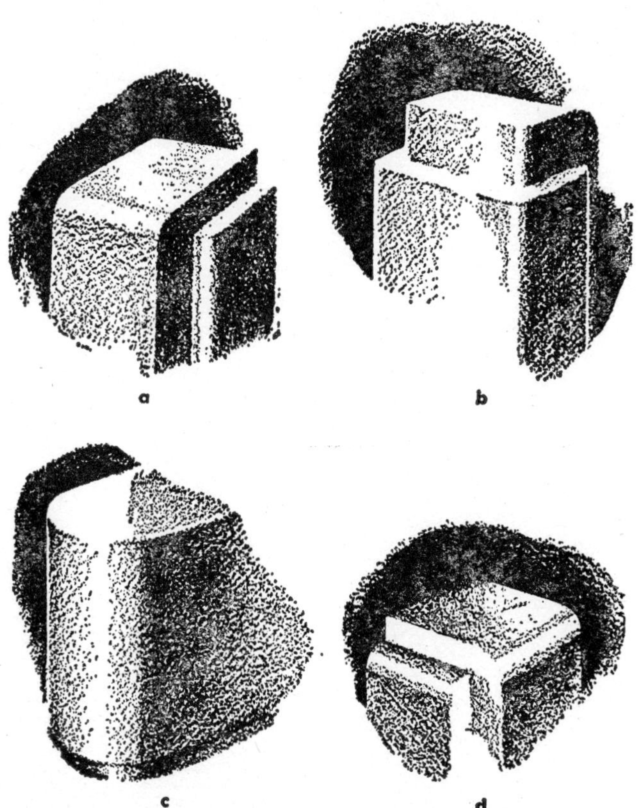

Harold van Doren, Streamlined corner treatments
Industrial Design, McGraw-Hill, New York, 1940

asking you to modernise them, to find the means for substituting curvilinear forms for rectilinear forms. He wants you to make cast iron and die-cast zinc and plastics and sheet metal conform to the current taste, or fad if you will, for cylinders and spheres or the soft flowing curves of the modern automobile in place of the harsh angles and ungainly shapes of a decade ago.

He expects, too, that unnecessary exposure of mechanical parts will be elimated, that buttons will be substituted for levers, and control panels and dials will be organised into simple and easily read groups, tied in wherever possible with related elements of the principal forms.

In ninety-nine cases out of a hundred, this procedure is utterly unrelated to genuine streamlining. Then why does the client refer to it as such? And why should designers be streamlining everything, from lipsticks to locomotives?

Simply because, in the unbelievably rapid growth of the American language, words soon lose their specific and restricted meanings and assume a general significance embracing far wider fields than originally intended. The streamlined laundry tub today means the modern laundry tub. It means the very latest up-to-the-minute laundry tub that can be bought, something so ultra-advanced that it is almost more of the future than the present ...

The real field of true streamlining is transportation, especially the airplane, although it has hydraulic applications as well. In both of these fields it is functional. It has been borrowed in many forms by industry for application to static objects, where its employment is due largely to popular fancy. This is not the place to debate the merits of borrowed streamlining, although if it helps sell merchandise that should go a long way towards justifying its use ...

The real populariser of the streamline idea was a genius of the theatre, who put his talent and enthusiasm into the visualisation of a world of the future, in which everything that moved through water or air or under the sea was somehow manipulated into the shape of a catfish, blunt before, slender and pointed behind. Still under middle age, Norman Bel-Geddes has lived to see buses and trains and some experimental automobiles created by other designers dashing across the continent in forms that are almost Chinese copies of the fantastic sketches he made only a few years before.

Streamlining of transportation was bound to come. It was in the air. What Geddes did was to dramatise it, well before it had really arrived, and so convincingly as to crystallise the scattered forces already tending in that direction, and bring reality to a tendency which up to then had consisted of theory and tentative experiment.

List of Sources

1 Louis Sullivan, 'Ornament in Architecture'. Originally published in *The Engineering Magazine* (New York), vol. III, no. 5, August 1892. This revised version printed in Louis Sullivan, *Kindergarten Chats*, New York, 1947.

2 Rioux de Maillou, 'The Decorative Arts and the Machine', *Revue des Arts Décoratifs* (Paris), vol. XV, 1895, pp. 225-67.

3 M. H. Baillie Scott, 'An Ideal Suburban House', *The Studio*, vol. IV, 1894-5, pp. 127-32.

4 Alfred Lichtwark, 'Palace Window and Folding Door', *Pan* (Berlin), vol. II, 1896, pp. 57-60.

5 Louis Sullivan, 'The Tall Office Building Artistically Considered'. Originally published in *Lippincott's Magazine* (Philadelphia), vol. 57, March 1896. This revised version printed in Louis Sullivan, *Kindergarten Chats*, New York, 1947.

6 Alfred Lichtwark, 'Practical Application', *Dekorative Kunst* (Munich), vol. I, October 1897, pp. 24-27.

7 Thiébault-Sisson, 'An Innovator: Victor Horta', *Art et Décoration* (Paris), vol. I, Jan.-June 1897, pp. 11-18.

8 Henry van de Velde, 'A Chapter on the Design and Construction of Modern Furniture', *Pan* (Berlin), vol. III, 1897, pp. 260-64.

9 Samuel Bing, 'Where are we going?', *Dekorative Kunst* (Munich), vol. I, 1897-8, pp. 1-3; 68-71; 173-77.

10 August Endell, 'The Beauty of Form and Decorative Art', *Dekorative Kunst* (Munich), vol. I, 1897-8, pp. 75-77; 119-25.

11 Adolf Loos, 'Potemkin's Town', *Ver Sacrum* (Vienna), vol. I, 1898, pp. 15-18.

12 Victor Champier, 'The Castel Béranger by Hector Guimard', *Revue des Arts Décoratifs* (Paris), vol. XIX, 1899, pp. 1-13.

13 Charles Plumet, 'The Modern Home', *Revue des Arts Décoratifs* (Paris), vol. XIX, 1899, pp. 179-91.

14 Emile Gallé, 'Modern Furniture Decorated According to Nature', *Revue des Arts Décoratifs* (Paris), vol. XX, 1900, pp. 333-41; 365-77.

15 Henry van de Velde, 'The New Ornament', *Die Renaissance im modernen Kunstgewerbe*, Cassirer, Berlin, 1901.

16 Henry van de Velde, 'The Rôle of the Engineer in Modern Architecture', *Die Renaissance im modernen Kunstgewerbe*, Cassirer, Berlin, 1901.

17 Hermann Muthesius, *The English House* (*Das Englische Haus*), Wasmuth, Berlin, 1904-5.

18 Josef Hoffmann and Koloman Moser, *Work-Programme of the Weiner Werkstätte* (*Katalog mit Arbeitsprogramm der Wiener Werkstätte*), Vienna, 1905.

19 Hermann Muthesius, *The Meaning of the Arts and Crafts* (*Die Bedeutung des Kunstgewerbes*),

Lecture at Handelschochschule, Berlin, Spring 1907.

20 Adolf Loos, 'Cultural Degeneracy', 1908. Reprinted in Adolf Loos, *Trotzdem, 1900-1930*, Vienna, 1931.

21 Adolf Loos, 'Architecture' written 1910 and published in various editions in German and French. Reprinted in Adolf Loos, *Trotzdem, 1900-1930*, Vienna, 1931.

22 C. R. Ashbee, 'A Chapter of Axioms', *Should we Stop Teaching Art?*, London, 1911, pp. 2-14.

23 Karl Grosz, 'Ornament', 1911, *Jahrbuch des Deutschen Werkbundes* (Jena), 1912, pp. 60-64.

24 Hermann Muthesius, 'Where do we Stand?', 1911, *Jahrbuch des Deutschen Werkbundes* (Jena), 1912, pp. 11-26.

25 K. E. Osthaus, C. J. Fuchs, H. Muthesius, *et al.* From the debate following Muthesius's speech, 1911. *Jahrbuch des Deutschen Werkbundes* (Jena), 1912, pp. 28-30; 34-36.

26 Walter Gropius, 'The Development of Modern Industrial Architecture', 1913, *Jahrbuch des Deutschen Werkbundes* (Jena), 1913, pp. 17-22.

27 W. R. Lethaby, 'Modern German Architecture and What we may Learn from it', 1915, W. R. Lethaby, *Form in Civilization*, London, 1922, Chapter 8, pp. 96-105.

28 Hermann Muthesius, *The Future of German Form (Die Zukunft der deutschen Form)*, Deutscher-verlags, Stuttgart and Berlin, 1915.

29 Hans Poelzig, 'The Architect', *Bauwelt* (Berlin), 24, 1931.

30 Frank Lloyd Wright, 'The Cardboard House', *Modern Architecture* (The Kahn lectures, Princeton University), 1931.

31 Victor Horta, 'Reminiscences of the Maison du Peuple', *Mémoires*, Horta Archive, Brussels (n.d.).

32 Antonio Sant'Elia, 'The New City', 1914, *Nuove Tendenze*, exhibition catalogue, Famiglia Artistica, Milan, May-June 1914.

33 Paul Scheerbart, *Glass Architecture (Glasarchitektur)*, Berlin, 1914, Chapters 1, 5, 13, 18, 29, 33, 35, 106, 111.

34 Erich Mendelsohn, 'Reflections on a New Architecture, 1914-17', Lecture to the Arbeitsrat für Kunst, Berlin, 1919. English translation from Erich Mendelsohn, *Structures and Sketches*, London, 1924.

35 Adolf Behne, 'Glass Architecture', *Wiederkehr der Kunst*, Leipzig, 1919.

36 Walter Gropius, *Programme of the Staatliche Bauhaus in Weimar* (*Programm das Staatliche Bauhaus, Weimar*), Four-page pamphlet, Weimar, April 1919.

37 Walter Gropius, 'Address to the Bauhaus Students'. *Erste Ansprache im Bauhaus.* Document in the Bauhaus-Archiv, Berlin, July 1919.

38 Bruno Taut, '"Ex Oriente Lux"! Call to Architects'. *Das Hohe Ufer* (Berlin), vol. I, no. 1, 1919.

39 Bruno Taut, *The City Crown* (*Die Stadtkrone*), Jena, 1919, pp. 62-70.

40 Nikolai Punin, 'Tatlin's Monument to thc Third International', *Iskusstvo Kommuny* (Petrograd), March 9, 1919.

41 Naum Gabo and Antoine Pevsner, *Realistic Manifesto*, Second State Printing House, Moscow, August 1920.

42 Le Corbusier and Amédée Ozenfant, 'Purism', *Esprit Nouveau* (Paris), 4, 1920, pp. 369-86.

43 Nikolai Punin, 'Tatlin's Monument to the Third International'. *Pamyatnik III Internatsionala*, Moscow, 1920.

44 A. Rodchenko and V. Stepanova, *The Programme of the Productivist Group*, Moscow, 1920.

45 Theo van Doesburg, 'The Will to Style: The Reconstruction of Life, Art and Technology'. Lecture given in Jena, Weimar and Berlin, *De Stijl* (Leiden), vol. V, no. 2, 1922, pp. 23-32; vol V, no. 3, 1922, pp. 33-41.

46 Vilmos Huszar, 'The Staatliche Bauhaus in Weimar', *De Stijl* (Leiden), vol. V, no. 9, 1922, pp. 135-37.

47 Lazlo Moholy-Nagy, 'Constructivism and the Proletariat'. *MA* (Hungary), May 1922.

48 Gino Severini, 'Machinery', *De Stijl* (Leiden), vol. V, no. 12, 1922.

49 Fernand Léger, 'The Machine Aesthetic: The Manufactured Object, the Artisan and the Artist', *Bulletin de l'Effort Moderne* (Paris), 1924.

50 Leon Trotsky, 'Tatlin's Monument'. From the chapter entitled 'Revolutionary and Socialist Art' in *Literature and Revolution*, English trs. New York, 1924, pp. 247-48.

51 M. Szczuka and T. Zarnower, 'What is Constructivism?', *Blok* (Warsaw), 6-7, 1924.

52 Hugo Häring, 'Approaches to Form', *Die Form* (Berlin), vol. I, 1925, pp. 3-5.

53 Frederick Kiesler, 'Manifesto', *De Stijl* (Leiden), vol. VI, nos. 10-11, 1925, pp. 141-46.

54 Hannes Meyer, 'The New World', *Das Werk* (Bern), vol. VII, 1926, pp. 205 and 221-24.

55 Kasimir Malevich, 'Suprematist Architecture', *Wasmuths Monatshefte für Baukunst* (Berlin), vol. XI, 1927, p. 412ff.

56 Rudolf Schindler, 'A Manifesto', Manuscript(?), 1912.

57 Herman Muthesius, 'The Problem of Form in Engineering', *Jahrbuch des Deutschen Werkbundes* (Jena), 1913, pp. 28-32

58 J. J. P. Oud, 'Architecture and Standardisation in Mass Construction', *De Stijl* (Leiden), vol. I, no. 7, 1918, pp. 77-79.

59 Walter Gropius, 'The Theory and Organisation of the Staatliche Bauhaus', *Staatliche Bauhaus Weimar, 1919-23*, Bauhaus-verlag, Weimar and Munich, 1923, pp. 7-18.

60 Oskar Schlemmer, 'The Staatliche Bauhaus in Weimar', Manifesto from the four-page publicity pamphlet *Die erste Bauhaus-Ausstellung in Weimar, Juli bis September, 1923*, 1923.

61 F. H. Ehmcke, 'The Bauhaus in Weimar', *Die Zeit* (Berlin), 4 January 1924.

62 K. Nonn, 'The State Garbage Supplies (The Staatliche Bauhaus in Weimar)', *Deutsche Zeitung* (Berlin), no. 178, 24 April 1924.

63 Robert Mallet-Stevens, 'Architecture and Geometry', *Bulletin de la Vie Moderne* (Paris), 1924, pp. 532-34.

64 Le Corbusier, 'The New Spirit in Architecture', *L'Almanach d'Architecture Moderne*, Crès, Paris, 1925, pp. 21-23.

65 Le Corbusier, 'Mass Produced Buildings', *L'Almanach d'Architecture Moderne*, Crès, Paris, 1925, pp. 77-81.

66 Le Corbusier, 'Appeal to Industrialists', *L'Almanach d'Architecture Moderne*, Crès, Paris, 1925, pp. 102-103.

67 Le Corbusier, 'A Single Trade', *L'Almanach d'Architecture Moderne*, Crès, Paris, 1925, pp. 109-13.

68 Le Corbusier, 'Standardisation Cannot Resolve an Architectural Difficulty, *L'Almanach d'Architecture Moderne*, Crès, Paris, 1925, pp. 114-15.

69 Le Corbusier, 'A Contemporary City with Three Million Inhabitants', *L'Almanach d'Architecture Moderne*, Crès, Paris, 1925, pp. 172-74.

70 Le Corbusier, 'Words', *L'Almanach d'Architecture Moderne*, Crès, Paris, 1925, pp. 182-84.

71 Walter C. Behrendt, 'The State of the Arts and Crafts', *Die Form* (Berlin), vol. I (new series), 1925-6, pp. 37-40.

72 Kurt Ewald, 'The Beauty of Machines', *Die Form* (Berlin), vol. I (new series), 1925-6, pp. 111-16.

73 Walter Gropius, 'Where Artists and Technicians Meet', *Die Form* (Berlin), vol. I (new series), 1925-6, pp. 117-20.

74 Walter Gropius, 'Bauhaus Dessau – Principles of Bauhaus Production' (*Bauhaus-Dessau, Grundsätze der Bauhausproduktion*). Printed sheet published by the Bauhaus, Dessau, March 1926.

75 Wassily Kandinsky, 'The Value of the Teaching of Theory in Painting', *Bauhaus* (Dessau), vol. I, no. 1, 1926.

76 Georg Muche, 'Fine Art and Industrial Form', *Bauhaus* (Dessau), vol. 1, no. 1, 1926.

77 Werner Gräff, 'The Dwelling' (Weissenhof Exhibition), *Die Form* (Berlin), vol. II, 1927, pp. 259-60.

78 Le Corbusier, 'Five Points of a New Architecture', *Die Form* (Berlin), vol. II, 1927, pp. 272-74.
79 W. Lotz, 'Weissenhof Exhibition', *Die Form* (Berlin), vol. II, 1927, p. 251.
80 Mies van der Rohe, 'Remarks on my Block of Flats', *Bau und Wohnung* (Stuttgart), 1927.
81 M. Ginzburg, 'Results and Prospects', *Sovremmenaya Arkhitektura* (Moscow), 4-5, 1927, pp. 112-18.
82 Gustav Platz, 'Elements in the Creation of a new Style' ('Die Elemente der Stilbildung: Stil'), *Die Baukunst der neuesten Zeit*, Propylaen-Verlag, Berlin, 1927, Chapter III, pp. 89-92.
83 Gerrit Rietveld, 'Utility: Construction (Beauty: Art)'. 1-10 (Amsterdam), vol. I, no. 3, 1927, pp. 89-92.
84 W. Lotz, 'Space in Transport Vehicles', *Die Form* (Berlin), vol. III, 1928, pp. 396-400.
85 Mies van der Rohe, 'On the Subject of Exhibitions', *Die Form* (Berlin), vol. III, 1928, p. 121.
86 Walter Riezler, 'The Purpose and Concept of Technical Beauty', *Die Form* (Berlin), vol. II, 1927, pp. 385-95.
87 Hannes Meyer, 'Address to the Student Representatives at the Bauhaus', Document in the Bauhaus-Archiv, Berlin, 1928.
88 Arthur Korn, 'Glass in Modern Architecture'. *Glas im Bau und als Gebrauchsgegenstand*, Pollak, Berlin, 1929.
89 Bruno Taut, 'Five Points', *Modern Architecture*, London, 1929.
90 Ernst Kallai, 'Ten Years of Bauhaus', *Die Weltbühne* (Berlin), no. 21, January 1930.
91 Reginald Blomfield, *Modernismus*, London, 1934, Chapter IV, pp. 51-83.
92 Marcel Breuer, *'Where do we Stand?'*, Lecture given in Zurich, 1933.
93 R. M. Schindler, 'Space Architecture', *Dune Forum* (Oceano, Calif.), February 1934, pp. 44-46.
94 Walter Gropius, 'Programme for the Establishment of a Company for the Provision of Housing on Aesthetically Consistent Principles', Manuscript, 1910.
95 Anon, 'Good and Cheap', Editorial, *Journal of the Design and Industries Association*, no. 8, 1918, pp. 3-9.
96 Alfred Simon, 'Good and Cheap – a Reply', *Journal of the Design and Industries Association*, no. 9, 1918, pp. 31-34.
97 M. H. Baillie Scott, 'Good and Cheap – a Reply', *Journal of the Design and Industries Association*, no. 10, 1918, pp. 23-25.
98 W. R. Lethaby, 'Housing and Furnishing', *The Athenaeum*, 21 May 1920. Reprinted in W. R. Lethaby, *Form in Civilization*, London, 1922, pp. 35-45.
99 W. Gropius, 'How can we Build Cheaper, Better, More Attractive Houses?', *Die Form* (Berlin), vol. II, 1927, pp. 275-77.
100 M. Stam, 'The Stam Houses', *Die Form* (Berlin), vol. II, 1927, p. 292.
101 W. F. Crittall, 'Silver End', *Design and Industries Association Journal*, no. 13, 1930, pp. 8-10.
102 Der Block, 'Manifesto', *Baukunst* (Munich), 1928, p. 128.
103 Congrès Internationaux d'Architecture Moderne (CIAM), 'Declaration of Aims', CIAM declaration at 1st Congress, La Sarraz, June 1928.
104 A. Gan, 'What is Constructivism?', *Sovremmenaya Arkhitektura* (Moscow), 3, 1928, pp. 79-81.
105 Karel Teige, 'Contemporary International Architecture', *Red* (Prague), 5, 1928, pp. 193-98.
106 Ernst May, 'Flats for Subsistence Living' (CIAM, Frankfurt, 1929), *Die Wohnung für Existenzminimum*, Frankfurt-am-Main, 1930, pp. 10-16.
107 Walter Riezler, 'The Fight for German Culture', *Die Form* (Berlin), vol. VII, 1932, pp. 325-28.
108 Philip Johnson, 'Architecture in the Third Reich', *Hound and Horn* (New York), 1933, pp. 137-39.
109 Jiři Krohá, 'Ideology of Architecture'. Unpublished Manuscript(?), 1933, printed in Josef Cisarovsky, *Jiři Krohá*, Prague, 1967, pp. 35-37.
110 Paul Schmitthenner, 'Tradition and New Build-

ings', *Deutsche Kulturwacht* (Berlin), 17, 1933.

111 F. Schuster, 'Five Years after Weissenhof', *Schwäbischer Heimatbuch* (Esslingen), 19, 1933, pp. 116-18.

112 F. R. Yerbury, 'In Germany Now', *Architectural Association Journal,* September 1933, pp. 126-33.

113 Wells Coates, 'The Conditions for an Architecture of Today', *Architectural Association Journal,* April 1938, pp. 447-57.

114 Werner Gräff, 'On the Form of the Motor Car', *Die Form* (Berlin), vol. I (new series), 1925-6, pp. 195-201.

115 J. Molzahn, 'Economics of the Advertising Mechanism', *Die Form* (Berlin), vol. I (new series), 1925-6, pp. 141-44.

116 Marcel Breuer 'Metal Furniture', in Werner Gräff, *Innenraume,* Stuttgart, 1928, pp. 133-34.

117 M. Stam, 'Away with Furniture Artists', in Werner Gräff, *Innenraume,* Stuttgart, 1928, pp. 128-30.

118 W. Lotz, 'Suites of Furniture and Standard Furniture Design', *Die Form* (Berlin), vol. II, 1927, pp. 161-69.

119 J. Gloag, 'Wood or Metal?', *The Studio,* 97, 1929, pp. 49-50.

120 C. Perriand, 'Wood or Metal?', *The Studio,* 97, 1929, pp. 278-79.

121 Le Corbusier, 'The Furniture Adventure', *Précisions,* Vincent Fréal, Paris, 1930, pp. 103-22.

122 Ernst May, 'Town Planning and Illuminated Advertising', in W. Lotz, ed., *Licht und Beleuchtung,* Berlin, 1928, pp. 44-7.

123 M. Dufrêne, 'A Survey of Modern Tendencies in Decorative Art', *The Studio Yearbook of Decorative Art,* 1931, pp. 1-4.

124 Harold Van Doren, 'Streamlining', in H. Van Doren, *Industrial Design: A Practical Guide,* McGraw-Hill, New York, 1940, pp. 137-52.

Index